MENTAL HEALTH

CONSULTATION

AND

COLLABORATION

Gerald Caplan
Ruth B. Caplan

Foreword by
Charles D. Spielberger

MENTAL HEALTH
CONSULTATION
AND
COLLABORATION

Jossey-Bass Publishers · San Francisco

Substantial discounts on bulk quantities of Jossey-Bass books are available to corporations, professional associations, and other organizations. For details and discount information, contact the special sales department at Jossey-Bass Inc., Publishers (415) 433-1740; Fax (800) 605-2665.

For sales outside the United States, please contact your local Simon & Schuster International Office.

Jossey-Bass Web address: http://www.josseybass.com

Manufactured in the United States of America

Library of Congress Cataloging-in-Publication Data
Caplan, Gerald.
    Mental health consultation and collaboration / Gerald Caplan, Ruth B. Caplan.—1st ed.
      p.   cm.—(The Jossey-Bass social and behavioral science series)
    Includes bibliographical references and index.
    ISBN 1-55542-478-3 (alk. paper)
    1. Mental health consultation. I. Caplan, Ruth B. II. Title. III. Series.
    [DNLM: 1. Community Mental Health Services. 2. Referral and Consultation.
WM 30 C244m]
RA790.95C36   1993
362.2'2—dc20
DNLM/DLC
for Library of Congress   92-20621

FIRST EDITION
HB Printing   10 9 8 7 6 5 4 3 2

The Jossey-Bass
Social and Behavioral Science Series

CONTENTS

FOREWORD

The contributions of Gerald and Ruth B. Caplan to community mental health and community psychiatry and psychology over the past forty years have been monumental and without parallel. The impact of their work on traditional modes for providing mental health services has substantially broadened the roles and horizons of professionals in all of the mental health disciplines. Through their contributions to the early detection and prevention of emotional disorders, they have markedly facilitated the delivery of services to a much larger circle of those in need.

From the origins of the Caplans' early work in counseling teachers of emotionally disturbed adolescents at the Lasker Child Guidance Center in Jerusalem to the pioneering mental health consultation programs at the Harvard School of Public Health and the Wellesley Human Relations Service where Gerald Caplan collaborated with Eric Lindemann, the innovative contributions of Gerald and Ruth Caplan have continued to evolve at the Harvard Medical School and, more recently, at the Jerusalem Institute for the Study of Psychological Stress. The methods and techniques of individual and group consultation developed by the Caplans have had a significant beneficial impact on both the caregivers who use them and the recipients of their service.

This volume provides a comprehensive and systematic presentation of the theory and practice of community mental health consultation and population-oriented psychiatry, and outlines the Caplans' recent concepts of collaboration through which mental health specialists develop fruitful partnerships with professional colleagues in a variety of health, education, welfare, and religious organizations. In addition to presenting a lucid description of the evolution, development, and current status of their pioneering techniques, many of which have become standard practice in the mental health disciplines, the book clearly articulates the fundamental theoretical principles on which these techniques are based.

The range of influence of Gerald Caplan's work on the mental health disciplines is truly remarkable, but nowhere has this impact been greater than in psychology. His emphasis on primary and secondary prevention and on the utilization of mental health consultation in working with a variety of caregivers has had an enormous and markedly beneficial influence on the practice of clinical, counseling, and school psychology. Caplan's work was instrumental in stimulating the establishment of the Division of Community Psychology within the American Psychological Association (APA).

The educational background and professional experience of Ruth B. Caplan have significantly complemented and enriched the pioneering contributions to mental health consultation and community psychiatry of her distinguished father. While working on advanced degrees in English literature at Harvard, she explored the origins of psychiatric concepts as historian for the Department of Mental Health of the Commonwealth of Massachusetts. She also taught courses on the history of psychiatric institutions and community psychiatry at the Harvard Medical School and, subsequently, at the Hebrew University in Jersusalem. While associated with Harvard's Laboratory of Community Psychiatry, Ruth Caplan helped to establish a unique mental health consultation program for parish priests in collaboration with the Episcopal Church of Massachusetts. Her 1972 book, *Helping the Helpers to Help,* based on her studies of consultation with clergy in helping them to develop greater skill, confidence, and effectiveness in working with their parishioners, provides an essential part of the theoretical and technical foundation for this volume.

The APA Division of School Psychology has recently honored Gerald Caplan, recognizing his many outstanding contributions to professional psychology in working with students, teachers, parents, and other caregivers in educational settings. This text partially incorporates and expands upon his classic volume, *The The-*

ory and Practice of Mental Health Consultation, published in 1970 but now out of print. That text has commanded a unique position in the school psychology literature as the book most frequently cited in articles published during the 1970s in the *Journal of School Psychology.*

The opportunity for me to acknowledge the powerful personal influence of Caplan's ideas and inspiration on my own formative professional development is especially pleasing. At Duke University in the fall of 1958, after moving to a full-time position in psychology from a joint appointment in psychiatry and the Psychiatric Outpatient Clinic, my new responsibilities involved the development of training opportunities in community mental health. I also had considerable time for clinical practice, but no longer had ready access to working with patients. In seeking opportunities to continue clinical work and to obtain first-hand experience in community mental health, I was fortunate to be invited to serve as a consultant to the New Hanover County Mental Health Association and Health Department, both located in Wilmington, North Carolina.

Funds were available for me to spend only one day each month in Wilmington, which is located approximately 150 miles from the Duke campus, with specific duties and responsibilities to be arranged. As was typically the case in most small American communities some thirty years ago, the mental health resources in Wilmington were extremely limited. A single psychiatrist was available to serve the mental health needs of a population of more than 150,000 people who resided in the city and in the surrounding rural area up to a distance of fifty to sixty miles. There were no other trained mental health professionals in the area. When I conferred with this terribly overburdened psychiatrist on how best to spend eight to ten hours a month, he was most insistent that this time be devoted to giving the Rorschach and other tests that would help him make decisions concerning the appropriateness of prescribing electroconvulsive shock or psychotropic drugs!

I am most grateful to Eliot Rodnick, then chair of the Duke Psychology Department and the person responsible for obtaining the funds from the National Institute of Mental Health for my new position, for calling the writings of Gerald Caplan to my attention.

Although Caplan's published work at that time focused on consultation with individual caregivers, given the limited time I would have in Wilmington, it seemed prudent to endeavor to develop a group consultation program rather than working with individual patients or consultees.

Since my base of operations and staff support would be in the New Hanover County Health Department, I considered working with public health nurses a major priority. Guided by Caplan's writings on the goals and techniques of mental health consultation and conferences with leaders of the County Mental Health Association, a mental health consultation program was developed that involved monthly meetings with caseworkers from the Department of Public Welfare and members of the Wilmington Ministerial Association, in addition to the public health nurses associated with the Health Department. Before each meeting, I met with the caregiver from each group who volunteered to present an ongoing case and, when possible, the individual patient, client, or parishioner whose case was to be presented.

The application of Caplan's principles and techniques to a case-seminar form of group mental health consultation worked surprisingly well. Indeed, over the more than five years that I worked in Wilmington, we evolved a form of mental health collaboration with community caregivers that, of logic and necessity, seems to have anticipated later developments in Caplan's theory and techniques. On being asked to expand the consultation program to two days each month, I agreed to do so on the condition that the second day would be invested entirely in the public schools, again following Caplan's views in regard to an optimal point for mental health intervention.

The development of the Wilmington community mental health consultation program was greatly facilitated through my personal contact with Gerald Caplan, who was most gracious in helping me to develop a summer placement program at the Harvard School of Public Health and its associated agencies for advanced graduate students in Duke's Clinical Psychology Program. These summer placements provided a unique opportunity for our students to experience and participate in mental health consultation, and for me to observe firsthand Caplan's masterly teaching and training of mental health professionals in consultation techniques. The visits to Boston to coordinate the training of our graduate students also put me in close touch with Saul Cooper, Ira Iscoe, and James Kelly, leaders in the emerging field of community psychology. They were all to become presidents of the APA Division of Community Psychology that was established in 1968.

Clinical, school, and community psychologists have greatly valued what we learned from Gerald Caplan, and we have all benefited from the relationships with esteemed colleagues in those formative years that were stimulated by our association with him. The debt that we owe to Gerald and Ruth Caplan is, indeed, enormous, and we will continue to benefit from the legacy of their teachings for many years to come.

The principles and techniques of mental health consultation and community collaboration that are presented in this volume will be of significant interest and exceptional value to all who are involved in applications of psychology in community settings. In addition to practitioners in the core mental health disciplines, ministers, teachers, marriage and family counselors, and colleagues trained in our health care disciplines will enjoy and profit from a careful reading of its contents.

September 1992   Charles D. Spielberger
                                                    President, 1991–1992
                                                    American Psychological Association

PREFACE

The plan to publish this book emerged from discussions with leading professors of educational psychology during the annual convention of the American Psychological Association in Boston in August 1990. A special session of the convention had been organized to celebrate the contributions of Gerald Caplan to American psychology (see Erchul, 1993), and in particular to commemorate the twentieth anniversary of the publication of his book *The Theory and Practice of Mental Health Consultation* (Caplan, 1970), which had recently gone out of print.

It became clear that this book had been widely accepted over the years as one of the basic conceptual and methodological systems underlying a major development in school psychology. The profession had moved beyond its traditional focus on identifying the intrapsychic idiosyncrasies of problem children, and beyond prescribing how the psychologist might *directly* remedy them by treating the child himself, toward a broader ecological perspective that focused on the contributions of the teachers and the school setting. School psychologists had begun to devote many of their efforts to influencing students *indirectly* through helping their educators find more effective ways of handling them; in this, consultation was an important tool.

Consultation between psychologists and educators had become a central element in the training and practice of school psychologists. *The Theory and Practice of Mental Health Consultation* was required reading in many university departments of school psychology, and one of the most cited references in hundreds of publications in the school psychology literature (Oakland, 1984), even though it had been written primarily for mental health clinicians in community mental health programs. Thus, its approach and terminology were sometimes more psychoanalytically clinical than educational psychologists could easily accept.

It appears that what made the book so attractive was that it provided a detailed set of systematic guidelines to the *process* of helping professionals of other disciplines overcome current work difficulties. It explained how to explore the relevant assets and liabilities of their institutional setting; how to promote the development of a supportive relationship and of a common language; how to assess the nature of their current work difficulty; and how to offer consultees acceptable assistance that would enable them to master their clients' predicaments.

Of particular value, apparently, were the book's many case examples, which illustrated expectable difficulties in assessment and intervention, provided authentic details of techniques, and made the abstract concepts come to life. This allowed readers to draw out the generalizable basic principles so that they might *work out for themselves* how to deal with similar issues in their own setting. This exemplified a basic message of the book—that consultees should be afforded the opportunity to *actively* derive *their own* ideas about how to deal with a current professional problem on the basis of the statements of their consultant, rather than be given specific prescriptions which, if accepted, remain somebody else's ideas, however sensible they may be.

The discussion at the 1990 convention in Boston emphasized that the unavailability of the 1970 book left a significant gap in the field. This is also true of its companion volume by Ruth Caplan, *Helping the Helpers to Help* (1972), which described the Harvard consultation program in the Episcopal church and which had also gone out of print.

In considering the publication of a new book to fill this gap, we concluded that special assets in the original texts should not be lightly discarded. Therefore, they have been retained, in large measure, in the present volume. Formulations and detailed practice examples drawn from the American scene of the 1950s and 1960s may evoke a rather quaint and old-fashioned world, one that was less violent, more sexually strict, and more racially divided; but the very obtrusive "there-and-then" quality makes it obvious that readers must perforce move beyond the text to construct *their own* maps for practice in the here and now.

We therefore decided that the new volume should incorporate relevant parts of the original texts of the two books largely unaltered, but that in addition, new material should be included that would bring the concepts and techniques up to date, based on the experience of both authors in many different work settings over the past twenty years.

We hope that in our new book we will succeed in preserving what has been found valuable in the two original volumes. Our focus will continue to be neither on such content areas as psychology or mental health, nor on standardized generic methods of problem solving, but on offering a detailed conceptual and methodological guide to specialist consultants on how to deal with problems of helping professional consultees to help their clients.

In our joint authorship, we hope that our different training and experience have enabled us to complement each other. One of us is a population-oriented psychiatrist who has worked for years as a consultant in health, welfare, and education organizations in many countries, and the other is a historian with special expertise in textual analysis and participant observation who has made a study of the history of the mental health field and of mental health consultation. The style of narrative voice changes from section to section according to which author has moved to the fore. The first-person pronoun in some of our case examples is that of Gerald Caplan, who was conducting the consultations described. We use this formulation to foster authenticity; but to preserve confidentiality, we have disguised all examples and hidden the identity of consultees, clients, and institutions.

We oppose sexist stereotyping, but in order to avoid clumsy formulations such as *he or she* and *his or her,* whenever we use the pronoun *he,* we wish to imply *he or she* unless we are denoting a specific individual. Consultants may be male or female, and so may consultees. Their sex is very rarely a significant issue, and if in any of our examples we judge it to be relevant we will point this out.

Audience

Our book is primarily addressed to population-oriented psychiatrists, psychologists, social workers, and social scientists who use consultation and collaboration techniques in agencies and institutions that provide health, education, welfare, legal, and correctional services. The book is designed to offer methodological guidance to school psychologists and to students of school psychology; by analyzing the examples of our operations in many different settings, they can draw out generic principles that they can apply in their own work. We also seek to convey our views about ways of improving mental health to non–mental health specialists who act as consultants to line staff and to managers and administrators in such organizations as religious denominations, business firms, industrial bodies, and the armed services.

In addition, we hope that our book will be read by potential consultees and by their managers and administrators who may seek the help of specialist consultants in their organizations. Our purpose is to increase their understanding of the way psychosocial factors at the individual, group, and organizational levels may complicate their daily work, and how different types of consultation and collaboration may improve matters. In particular, our book is addressed to clergy, who may learn from our experience in the Episcopal church how to capitalize on the benefits of traditional parish roles in helping congregants master life stress, and who may also, on their own, work out clergy-to-clergy support services similar to those developed by our Episcopal colleagues.

Overview of the Contents

Part One presents many aspects of the theory and practice of mental health consultation. The first chapter describes how the demands, opportunities, and constraints of the different settings in which we have worked as mental health specialists over the past forty years have stimulated us to develop our concepts and techniques, and to modify and enrich them in response to our continuing experience. The goal of this chapter is to show that our ideas and methods did not grow out of a systematic body of theory but accumulated as a collection of ad hoc responses to the practice demands of our service responsibilities, and were then molded by our search for generic elements that would also apply to other settings.

In Chapter Two, consultation is defined as a disciplined process of interaction between a specialist consultant and a consultee who is not a specialist in psychology, but whose caregiving profession pays attention to mental health issues. The particular characteristics of this method are described and differentiated from other types of interprofessional communication, such as education and supervision. A fourfold classification of consultation is proposed, which guides consultants in choosing their techniques.

Chapter Three describes the steps in deciding whether and how to develop a consultation program: choosing appropriate agencies and caregivers; exploring the community; and promoting initial contacts with a target organization.

Chapter Four describes the crucial step of building relationships with a consultee institution. The chapter shows how to negotiate a formal agreement that defines the terms of the partnership, and describes regularly occurring complications and ways of dealing with them.

An optimal supportive, nonhierarchical consultee-consultant relationship is the vehicle for all consultation. Chapter Five describes how such a relationship is actively promoted by the consultant, and offers guidance in counteracting covert manipulations that would influence the consultant to use psychotherapy techniques.

The next seven chapters provide detailed descriptions of techniques to accomplish the four categories of consultation. Chapter Six describes the steps in the first category of consultation, *client-centered case consultation*. The consultant must make a specialized assessment of the client by investigating him directly and then deciding on appropriate remedial action.

Chapter Seven discusses the second category, *consultee-centered case consultation*. The chapter focuses mainly on lack of professional objectivity, which may be due to overinvolvement, similarity between the consultee's life and that of the client, simple identification of the consultee with one of the actors in the client's case, unconscious transference links between the consultee's past and some element in the case, and characterological distortions of perception and behavior in the consultee.

Chapter Eight describes specific techniques to remedy the cognitive distortion that we call theme interference, where an unconscious cognitive constellation, a "theme," is triggered by the consultant's sensitivity to a particular element in the case.

Chapter Nine uses tape recordings to describe an unsuccessful group consultation. The case example highlights the ever-present hazard of personal overinvolvement and loss of professional objectivity.

Chapter Ten, in contrast, describes the details of a successful consultation in which a consultant and members of a consultation group helped a consultee overcome professional inhibitions produced by subjective distortions.

Chapter Eleven describes the third type of consultation—*program-centered administrative consultation*—and includes case examples of techniques to deal with the complications of this process, where the consultant is asked to help with administrative or policy problems.

Consultee-centered administrative consultation, the fourth type, is the most complicated. Here the consultant has the mission of modifying the attitudes and practices of staff, including helping them to change policies as a way to improve the efficiency and effectiveness of their enterprise. Chapter Twelve shows how principles of consultee-centered case consultation may guide the consultant in dealing with individuals and groups of staff.

Part Two takes up the alternative technique of mental health *collaboration*. Chapter Thirteen defines the nature and purpose of collaboration, and differentiates it from consultation, the main difference being that in collaboration the specialist *accepts responsibility* for the mental health outcome of the clients. Techniques are discussed to handle expectable problems in this process.

The challenges of collaboration will vary according to the realities inside the host institution, and a collaborating specialist must use special techniques geared to the various effectiveness levels he encounters. Chapter Fourteen describes how he deals with the problems and opportunities in a well-organized institution, using as an example the experience of a child psychiatrist working in a pediatric surgery department of a general hospital.

Chapter Fifteen describes a collaboration attempt with the staff of a poorly organized children's rehabilitation hospital. Experience with this example raises the question of the viability of intervention by collaborating specialists who penetrate a poorly organized institution from an outside base.

Part Three examines certain methodological and technical issues. Chapter Sixteen discusses how school psychologists use our methods, primarily collaboration.

Chapter Seventeen focuses on a controversial characteristic of our techniques of mental health consultation. We advocate that the consultant in consultee-centered consultation covertly collect information about the consultee's sensitivities to aspects of the case and decide whether they are distorting his professional objectivity. The consultant then influences the consultee to modify his expectations about the case, but without making his operations explicit. This aspect of our technique is manipulative, and in this chapter we analyze how manipulation operates as a covert method of influence.

Chapter Eighteen examines the present-day implications of the past twenty years' experience in this field. Consultation by mental health specialists has stood the test of time, and techniques pioneered by mental health consultants have achieved widespread acceptance. The chapter summarizes these techniques and emphasizes that the underlying principles are the results of our practical experience in the field.

Our final chapter sounds a note of caution. All mental health specialists who use mental health consultation and other preventively oriented techniques must realize that non–mental health professionals may misinterpret our messages and misuse our concepts to weaken, rather than strengthen, their clients. Our population orientation calls on us to spread our mental health messages widely; the danger of distortion in the way our ideas are interpreted and implemented increases the more we disseminate them. The chapter suggests ways of combating this difficulty.

Acknowledgments

We are very pleased to acknowledge the special help we received in preparing this book from Judie L. Alpert, Jan Close Conoley, William P. Erchul, Terry B. Gutkin, Jan N. Hughes, Nadine Lambert, Joel Meyers, Walter B. Pryzwansky, and Ann C. Schulte. Each of these professors of psychology is responsible for university training of school psychologists in methods of consultation. They advised us on how to address the urgent needs of their students and colleagues in the field of educational psychology, and they prepared specific questions for us to address in Chapter Sixteen.

We are particularly indebted to William P. Erchul, director of the school psychology program at North Carolina State University, who encouraged us to write the book at this time, reviewed sections of the manuscript, and mobilized his colleagues to volunteer their assistance.

Jerusalem, Israel   Gerald Caplan
September 1992   Ruth B. Caplan

THE AUTHORS

Gerald Caplan is professor of psychiatry, emeritus, of Harvard University and professor of child psychiatry, emeritus, of the Hebrew University of Jerusalem, Israel. He received his B.Sc. degree (1937) in anatomy and physiology, his M.B.Ch.B. degree (1940) in medicine, and his M.D. degree (1945), all from the Victoria University of Manchester, England. He received his D.P.M. (1942) from the Royal Colleges of Physicians and Surgeons, London, his honorary M.A. degree (1970) from Harvard University, and his F.R.C.Psych. degree (1981) from the Royal College of Psychiatrists of England. He was trained in general psychiatry at Birmingham University, England, in child psychiatry at the Tavistock Clinic, London, England, and in psychoanalysis at the London Institute of Psychoanalysis and the Boston Psychoanalytic Institute. He has been a full member of the British Psychoanalytic Society and of the International Psychoanalytic Association since 1975. He has been a fellow of the American Psychiatric Association since 1965 and a member of the executive committee of the International Association of Child and Adolescent Psychiatry and Allied Professions since he helped establish it in 1948; he has been its honorary president since 1970.

Gerald Caplan is a world leader in the fields of preventive psychiatry; adult, child, and family psychiatry; and community mental health. He and his colleagues at the Harvard School of Public Health, and later at Harvard Medical School, conducted a series of studies on responses to stress and individual, family, and population factors responsible for mental illness, and they developed the concepts, techniques, and organizational models that were a main basis for the community mental health center movement in the United States. They trained a multidisciplinary cadre of specialists in this field, who now occupy leadership positions in federal and state programs and in universities in the United States. Gerald Caplan has influenced the development of community mental health programs in many countries of Europe, where he has spread his influence through consultation and teaching, and through his writings, many of which have been translated into other languages. He has been particularly influential in promoting public health approaches to preventing mental disorder, crisis theory and practice, support system theory and practice, and techniques of anticipatory guidance, preventive intervention, mental health consultation, mental health collaboration, and mediation. He has written 150 journal articles and 17 books, the best known of which are *An Approach to Community Mental Health* (1961), *Principles of Preventive Psychiatry* (1964), *Theory and Practice of Mental Health Consultation* (1970), *Support Systems and Community Mental Health* (1974), *Arab and Jew in Jerusalem* (1980, with R. B. Caplan), and *Population-Oriented Psychiatry* (1989).

Gerald Caplan worked as deputy medical superintendent at Swansea Mental Hospital in Wales from 1943 to 1945; he worked as psychiatrist in the adult department of Tavistock Clinic in London from 1945 to 1948 and in its children's department from 1946 to 1948. He was adviser in psychiatry to the Ministry of Health of Israel from 1948 to 1949 and psychiatric director of the Lasker Mental Hygiene and Child Guidance Center of Hadassah in Jerusalem, Israel, from 1949 to 1952. Between 1952 and 1964 he worked at the Harvard School of Public Health, where he was head of its Community Mental Health Program (1954 to 1964) with the title of associate professor of mental health. In 1964 he moved to Harvard Medical School to establish and direct its Laboratory of Community Psychiatry and was there until 1978 as clinical professor of psychiatry and later as professor of psychiatry. When he retired to emeritus status, he was appointed professor of child psychiatry and chairman of the department of child and adolescent psychiatry at the Hadassah–Hebrew University Hospitals in Jerusalem. Since 1984 he has worked as scientific director of the Jerusalem Institute for the Study of Psychological Stress and of its Jerusalem Family Center.

Ruth B. Caplan, who currently devotes most of her energies to bringing up her five children, received her B.A. degree (1965), magna cum laude, from Radcliffe College and her M.A. (1969) and Ph.D. (1974) degrees from Harvard University in English literature.

Her main research interests have focused on the development of psychiatric concepts and institutions in the United States, and on the development and techniques of mental health consultation, based on participant observation of mental health consultation groups with parish priests of the Episcopal church in Massachusetts. She also collaborated in the research on the relationships of Arabs and Jews in Jerusalem conducted by her father, Gerald Caplan, from 1969 to 1977. She has published a series of articles on the development of community psychiatry concepts and on distributive-statistical techniques in linguistic and literary research, as well as three books: *Psychiatry and the Community in Nineteenth-Century America* (1969), *Helping the Helpers to Help* (1972), and *Arab and Jew in Jerusalem* (1980, with G. Caplan).

Ruth Caplan worked as historian in the Division of Mental Hygiene of the Department of Mental Health of the Commonwealth of Massachusetts from 1965 to 1968; as visiting assistant in community psychiatry at the Laboratory of Community Psychiatry, Harvard Medical School, from 1967 to 1969; as associate in psychiatry, Harvard Medical School, from 1969 to 1972; as assistant in the English literature department, Hebrew University of Jerusalem, from 1971 to 1975; and as lecturer in that department from 1975 to 1980. She taught courses to medical students, psychiatric residents, and community mental health specialists at Harvard Medical School on history of community psychiatry, history of psychological theories, and history of psychiatric institutions from 1966 to 1972. She taught courses to undergraduate and graduate students at the Hebrew University of Jerusalem from 1971 to 1980.

MENTAL HEALTH

CONSULTATION AND COLLABORATION

PART I

Theory and Practice of Mental Health Consultation

CHAPTER ONE

The Evolution
of Our Work

In 1949 I (Gerald Caplan) worked at the Lasker Mental Hygiene and Child Guidance Center in Jerusalem. Part of my duties included supervising the mental health of about sixteen thousand new-immigrant children in the Youth Aliyah organization, an Israeli organization for the absorption and education of child immigrants. These children, aged fourteen to eighteen, were cared for in more than a hundred residential institutions, situated mainly in the communal settlements up and down the country and staffed by nonprofessional child-care workers and educators. Our small team of psychologists and social workers was expected to diagnose and treat children who were emotionally disturbed but not to the degree that they had to be removed from their regular educational setting. We rapidly discovered that this was an impossible task if we operated along traditional lines of accepting referrals and diagnosing individual children. During our first year we had about a thousand referrals, and however fast we worked we could never keep up with the demand.

Counseling the Counselors

Transportation in Israel was often difficult, and it was sometimes more feasible to send a staff member out to an institution to investigate a batch of referrals than to bring the children to one of our central clinics. Since we could not provide psychotherapy for the disturbed children, our psychologists began to talk informally with the institutions' staff about ways to reduce the pressure on the children or support them in working through their problems themselves. We spent more and more time talking to the instructors and housemothers about the children we were seeing. We discovered that often children referred to us did not appear to be mentally ill. The problem seemed rather that they were getting on the adults' nerves.

We found that many instructors and institutions appeared to have special difficulties with children of certain types. Although the population of immigrant children was fairly randomly distributed among the different institutions and did not appear to vary much in its composition, we began to notice that one institution was continually referring bedwetters, while another was referring children with learning difficulties, and a third was plagued by aggressive children. If we asked the staff of the first institution whether they had children with learning or aggression problems, the typical reply was "Of course! How could one expect that children who have been brought up in the slums of Casablanca and have never been to school would not have difficulty adjusting to sitting on a school bench at the age of fifteen and would not let off steam by occasional violent outbursts?" Similarly, if we asked the staff of the other institutions whether any of their children wet the bed, we were told that this was a normal and predictable reaction of children made miserable by separation from their parents and families. It seemed that the staff members of each institution shared idiosyncratic sensitivities.

Gradually, we changed fundamentally our ways of working. Apart from exceptional cases, we used our staff in what we then called "counseling the instructors" instead of investigating and reporting on the children. We began to spend most of our time discussing, not the diagnostic classification of the child, but the various management possibilities that were available to the instructor. We concentrated on an instructor's perception of his pupil and tried to help him deal with the child's problem as he saw it.

A number of interesting findings began to emerge. Many times we saw instructors who were at their wits' end with a child. After a sympathetic and objective discussion, their range of alternatives seemed to widen, and their chances of finding something that

would work improved. Second, we were impressed by gross misperceptions of the children revealed in instructors' reports. We began
to see that an important goal of our counseling was to undo these
stereotyped perceptions. This proved relatively easy to accomplish.
After discussing the case with a psychologist, who introduced his
own observation of the child as a human being in difficulties rather
than as a "problem child," the instructors usually abandoned their
stereotypes of the child. Their attitude changed dramatically and
their management of the case improved.

The third significant finding involved instructors who
seemed quite upset themselves. They had called on us for help with
a problem child, but it seemed to us that their stereotyping and
narrowing of focus were symptoms of emotional crisis in their own
personal life or in the social system of their institution. At first our
workers felt rather uncomfortable in these situations; but soon we
found that our best results seemed to occur with instructors who
were most upset. In fact, we developed a system of priorities for
consultation, choosing cases where the instructors seemed to be in
the most intense crisis. In this way we felt we could use our limited
staff to best advantage.

It is of interest to note that we did not choose to treat these
instructors with psychotherapy, which would have confronted them
with the fact that they were displacing onto the child problems in
themselves and their institution, and then would have helped them
work directly on these problems. This approach might have come
most naturally to a psychoanalytic psychiatrist such as myself. Several factors worked against this happening.

First, we were at that time engaged in some interesting research in the well-baby clinics of Jerusalem, where we were trying
to prevent emotional disorder in infants by identifying and remedying disorders of the mother-infant relationship. We were developing methods of focused casework to "unlink" a mother's personal
disturbance from its displacement onto her new baby. We believed
this might be accomplished in a few therapeutic sessions if we kept
the focus on the mother-child relationship and prevented the discussions from veering over into an examination of the mother's
nonmaternal problems. Counseling instructors about their relationships with their pupils seemed to us very similar to this preventive

work with mothers and babies, and we began to use a similar, carefully focused interviewing technique.

The second factor was that the directors of Youth Aliyah were watching our novel methods with some suspicion. They were paying for the treatment of the children under their care, and they were quite wary of our switch of focus to the instructors. They required continual assurance that the welfare of the children was our primary goal. The instructors were mainly volunteers from the communal settlements, and the directors of Youth Aliyah were quite sensitive to anything that might interfere with the instructors' motivation. They did not want us to upset the instructors by turning them into patients. Indeed, after I left Israel, the staff of the Lasker Center gradually changed its counseling approach, focusing more and more openly on instructors' personal problems and on social issues in their institutions. This aroused increasing resistance, and eventually the whole counseling program fell into disrepute and was terminated.

Before leaving this brief discussion of the Israeli experience, Ruth and I want to emphasize one other issue. Because of the chance nature of the situation, my team at the Lasker Center conducted most of our consultation in the institutions and not in our central offices. We soon discovered that this was most important. We could quickly pick up much more relevant information about the crucial issues by actually going into the institutions. Also, the instructors felt freer to give an authentic account of their perceptions on their home ground. We believe this aspect of our Israeli program was an important formative influence on the style of later mental health consultation programs.

Mental Health Consultation

In 1952 I came to Boston and began my work at the Harvard School of Public Health. During the first few years I collaborated closely with Erich Lindemann in his preventive psychiatry program at the Wellesley Human Relations Service. The work of Lindemann and his colleagues exerted a considerable influence on my thinking and on the pattern of development of what I began to call "mental health consultation" rather than "counseling."

By the time I joined them, Lindemann and his team had worked out a consultation method that was essentially the same as the Israeli counseling approach. They too had moved into this style, not as a result of planning based on theory, but as a pragmatic reaction to the demands of their field. The Wellesley group had been interested in developing methods of observing and analyzing the behavior of children in the classroom as an objective way of screening a school population for disturbed children. Their psychologists had obtained permission to sit at the back of the classrooms in the Wellesley schools and record behavior. Soon the researchers began to be inconvenienced by teachers wanting to talk about their observations before the researchers felt they had anything scientifically valid to report. Nevertheless, as guests in the schools, they felt obliged to be polite to their hosts. Little by little, they discovered that these talks with the teachers seemed to have meaning in their own right. The teachers, on their side, found that these informal chats helped increase their understanding of problem children. Before long, what had originally been a side issue, even an interference, became a formally recognized collaborative effort between the Wellesley school system and the Human Relations Service.

For many years, the Wellesley consultation program involved the use of classroom observation by the consultant as a basis for discussions with the teachers. The Wellesley consultants learned to rely on their own observation of a child's behavior to identify disordered perceptions in the teacher's story about the student. They also used joint observation to help the teachers modify their unrealistic perceptions.

In 1954 I was asked to set up a mental health segment in the field training unit of the Harvard School of Public Health at the Whittier Street Health Center, run by the city health department. This quickly led to the establishment of the Whittier Street Family Guidance Center, which continued its research and training operations until 1962. During most of this period the focus was an intensive study of mental health consultation with public health nurses. We chose this professional group as consultees because we wanted to develop a collaborative relationship with public health workers as a focal point of our community mental health program at the Harvard School of Public Health, and because the nurses were the line workers who were most keen to collaborate with us.

Working with public health nurses also had particular meaning in the light of the theoretical framework of preventive psychiatry that we were developing in cooperation with the Lindemann group at Wellesley. This framework emphasized the significance of periods of life crisis as turning points in psychological development, and the importance of the intervention of caregiving professionals. Our consultation with public health nurses took on a similar focus: primary prevention. These workers are in the front line of contact with those in a lower socioeconomic class, a particularly vulnerable population with whom they have close and continuing relationships. They visit patients in their homes during periods of life crisis: childbirth, especially the birth of premature or congenitally deformed babies; infectious disease; and the disorders of old age. We began to see the role of our consultation program as providing support and guidance to the nurses so that in their everyday work with their patients they could promote healthy coping with life crises and thus reduce the risk of mental disorder in a widespread population.

For a period, our method was called "crisis consultation." Two crises were involved—the crisis in the client and the crisis in the consultee. As we gained more experience, we realized that many nurses came to us for help with patients who were not currently in crisis but who presented management problems because of personality difficulties or mental disorder. We began to realize that mental health consultation could be a method of secondary and tertiary prevention of mental disorder, reducing its prevalence by early diagnosis and prompt effective treatment and reducing the rate of residual disability (Caplan, 1964). We also discovered that only a small proportion of consultees were themselves in manifest crisis. This led us to our formulations on "theme interference" in consultees—namely, idiosyncratic sensitivities that caused subjective interference with professional functioning and a range of psychological disequilibrium, of which a crisis or major upset was an extreme example.

The program at the Whittier Street Health Center, and later in the rest of the city health department, provided us with an excellent opportunity to refine our consultation method. Eventually, we set up a formal research project to evaluate the main technique that had emerged: "theme interference reduction."

Exploring New Settings

In 1962 our team ended the evaluative research program on theme interference reduction with public health nurses, and we moved in 1964 from the Harvard School of Public Health to an expanded teaching and research program in the Laboratory of Community Psychiatry at Harvard Medical School's psychiatry department. Ruth Caplan joined our team, and we began to do much more group consultation and to offer consultation to other agencies. Our experience in these settings provides the basis for many of the examples cited in this book.

Also mirrored in the book are historical developments in which we have been involved, particularly the use of our ideas in the community mental health movement. Mental health consultation to caregivers in other professions has been considered the leading edge of the community mental health center's outreach approach. One indication is its inclusion in the list of obligatory elements in all programs eligible for federal funding.

Although both of us were happy that our ideas and techniques and the specialists we trained played so important a part in the development of this revolutionary service, it is worth emphasizing that we ourselves never actually worked in a community mental health center. From our point of view, the community mental health center represents one of several possible models for providing remedial and preventive services to a *population*. We have come to see mental health consultation itself as one of a number of specialized techniques in what we nowadays call "population-oriented" psychiatry or psychology (G. Caplan, 1989). The term refers to organized programs that seek to satisfy the psychological and psychiatric needs of entire populations, however they may be defined. *Population* is broader than *community*. The term *community* implies a collectivity that is part of the population but bound together by a common origin, history, culture, and identification, usually

residing in a particular locality—characteristics of the potential recipients of the services of the community mental health center.

This population orientation influenced us to move into
many different organizational settings as we sought to capitalize on
our specialized knowledge of human nature to improve the lives of
people who lived, worked, studied, prayed, socialized, or were being
treated in such settings. We hoped to accomplish this by influencing the way the practitioners and administrators inside these organizations dealt with the people whom they served. Our book
provides details of our experiences as we moved beyond public
health centers into the Episcopal church, the Peace Corps, the Job
Corps and other antipoverty programs, the court system, hospitals,
and other health, education, and welfare services.

As we focused on problems we encountered in these different
settings, we had to develop new methods and techniques. Two were
particularly important: group methods of mental health consultation (with the Episcopal clergy in the United States) and methods
of mental health collaboration (on the wards of general hospitals
in Jerusalem, where we built partnerships with our medical and
surgical colleagues). Over the years we have maintained our earlier
interests in using mental health consultation in the school setting,
and we have also begun to add techniques of collaboration. This
produces a mixture that is likely to be more applicable for specialists such as school psychologists, whose staff position affords them
both opportunities and constraints that are lacking for specialists
invited in from the outside.

CHAPTER TWO

A Definition
of Mental Health
Consultation

The term *consultation* is used in many different ways. Some apply it to almost any professional activity carried out by a specialist; in England the professional office of a specialist physician is known as the consulting room, and when he is interviewing or treating a patient, his secretary says he is "in consultation." Others use the term to denote specialized professional activity between two persons in regard to a third; two physicians "consult" about a patient, or a physician "consults" with a mother about her child. Some use the term to describe the work done by a highly trained person—a "consultant."

In this book the term *consultation* is used in a quite restricted sense: a process of interaction between two professionals—the consultant, who is a specialist, and the consultee, who invokes the consultant's help in a current work problem that he believes is within the consultant's area of specialized competence. The work problem involves managing or treating one or more clients of the consultee, or planning or implementing a program to cater to the clients. *Client* is used to denote the layperson who is the focus of the consultee's professional operations; the client could be a teacher's student, a nurse or physician's patient, a clergyman's congregant, or a lawyer's client.

In our definition of *consultation,* the consultant accepts no direct responsibility for implementing remedial action for the client; professional responsibility for the client remains with the consultee just as much as it did before he asked the consultant for help. The consultant may offer helpful clarifications, diagnostic

11

formulations, or advice on treatment; but the consultee will be free to accept or reject all or part of this help. In other words, the consultant exercises no administrative or coercive authority over the consultee; and unless the latter completely implements his prescriptions, the consultant is not liable for the outcome.

Another essential aspect of this type of consultation is that the consultant engages in the activity not only to help the consultee with his current work problem but also to add to the consultee's knowledge so that in the future he can deal more effectively with this category of problem on his own.

In this book the term *mental health consultation* means using this kind of consultation as part of a community program for the promotion of mental health and for the prevention, treatment, and rehabilitation of mental disorders. In this case, the consultants are those with a specialized knowledge of the issues involved—psychiatrists, psychologists, psychiatric social workers, social scientists, mental health nurses, and psychiatric nurses. The consultees are caregiving professionals who play a major role in preventing or treating mental disorders but who have no specialized training in psychiatry and its allied disciplines. They include family doctors, pediatricians, and other medical specialists, hospital and public health nurses, teachers, clergy, lawyers, welfare workers, probation officers, and police. Although the primary role of these professionals does not relate to mental disorders, all of them may at times encounter a mentally disordered person among their clients. They may also encounter idiosyncrasies in a client that overtax their knowledge of psychology, and they may seek help from a mental health consultant. In addition, they may be interested in how their routine professional operations affect the future mental health of their clients, and may ask for guidance in preventing mental disorders and promoting mental health.

From a logistic point of view mental health consultation has special merit in a community program, since a relatively small number of consultants can exert a widespread effect through the intermediation of a large group of consultees, each of whom is in contact with many clients. For consultants to be effective along these lines, they must limit the amount of time devoted to helping any one consultee deal with a current case, and there must be a maximum educational carryover to the consultee's work with other cases.

How Consultation Differs from Other Specialized Methods

A mental health specialist who is formally or informally designated a "consultant" may engage in many types of professional activity—supervision, education, psychotherapy, casework, counseling, administrative inspection, negotiation, liaison, collaboration, coordination, and mediation—all based on his fundamental knowledge of human motivation and human relations. To some extent these activities are similar in goals, methods, and techniques, but we will achieve a higher level of professional functioning when the specialist is able to differentiate these various activities and employ each of them consistently in relation to his current assignment, his professional goals, and his understanding of the situation.

To highlight the specific characteristics of consultation it may be useful to emphasize the differences between it and some of these other activities, particularly supervision, education, psychotherapy, and collaboration.

Regarding supervision, one chief difference is that the supervisor is usually a senior member of the same professional specialty as the supervisee, whereas a consultant is usually of a different specialty from the consultee. The supervisor has some administrative responsibility for the supervisee's work and represents the agency in which both work. The supervisor's task is to safeguard the quality of care for the agency's clients, with special reference to the fact that supervisees have limited experience and may not yet be fully independent professionals. In contrast, the consultant usually comes into the agency from outside; he bears no administrative responsibility for the quality of the consultee's work or for the care of the clients.

Supervision is a continuous process. The supervisor's responsibilities include inspecting the supervisee's work and initiating discussion about any aspects that do not appear satisfactory. Consultation is initiated by the consultee or by the consultee's supervisor. It usually takes place in an ad hoc pattern as a short series of interactions that arise in relation to a current work difficulty and terminate when this has been dealt with. Any continuing relationship between a consultee and a consultant is activated in the future when help is sought for a fresh problem.

A supervisor has a higher position in the hierarchy of the institution and can enforce decisions on the supervisee. In contrast, there is no power differential between consultant and consultee; the consultee is free to accept or reject any message or prescription. Ideally, the only difference in status derives from the authority of ideas; the consultant's extra competence in his own specialty is explicitly or implicitly recognized by the consultee when he asks for help. On the other hand, the consultant should reciprocally respect the consultee in his own professional specialty in which the consultant is not expert; for example, a consultant psychiatrist arouses the respect of the consultee teacher because of the psychiatrist's knowledge of interpersonal relations, and in turn the psychiatrist respects the teacher's special competence in pedagogy. This is a coordinate relationship, as contrasted with the superior-subordinate relationship of supervision.

One type of supervision resembles consultation—supervision of a special skill or technique as part of a staff in-service training program; for example, a psychiatrist supervising psychologists doing psychotherapy in a mental hospital or psychiatric clinic. Often these supervisors may not be full-time staff members but may be hired on a sessional basis purely as a supervisor. As staff workers rather than line workers, they have very little administrative authority over their supervisees, and they may not be responsible for inspecting the quality of patient care. Variations of such a role shade off to become almost indistinguishable from consultation. However, close inspection may reveal an unstated or unexercised authority differential and an administrative responsibility for the client's treatment; these are the essential differences between the two roles.

Supervision of a skill or tutoring is one form of education, and it is used widely in programs of professional training. Here the supervisor, or tutor, is clearly seen as a teacher and the supervisee as the student. How do these and other educational situations differ from consultation? Since consultation has been defined as "help" plus "education," there is clearly some overlap. The difference between consultation and most other types of education lies mainly

in the relationships—the special coordinate, facilitative relationship between consultee and consultant, contrasted with the
hierarchical, obligatory relationship between student and teacher. A
student may be free to choose a particular course, but once enrolled
he undertakes to pay attention to the teacher, to do his exercises, and
to carry out the precepts of his teacher. This contrasts with consultation, in which the consultee is continually free to come and go
and to accept or reject. Most education is organized in the form of
courses with a set structure, or in the form of continuous exposure
of the students to the influence of the teachers for a period of time,
limited by contract. In contrast, consultation may be invoked from
time to time on an indefinite basis.

Another difference is that in most education the teacher has
some clear idea of the content he intends to impart to the student,
whether this be factual knowledge or a range of skills or attitudes.
This content may be imparted in various ways, systematic and less
systematic. In contrast, the consultant usually has no preconceived
idea of a content area he wishes to impart to his consultee. Like the
teacher, his goal is to increase the consultee's insight, sensitivity, or
skill and also, perhaps, evaluate the extent to which he has succeeded in this; but his responsibility does not include appraising the
consultee's handling of problems for which he has not sought help,
and he takes it for granted that his efforts will remain focused only
on specific segments of the consultee's functioning. Teachers who
conduct problem-centered case seminars come closest to consultation, but even they are not entirely nondirective. And although they
use material of current interest presented by a seminar member, they
guide the discussions in channels that will eventually cover the
content area they are trying to teach.

However proficient a consultee may become in handling certain categories of work problem, there is always the possibility of
facing unusual cases that he may not know how to handle, and in
which he may be helped by consulting an expert. A professional
worker should ideally continue learning all his life, and from this
point of view there should be no end to education. But education
defined in a somewhat narrower sense—a specific activity that promotes a high level of competence—should be needed less and less
as professionals become more competent. Experience shows that, in

contrast, the need for consultation and its value may *rise* with increasing competence of the consultee. A public health nurse who has become quite sophisticated in the mental health dimensions of her work is more likely to ask for, and profit from, mental health consultation than a nurse who does not have the insight and skill to identify the psychological complications of her cases.

The effectiveness of a professional worker—a physician, a nurse, a schoolteacher—who is dealing with the mental health problems of a client is likely to be influenced by personal subjective factors. Longstanding personality difficulties, personal or cultural prejudices or sensitivities, and current emotional upsets in the professional worker may distort his perceptions of his client and his remedial efforts. Some mental health authorities have suggested that the solution is to provide psychotherapeutic help, usually in the form of group psychotherapy that focuses on the personality problems that are most intrusive into the work field.

Mental health consultation deals with this problem in another way, different from techniques of psychotherapy. Psychotherapy is here defined as a treatment procedure undertaken by a helping professional to cure or relieve the symptoms of a mental disorder in someone who conceives of himself as a patient. The person seeks diagnosis and treatment because he is aware of personal pain or discomfort that he defines as an illness. In entering into a relationship with the therapist, he agrees to an infringement of his customary privacy, sometimes in bodily matters, such as undressing for a physical examination or allowing his bodily fluids to be taken for investigation, and invariably in the psychological sphere—for example, talking about thoughts, memories, and feelings that are usually hidden from others. This relationship gives the therapist special power over the patient, which has led to a system of controls over the professional conduct of therapists; patients rely on these controls when they invest their trust in a psychotherapist.

In contrast, a consultee usually has no awareness of personal disorder other than his anxiety and frustration regarding his client. He may sometimes be aware of his own psychological problems and their intrusion into the work field, but he is asking for consultation about the work difficulty and expects his own privacy to be respected. The consultant takes care not to intrude on this privacy, and he does not direct the discussion into an appraisal of the consultee's personal life or, in some types of consultation described in this book, even the consultee's feelings about his work. The consultant takes it for granted that, like himself, the consultee has personal feelings and psychological complications, but the consultation discussions focus on the client's problem and the professional task of dealing with it. Instead of the hierarchical doctor-patient relationship, there is the coordinate relationship of two professional colleagues working together on a case, and personal matters are equally excluded by both.

Another difference, even when psychotherapy is invoked because of work problems, is that the primary goal of consultation is increased effectiveness in the work setting, whereas the primary goal of psychotherapy is cure for the patient. To cure the patient may mean lowering his productivity, if it was at too high a level for his personal comfort, or it may mean leaving that job altogether.

A source of confusion in differentiating consultation and psychotherapy lies in the terms *therapeutic* and *psychotherapeutic*. Effective consultation will be helpful not only to the client but also to the consultee. The negative reactions of anxiety, frustration, shame, and guilt, which may have been provoked by the work impasse, will give way to feelings of gratification, confidence, and happiness. In certain cases where the work problem was linked with a consultee's personal problem, his experience of success in his dealings with the client may have a reflexive meaning for his own life; a topic that previously provoked insecurity may henceforward be handled confidently and effectively. In these cases a secondary result of the consultation is an increased state of psychological well-being in the consultee, and this may amount to a very real personality growth and development. The consultation may then clearly be said to have had a "psychotherapeutic" effect on the consultee.

Another activity in which mental health and other specialists commonly engage is collaboration. We use this term to designate the functioning of a specialist who is called in by another professional to help deal with a specialized problem arising in the condition of the latter's client. The specialist is invited not merely to enlarge his colleague's understanding of the case and to advise on action but also to take part in implementing the action plan. We will deal with the differences between collaboration and consultation in Part Two.

Four Types of Mental Health Consultation

A mental health consultant has no predetermined ground to cover with his consultees. His job calls for him to react to their temporary feelings of need for help with current problems in their work field. These may involve the difficulties of a line worker in handling a particular client, or the problems of a group of administrators in developing or improving a program for part or all of the organization. The consultant must therefore be prepared for unexpected shifts of focus both in content and scope of consultation problems and in the position of his consultees within their organizational structure.

Since this setting rarely provides him with the clear set of mutual expectations to which he has become accustomed in his traditional work as a teacher, psychotherapist, clinical psychologist, or agency caseworker, he must develop an internal conceptual map that he carries into the sphere of consultation operations so that he can quickly choose an appropriate response to the demands of the situation.

This conceptual map must indicate the limits of the consultant's professional domain. Although his role may not be obviously prestructured, he is not in fact free to do anything that comes into his head or to respond completely to all requests from would-be consultees. He is constrained by the policies of his own agency, which, for instance, may permit him to work with the consultee institution only to the extent that he helps prevent disability or defect due to mental disorder in the community. These policies probably do not allow him to spend time on problems that have no clear connection with the mental health of the community. He is also constrained by the policies of the consultee institution, which restrict him to working with certain staff members in a way that will promote their accomplishment of its mission and avoid upsetting its accepted patterns of communication and authority. His intervention is not likely to be welcomed if, at the invitation of an individual consultee, he takes sides in informal power struggles among the staff or if he suddenly disrupts the traditional processes of decision making.

In these constraints on his consultation operations, the consultant is helped by a classification system that allows him to categorize each situation so that he knows in general how it may be expected to unfold and what the most promising methods of dealing with it are likely to be. There are many useful ways of classifying mental health consultation for this purpose. We have developed a fourfold classification based on two major divisions: a primary focus on a case problem versus an administrative problem, and a primary interest in giving a recommendation for solution of the work difficulty versus attempting to improve the problem-solving capacity of the consultees and leaving them to work out their own way of solving it.

In practice, consultation situations rarely fall neatly into one of these four categories; most are mixed. The details of the mixture may alter over time as the interactions of consultant and consultee change in relation to the unfolding of the situation. But if the consultant continually assesses the type of process in which he is involved and maintains an awareness of the relative loading of its different elements, he will find it easier to choose an effective general pattern of response.

The four consultation types are described below.

A-1. Client-Centered Case Consultation

The consultee's work difficulty relates to the management of a particular case or group of cases. The consultant helps by using his specialized knowledge and skills to make an expert assessment of the client's problem and to recommend how the consultee should deal with the case. The primary goal of the consultation is for the consultant to communicate to the consultee how this client can be helped. A subsidiary goal is that the consultee may use his experience with this case to improve his knowledge and skills, so that he will be better able in the future to handle comparable problems on his own. This is the traditional type of specialist consultation of medical practice, as when a general practitioner asks for an expert opinion from a cardiologist, when one of his patients is suffering from a complicated heart condition that he does not feel competent to handle satisfactorily on his own.

A-2. Consultee-Centered Case Consultation

Here, too, the consultee's work problem relates to the management of a particular client, and he invokes the consultant's help to improve his handling of the case. In this type of consultation the consultant focuses his main attention on trying to understand the consultee's difficulty with the case and to help him remedy this. The consultee's difficulty may be caused by lack of knowledge about the type of problem, lack of skill in making use of such knowledge, lack of self-confidence so that he is uncertain in using his knowledge and skills, or lack of professional objectivity due to the interference of subjective emotional complications.

The primary goal of the consultant is to help the consultee remedy whichever of these shortcomings he judges to be present. The consultant may help the consultee increase his knowledge or skills, he may support and reassure him to increase his self-confidence, or he may help him increase his professional objectivity. The purpose is to improve professional functioning so that the consultee can solve the client's problems and those of future clients with similar difficulties. The aim of this type of consultation is frankly to educate the consultee, using his problems with the current client as a lever and a learning opportunity; the expertness of the consultant is focused on this task rather than, as in a client-centered case consultation, on diagnosing the client and developing a prescription for his treatment.

B-1. Program-Centered Administrative Consultation

Here the work problem is in the area of planning and administration—how to develop a new program or to improve an existing one. The consultant helps by using his knowledge of administration and social systems, as well as his expert knowledge and experience of mental health theory and practice and of program development in other institutions, to collect and analyze data about the points at issue. On the basis of this he suggests short-term and long-term solutions for the organization's administrative questions. As with category A-1, his primary goal is to prescribe an effective course of action. He hopes that a side effect will be that the consultees will learn something from his analysis and recommendations that they can use, on their own, in dealing with similar administrative problems in the future.

B-2. Consultee-Centered Administrative Consultation

This is the analogue of category A-2, but with a focus on problems of programming and organization instead of on dealing with a particular client. Here, too, the primary concern of the consultant is not to collect and analyze administrative data relating to the mission of the institution but to remedy difficulties and shortcomings among the consultees that interfere with their ability to grapple with tasks of program development and organization.

In addition to lack of knowledge, skills, self-confidence, and objectivity in individuals, the consultees' problem may be the result of group difficulties—poor leadership, authority problems, lack of role complementarity, communication blocks, and the like. The consultant's primary goal is to understand and help remedy these; and his hope is that his successful accomplishment of this task will enable the consultees to develop and implement effective plans, on their own, to accomplish the mission of their organization.

Summary of Characteristics of Mental Health Consultation

Let us now review our preceding discussion by briefly summarizing the characteristics of mental health consultation as we are defining it in this book.

1. Mental health consultation is used between two professionals—consultant and consultee—in respect to a lay client or a program for such clients.

2. The consultee's work problem must be defined by him as being in the mental health area, relating to (a) mental disorder or personality idiosyncrasies of the client, (b) promotion of mental health in the client, or (c) interpersonal aspects of the work situation. The consultant must have expert knowledge in these areas.

3. The consultant has no administrative responsibility for the consultee's work or professional responsibility for the outcome of the client's case. He is under no compulsion to modify the consultee's conduct of the case.

4. The consultee is under no compulsion to accept the consultant's ideas or suggestions.

5. The basic relationship between the two is coordinate. There is no built-in hierarchy. This is a situation that in our culture potentiates the influence of ideas. The consultee's freedom to accept or reject what the consultant says enables him to take quickly as his own any ideas that appeal to him.

6. The coordinate relationship is fostered by the consultant's being a member of another profession (usually) and coming briefly into the consultee's institution from the outside.

7. It is further supported by the fact that consultation is usually given as a short series of interviews—two or three, on the average—that take place intermittently in response to the consultee's awareness of need for help. The relationship in individual consultation is not maintained or dependency fostered by continuing contact. In group consultation there may be regular meetings, but dependency is reduced by peer support.

8. Consultation is expected to continue indefinitely. Consultees can be expected to encounter unusual work problems throughout their careers. Increasing competence and sophistication of consultees in their own profession increase the likelihood of their recognizing mental health complications and asking for consultation.

9. A consultant has no predetermined body of information that he intends to impart to a particular consultee. He responds only to the segment of the problem that the consultee exposes. The consultant does not seek to remedy other areas of inadequacy in the consultee. He expects other issues to be raised in future consultations.

10. The twin goals of consultation are to help the consultee improve his handling or understanding of the current work difficulty and through this to increase his capacity to master future problems of a similar type.

11. The aim is to improve the consultee's job performance and not his sense of well-being. It is envisaged, however, that since the two are linked, a consultee's feelings of personal worth will

probably be increased by a successful consultation, as will also his capacity to deal in a reality-based socially acceptable way with certain of his life difficulties. In other words, a successful consultation may have the secondary effect of being therapeutic to the consultee.

12. Consultation does not focus overtly on personal problems and feelings of the consultee. It respects his privacy. The consultant does not allow the discussion of personal and private material in the consultation interview. This does not mean that the consultant disregards the consultee's feelings. He is particularly sensitive to these and to the disturbance of task functioning produced by personal problems. He deals with personal problems, however, in a special way, such as by discussing how the consultee has displaced them onto the client's case and the work setting.

13. Consultation is usually only one of the professional functions of a specialist, even if he is formally entitled "consultant." He should use the consultation method only when it is appropriate. At other times he should use different methods. Sometimes the demands of a situation will cause him to put aside his consultation. For instance, if he gets information during a consultation interview that leads him to judge that the consultee's actions are seriously endangering the client, such as by not preventing suicide or not leading toward treatment for a dangerous psychosis, he should set aside his consultant role and revert to his basic role as a psychiatrist, psychologist, or social worker. He will then give advice or take action that he does not allow the consultee the freedom to reject. This destroys the coordinate relationship and interrupts the consultation contact in favor of a higher goal. Such dramatic occasions have been rare in our experience, but consultants must constantly keep the possibility in mind as a realization of the realistic limits of this method.

14. Finally, it is worth emphasizing that mental health consultation is a method of communication between a mental health specialist and other professionals. It does not denote a new profession, merely a special way in which existing professionals may operate.

CHAPTER THREE

Developing
a Consultation Program
in a Community

Mental health consultation is usually part of an organized program of community mental health that is designed to promote the mental health of the population and to reduce community rates of mental disorder. In this setting a mental health consultant is not an independent practitioner who responds to ad hoc invitations from other professionals to help them by using skills he happens to possess. He is one of the emissaries of his organization, who operates in the field as part of a carefully conceived institutional plan to deal with a community problem.

In planning a consultation program, certain organizational issues are relevant; in this chapter we consider these issues.

Establishing Basic Philosophy and Mission

The overall mission of the mental health agency is primarily derived from the mandate it receives from the community. Its domain is officially defined by federal, state, county, or local government, or by formal decisions taken by voluntary associations and planning councils. This mandate is accepted by its governing body, which is either an administrative unit of the executive branch of government or is a local incorporated board of directors. In any case, it is able to accept legal responsibility for such tasks as collecting and disbursing funds, renting premises, hiring staff, and directing the other operations designed to fulfill its mission, including reporting back to its sponsors on the use of funds and achievement of goals.

24

In the United States, the mission of a particular mental health agency is very much molded by public opinion, which mirrors the spirit of the times and which is expressed through current legislation, governmental administrative practices, and the policies of voluntary civic organizations. The feelings of need of the local community are communicated to the governing body of the agency and to its professional staff along these channels by its elected or appointed representatives, and also by direct communication of individuals and special interest groups, such as parents of retarded or emotionally ill children.

A factor of increasing importance during the 1960s was the influence of "consumers" in the health and welfare field, namely the population that is supposed to be served. This was related to a significant change in the philosophy of civic and legislative leaders, who were becoming alert to the delivery of services to populations in need of them, rather than, as in the past, restricting themselves to establishing institutions and agencies to which appropriate clients might be admitted. This in turn was related to an increasing militancy on the part of the deprived segments of the population, such as minority groups and the poverty-stricken inhabitants of metropolitan slums. This participation of the consumers was linked with civil rights, urban development, and antipoverty legislation.

The third factor that is significant in determining the mission of a mental health agency is the point of view and the professional skills of its staff. These are to some extent determined by the attitudes of the governing board, which selects the director and possibly ratifies the appointment of other staff. An important aspect of appointing the director is exploring his views about the mission of the agency. The need for consonance of views between the director and the board does not end when the appointment decision has been made. Throughout his service, the director must pay particular attention to his sources of sanction, and must carefully define the extent to which the agency's mission is molded by the board and the public. The mission is also influenced by the special interests and competence of himself and his staff, which in turn are modified by current ideologies within their professional reference groups.

How much leadership and initiative the professional staff

should exercise in persuading its governing board to bring the agency's mission into line with current professional ideology is a complicated question. If the staff exercises too powerful a voice in the matter, there is always the danger of deviating too far from the will of the population and its leaders. On the other hand, it is the staff's obligation to communicate adequately to its board the results of professional research, so that the representatives of the consumers and of the providers of resources may base their policy decisions on as wide as possible a fund of information about realistic possibilities of accomplishment. They must take account of the size and skills of the staff, their knowledge of latest scientific and technical experience, and their information about innovative thinking in other places.

The dynamic interplay of all these factors leads to fundamental decisions, which are continually being modified, about the overall goals of the mental health agency, and about the relative priority of these goals in the light of the most pressing needs of the population, the supply of resources, the availability of other services in the community with which the efforts of the agency can be coordinated, and, most important, the value systems of the leaders. These decisions will determine, for instance, which subpopulations at special risk should have highest priority, for example, expectant mothers, young children, widows, old people in urban relocation areas, or socially deprived children. The decisions will determine how much staff time is spent treating different categories of the mentally ill, and how much is devoted to prevention of mental disorders or promotion of mental health. They will determine the agency's relative responsibility for dealing with cases within its own walls as compared with helping others in the community improve their handling of the mental health dimension of their work.

By such decisions, the agency will divide its staff services between intramural and extramural activities, and in the latter category will develop an appropriate balance among such activities as education of community professionals, collaboration, public information and public relations, liaison, case finding, and consultation. This in turn will affect recruitment and in-service training policies, so that the agency will be able to provide those technical services, such as mental health consultation, that are needed to fulfill its mission.

Two further points are worthy of emphasis. First, an essential aspect of the leadership role of the agency director is the continual redefinition of the organization's mission, which must be kept in focus by his staff as the superordinate set of goals of all their efforts. Second, the mission must be understood in terms of solving problems of mental health and mental disorder of the population by using whatever people and methods seem best fitted for this, and not in terms of categorical services or methods. The task of the agency should be to treat and rehabilitate mentally ill people, or to prevent mental disorder. It should not be seen as the provision of analytic psychotherapy, or casework, or mental health consultation. The latter approach leads inevitably to undue emphasis on role definition and restrictive specialization practices, and on bureaucratic procedures and hierarchies; on recruiting "good" cases to cater to the needs of particular methods and team members; and on rejecting or avoiding "unsuitable" cases that are not appropriate grist for the mill.

Developing a Conceptual Framework

A fundamental task for the professional staff of the mental health agency is to develop an overall map of the goals that are involved in its mission and of the concepts that can be used to guide its achievement. The coordination of activities of staff members in developing this map can be managed in two main ways. One approach, derived from traditional bureaucratic administrative practice, is to draw up a rational organizational chart and to parcel out the tasks among various officeholders, each of whom has a defined role that articulates with neighboring positions. The effects of personal idiosyncrasies and shortcomings that may upset the system are minimized by procedure manuals and a body of normative oral traditions that can be communicated to newcomers. This system works reasonably well in dealing with known problems in a relatively stable environment.

In recent years, a different approach has been developed, one that relies less on the organization chart and the procedure manuals, although these must always be used to some extent, especially in a large organization, to formalize lines of authority and communication and to minimize arbitrary personal action. This new approach develops shared concepts among staff members and a common view of immediate and distant goals, and then leaves it to individuals and groups to work out ways of pooling their energies to achieve these goals. Coordination is ensured by shared values and theoretical models and by free communication and movement, rather than by restricting activities within contiguous role boundaries. Personal commitment to the current task is promoted because each person must use his own initiative and creativity to determine his contribution to the common goal; he has to reach out actively to others whose help he needs in solving his work problems. This is a particularly appropriate way of dealing with the novel difficulties that develop in a rapidly changing environment, because it increases the potential for innovation; each problem is dealt with in its own right rather than by a preplanned routine.

In this new approach the crucial question, beyond that of establishing consensus about the agency's mission, is how to develop an appropriate set of conceptual models to provide staff members with common guidelines and language with which to analyze and plan their operations. In my book *Principles of Prevention Psychiatry* (G. Caplan, 1964), I described such a set of conceptual models for community mental health that have proved valuable in developing population-focused programs.

Mental health consultation is one of the methods that may be used by the staff of a community mental health agency to facilitate the operations of other professionals in promoting mental health and reducing the incidence of mental disorders (primary prevention); to shorten the period of disability of mental disorders by early recognition and prompt and effective treatment (secondary prevention); and to reduce the rate of residual defect following mental disorder in the population (tertiary prevention). The amount of staff time to be devoted to mental health consultation in contrast to other methods, the decision as to which staff members should act as consultants, and the choice of professionals and caregiving agencies in the community who will be provided with mental health consultation services will be determined by judging which current problems must be attacked, in what order, and with what intensity, so as most effectively and efficiently to carry out the defined mission of the program. This demands not a detailed blueprint of operations but a continuing process of collecting information about the community, and a succession of planning judgments about salient and practicable goals and about ways of achieving them through individual and joint staff action. This must be followed by evaluation of results, both in terms of cost and in regard to their contribution to the fulfillment of the mission.

Establishing Goals

Two aspects of goal setting are significant: salience and feasibility.

Salience

Goals can be rank ordered by their importance in satisfying current feelings of need in the community. The needs themselves will be felt with different degrees of urgency, and they will be felt by smaller or larger sections of the population, both consumers and civic leaders. In judging the salience of a goal, all these issues must be taken into account, including the fact that although it may be natural to oil the wheel that squeaks loudest, a bearing that is quietly rusting away may finally bring the machine to a halt. Ways must therefore be found to increase the flow of information from those people who may be in greatest need but whose plight may be hidden because of inadequate communication or cultural blocks.

Salience of a goal is to be judged not only in regard to the need of those involved but also its effect on the program's mission. For instance, the continuing need of a chronically dependent group may be salient in its own right, but it may be less significant for achieving the overall mission than the need of others whose current crisis provides a leverage point for expanding the helping potential of the agency, or less than that of influential groups who, if helped, may act as a catalyst to many others.

Similarly, the choice of salient target groups must contribute to the overall balance of the program. For example, the different levels of prevention are likely to be differentially weighted in accordance with the agency's current mandate. The salience of need of widows adjusting to the death of their husbands, and the possibility of using staff time in consultation to clergy and undertakers to help them to satisfy this need, will be judged quite differently in accordance with whether primary, secondary, or tertiary prevention dominates the philosophy of the mental health program.

Community leaders may feel that we should place our main emphasis on the treatment of psychotic patients in improved mental hospitals and may question the validity of using scarce community resources on primary prevention. An agency operating in line with this philosophy would devote little if any time to helping widows who were not currently ill. The leaders, on the other hand, may urge a change from our traditional focus on erecting institutions and recruiting appropriate patients, to assuming responsibility for identifying the salient mental health needs of the population and to concentrating resources on preventing healthy people from becoming sick. An agency identified with this philosophy would probably deploy significant resources in such programs as helping widows to adjust in a healthy way to the consequences of their bereavement, so as to reduce the number who would eventually break down psychiatrically.

Of course judging the salience of a goal is relatively arbitrary, involving, as it does, a complicated tangle of factors. It is particularly susceptible to influence by the spirit and value system of the time and by fashions in professional style. These will, in turn, reflect both long-term and short-term historical trends. For instance, despite all the available evidence that mental disorder was most pressing among the poor and was so widespread as to overburden all efforts at direct professional action, it was not till the 1960s that it seemed important to focus specialized mental health attention on metropolitan slums, and to do so with a self-help approach.

Feasibility

Discussions about priorities of goals also involve judgments on their feasibility. Resources are too limited to be dissipated in futile efforts toward currently unattainable ends. Practicability depends, of course, on whether effective methods are available and on the number and skill of staff. In addition, this judgment depends on a prediction about the chances of changing target individuals, groups, and institutions. Their rigidity and their current openness to outside influences of different types must thus be assessed. Here again, crisis concepts are important. Systems are more susceptible to change and more open to outside influence during periods of disequilibrium. At such times, an agency mobilized and ready to move in, if invited, with a concrete offer of help is likely to produce a far greater effect than would be possible during more stable times. On the other hand, individuals and institutions, whatever their level of equilibrium, differ in their receptivity to modification; this must be taken into account in deciding where to work.

Current events may, however, modify feasibility. A new mayor is elected, forcing a shakeup of his police force. The police commissioner reached retirement age, and a new director appointed from outside embarks on a policy of reform. Because of such changes, the police force might now be judged more amenable to influence by mental health workers; in fact the administrative officers might even be eager to secure their help in furthering their own policies.

It goes without saying that all change infringes on the rights or comfort of some people and consequently is likely to provoke opposition. Mental health planners and organizers must be continually alert to the probable ripple effects of changes that satisfy the felt needs of certain people and fit in with their own agency mission and professional concepts. What will be the inevitable opposition? Whose comfort will be upset? Whose rights will be threatened? Can this damage be overcome or minimized? Will the cost of the side effects be worth the central achievement? Rarely can the answers to these questions be known in advance. But unless the questions are seriously asked, and there is reasonable assurance that the answers will be generally satisfactory, a judgment on feasibility must remain uncertain.

An important safeguard is to make every judgment contingent on continuing feedback about unexpected opposition and undesirable side effects, and to allot some resources to checks and balances and to mechanisms for modifying the program in the light of local conditions. However small the agency, this means creating maximum decentralization, so that as many decisions as possible are made by the people in the field, those in the best position to understand the idiosyncratic details of the local situation and to assess the immediate reactions of those affected.

Choosing Target Institutions for a Consultation Program

The best approach in developing a consultation program for a community mental health program is to focus for a relatively short period on a series of agencies and institutions, each of which appears to offer the most rewarding avenue for action in light of all the previously mentioned factors. This demands a pragmatic approach. Opportunities that happen to present themselves should be grasped if they hold promise of achieving salient and feasible goals in line with the program's mission and the knowledge of the community.

To spread the results of mental health intervention throughout the community, ripple effects are important. Wherever possible, one should choose to work with highly visible agencies, so that information about the mental health program will be widely disseminated, and with caregivers who occupy key positions in the community service network, so that improved procedures have a better chance of being copied by others. Obviously, institutions that reach large numbers of high-risk clients are preferred. A pragmatic approach does not mean inactivity, not even alert inactivity. Agencies with which one would eventually like to develop a mental health consultation program because they rate high on the previously discussed scales can be involved in minor types of collaboration that promote enough contact to begin forming relationships. For instance, they can be approached for information about their areas of community life, or they can be involved in simple studies that may yield results of value to them as well as to the mental health agency. Such contacts should not unduly burden either side, and since the expenditure of time for the mental health workers will be minimal, they will be able to contact a wide pool of agencies from which ripe targets may eventually emerge.

Promoting Initial Contacts

The fundamental principle that improves the promotion of initial contacts is to create proximity and establish the reputation of being trustworthy, competent, and eager to help without infringing on the rights of other agencies or endangering their programs.

The firmest basis for initial contact is the offer of collaborative service for those clients whom the staff wishes to refer for psychiatric diagnosis or therapy. Such referrals should be accepted on a demonstration basis. The mental health workers should understand that their operations are being carefully observed to assess their willingness and capacity to collaborate with the other agency and to help its clients. It is particularly important, therefore, to take a referred case without delay and to accept it even though it might be an "unsuitable" or troublesome case. In fact, it has usually been carefully chosen, whether by conscious or unconscious design, precisely as a test case to establish the bona fides of the mental health workers. If they realize that the case is being used as a means of exploratory communication, they are less likely to treat it solely on its own merits and to deal with it in a routine traditional style that includes walling it off from scrutiny by the other community workers.

The rights of the patient to confidentiality and competent diagnosis and treatment can be safeguarded even while relationships with the other agency are being built. This means, however, sending an immediate written diagnostic and dispositional report and subsequent information on the progress of treatment or management to the other agency in language that its staff can readily understand. These reports should also provide opportunities for mental health workers to visit the community agency to discuss the case with as many of its staff as possible, thus initiating personal relationships and beginning to build a picture of its social system and culture. During these visits guidance can be offered on the current management of the client if he continues with the agency. For instance, classroom management of a young patient can be discussed with his teachers, principal, and guidance counselor in the school that referred him. Further visits to deepen these initial relationships can be made to gather information about the child's school progress and to report on the developments in his therapy. Once again, there need be no breach in confidentiality, because these developments need be discussed only in the most general terms. This is usually the level at which the educators wish to learn about the case anyway; they are rarely interested in its deeper dynamics, contrary to the stereotyped fantasy of many mental health workers. During these discussions the mental health worker has an opportunity to establish his trustworthiness and his competence. He can also talk, in passing, about some of the other services of the mental health program.

Wherever possible, a single worker should be assigned to a particular target institution, so that he can build a personal knowledge of its social system and of its staff. He may act in liaison to communicate with both staffs about referred cases; eventually he may be asked informally, and later formally, to lead discussions or seminars about mental health in other institutions, to collaborate in the joint management of cases with mental health problems, and finally to act as a mental health consultant.

Distributing Staff Among Community Agencies

The progress of consultation relationships with community agencies should be monitored. Stabilized and set patterns should generally be avoided. The program should be intensified or reduced with particular agencies so that it spreads increasingly from those which are most feasible to those which are most salient.

When indicated, regular consultation contact with one agency should be terminated and the workers transferred to a new one, leaving the communication channels open with the old agency for ad hoc "consultation on request." The hazard of dealing just with old friends because of habit or ease should be avoided. Eventually, a consultant may become so integrated within the structure of a consultee agency that he ceases to be effective. He may identify so much with its culture that he can no longer penetrate its blind spots and biases, and he may be so highly regarded that its workers do not wish to upset him with its less savory problems. Even if the results of the monitoring indicate the need for a long-term continuing consultation program with a community institution, such as a school system or a particular school, it may often be advisable to rotate consultants so that they do not spend more than two or three years in one place.

CHAPTER FOUR

Building Relationships
with a Consultee Institution

In preparing the ground for a consultation program in a caregiving setting, the consultant must go through a complicated and sometimes lengthy operation of building up relationships. His entry into the potential consultee institution may result from a planning decision that he and his colleagues have made in line with the considerations discussed in the previous chapter. It may be a response to a formal invitation by the authorities of the institution, who are aware of certain needs that they believe the consultant agency may be able to satisfy. The consultant's entry may also be in response to an informal contact, such as a request for ad hoc help with a case by a staff member who may not have obtained explicit sanction from his superiors. The first contact may be a visit by the consultant to obtain information about a case that has been referred to his clinic for diagnosis and treatment; in that instance, too, he may be in touch with line workers or those in intermediate positions in one of the institution's subsidiary units.

Elements in Building a Relationship

As soon as the consultant decides that he is engaged in a process of preparing for a potential program of mental health consultation, there are certain issues to which he must pay attention so that his relationship building may pursue an orderly course.

First, he must be aware that in interactions with the staff of the institution both he and they are emissaries of their respective agencies, not simply individual professional workers. This means that he must consciously shape his own actions in line with the policies of his agency, and must keep its staff informed of the progress of his operations, so that they may have an adequate opportunity to guide him and to articulate their work with his. He must also realize that the actions of the workers of the consultee institution are being similarly molded by their colleagues, and he must take into account that they are probably reporting back to their superiors and peers on what transpires in their interactions with him.

Second, the consultant must realize the importance of making personal contact with the authority figures of the consultee institution as soon after his initial entry as possible, no matter how or at what level he came into the system. The purpose of this contact is to obtain sanction for his exploratory and negotiatory operations in the institution. This is particularly important if he was called in informally to deal with a case by a subordinate member of staff. He should inform the staff person that he wishes to introduce himself to the director of the institution. He can deal with any embarrassment of the staff worker by saying something like, "In our agency we have a rule that we must always make a call on the director of any institution we enter, in order to introduce ourselves, tell him about our agency, discuss our purpose in his institution, and get his formal permission to remain in his domain." This approach relieves the staff worker of the responsibility for making the introduction, which is important if this worker does not have easy access to the director.

Such a situation is not uncommon. Often, the staff member who first reaches out for help to a mental health agency is marginal or deviant in his own social system. He does not find it easy to get help and support with his problems inside his own system and therefore may more actively search for outside assistance. He is a useful bridge in bringing the consultant in, but the consultant must beware lest he become too closely identified with the marginal person and be perceived by the other staff as also deviant and therefore to be similarly walled off and kept out of its central communication network. This may be prevented if the consultant makes rapid contact with the director of the institution and through him with other key members of its staff.

This leads us to the third fundamental issue. The mental health worker must, as quickly as possible, explore the organizational pattern and social system of the institution to elucidate its authority and communication networks. He must take care not to get a distorted view by relying too much on information given by the individual or group that called him in; wherever possible, he should aim to corroborate all the information they give him by talking with others.

In these preliminary explorations, the mental health worker is trying to learn enough about the institution and its workers to determine the nature of their problems and to decide whether he can help solve them and at the same time fulfill the mission of his own agency. As far as possible, he will foster relationships of mutual trust and respect that may form a basis for such collaboration. He will get to know the staff of the institution and help them get to know him and understand the nature of the expert assistance he is able to offer. He will also communicate his readiness and availability to work with them in pursuit of mutual goals.

This process may focus on joint work with a mentally disordered client, who has been referred to his agency for diagnosis and treatment. At the other end of the spectrum, such a case may provide an opportunity for a wider-ranging discussion about the two institutions and their staffs and the possibilities of collaboration in pursuit of superordinate goals—that is, goals of value to each, which cannot be achieved alone but only by a pooling of resources and a joining of efforts.

In such discussions it is important for the mental health worker to realize, and to communicate to the other professionals, that he is not being purely altruistic in offering to help them with the problems, but that he cannot achieve his own professional goals of communitywide improvement in mental health unless the other caregiving professionals in the community understand the mental health dimension of their work and use it in their everyday operations. He needs the opportunity of working with them on demonstration cases to deepen their understanding of this aspect of their roles. He stands to gain as much out of this interaction as they do, and he is not just being kindhearted in offering his help on their cases. Such a message sets the stage for the kind of coordinate relationship of mutual involvement and interdependence that is the foundation for the type of consultation advocated in this book.

While this exploration is being carried out, the mental health worker is trying to achieve two other goals. He is building channels of communication to key members of staff of the institution, and with them he is developing a common verbal and nonverbal language.

Building Channels of Communication

Developing communication channels involves finding key members of the communication network who have easy access to significant groups of line workers and also to the authority system, and then building relationships of trust and respect with them so that they will act as communication bridges between the consultant and the staff of the institution. In certain cases, the director of the institution will himself nominate such people—for example, the head guidance counselor and the nurse in a high school—and will ask the consultant to communicate with the system through them. In many cases the mental health worker will have to identify such people himself and to work out the arrangements whereby messages are transferred to and from the rest of the staff. Occasionally the director of the institution will himself act as the communication bridge, perhaps because he wishes to exercise special surveillance over the consultant's work. On the other hand, this pattern has the advantage that through his office the consultant has potential access to the total institution, whereas most other communication bridges are likely to cover parts of the system less adequately than others.

The dissemination of messages is a complicated process. The communication link person is a gatekeeper as well as a message-exchange point. In the case of the director, the effect of the surveillance is obvious. He needs to satisfy himself that the operations of the mental health worker are conducive to the welfare of the institution before he will allow messages to pass freely. Until he is satisfied, he is likely to be highly selective in deciding what types of communications are allowed. At the beginning, he may permit only requests for consultation from senior and trustworthy staff who are able to defend themselves and the good name of the institution against any possible harmful effects of this "newfangled" psychological work—the so-called Horatio-at-the-bridge approach. Alternatively, he may promote requests for consultation from the weakest and most expendable members of staff and watch to see if the mental health worker damages them—the "human cannon-fodder approach." In any case, he will allow the communication channels to become free both in content and destination of messages only if he believes that the mental health worker is both trustworthy and effective. When he hands the matter over to his secretary as a routine mechanical operation involving transfer of messages between the mental health worker and anyone on his staff, the consultant may congratulate himself that he has established top sanction within the institution.

When the director deputizes somebody else to act as communications gatekeeper, added complications are often involved. The person chosen is usually someone whose role domain is bordered by, or overlaps, that of the would-be consultant, such as the head guidance counselor or psychologist of a school, or the chief supervisor of a public health nursing unit. They are particularly sensitive to the implications that a possible new program of mental health consultation may have for their own vested interests. Until they are satisfied that their own status will not be endangered by the mental health worker, they are likely to restrict the messages they transmit. Often they will not permit direct interaction between the would-be consultant and the line workers but will themselves act as intermediaries; for example, the guidance counselor will collect from the teachers all the information about a problem child and will himself discuss the case with the consultant. Such a situation may be quite frustrating to the mental health specialist. He will do well, however, to realize that he must try to satisfy the gatekeeper that his fears of being superseded are unfounded, so that eventually this defensive obstructionism can be laid aside. He should avoid early attempts to bypass the communication block, and he should not complain to the school principal and demand a less obstructive gatekeeper. Bypassing the obstacle will leave it actively operating at his rear, which may be hazardous. The guidance counselor's suspicions and insecurities will be aggravated by the maneuver, and he will probably find ways of making a nuisance of himself. He is usually a senior staff member of the institution and probably has many friends in positions of influence.

The second approach, via the principal, may not succeed because he probably intended the guidance counselor to act as a specially vigilant gatekeeper. Even if he authorizes bypassing the guidance counselor, the situation can still develop as described above unless the mental health worker has managed to build up a very positive reputation and the behavior of the guidance counselor is so irrational and out of line with the rest of the staff that they wholeheartedly support the decision to bypass him. This is unlikely unless the consultant has been working in the institution for a long time, painstakingly building his equity with the staff.

The best way of dealing with the problem of an obstructive gatekeeper is to work patiently with him, and with whomever he will allow to have limited access to the mental health worker, until suspicions and insecurity have had a chance to die down.

When the director of the institution gives the mental health worker *carte blanche* in choosing his own channels of communication to the staff, the consultant will do well not to view this as a purely mechanical matter that can be accomplished by putting notices in the staff common room or leaving notes in staff pigeonholes, but to search out the natural communication links and gatekeepers in the system and use them as message carriers—for example, the supervisors in a public health nursing agency. If and when these people suggest simple channels through secretaries or notice boards, the mental health worker can feel confident that he has dealt with the major obstacles to communication and can settle down to a routine.

Obstacles to Communication

There are two types of obstacles to free communication, apart from the language barrier that we will discuss in a moment. The first is connected with realistic conflicts of interest between the mental health worker and some or all of the staff, who feel obliged to reduce his operations by interfering with his data collection or his messages. The second involves distorted perceptions and irrational expectations of staff members that make the consultant appear dangerous, even though in reality he intends to be helpful.

Conflicts of Interest

Conflicts of interest between the consultant and members of the problem-solving staff of the consultee institution can easily occur. The would-be consultant should always be on the alert to identify them and not fall into the trap of considering all opposition to his operations as irrational resistance. In a school, for example, it is likely that a variety of ways of dealing with mental disorder among the students have developed over the years, and that various staff members have been allotted functions that have become part of their professional domains. These will probably include the principal, the educational supervisors, the school physician, the school nurse, the truant officer, the guidance counselors, the remedial reading and arithmetic staff, and possibly a school psychologist and a school social worker. Each will have his part to play, and each may feel, with some justification, that a mental health consultant will trespass on his preserves and oblige him to change his ways of operating. It may well be that the consultant will fulfill functions that none of them is equipped to undertake, and that he may help them to do better and more easily what they were already doing before he came. But unless the consultant finds out what each has been doing and carefully defines his own role so as not to overlap their domains, and unless he succeeds in communicating this clearly to them, it is likely that some of them will overtly or covertly oppose his entry into their system. If he comes in with the sanction of higher authorities, such as the superintendent of schools or the school board, overt opposition may not be feasible. In that case, they will covertly obstruct him as an intruder who is threatening their interests. Hidden opposition of this type should not be mistaken for unconsciously energized acting-out behavior. It must be dealt with by negotiation and not by manipulation or interpretation.

Distortions of Perception and Expectation

The second type of opposition is more familiar to mental health specialists because it is similar to the resistance they regularly encounter in casework or psychotherapy. It is likely that the staff's perceptions of the would-be consultant will be colored by a variety of anxiety-provoking fantasies, and these will block and distort communication with him.

Some of the distortions of perception and expectation will be cultural—that is, they will be shared by most of the staff and will be based on the ideologies they hold in common. Examples are the fearful perceptions of a mental health specialist as a "mind reader," who will lay bare one's forbidden thoughts; as a therapist, who will uncover one's psychological weaknesses and treat one as a dependent patient; as a psychoanalyst, who will weaken defenses and advocate sexual and aggressive license; and as a judge, who will condemn one and make one lose face because of one's professional and personal mistakes or inefficiencies. A common fantasy is that a mental health specialist will make one talk about unmentionable topics.

To these specific mental health fantasies are likely to be added stereotyped expectations associated with strangers, who may blunder about inside the institution and open up channels of communication that should remain closed or who may discover the skeletons in the closet and communicate this information to outside critics. If the consultant enters the system with the sanction of a higher authority, such as the superintendent of schools, he may be perceived as that person's spy.

If the consultant comes from an agency with which the institution has had previous dealings, he is likely to inherit past difficulties. Institutional memories are long. It is important for the consultant to investigate the history of transactions between his agency and the institution as far back as possible. In one case a consultant, who was at a loss to understand the prolonged suspicion that greeted all his efforts to establish his trustworthiness in a public health nursing unit, eventually discovered that fifteen years earlier a director of his agency had been extremely rude and critical toward the public health nurses. Since that time, an attitude of deep suspicion of his agency had become part of the culture of the nursing unit. The image he had inherited was that, despite his initial placatory behavior, he would eventually deliver a devastating attack on the nurses, just as his predecessor had done in the past.

The investigation of the past relationships should be carried out before the consultant's initial visit. He should find out as much as possible by talking to staff members in his own organization, particularly the oldtimers, and he should be alert to memories of previous contacts that had been interrupted, especially in an atmosphere of conflict. Wherever possible, he should read old case reports and comb the correspondence files for insight on the social structure and culture of the target institution, especially its traditions of dealing with the mental health problems of clients, and also on the vicissitudes of its transactions with his own organization.

Personal characteristics of the consultant may also stimulate stereotyped distortions of perception and expectation. A Jewish consultant in a Catholic agency was initially perceived as someone who would be likely to ride roughshod over the religious sensitivities of his consultees, advocate contraceptives and abortion, and attack their belief in God and the discipline of their church.

In dealings with particular consultees, these culturally based stereotypes are, of course, likely to be compounded by individual transference distortions. Since a consultant often comes into an institution during periods of heightened tension, precipitated by mental health crises in its clientele and by the difficulties of handling them, people's normal defensive structure may be weakened. This catalyzes a quicker and more regressive transference to a newcomer than would usually be expected. Mental health specialists whose experience of transference has been confined to psychotherapy, especially with neurotic patients, are likely to be surprised by the rapid appearance of significant transference manifestations in initial consultation situations. They may either dismiss the evidence of their senses or wrongly ascribe these reactions to psychopathology in the institution staff.

Dissipating Distortions

An essential part of a consultant's task is to explore these irrational perceptual stereotypes and to counteract their effects. He learns about them by paying attention to behavioral cues and by being sensitive to the inner meaning of the words and actions of the institution staff, particularly their defensive maneuvers. He should allow the staff full freedom to manipulate him and to ascribe the roles to him that reveal their stereotyped fears, their testing out to confirm their suspicions, and also their ways of warding him off. As soon as he has identified these, he should take steps to dissipate the distortions of perception and expectation and to replace them by providing the consultees with opportunities to see him as he is.

The most important thing is to interact with as many people as possible in the institution, so that they can have personal experience of him and not feed their fantasies from the distorted reports of others. As soon as he can, he should make the rounds of all the staff. In this connection he is often helped by being invited to give a lecture or to explain the work of his agency at a staff meeting. He should always accept such an invitation, even if he doubts the value of communicating to a group of strangers by means of a formal lecture.

Such a situation provides the mental health specialist with an invaluable opportunity to show himself publicly to the institution staff. Whatever the topic of his lecture, he should try to include in it, often in the form of asides or by indirect allusions, messages designed to counteract their fantasies. He can mention popular misconceptions about psychoanalysts, establish his belief in the importance of impulse control, clarify his attitudes of respect for colleagues of other professions, and emphasize the importance of a nonjudgmental approach and of confidentiality. The Jewish consultant used such a lecture to tell his Catholic audience that he respected people of other religions, that it was important, from the point of view of mental health, to support religious adherence and, for example, to respect the strictures of the church against contraceptives.

The main method of dissipating these stereotypes is repeated personal interaction between the consultant and the staff, particularly key individuals who act as the opinion molders of their fellows. These interactions have a variety of manifest contents, such as discussion of cases, exploration of the operations of each other's institution, negotiation of a collaborative agreement, and definition of domain boundaries. Whatever the manifest content, the consultant must constantly be alert to the latent content, which includes staff members' repeated testing out to validate their fearful stereotypes and his equally repeated invalidation of these stereotypes by his verbal and nonverbal behavior.

For instance, when the consultant in the public health nursing unit learned about his critical predecessor, he repeatedly sought situations in which the nurses might expect him to show criticism of their performance, and in each case he demonstrated his nonjudgmental and respectful approach. He demonstrated similar attitudes when discussing the work of other professionals and the behavior of people in case histories that were discussed with him. In many different ways he communicated over and over again to the public health nurses, "You can trust me to be consistently respectful of other people, especially those with less power and authority than me, because I am sensitive to the basic importance of human dignity, even though I do come from the same agency as the man who insulted and shamed your colleagues years ago."

While the mental health specialist's image is being actively explored by the staff of the institution, he should be alert to their ways of testing him out, through the cases they refer, the situations with which they confront him, and the questions they ask. He should take into account that practically every one of these is a test case, with a latent content involving some question about his attitudes and ideology as well as a manifest content related to the real predicament in the current work situation. The consultant should try to identify these latent questions and then answer them, while at the same time talking sensibly in relation to the manifest content level.

Particularly significant are jokes on the subject of mental health and psychologists. These are important ways of manifesting and releasing tension, but they are also opportunities for the consultant to communicate meaningful messages that will dissipate distorting fantasies. Banter such as "Have you brought your couch today?" or "I'm glad you've come, I am being driven crazy by these kids—I need treatment myself" or "Watch your tongue, Phyllis, the headshrinker is listening to you" should never be allowed to slip past without a corrective response. The response should be in line with the humor of the provocation; for example, "When I come here I leave my couch at home" or "We all feel at the end of our rope at times; it's a good thing we are sane enough to stand plenty of punishment" or "I had better watch out myself in front of so astute an observer; it's a good thing mind reading only works on the stage."

Testing out the consultant in relation to individual transference distortions goes on indefinitely in the consultation relationship, but at the institution level it usually dies down as the consultant establishes his reputation as a person worthy of trust and respect, and as he gradually works his way through the initial suspicions.

Establishing Trust and Respect

For the consultant to be perceived as trustworthy, the staff must be convinced that he is in general sympathy with the goals of their program and that he will not endanger their ways of working and their personal status. He must establish himself as honest, reliable, and consistent. He must also satisfy them that he will maintain confidentiality both inside and outside the institution, and that he will not use the information he obtains about them to do them any harm.

To gain the respect of the staff, the consultant must make them feel that in his field he has expert knowledge that is directly applicable to some of their work problems; that he can understand these problems from their point of view; and that he is willing and able to make his knowledge and skill available to them to help them overcome their difficulties. He is expected to be aware of their psychological sensitivities, and to assist them in their predicaments without overburdening them. Particularly important is the requirement that he should be able to communicate with them at their own level, and that his messages not be academic but focus specifically on the practical issues that are important to them.

By and large, the consultant earns the respect of the consultees by his reactions to the predicaments they ask him about. His principal mode of communication is not stating his assessment of the situations or giving advice (although when appropriate he may do both), but the questions he asks. These do not take the form of an interrogation of the consultee. Instead, the consultant sits beside the consultee, as it were, and engages in a joint pondering about the complexities of the problem. His contribution mainly takes the form of widening and deepening the focus of discussion by suggesting new avenues for collecting information, new possibilities for understanding the motivations and reactions of the characters in the case history, and new ways to handle the situation.

Distortions of the Consultant

The dissipation of perceptual stereotypes is not only a problem for the consultee. It is important also for the consultant. He too may suffer from preconceptions and culturally based distortions in regard to the consultees, especially in a new institution or a new consultee profession with which he has had no previous professional experience but about which he has heard from others or experienced himself in a nonprofessional role. For instance, a consultant who has never before worked in a school system may have preconceptions about schoolteachers and school principals based on his own experience as a student. Or a consultant who has not previously worked with clergy may have difficulty relating freely and realistically to religious leaders, especially those high up in the hierarchy. The same may apply to consulting with senior army officers.

By the same token, a consultant may have difficulty realizing the professional worth of consultees or professions of lower status than his own. It is not uncommon for psychologists to begin working with public health nurses, sanitarians, or public welfare officials with some feelings of condescension, revealed in the surprise with which the consultant reports the intelligent ways his consultees deal with their problems.

This belittling of the other profession is a major obstacle to effective consultation. Apart from anything else, it is likely to be picked up by the consultees, who are very sensitive to the consultant's underlying feelings and attitudes toward them. Consultants must constantly scrutinize themselves for such evidences of prejudices or stereotypes, and must try to overcome them in the same way in which they deal with this in their consultees—by honestly trying to get to know the consultees through repeated interaction and observation.

Consultants, like consultees, are also apt to have their perceptions distorted by individual transference reactions. A consultant too has a private life and is a member of an agency, and in both areas intercurrent upsets may affect his emotional equilibrium. He must pay special attention to the effects of such matters on his professional balance, and must be particularly alert to a possible consonance between a private crisis and the predicaments of his consultees. It is not at all unusual for a crisis in a client to link with a current upset in a consultee and also with a disequilibrium in the consultant.

Developing a Common Language

The removal of distortions of perception between consultant and consultees provides an opportunity for free communication, but for the communication to be effective the two sides must share a common language. It is not enough for the consultant to avoid the technical jargon of his specialty in talking with his consultees. He must realize that he has to make a special effort to learn the relatively private and idiosyncratic modes of communication of the consultee institution. These relate not only to vocabulary but also to such nonverbal behavior as gestures, comfort distance between people, punctuality, degree of interpersonal formality, signs of deference and respect, and ways of making appointments.

The consultant must constantly search for feedback from his consultees to validate that they have understood his messages, and he must check to see that he has understood their verbal and nonverbal communications. In the beginning he will often be surprised at the divergences in meaning that he will uncover by his cross checking. If he omits it, he will undoubtedly run into difficulties.

Ground Rules for Cooperation

Associated with the task of developing a joint language is the need to work out and maintain consensus on the ground rules for cooperation. The nature of the consultant's operations in the institution and the problems he is dealing with will change over time; so will the people who ask him for help and their reasons for seeking his services. At each stage the consultant should ensure that his current role is clearly defined and that the staff knows what kinds of situation are appropriate to discuss with him and what they may expect from the partnership. These ground rules should include a clear awareness of the source of sanction for this joint activity and also its limits—who is or is not allowed to contact the consultant, where, at what time, for how long, how often, through which channels, and for what purpose. What can the consultant be expected to do, what must he do, what will he not do?

Successive Stages of the Specialist Role

At first, the consultant may be a relatively unknown and unsanctioned visitor, whose operations are confined to helping a single staff member with a particular client. The specialist may observe or examine this client in order to make a diagnosis, prescribe treatment, or refer to another agency. In effect, he may be seen as a link with his own clinic, to which he will be expected to refer patients who need investigation or therapy.

At a later stage, the consultant may have received permission from the director of the institution to explore possibilities for more extensive cooperation. He may be invited to help staff members increase their knowledge of mental health matters by giving them a lecture, leading a discussion, or directing a seminar. During such interactions he will learn about their work problems and the common difficulties they encounter in their clients, and they will discover whether his expert knowledge is relevant to their concerns and whether he is willing and able to assist them with the problems they consider important. He is seen mainly as a visiting expert, whose role is that of staff educator.

At that point the mental health specialist may be invited in, on an occasional or a regular basis, to talk with individuals or groups of the staff about problem clients. He will be expected to screen them and either refer them to his clinic for investigation and treatment or suggest disposition to an outside agency, or else he may be expected to offer advice on appropriate management within the consultee institution. He may also be expected to act as a collaborator in certain cases, and to treat some of the clients himself, either during his visits to the institution or back in his own clinic. He is, in addition, likely to be asked to carry back messages about clients who are being treated in his clinic and to provide reports from his colleagues about the progress of these cases.

At this stage, his role may have a variety of segments—liaison, staff educator, screener and diagnostician of clients, collaborator in treating clients of the institution, and client-centered case consultant. As he continues with his work in the institution, these role segments may continue and may be supplemented by additional elements, or he may give up certain functions as he takes on others. For instance, as he moves more into a consultant role, he may no longer personally take on as patients the clients of that institution, who may be dealt with by his colleagues back at the clinic; or reports on the progress of patients in therapy may be made directly by his colleagues without his intermediation.

At about that stage, it may become obvious to the consultee staff that they can receive adequate help if they discuss their cases with the consultant rather than asking him to examine each client, and that this conserves time and allows the consultant to assist them with more cases. This usually leads to a move from client-centered to consultee-centered case consultation. Eventually, the administrators of the institution develop enough trust and respect for the consultant to invite his advice on policy and program development, and he is asked to give program-centered and, later, consultee-centered administrative consultation.

This succession of phases may take a varying amount of time to unfold. It is usually a lengthy process. The process may not develop beyond a particular phase because of the complications of the situation or because of the talents and interests of the consultant. It is important that the mental health worker be fully aware of the phase that the process has reached. Further, he must ensure this is made explicit to both his clinic and the consultee institution by a series of agreements or contracts governing his operations as they develop over time.

The Consultation Contract

It has become customary to use the term *consultation contract* for the agreement between the consultant and consultees about their complementary roles. There has to be negotiation between them that leads to a formal or informal agreement, involving sanctioned mutual behavior and some sort of exchange of goods or services. When the situation of the two parties alters with the passage of time, renegotiation of the agreement is needed.

Obtaining Sanction

Initial sanction for the consultant's entry into the consultee institution is obtained from the director or one of his representatives. As the consultant develops his successive roles, he must take care to obtain sanction for his operations also from people in the intermediate layers of the institution, down to and including the line workers with whom he will be working. For instance, in a school where he will be working with classroom teachers to help with problem children, he should clarify what he will be doing not only with the principal, but also with the vice principal, the educational supervisors, and the teachers' group. All these people must understand the nature of his activities and agree in general with his goals and methods. If he misses people in any of the layers, he is likely to run into difficulty, because they may undermine his program overtly or covertly. Of particular importance is the sanction of the middle management or supervisory group. They are usually in a position to exert a great deal of influence on the line workers, and their support is essential for a smoothly running program.

Obtaining sanction is basically a simple matter, once the consultant has explicitly recognized that he needs to do it. Usually all that is necessary, in addition to his general activities in arousing trust and respect, is for him to go from one person or group to another in the system, as he learns about their needs and works out what he is able and willing to do to satisfy them, and explore with them whether what he has in mind seems sensible to them. He also elicits their reactions and suggestions for modification, so that he, in effect, gives them a hand in molding his program to suit their perceptions of their work problems and of the ways he can help. What emerges then is a joint plan, or rather a series of modifications of the joint plan, as he discusses it with the various workers and authority figures concerned. Eventually, when the details of the plan have been worked out, all the relevant people have been involved and know about him. They have all had an opportunity to modify the plan and therefore have a personal commitment to supporting it.

Obviously this type of careful layered working through can be time consuming. It should not be hurried. The consultant should allow time for the people in different positions in the institution to consider the implications of his operations for their own work, and to think out ways in which he can best help without interfering too much with their traditional ways of managing their affairs. The introduction of a new person into a system invariably involves some disruption. This cautious approach minimizes the disruption and provides an opportunity for integrating the consultant's efforts into the existing problem-solving system.

Content of the Contract

In the early stages of the consultant's work in an institution, both sides may have only vague ideas about how they should cooperate. The contract at that time will mirror this by stating that the mental health specialist and the staff of the institution are engaging in explorations to see whether they can work out mutually acceptable goals and methods of cooperation. Such a contract may not be formalized in writing but may be implicit in the discussions between the would-be consultant and the potential consultees. We have found it advantageous, even in these early stages, to make this type of agreement explicit, and to emphasize that we expect the exploratory phase to lead to concrete findings that will eventually be included in a new agreement between the parties concerned.

We have also come to the conclusion that as early as possible, and certainly as soon as clear details of complementary roles begin to emerge, it is advantageous to begin formulating the contract in writing. The written word is an excellent way of revealing misunderstandings that may be obscured in verbal discussions. It is important that these be corrected as early as possible.

This does not have to be a formal document; usually it takes the form of an exchange of letters. These letters should specify how often and for how long the consultant will visit; how potential consultees will communicate with him; the type of cases that it is appropriate to discuss with him; the kind of consultation to be involved (case consultation or administrative consultation, client-centered or consultee-centered); what help he will offer (advice, referral, collaboration or not, enlargement of the consultee's understanding, and so on); and the nature and limits of confidentiality.

The contract should also specify what the consultant will *not* do; for example, psychotherapy for personal problems of consultees, discussion of intrastaff problems such as relationships of line workers and supervisors, or intervention in staff conflicts. It should also specify how the consultant and his agency will benefit from the program, for example the amount and type of payment; or if no direct payment is involved, the professional rewards, such as the consultee group's contribution to the consultant's mission of promoting mental health in the population for whose well-being he has some responsibility. See Exhibit 4.1 for a sample contract.

Renegotiation of Sanction and Contract

Negotiation of the initial contract takes the form of a series of steps toward an agreement between the parties. This agreement should be expected to change with the passage of time, because the situation of the consultant and the consultee agencies and of the community in which they operate will inevitably change.

The term *consultation contract* may obscure this, because most contracts can be relied upon not to change for long periods, even though occasionally they may need review and modification. Consultants should always write into the contract a clause dealing with systematic review and revision; for example, that the parties should meet once a year to evaluate the consultation program and suggest improvements in the agreement.

It is particularly important to initiate such a review if there is a change in any of the key posts of the consultee institution that may affect the sanction of the consultation program; for example, a change of school principal or of nursing supervisor in a public health agency. On such occasions, it is rarely wise to assume that the new office holder will be adequately briefed about the program or will fully agree with the terms of a contract he did not help formulate. Instead, the consultant should realize that he must start

Exhibit 4.1. Example of a Consultation Contract.

Frobisher Public School
City of Greenfield

Dr. Walter Simpson
Psychiatric Director
Greenfield Mental Health Center

Dear Dr. Simpson,

I write to confirm the plan we worked out at our meeting last Wednesday, when we reviewed the experience of your child psychiatrist Dr. Ursula Walters and our staff during the first exploratory year of the new mental health consultation program.

It is my understanding that within the framework of the contract signed between you and our Superintendent of Schools, under which your agency is remunerated by the Greenfield School Board, you will make available to us, free of extra charge, the services of Dr. Walters every Thursday morning from 9:00 a.m. until noon. We will provide her with a room next to our nurse's office, where she will offer consultation to members of our staff, on an individual or group basis.

The program will be coordinated by Mr. Jerome Robbins, our Assistant Principal. He will maintain a list of those who have requested consultation. Any teacher or other member of our staff who seeks help in dealing with mental health problems of a student and his or her family may ask Mr. Robbins to arrange an appointment with Dr. Walters. The content of these consultations will be confidential, and neither Dr. Walters nor our staff member will be expected to report them.

The focus of consultations will be restricted to psychosocial problems of students and how to handle them in school. Personal problems of staff and problems of intra-staff relationships will not be dealt with. If on the basis of her experience with a number of cases, Dr. Walters wishes to suggest modifications in curriculum content or school policies she should feel free to communicate with me, but without reporting details of her individual consultations. She may also suggest a group staff meeting to discuss common mental health problems of students. Mr. Robbins will be pleased to organize such a meeting.

At the end of next school year we will review our experience in this program and we may modify it. During the year either side may arrange an ad hoc review to be organized by Mr. Robbins.

We are most grateful for the services of Dr. Walters and for her enrichment of our school program. We are pleased to be working with you to improve the mental health of the people of Greenfield.

Yours sincerely,

James Connors, Principal

---

almost from the beginning to negotiate sanction with the new worker and to involve him in a major review and possibly a detailed reformulation of the content of the contract. The goal is that the new worker should feel that this is a program he has had a chance to mold and to which he can wholeheartedly commit, rather than somebody else's project that he has inherited.

Sanction Maintenance

The consultant must ensure that significant figures of power and influence in the consultee organization are continually kept informed of his operations and are stimulated to support him. These people are usually very busy and the consultant should not annoy them by intruding unduly on their time; but every once in a while he should seize an appropriate opportunity to send them a short report about the consultation program or to visit them for an informal chat about his work, so that they may keep abreast of his progress and have a chance to make explicit their support.

Common Technical Issues

The following issues are frequently encountered by consultants engaged in building relationships in consultee institutions.

Ensuring Adequate Communication of the Contract to Consultees

The consultant can rarely rely on the communication network of the consultee institution to convey undistorted messages about the details of the contract. He should therefore take every opportunity to clarify and confirm the essential points himself, particularly those that are emotionally complicated. He should repeat them over and over again whenever he is talking to individual staff members. For instance, he should repeatedly tell them that consultation deals only with work difficulties and never with private issues, that the consultation discussions are confidential, that he will not take sides in differences of opinion among staff members, and (if the contract includes consultee-centered consultation) that the help the staff can expect from him will lead to deepening their understanding of the psychological aspects of their clients so that they can develop more effective ways of handling their work problems.

Dealing with Status Problems

The goal of relationship building is to achieve a nonhierarchical relationship with the consultees, so that they will not feel coerced to accept what the consultant says just because he says it. Since they will be free to accept or reject, they will quickly and without dependency tensions be able to take as their own any ideas that make sense to them. This desirable situation is achieved by the consultant's noncoercive and respectful behavior and by various techniques that will be discussed in the next chapter. But the development of such a relationship will be obstructed if in fact the consultee has very low status in the consultee organization while the consultant is a senior member of the consulting agency; for instance, if the psychiatric director of the community mental health program offers consultation to a junior nurse's aide or a student teacher. When this happens, the consultant must take special steps to divest himself of rank.

This is particularly difficult if the consultant and consultee are respectively senior and junior members of the same profession. When this is the case, it is very hard for the consultee not to see the consultant as a role model and to feel compelled to do whatever he says, despite being admonished to feel free to reject any part of the consultant's statements. The best way of handling this problem is to avoid it, by taking care to appoint a consultant who is of a different profession from the majority of staff members of the consultee institution.

Another common status difficulty that complicates the task of relationship building arises when the would-be consultant is of obviously lower status than the authority figures in the consultee institution; for instance, when a junior social worker attempts to negotiate a contract with the superintendent of schools. A useful way of dealing with this is for a senior member of the consultant organization to open the negotiations with the authority figure and, after the initial phases, to introduce the junior staff member as his personal representative, upon whom, as it were, he confers his own power and status.

In dealing with a large organization, it may be necessary for negotiations to be carried out at a variety of levels by representatives of appropriate rank. In an army mental hygiene service, for instance, the psychiatric director, who is a major, will negotiate with the general commanding the camp; the social worker, who is a lieutenant, will negotiate with the captain who commands a unit; and the enlisted man social work technician will negotiate with the noncommissioned officers of a company. After the initial contacts, it may be possible for some of the negotiation to be delegated to lower-status representatives, but there are obvious limits to this; the general is not likely to take kindly to negotiating a consultation contract with an enlisted man. Although the army is an extreme example, this principle also holds in less hierarchical settings. Free communication requires a culturally acceptable consonance between the rank of parties to a negotiation.

Resistance to Consultation as a Sign of Inadequacy

In many potential consultee institutions the development of a consultation program is hindered by the attitude that asking for consultation is an admission of professional incompetence. This would be especially true with consultee-centered consultation. To overcome this problem, the consultant must emphasize that consultation deals with cases in which the *problems of clients* are complicated, unclear, and confusing, rather than saying that the aim is to help *consultees* who are confused about their clients.

The first viewpoint allows the consultant to educate the staff to the realization that for them to recognize clients whose problems are particularly complex demands professional sophistication in mental health matters. Thus the ability to identify a case as appropriate for consultation is a sign of professional merit, instead of inadequacy.

The consultant must direct this message to the influential figures of the institution, particularly the supervisory group. If they accept the message and its associated value judgment, they will set the pattern for the rest of the staff.

Avoidance of Undue Dependency Among Consultees

This is, of course, largely determined by the transactions between the consultant and individual consultees, and it will be dealt with at this level in the next chapter. The question of dependency does, however, have an institutional aspect. The consultant can make his task with individual consultees much easier if he handles appropriately his relationship with the staff as a whole.

To foster their respect and their expectation that they will be helped if they consult him when they encounter a mental health difficulty in their work, he must establish himself as an expert in a field of mental health. But he must make it clear to all concerned that outside his own field he is a layman who is perfectly comfortable about confessing his ignorance and uncertainty and in asking others for clarification and guidance. In particular, he must not be bashful in communicating his lack of knowledge about the professional fields of his consultees, and he should sincerely ask them to educate him in the realities of their professional work. He should encourage the consultee group to actively teach him to understand their work problems as they see them and the range of ways they have developed for dealing with them. In other words, he must help them see that the role of consultee is an active one, and that in large measure they will be responsible for making optimal use of what he brings to them.

In fact, the fundamental difference between a mental health specialist dealing directly with his own patient and a consultant dealing indirectly with a client through the intermediation of a consultee is his ability to understand the consultee's point of view and potential for action with the client. The consultant must be a student of the social system and the role problems of the consultee, and his best teachers will be the consultees themselves.

CHAPTER FIVE

Fostering
Effective Relationships
with the Consultee

Whatever the type of consultation, the effect of the consultant's intervention is mediated by his relationship with the consultee. This must be a relationship of mutual trust and respect, so that what each expresses has importance and significance for the other. The consultee must be open to the cognitive and affective influence of the consultant, but at the same time he must feel sufficiently independent to accept only those aspects of the consultant's ideas that fit in with his own needs and with his subjective impressions of the realities of his current professional situation.

The ideal consultation relationship is one of *coordinate interdependence*, in which each side gives to and takes from the other. The consultee must educate the consultant about his work setting and about the complications of his role *vis-à-vis* the client. He must also help the consultant pinpoint the special difficulties of the case, so that he can usefully plan his consultation intervention. The consultee must then work out a new approach to the client based on selected aspects of the consultant's suggestions. The role of consultee certainly includes dependence on the consultant, who gives him both emotional support and cognitive guidance. In this process the consultant brings to bear expert knowledge not normally available to the consultee. But the dependent role of the consultee is fulfilled mainly by an active process of drawing what is needed from the consultant and not by merely passively receiving what he offers.

The consultant, on his side, is striving to understand the realities of the consultee's present professional problems. Even in client-centered case consultation, where his major focus will be on elucidating the intricacies and implications of the client's case, he knows that his recommendations will be of value only if they are acceptable to the consultee. In consultee-centered consultation, his dependence on the consultee, who is the arbiter of the action outcome, is even more obvious. As a consultant, his expertness improves the situation only if it serves the current needs and capabilities of the consultee. However much the consultant may know about the culture of the institution and the consultee profession, or the personality and history of the consultee, or the details of the client's case, he will never be able to formulate a contribution to the consultee's knowledge and skill that is *exactly* consonant with his needs and capacities and those of his social system. Nor can he absolutely ensure that this formulation will be used as he intends it. If he had coercive power over the consultee he could force him to accept the formulation, but such coercion would probably mean that the suggestions would remain a foreign element in the consultee's thinking and would take a long time to be integrated, or perhaps would be rejected as soon as the consultant left the scene.

In our culture, consultees usually have little difficulty realizing their dependence on consultants for emotional support and for contributions of expert knowledge and skill. They find it harder to understand the demand the consultation situation makes on them for activity in teaching the consultant to understand their professional predicament and role complications. On the other hand, consultants readily perceive the need to provide support and guidance but find it difficult to realize the extent of their real dependence on the consultees, not only for essential information about the consultee's profession but also to achieve his own fundamental community mental health goals of population-focused prevention.

Getting to Know the Consultee

Before the consultant can build a relationship with the consultee, the two professionals must get to know each other. This can be accomplished in two main ways: by establishing "spontaneous" proximity and by scheduling formal interviews.

Establishing Proximity

Proximity may be engineered by means of informal social gatherings, such as by accepting an invitation to coffee with the group of public health nurses or by sitting around chatting in the staff common room or the cafeteria. It may also be achieved as a side effect of some formal activity, such as in a group discussion following a lecture or in "hanging around" after the lecture is over.

The essential point is for the consultant to bring himself within talking distance of the consultee in a setting where it is socially acceptable for them to talk informally without significant commitment on either side. In this situation, the consultant should appear approachable, and should perhaps initiate the contact with some informal bridge comments about the weather or questions about the institution.

Scheduling Meetings

On many occasions we have found it valuable to arrange with a public health nurse supervisor or school principal for a series of scheduled interviews with members of their staff in systematic rotation. These interviews are set up quite explicitly so that the potential consultees may get to know the consultant and he can learn something about the clientele of the institution. It is often important to keep the focus off the work of the consultees, to reassure them that the concern is the problems posed by their clients and not their own personal methods of working.

In some cases, nurses or teachers may be reluctant to spend time alone in a room with a consultant, who they may misperceive as a dangerous figure or as someone who has nothing valuable to offer them. It is they who probably have most to gain from scheduled interviews. Therefore, these interviews should, if possible, not be voluntary. It does not matter if the unwilling potential consultee is urged into the room by his supervisor. The essential issue is for the consultant to prove during the interview that he is a friendly person, someone who is interested in the mission of the agency in dealing with the problems of its clients, who is worthy of trust and respect, and who is not dangerous. The consultant's job is to demonstrate that he is not seductive or critical, will not attack defenses, and will not uncover weakness or unacceptable thoughts.

In such interviews, as well as in the informal contacts, the consultant should set the stage for coordinate relationships by talking spontaneously and frankly about himself and his institution, about the goals and methods of his own work, and about his reasons for being in the consultee institution. He should freely discuss the current stage of the consultation contract, even if it is still in its preliminary phases. Also, he should take an appropriate opportunity to mention some of the main things that will not be included in his operations, such as diagnosis and psychotherapy of the staff, intervening in intrastaff tensions and conflicts, and leaking confidential information between levels of the institutional hierarchical structure.

In getting to know his potential consultees, the consultant must act in ways that conform with the institution's culture. The best way of finding out what would be expectable and acceptable is to discuss the matter with the gatekeepers, such as the principal in a school or the supervisors in a public health nursing unit. The consultant should be flexible and fit in with their suggestions and arrangements. He may quickly learn that the gatekeeper does not yet sanction free contact with subordinate staff, so he will focus on reducing the gatekeeper's ambivalence until he gets the necessary sanction for formal contact with potential consultees. While this process is developing, he may also move along informal lines of establishing proximity with consultees, if he has meanwhile obtained the necessary sanction for free movement within the life space of the institution, such as permission to enter the staff room or cafeteria. It is important that in these situations his presence should be acceptable, and that he not be perceived as an intruder or uninvited guest.

Relationship Building as a Directed Process

In psychotherapy, the therapeutic relationship often develops spontaneously, without the active direction of the therapist. It is usually conceived that transference emerges from the unconscious of the patient and, as it were, is invested in the therapist, who presents himself as a new object partially to replace some of the former ones. "Uncovering" types of psychotherapy emphasize a nondirective approach, more so than supportive and manipulative psychotherapy.

In mental health consultation, the techniques we have developed are an amalgam of the uncovering and the supportive approach. On the one hand, they are quite directive. The consultant must accept the responsibility for actively fostering the optimal relationship between the consultee and himself; he must decide what content to permit in their discussions and what to prohibit. On the other hand, within those constraints he fosters the consultee's freest possible expression of his perceptions of the client. He uses these expressions, both verbal and nonverbal, as projective material whose inner meaning he must interpret to himself in order to understand the unconscious aspect of the consultee's predicament. This understanding is the basis for his every intervention.

In contrast to the techniques of uncovering types of psychotherapy, which seek to promote the patient's insight into the personal sources of his distortions, the consultant seeks to support and maintain the defensive displacement of the consultee's problems onto the story he tells about the client. The psychotherapist often confronts the patient with evidences of distortion in his story and forces him to try to understand his feelings about the issues and the source of these feelings in his current or past experience. The consultant, on the other hand, studiously avoids raising any question about the authenticity of the consultee's perceptions of the client's case, and keeps the focus on the client rather than on those who are discussing him.

A major problem in technique for the consultant is maintaining a level of communication with the consultee during the early stages so that the optimal relationship is fostered, while encouraging the consultee to speak freely about the case. Each consultant will handle this dilemma in his own characteristic way. I deal with it by a special type of interviewing technique.

I sit beside the consultee, actually or metaphorically, and I involve him by questioning the material he presents about the case. I do not allow the consultee to talk for more than a few minutes without interrupting him with a question. I avoid, under all circumstances, a situation in which I listen in relative silence while the consultee tells a long story about the client and then turns to me and says, "What do you think about it and what should I do?" First, I probably will not know what he should do. Second, since I may not yet know what the elements in the story really mean to the consultee, I risk saying something that has an inner meaning to the consultee. Third, by then my silence will have allowed the consultee to develop doubts about my attitude to him, and when he asks, "What do you think?" he may mean "about me?" I prefer him to know the answer to that question without having to ask.

My constant interruptions of the consultee's story are made tactfully, so that he will not consider them a hindrance or a frustration. On the contrary, the questions I ask always give him the chance to enrich his story by bringing in additional details about the client and his human predicament. My questioning never takes the form of a cross examination of the consultee. He does not feel that I am scrutinizing or testing his knowledge, actions, or attitudes. I accept and respect his current state of knowledge about the case. The purpose of my questions is to get as full a statement of this knowledge as possible, so that the two of us may try to understand the complications of the case and jointly wonder about possible patterns of forces and inner meanings in the client's life.

My questions demonstrate my own expert knowledge by bringing into focus a wider series of issues that the consultee may previously have considered irrelevant and therefore not worthy of his attention. In this way I am also continually showing my respect for the consultee's powers of observation and for the privileged position of his profession in being able to get such significant data. I am careful to avoid questions that the consultee is likely not to be able to answer; where I am in doubt I phrase the questions in such a way that he does not lose face if he has not made the necessary observations. In fact, consultees usually have a wealth of detailed information about cases they present. This information has often not been collected systematically, or with the same system as that involved in a psychiatric investigation; but since the consultee is likely to be especially concerned about this case, he will have observed a great deal more than he himself believes to be relevant.

The net result of such an interview technique is that, as the consultation discussion progresses, the consultee's thinking about the case gradually becomes richer and more complicated, and at the same time he feels supported, because the consultant is working actively with him in a joint endeavor to make sense out of the confusing material. He feels that his confusion is shared by the consultant, and he is reassured that this lack of clarity is an expectable stage in solving the mysteries of the client's predicament.

Fostering the Consultee's Self-Respect

This side-by-side wrestling with the complexities of the case is the basis for an appropriate relationship between consultee and consultant. It provides the consultee with expert help and support, while emphasizing his own specialized role as the contributor of important information. This fosters his professional and personal self-respect, which may previously have been weakened by his feelings of confusion and helplessness about the case.

The consultee may also be feeling a loss of face: asking for consultation help is an open confession of professional failure. This may have a personal basis in some unsolved dependency problems. In some agencies competent professionals are expected to deal with work problems on their own. No matter what the official policy may be, the informal culture of the agency says that asking for help is a sign of inadequacy. In these cases, the line workers think a consultant is useful only to new and inexperienced professionals.

One way of handling this has been described in the last chapter: communicating to the staff that consultation is to be invoked whenever they encounter a complicated or confusing *situation*, to help them clarify it rather than to help them with their own confusions. This often leads to a situation in which identifying a case situation as being complicated enough to merit consultation is a mark of professional sophistication. The consultant's explicit focus on the client and his case, rather than on the consultee and his handling of the case, is in line with this approach.

Another technique is for the consultant to make it clear to his consultees that their cases are intellectually taxing to him just as much as to them. A consultee must feel confident that the consultant is taking the case predicament seriously. There must be no question but that the case is a suitable issue for consultation. Consultees sometimes fear making fools of themselves, wasting a consultant's time on a simple case and thus revealing the depths of their ignorance in mental health matters. From the point of view of relationship building, a consultant will be well advised not to demonstrate his brilliance by snap diagnostic judgments and prescriptions. He may, indeed, hit the nail on the head as far as the client is concerned, but he may leave the consultee in a state of self-deprecation over his own inadequacies in not being able to recognize the obvious, or in a state of intimidation in the face of the omniscient expert—both of which are inimical to a future coordinate relationship.

If the consultant can be protected from loss of face, the more involved and upset he is about a case, the quicker he will develop a meaningful relationship with the consultant. His increased frustration at not being able to understand and act renders him more open to the consultant's intervention; at the same time, the consultant's handling of the situation prevents continuing dependency and fosters the consultee's professional autonomy. The consultant makes his specialist skills available and acts, as it were, as a supplementary ego during the consultation while stimulating the ego strength of the consultee so that the consultee increases his own feeling of mastery.

Dealing with the Consultee's Anxiety

A consultant must differentiate two main types of anxiety in consultees: anxiety about the case and about the consultant.

Anxiety About the Case. Especially in a first contact with a new consultee or where a stable relationship has not yet developed, the consultant must be careful not to reduce this case anxiety too soon or the consultee will have no reason to continue the contact. It is particularly important not to lower anxiety about the case by techniques of reassurance. This will only attack the ego strength of the consultee as a mature adult and induce him to accept a childlike dependency on the consultant, who because of his high status and superior knowledge can assure the consultee that his fears are exaggerated or unfounded.

Instead of such reassurance, the consultant should offer the ego support of a joint examination of the facts and a sharing of concern. If the consultee feels that the consultant has truly understood the intricacies of the case and takes the client's predicament seriously, and yet remains professionally calm, he will identify with these attitudes, and his own anxiety level and fear for the client will be reduced. This type of anxiety reduction will not interrupt the consultation, because it is the result of the consultee's growing trust and respect for the consultant, and this is what now holds them together.

There is one situation in which this approach may not work. If the consultee is so upset about the case that he becomes panicky, and the consultant fears that he may engage in impulsive activity, it may be necessary to use reassurance, at least to reduce the tension to bearable limits. An alternative is for the consultant to increase his own involvement in the case, by asking the consultee to report developments by telephone or by increasing the frequency of consultation sessions. The effect of this is not so much to reduce anxiety—in fact, the consultant's actively demonstrating his own concern may appear to validate the consultee's fearful judgment— as to help the consultee to put up with it, through the consultant's sharing the responsibility for a possible unfortunate outcome.

It is worth emphasizing that standing firm against the consultee's anxiety has its limits. The client may indeed be in danger. We have in mind actual danger to life, such as the possibility of suicide or homicide, or a major psychosis that demands immediate attention. Under these circumstances, the consultant must be guided by his fundamental responsibilities as a mental health specialist rather than by the niceties of relationship-building technique. He must explain to the consultee that in his judgment the situation merits emergency action that must take precedence over the consultation contract; and he must, if necessary, personally intervene to ensure the safety of the client and his family. If the consultee agrees, the resulting action will be collaborative. If he disagrees, the consultant will be forced to take unilateral action.

This may upset the consultation relationship, but it cannot be helped.

In my nearly forty years of experience as a consultant and supervisor of consultants, involving thousands of cases, although I and many consultants have often wrestled in our own minds with the possibility of serious danger to the client, I can recall no more than four instances of our being forced to abort the consultation. It appears that in all social systems in which consultants are used, there are other formal and informal safety valves for serious emergencies, so that they are not brought into the consultation setting.

Anxiety About the Consultant. This acts in the opposite direction from anxiety about the case. It tends to prevent or to cut short contact between the consultee and the consultant and therefore should be actively combatted at every opportunity. This anxiety usually occurs in the early stages of contact with a consultant. As he becomes better known and his reputation as a trustworthy and competent specialist becomes established, the anxieties about him are reduced. New staff members may, however, need to discover for themselves that he is safe and dependable.

The two sources of anxiety about the consultant are the quasirealistic expectation that he will uncover their work deficiencies and shame or blame them, or make them dependent on him, and the unrealistic, irrational fantasies discussed previously: that he will read their minds and reveal guilty secrets, or that he will attack their defenses.

Consultants must be prepared for constant testing out in the early stages and must beware of saying anything that can be interpreted as judging the quality of the consultee's work. For example, we have found it advisable not to compliment consultees on good work they may have done on the case; although this may be ego supportive, it also carries the implication that we are indeed making a judgment about work performance. This particular judgment is positive, but the consultee may be left with the worry that we have made negative judgments about other aspects of his work, which we are tactfully concealing or perhaps reserving for future communication.

It is important to be entirely nonjudgmental and to make this very obvious, particularly when the consultee appears to be especially fearful. In such situations the consultee will often bait a trap by mentioning examples of obviously ineffectual professional behavior. The response should be a clear reaction, not to the consultee's behavior but in terms of the client. An exaggerated example of this from my own experience was a public health nurse who, in orienting me to the low-income neighborhood in which she had worked for years, told me that she constantly carried a "bottle of vitriol" to spray in the face of the first man who tried to rape her in a dark passageway of one of the housing projects. I had no way of telling whether she was pulling my leg, but I reacted by engaging her in serious discussion of helping people improve their impulse control, and then suggested that I would be interested in discussing details of a case example, if not of attempted rape, at least of some lesser antisocial behavior among her patients, so that we could better understand some of the complicated factors involved.

Fear of the consultant will usually be easy to detect, even without verbal and nonverbal signs of overt anxiety. Clues are elaborate preparation of the case report, demonstration of sophistication in mental health matters and knowledge of psychological terminology, or the fact that the consultee has asked for help on a case in which there is no significant problem.

Faced with this anxiety, the consultant's first goal is not to understand the intricacies of the case or to assess the nature of possible theme interference but to understand and handle the consultee's anxieties about him. This must be done without making the issue explicit. A psychotherapist in such a situation might well openly refer to the anxiety and might talk with his patient about possible causes. A consultant must understand in his own mind the nature of the fear from the implications of the consultee's behavior and then invalidate the distorted perception. He does this by his remarks about *the client*, which reveal to the consultee the consultant's basic attitudes of friendly sympathy and personal respect for people.

For example, a young public health nurse brought as her first consultation case a teenage patient who was continually browbeaten by her father, a successful drugstore operator, who had worked his way up from a deprived background and who was driving his daughter beyond her capacities. The nurse presented the story very tentatively. She kept repeating to the consultant, who was a senior psychiatrist, that she was not sure of the facts, that she had not had time to work the case up properly, and that if he wished she would go back and get further information. The consultant realized that both the content and manner of presentation were evidence of the nurse's fear of him, and he was very careful to show his respect for her privileged status as a professional who had access to a wealth of information from her field contacts that psychiatrists only rarely can obtain in office visits. He gave her the opportunity to demonstrate to him and to herself the richness of her observations. By his aligning himself with her in confronting the problem of her patient, he was able to show her that she already had so much data that it would probably take them at least one or more consultation sessions to digest it.

The Consultant as Role Model

In the highly charged atmosphere of the consultation setting, especially when the consultee is upset by a work impasse, the consultant takes on a supplementary ego role not only actively but passively, by his mere presence as a trusted and respected person. To the consultee, he becomes an ego-ideal figure. His attitudes are likely to be incorporated in the consultee's self-assessment and to his personal prescriptions for his own behavior.

The consultant must consciously try to keep his own overt reactions in consonance with the style he would like the consultee to identify with. He must avoid role identity distortion by taking care to keep his own specialized professional thinking in the background. For instance, although the case may arouse his psychiatric interest, he should discuss it only at the level of general human relationships or on the plane that he knows to be of direct relevance to the professional style of his consultee. In the previous example of the teenage girl and her pharmacist father, for instance, there was evidence that incestuous fantasies were being stimulated both in father and daughter. The consultant had consciously to set aside such specialized psychiatric inquiry, as not being relevant to the current level of the public health nurse's concerns and to her professional role.

There are three aspects of functioning, which probably are common and acceptable to all caregiving professions, which mental health consultants should try to demonstrate in their reactions to the cases presented by their consultees: empathy, tolerance of feelings, and the conviction that with enough information all human behavior is understandable.

By empathy, we mean the capacity to look objectively at the realities of the client and the people with whom he is related, and at the same time to have some subjective experience of their feelings, to resonate with them at the feeling level and thus share their experience even at a distance.

By tolerance of feelings, we refer to the consultant's demonstration that he retains his professional equanimity despite free expression of feeling in regard to the *dramatis personae* of the case. We do not mean that he uncovers feelings related to his own private life. On the contrary, he demonstrates his human affective resonance with the client as part of his professional style of functioning while maintaining the boundaries of his own private life. By example he encourages the consultee to do the same. We will discuss this further later in this chapter, in connection with the avoidance of psychotherapy.

The third point is particularly important. We believe that much of the upset felt by consultees is linked with their fear of irrationality in their clients, which is probably related to their anxiety about their own irrational impulses. A fundamental message of consultation is that if one spends enough time and collects enough information, one can eventually discover the patterns of forces in the case and then understand the attitudes and behavior of the people involved.

Clarification of Consultation Contract

In initial sessions with a new consultee a consultant should informally discuss the main points of the consultation contract. In our experience, this must be done repeatedly, to make sure that consultees really understand it, especially if the contract calls for consultee-centered consultation. The communication should be made piecemeal, as may appear appropriate during the session, rather than as a pat "lecture."

Maintaining Confidentiality

One more message must be conveyed explicitly and repeatedly in these early contacts: that the consultant undertakes to preserve the confidentiality of material communicated to him. In particular, he promises not to tell the consultee's superiors anything about the consultee's handling of the case, even though he may be expected to discuss the client's problems with them.

The development of trust between consultee and consultant will to a large extent depend on how the consultant fulfills this promise. This is not a simple matter. In institutions with a technical or administrative supervisory system, supervisors are likely to be interested in the consultant's views on the case, and often also in his judgment of the consultee.

In negotiating the consultation contract, the consultant can obtain administrative sanction for not making reports on his consultees to their supervisors, but he cannot sidestep the predicament of talking with them about their clients. A supervisor can legitimately request formal or informal consultation about a client. ← not a consultee

Moreover, it is important for the consultant to build and maintain a good working relationship with the supervisory group, for they are the gatekeepers who exercise major control over the flow of consultees. Such a relationship necessitates regular interaction; most consultants find it advisable to meet, if only briefly, with the supervisors at the beginning and end of every visit to the consultee institution. It is almost inevitable that during such interactions there will be some discussion of those clients who are currently a source of concern to the staff.

This complication should be discussed with consultees, and they should be assured that in a discussion with a supervisor the consultant will talk only about the client, basing his remarks on information the supervisor probably already knows, and never about the way the consultee is dealing with the case.

Many consultees will not trust the consultant in the early stages of their relationship, and will test his sincerity by finding out afterward what he told the supervisor. If he is meticulous in keeping his promise, they will eventually realize this; and he will soon develop a reputation for trustworthiness that will make it easier for him to build relationships with new consultees in that institution.

Consultation confidentiality is one-sided. The consultant binds himself not to divulge what transpired. The consultee is not similarly bound, and must be free to use whatever went on in the consultation session in whatever way he sees fit. Moreover, the consultant is not in a position to interfere between a supervisor and a supervisee; he cannot prevent the supervisor from asking the supervisee about the consultation. The upshot of all this is that even though the consultant will not talk, the consultee can have no confidence that the discussions can be kept secret from the supervisor. This introduces a constraint that prevents the consultee from freely sharing perceptions and expectations about cases, which is an essential prerequisite for consultee-centered consultation.

One way of handling this problem is for the consultant to redouble his efforts to develop a better relationship with the supervisors and to convince them that he respects their domain prerogatives. Another way, which we have found successful, is to raise the issue as a technical problem in meetings with the group of supervisors. Without divulging the identity of the supervisor causing the trouble, and sometimes without even discussing it as an actual problem but as one that has happened in the past and must therefore be prevented in this program, the consultant can emphasize how important it is for supervisors to allow their supervisees to keep to themselves the details of what they say to the consultant about their management of their cases. The supervisors as a group then constrain each of the members to avoid such inadvertent interference with the confidentiality of the consultation interviews.

"One-Downsmanship"

This negative variation on the well-known Potterism expresses graphically an important issue in consultation relationship building. Consultees, whether testing the consultant's assertion of his coordinate status or expressing a sincere feeling of inferiority, will often manipulate the consultation situation to demonstrate their lower status or to maneuver the consultant into showing his superiority. Common examples are expressing undue deference to the consultant's opinions, inviting him to make the next appointment at a time inconvenient to the consultee, or offering to accept unaccustomed burdens in collecting additional information about the case. It is essential that the consultant not acquiesce in this one-downsmanship manipulation.

The consultant must be alert to such a possibility, and whenever he identifies it he should counter in similar manner. For example, he should answer deference by deference, both in his tone of voice and in his attention to the opinions and comfort of the consultee; he should make it clear that he recognizes that the consultee is a busy person and that the next appointment must be at a time that suits his convenience; and he must emphasize that the purpose of consultation is to lighten the load on the consultee and not to increase it, so it is not appropriate for the consultee to collect information over and above that which is readily available during his ordinary work on the case.

If there is a major formal status differential in the consultant's favor, he must himself make use of one-downsmanship to set the consultee at ease and emphasize that in this setting they are meeting each other on an equal footing.

Avoidance of Psychotherapy

Assuming the role of a psychotherapeutic patient is a particularly difficult type of one-downsmanship. Sometimes the consultee may slide into this maneuver in so subtle a way that it may initially escape the consultant's attention, until he suddenly discovers that he is involved in a clearly hierarchical relationship. One common example of this occurs when the consultee in a most natural manner begins to talk of his feelings of anxiety about the client, and then about his feelings of inadequacy, frustration, shame, or hopelessness about his conduct of the case. If the consultant's response is the equally natural expression of his understanding and sympathy for the consultee, this may appear to be merely an ego-supportive maneuver. Certainly it is a response that would come easily to a caseworker, or a psychotherapist, or even to a nonprofessional friend.

Unfortunately, because at the moment one party is expressing emotional disturbance and is communicating this inferiority to the other, who is exhibiting emotional stability and is expressing sympathy and encouragement, this means that from his position of superior strength the consultant is providing emotional supplies to the consultee and nurturantly catering to his dependent needs.

In consultation, both parties must be on an equal footing. This situation will be strained if the consultee is in fact psychologically upset by his impasse with the case. If, however, he is allowed to save face by not having to express his upset openly, the subjective disturbance can remain a private matter, which, like many other private problems, can be kept apart from his professional operations and need not significantly affect them. In particular it will not interfere with his relationship with the consultant.

Apart from its interference with the nonhierarchical relationship of the consultation setting, there are other reasons a consultant should avoid psychotherapy. First, a definition. Here we use the term *psychotherapy* to denote an explicit professional method in which a therapist, who is a recognized healing person, treats a patient, who feels or is felt by others to be psychologically sick, with the goal of shortening or reducing his illness and returning him to healthy mental functioning.

For our present purposes certain elements of the relationship between patient and psychotherapist are significant. First, the patient is dependent on the therapist, and this dependency involves vulnerability. Society protects the patient by a code of ethics to which the therapist must adhere. The patient feels free to place himself in the power of the therapist because he can rely on this societal surveillance and control. Second, the relationship of the patient and therapist is governed by a contract, either explicitly negotiated between them or covertly understood by both because of common usage in their culture. The patient asks to be cured of his illness and offers some form of payment. He also undertakes to adhere to the therapist's requirements both in the investigation and in the treatment process. The therapist offers to use his best diagnostic and therapeutic efforts. He also requires the patient to adhere to his professional demands, such as the open expression of feeling and thoughts, including those normally kept private, despite the pain and embarrassment this might cause the patient. Finally, it is expected that however positive the initial relationship between patient and therapist, negative features will eventually appear because of the invasion of the patient's privacy and because the therapist will influence the patient to confront aspects of his functioning that he was previously repressing or in some other way avoiding, and that are likely to upset him. Transference, which originally may be positive, will soon pass through negative phases. Resistance is an inevitable aspect of psychotherapy. The contract between patient and therapist guarantees that they will continue meeting during these negative phases, and that they will have an opportunity to understand and deal with the resistances and negative transference.

In contrast, the consultation contract provides no sanction for invasion of the consultee's privacy, no societal guarantee that the consultant will not make illicit use of knowledge about the consultee's weakness, and no assurance to the consultant that the consultee will continue to see him if resistance and negative transference are aroused. The consultant has no hold, as it were, on the consultee. The consultee, on the other hand, has no right to use the consultation setting to deal explicitly with his personal problems, because it has been established by the administrators of the institution to help him improve his professional handling of his clients and not to deal with private matters.

Sometimes a consultee develops a trusting relationship with a consultant and a deep respect for his psychological acumen as a result of their discussion of a client's case and asks the consultant to help him with one of his personal problems, possibly a problem similar to the client's. If the consultant agrees, and turns the consultation interview into a psychotherapeutic session, both parties will be misusing company time. Some may think that this infraction of the rules is not significant, since good is being done. But the consultant must realize that if he breaks the rules on this occasion, the consultee may later fear that he will deviate from the contract in other areas, such as in reporting on him to his superiors.

Moreover, the consultant will not be able to give the consultee effective treatment for his problem, because he will not be able to use his ordinary diagnostic or psychotherapeutic techniques in the absence of a proper therapeutic contract. The superficial counseling, which is all that is likely to be possible, probably will not do enough good to offset the upset in the coordinate nature of the consultation relationship. This may not matter if the consultation on the current case has already been satisfactorily concluded, but it is likely to color their ongoing relationship and prevent future consultations. Almost inevitably, the consultee will leave the session with unresolved feelings of personal dependency on the consultant, and this will weaken rather than strengthen his feelings of professional autonomy, especially if he sees a link between unsolved problems in his private life and work difficulties.

Consider, too, the implications for the consultant's ongoing work in the consultee institution as a whole. Consultants must remember that the rules of confidentiality apply to them only; consultees cannot be forced to keep interview material secret. They may talk to some of their friends in the agency about what went on. The communication may sound innocent: "I had such a good session with Dr. Smith today. He is really a very kind and wise man. He was a great help to me in dealing with a problem I am having with my mother." In the relatively closed social system of a consultee institution, in which outsiders, especially interesting outsiders like mental health consultants, are a welcome subject for gossip, the implications of such an innocent remark will be rapidly disseminated. Potential consultees who have problems in their own personal life—and who has not?—may then become afraid of asking for consultation, lest the consultant breach the barrier between the professional and the private spheres. The incident will be taken as proof that the mental health specialist, despite all his protestations to the contrary, is really interested in making the staff into patients.

Ways to Avoid Psychotherapy

The best way of handling this problem is to prevent it. The danger is greatest in individual consultee-centered case consultation, especially cases involving theme interference in which a personal problem of the consultee has been displaced onto the job situation. The consultation techniques for dealing with this will be discussed in Chapters Seven and Eight.

In other types of individual consultation and in group consultation, it is relatively simple for the consultant to help his consultee realize that such feelings as anxiety, shame, guilt, and anger are a natural reaction in a mature professional who is struggling to assist a distressed client. The consultee's emotional upset is the more expectable because the case impasse that occasioned the consultation is likely to make him feel frustrated. The consultant can help his consultee express his feelings and increase his tolerance for them by talking about his own similar reactions in such cases. In group consultation, other members of the group can validate these feelings. The consultant's main task is to demonstrate that a professional can freely discuss his feelings about a case without talking about his private life, even if the case stimulates associations to personal matters.

In individual consultee-centered case consultation, on the other hand, group support is missing, and the influence of the consultant's example may not be sufficient to counteract the pressure of the consultee's personal problem. This is rendered more likely because of the privacy and confidentiality of the setting, the image of the consultant as a clinician with whom it is natural to share personal feelings, and the development of a consultation relationship of trust and respect.

Experience with many consultees suffering from theme interference has demonstrated that there is an expectable chain of associations, which, if not interrupted, leads from talking about the client to talking about private matters. This chain of associations starts with the consultee's reported perceptions of the client, and continues to his feelings about the difficulties of the case, to his feelings about personally significant details of the case, to memories of similar feelings about this whole category of problem, to memories of similar feelings about examples of this problem category in his own life, to details of his current personal problems that are similar, and then to links with significant personal problems of his past life, followed by the explicit or implicit request for the consultant's counsel. It is precisely this chain of associations that therapists try to energize when they focus discussion on a patient's feelings about an incident in an objectively told story. Their goal is to stimulate the emergence into consciousness of the underlying

keep going
back to client

present and past problems. The consultant's goal, on the other hand, is to avoid this process, and to keep the consultation discussion focused on the apparently external and personally unrelated story of the client's life.

Accordingly, the consultant in individual theme interference cases should never ask the consultee how he feels about the case or about any of the incidents described. All questions should be phrased to elicit an objective answer. "What went on?" "What kind of woman was the mother?" "What did the baby look like?" Avoid questions such as "What did you think went on?" and "What was your impression of the mother?" They may lead the consultee to a discussion of his personal reaction. And obviously questions such as "How did you feel about the mother?" and "What were your feelings about the way the mother handled the baby?" should be avoided.

If the consultee spontaneously begins to talk about his feelings, the consultant should as soon as possible interrupt and divert the discussion to some aspect of the client, usually by asking a question to elicit further facts or making a comment about the case. The consultant should not talk about the consultee's feelings, even supportively.

On occasion the consultee manages to verbalize strong feelings about the case, often negative feelings such as disappointment, shame, anger, guilt, or frustration, before the consultant can stop him. If the consultant ignores this expression, it might be felt as a personal rebuff. In such a situation, we have found it valuable to let the consultee know that we have heard his cry of pain, emphasizing by our response that we do not regard it as a sign of weakness but the natural human reaction of a respected colleague with whom we are having a task-oriented professional discussion. We do this by briefly noting that sensitive professionals frequently have a subjective affective resonance as they empathize with their clients, and we put ourselves in the same boat so that we get back onto the same level in continuing to discuss the case. To a consultee who voices hopelessness about the case, we might say, "I know from experience how you must feel. *We* professionals often react strongly to cases like this. It is just this empathy with the client that assures him that we care about his predicament. Let us once more try to understand how this man sees his problem. What makes him feel so hopeless?" Apart from our one-downsmanship response, we are implying that our emotional reaction is a source of strength in our conduct of the case, which is likely to be perceived as such by the client, and that it need not impede our continued joint attempt to unravel the complexities of the case. Also, we deal with the hopelessness of the consultee by directing the discussion not toward him but toward the possible displacement object: the client.

Discussion of the client is the safety zone of consultation. Whenever a consultation interview threatens to get out of hand— the consultee begins to discuss his personal feelings, incidents from his private life, details of his relationship with his peers or administrative superiors, or problems of the social system of his agency in which he is trying to get the consultant to intervene despite the terms of the consultation contract—the consultant should try to get back as soon and as smoothly as possible to a discussion of the client's situation. Experienced consultants use this as an almost reflexive safety device whenever they get into interviewing difficulties. As long as they are talking about the client's predicament, the consultant can be sure that he is within the sanctioned terms of his contract and that he can have the breathing space to consider how to react to the conscious or unconscious manipulations of his consultee.

If a consultee is obviously tense and upset, the consultant should be especially careful not to allow him to gain control over the interview by embarking on a long and rapid monologue. Interrupt frequently with questions to clarify the facts of the case, and begin as soon as possible to offer some conceptual framework that might suggest how the different elements are linked or what factors seem to be particularly significant.

The consultant should beware of generalizations by the consultee—discussions of enuretic children, rebellious adolescents, or engaged couples—especially if he suspects any personal link with the general category. As soon as the discussion gets properly under way, there is little to stop the consultee's suddenly saying, "All this has special meaning to me because I, too, have this problem." When that happens the consultant will have no case to retreat to for safety, because no specific case has been discussed. He will have to discontinue the discussion on the basis of the terms of the consultation contract, which almost certainly will mean loss of face to the consultee and a blow to the relationship.

This matter should be dealt with preventively by ensuring that early on every consultation focuses on the details of a specific client and his family or social situation. Whenever the consultee makes a generalization about categorical issues, the consultant should respond by asking how this relates to the case under discussion, and should then continue the analysis of the case. In this way he supports and strengthens the element of displacement and prevents the consultee's thinking about, or talking about, his personal problems.

If the consultee manages to elude the consultant's preventive efforts and does begin to talk about his private life, this should be tactfully but quickly interrupted. Then, after a suitable supportive bridge comment that affirms the consultant's continued respect for the consultee despite his confession, and possibly some form of one-downsmanship to reestablish the nonhierarchical nature of the relationship, the consultant should get the focus back onto the client. For instance, during a discussion of an enuretic child a teacher said to the consultant, "I feel especially upset about Johnny because for years now I have been plagued with this bed-wetting problem with my own son." The consultant did not say, "I am sorry to hear that. What form does the bed-wetting take with your boy?" Instead, he said, "I am sure your own experience has made you especially sensitive to the feelings of Johnny and his mother. How do you think Mrs. Brown dealt with the problem of other people knowing about Johnny? Has she felt a sense of personal failure, as though others condemn her as a poor mother?" At some stage it might be possible to say something like "It is sometimes a good thing for our clients that *we* professional people are also human and have problems, so that we can more sympathetically understand theirs."

The consultant in such instances must try to convey the implication that most of us professionals have personal problems but that usually we can keep them confined to our private lives, so that they need not intrude into the work sphere, and that often we can capitalize on our past or present private turmoil with greater empathy in our professional operations.

How should a consultant handle explicit requests for psychotherapy or for a referral to a therapist? Actually, experienced consultants who operate along the lines described in this chapter rarely encounter direct requests for psychotherapy. The consultees quickly learn by implication that such requests would not be appropriate in this setting. However, consultees do sometimes ask for advice about getting personal therapy, either as a way of testing the consultant's promise that he will not act as a psychotherapist or as a more or less conscious deviation from the consultation contract under the pressure of personal problems.

The important thing to realize is that, except in the excessively rare emergencies of an acutely psychotic consultee who is a potential danger to himself or others, there is no realistic reason for the consultant to deal with this matter. He can say something like this: "It is true that I am a psychiatrist, but in this setting I have been hired as a mental health consultant to work with you and other staff to improve our service to the institution's clients. I cannot give you valid advice about private matters, because in order to do so we would have to discuss your personal affairs so that I can satisfy myself that you do indeed need psychiatric attention. After all, most of us have various problems of life adjustment and psychological complications, but very few people need to see a psychiatrist. If we spent our time in my giving you a screening or diagnostic interview, this would not be what you and I are being paid for here. If I give you an appointment to come and see me in the clinic, this will complicate our future consultation work, because the relationship between a psychiatrist and a patient is very different from that between us two operating as colleagues working together on consultation cases. I am proud that you have enough trust in my judgment to ask for my counsel in this matter, but I suggest that under the circumstances it would be better for you to talk about this with your own doctor or with some other person you trust and respect."

In this example, the consultant may be forced to mention the terms of the consultation contract. This should be done lightly and tactfully, because it is a form of coercion. Even though its terms apply to both sides, the consultee will usually construe this as implying the use of force. This will probably be a major blow to his future working relationship with that consultee, but will safeguard the relationship with the other consultees in the institution. In some cases, despite initial frustration, it may also reassure that consultee about the consultant's steadfast and nonpunitive adherence to the contract, and he may decide in the future to return for consultation on the consultant's terms and to build a coordinate relationship with him.

Ending the Initial Session

Unlike most other interprofessional operations, in which both sides have a clear expectation about future contacts, consultation presents a situation of ambiguity. During the process of negotiating the consultation contract, the consultant talks in terms of one to four sessions for most cases. But when a consultee comes for the initial session, neither party can be sure whether this case will require more than a single session. Before a firm relationship has been established, there will be a tendency for consultees to want to interrupt or to postpone the second contact. This is because anxiety about the *case* will probably have been reduced and yet the relationship may not yet be sufficiently strong to bring the consultee back against the centrifugal forces of his yet unallayed anxieties about the *consultant*.

It is therefore unwise for the consultant to end an initial session by saying, "Whenever you feel like it, please come and see me again for further discussion of this case." The consultee may wrongly interpret this as meaning that the consultant does not really want to go on talking about the case, which must somehow have been unsuitable, and yet is too polite to say so openly—sort of a "don't call us, we'll call you" attitude.

If the consultant has clear indications that he will complete the consultation in the one session, there is no problem. If, as is more usual, especially with a new consultee, he feels halfway through that at least one more session is needed, both to continue exploring and building the relationship and also to deal with the case consultation itself, he should begin to prepare for the ending of this session in terms of ensuring the second meeting. Experienced consultants do not leave this to a sudden decision in the last few minutes of the interview. Instead, they begin about halfway through the session to make remarks about how complicated the case seems, how much material there is to try to understand, how interesting are the patterns that are beginning to emerge. Having laid this groundwork, it emerges as perfectly natural, almost not worth mentioning at the end, that a second session is essential. The consultee should by then have no doubt that the consultant is deeply involved in the case. The consultee should also not feel any pressure from the consultant to collect more data before the next session, although he himself may wish to return to the client to get more information about particular issues.

The consultant should not try to pull together the discussion at the end of the first session but should leave it in an interrupted state with many obviously unanswered questions. He should avoid summarizing formulations, for four reasons: (1) They may lead to premature closure, which will reduce the likelihood of the consultee's return, and which may be wrong because of lack of information. (2) They may unduly lower consultee anxiety about the case because they imply that it is already solved. (3) They may produce unlinking, in cases of theme interference, because the consultant still has no clear idea about the patterned way in which the consultee's subjective problems are distorting his perceptions and expectations of the client (this technical problem will be fully discussed in Chapter Seven). (4) They may break the displacement by allowing the consultee to leave the session with an awareness of the general outlines of the case such that on his own he will see its implications for his personal problems, a process that the consultant might have been able to prevent if it had begun to happen during a consultation discussion.

CHAPTER SIX

Client-Centered
Case Consultation

In client-centered case consultation—the most familiar type—a consultee who has difficulty dealing with the mental health aspects of one of his clients calls in a specialist for advice. Usually the specialist personally examines the client, makes a diagnosis, and writes a report with recommendations for disposition and management. The consultee translates appropriate aspects of the recommendations into a plan that he considers feasible and then takes action.

The primary goal of this type of consultation is to develop a plan that will help the client. A subsidiary, but not unimportant, goal is education: the consultee should learn something from the encounter with the consultant that will increase his ability to handle similar cases better in the future. The secondary goal is limited because the client's difficulties are unusual and probably future clients of the same type will also need to be seen by a specialist. Also, there is little opportunity for education since the interaction between consultant and consultee is minimal—most of the consultant's time is spent with the client.

Consultants who place greater emphasis on the educational goal will try to increase the proportion of their consulting time spent with the consultee. Some do this by collecting all or most of their information from the consultee, rather than from personal investigation of the client. The more they do this, the closer their operations get to consultee-centered case consultation. This is not without hazard. In consultee-centered consultation there is no expectation that the consultant will provide an expert assessment of the client. He is required only to add to the consultee's understanding of certain aspects of the case. In client-centered case consultation, on the other hand, the consultant is specifically asked to evaluate the client and give advice on management. It is essential that the advice be correct. This depends on the consultant having accurate information, which usually means that he must investigate the client himself—rarely can he rely on a consultee to provide him with an undistorted view of a client with whom he is having difficulty. Also, the investigation often requires specialized data collection in the form of psychiatric or casework interviews or psychological testing.

A consultant who has worked with particular consultees on many cases may come to rely on certain types of information they can give him and may feel less need for validating these data with his own investigations. He may also be able to triangulate, as it were, by collecting information from several informants, for example, three or four teachers and the nurse in a high school, all of whom are involved with the same student. In this way he can explore for consonance or discrepancies in their stories and begin to build up a valid picture of the client, which will reduce his need for personal contact. However, since he has to take responsibility for a diagnostic assessment, he will be wise to see the client for at least a short time himself.

In some types of client-centered case consultation the consultant is not required to commit himself to a diagnostic judgment but only to a screening assessment; in these situations there may be no need for him to see the client. For instance, in some school systems a committee consisting of guidance personnel, a school psychologist, a social worker, a nurse, and some of the educators meet regularly to review problem cases and decide on special education within the school or on referral of the children to specialized outside agencies. A psychiatrist may be called in to offer consultation to this group, either occasionally in relation to an unusually difficult case or on a regular basis to review routine problems. Here the consultant may feel comfortable giving his opinion on the basis of the documents and the accounts of the individuals present, without needing to see the children himself.

When the consultant spends little or no time with the client, he will have a good opportunity to get to know the consultees. In the more usual cases, where the consultant spends most of his time with the client and hardly sees the consultee at all, the consultant must make a special effort to get to know the consultee and to learn how to communicate with him. No matter how accurate the diagnostic formulation and how wise the prescriptions for disposition and management of the client, these will achieve little unless they are understandable, acceptable, and feasible to the consultee.

Steps in the Consultation Process

Consultants should organize the process of consultation in an orderly series of steps.

Consultation Request

The request for consultation help may come directly to the consultant through personal contact, by telephone, in writing, or indirectly through secretaries or other staff. It may take the form of a detailed account of the client's condition, the difficulties in his management, and a specific set of questions about the problem and how to deal with it.

   If there is direct communication, either face to face or by telephone, the consultant can ask for supplementary information not only about the client's condition and history but also about the consultee's work situation and the feasible possibilities for referral and modifications in management. If the consultation request comes in writing or through secretaries or other staff, it may occasionally contain the essential information about the client and the consultee, but often this is not so. It is common for a consultation request to consist of a short note: "Please see and advise" or "Consultation requested on this case of enuresis."

   Especially if this is a new consultee, such laconic requests should be treated with caution. The person asking for help may use the term *consultation*, but this may mean something different to him from what it does to the mental health specialist. He may be having difficulty with the client and may wish the specialist to take over the case, either completely or partially. The apparent request for consultation may in fact be a referral. In that event he will be angry if the consultant sends the client back with a message about disposition and management. On the other hand, a message that seems like a referral may be intended as a request for consultation advice, and the consultee will be even angrier if the consultant does not return the client but takes him over as his own patient.

The best way of dealing with this is, wherever possible, to talk directly to the consultee and clarify the specific request. Even busy consultees will rarely resent such contacts by the consultant, but will see them as a sign that the consultant is eager to be helpful. This contact will also establish proximity for beginning to build the relationship that is the basis for all consultation, even the most client-centered.

Assessment of the Consultation Problem

It is already clear that in this type of consultation the consultant must assess two problems: (1) the nature of the client's difficulties and (2) the liabilities and resources of the consultee and his work situation in relation to this client.

Assessment of the Client. There is no need to dwell on the assessment of the client, except to emphasize that the consultant must keep in mind the immediate purpose of his investigation and must plan his evaluative strategy accordingly. The consultee will usually want a quick answer, and so the investigation should be as short as reasonably possible. The consultant will usually have to answer two fundamental questions: Should the client be referred to a specialized professional or agency for further investigation or treatment? Whether or not the client should be referred, what can the consultee do, within the usual work setting, to help the client?

The answer to the first question usually requires collecting enough information, by interviewing the client and possibly members of his family, to permit a general evaluative formulation. A precise diagnosis may not be required, and so lengthy interviewing, diagnostic testing, and home visiting may not be necessary. If they are, this should be done as a second stage, probably after the client has been referred to a specialized mental health agency.

The answer to the second question demands, not the usual

kind of clinical diagnosis, but an assessment of the client's current human predicament in terms of the practical and psychological tasks that confront him and his involvement with significant others and with the caregiving persons to whom he turns for help, such as the consultee and the other professionals in his community. Recommendations that may emerge from an assessment on this plane will deal with modifying the client's network of role expectations and associated positive reinforcements and negative sanctions; providing advice and guidance about dealing with current life problems; and giving emotional support to relieve anxiety, guilt, and depression and to help the client tolerate confusion and persevere in grappling with his difficulties.

In making this type of assessment, the consultant will interest himself in the details of the human predicament in which the client is currently involved, not as a set of precipitants or consequences of his psychopathological deviations but as the central focus for the investigation. In the army, for example, as Bushard (1958) so vividly points out, the consultant would not focus so much on the investigation of a soldier's symptomatic picture as on his relationships with peers and superiors and on the details of his work difficulties. The consultant may, for instance, discover that some difference in culture, possibly linked with race, religion, or class, has initially interfered with free communication between the soldier and his peer group. This isolation may not have been significant until the soldier was burdened by the demand to perform some duty that strained his resources, or by a personal problem. Lack of communication with his peer group and superiors then means not only that he lacks support for the problem but that others do not understand the reason for his poor performance and punish him for it, indeed may even increase his duty burdens. Eventually, the soldier might try to escape by going AWOL or by developing symptoms of mental illness. Once he has cast himself into the role of delinquent or patient, the others in his unit move the focus of their attention from his real problems to his deviant behavior. The consultant's purpose should be to reverse this process, to uncover information about both the soldier's predicament and the blocks in his communications, so that the significant people around him may understand the nature of his human difficulties, learn how to communicate with him, and proffer their usual methods of support. Such an assessment implies that the consultant should investigate not only the client but also his life circumstances, particularly his relationship with the consultee.

Assessment of the Consultee Setting. This brings us to the consultant's second area of assessment—the liabilities and resources of the consultee and his work situation in relation to the client. A great deal of traditional client-centered case consultation is carried out in the specialist's office, as when a patient is referred by a general practitioner or a student by a schoolteacher. In this situation of isolation, it is very difficult for the consultant to do any more than investigate the client. Information about the client's relationship with the consultee must mainly be based on the client's statements. If the consultee and his institution are not known to the consultant, he can only use his imagination or his general knowledge to guess their relevant liabilities and resources. The best procedure for the consultant is to enter the consultee's environment, to see the student in the school, the patient on the ward, the soldier in his unit, and the disabled person in the vocational rehabilitation office.

There are many advantages in this method, such as the opportunity for relationship building and the ease of effectively communicating the consultant's opinion; but the main benefit is that the consultant can explore directly the links between client and consultee. The blockage of communication may not be due entirely to a deficiency in the client. It may be influenced by the consultee's inability to hear or to understand what the client is trying to say. An important part of the consultant's task is to act as a communication bridge between the two, but to do so he must be able to assess both sides of the system.

In a well-baby clinic, for example, the pediatrician asked a consultant for help with a woman whose fifteen-month-old son was suffering from head banging, which appeared to be due to maternal neglect of the child. The consultant saw the woman in the clinic and found her to be suffering from feelings of deprivation and a mild reactive depression, which were interfering with her relationship with her child. After some initial difficulty, he was able to get through to her, and gradually she told him her story. Her husband had lost his job eight months previously because of a fight with the foreman. He was drinking heavily and he could not get another job. He began to stay out nights, and she suspected that he was with other women. She applied for welfare, but was told she would get support only if her husband formally left her. The welfare worker made her take her husband to court, get a formal separation, and sue him for nonsupport of the child. The husband was forced to run away altogether to avoid being jailed. The worry over the whole affair had made her depressed.

The consultant wondered to himself why this fairly characteristic story was not known to the workers in the well-baby clinic. He was struck by the lack of rapport between the pediatrician and the woman, and also the lack of communication between the clinic personnel and the workers in the welfare department.

He noticed, too, that the pediatrician seemed hurried in his dealings with the clinic patients, and in particular that he did not have much time to talk with the public health nurses. They seemed to know a fair amount about the patient's family problems, but they ascribed her neglect of the child to low intelligence. They had been angry for some time about the policy of forcing welfare mothers to bring their husbands into court for nonsupport, and because of this anger they did not readily communicate with the social workers.

The pediatrician appeared to be a warm and kindly man. His hurry at the clinic, where part-time employees were poorly paid by the city health department, seemed to come from pressure to get back to his middle-class private practice. His lack of communication with the public health nurses stemmed partly from strained relations with their supervisor, who felt he was short-changing the clinic because he rushed in and out so quickly, and partly from his low opinion of the nurses because of the poor quality of their written reports. Since he rarely discussed cases personally with the nurses, he had no realization of the richness of their information about many of his patients.

The mother's depression and its origins could have been adequately assessed by the consultant even had he seen her in his own office. To obtain the other information—information that was vital to a meaningful plan—he had to spend some time in the clinic. The alienation of the mother from her baby was only part of a total picture of communication blocks—between the woman and her husband, between the woman and the pediatrician, between the pediatrician and the public health nurses, between the nurses and the welfare workers. Moreover, despite the sad realities of slum life and inadequate medical care and welfare services in the urban ghetto, there were many assets in the situation that might be mobilized in behalf of the woman and her baby—the warmth and interest of the pediatrician, the public health nurses' knowledge of local conditions and local resources, and the potential of using the welfare workers for constructive rather than destructive purposes by helping them to deal with this case more flexibly.

The consultant might have diagnosed depression in the mother and recommended that she be referred for antidepressant medication. A more significant consultation, however, would focus on building communication bridges among the participants, and on enabling the pediatrician to understand the woman's predicament and to find a way to mobilize the existing resources in his professional domain to help with her major life problem.

What might the consultant have done if he had been using consultee-centered case consultation? He would probably not have seen the woman at all but would have spent all his time talking with the pediatrician about the patient. He would undoubtedly have noticed that the consultee's view of the woman was unduly restricted and that he had not collected additional information from the public health nurses. Unless the nurses were also included among his consultee group, he would not have had access to the detailed information about the woman's marital history or about the influence of the welfare workers. If the consultee group did include all the clinic workers he probably would have obtained most of the story in a single session. He might not have been able to rule out an intellectual deficit in the patient, as he was in fact able to do from his own interview with her, but he would have been able to raise the question of mental retardation versus depression and to help the clinic workers differentiate the two. He would probably have been in a better position to understand the communication blocks in the pediatrician and the public health nurses, because he would have had more time to explore them. And this knowledge would probably have given him more leverage to remedy the situation than he had with a client-centered approach, where his contact with consultees was shorter.

In actuality, in this example the communication blocks were mainly situational and were little influenced by the personal idiosyncrasies of the health workers. It was therefore possible for the consultant to ameliorate the pattern with a relatively short communication in the form of advice on case management. This would not have worked if the blocks had been rooted in deep prejudice or in theme interference. Had this been so, the theme interference reduction techniques of consultee-centered case consultation would have been essential. The consultation probably would have required two or three sessions, for the consultant to obtain the necessary information and to build a relationship of sufficient intensity to provide enough leverage.

In contrast, the client-centered approach enabled the consultant to complete his main work in one session. Although he spent much of his time with the client, he did spend about thirty minutes in all with the pediatrician and the public health nurses, enough time for him to collect the necessary information about their social system and their involvement in the case, as well as to make his consultant intervention. Information about the consultees and their work situation can be rapidly obtained by observing interactional cues and by sensitive interviewing. In this example, for instance, the consultant observed the hurried manner of the pediatrician and his lack of rapport with the mother. He asked him a few questions about the patient and about the work situation in the clinic. Then he talked briefly to the nurses and their supervisor about the patient, the policies and practices of the welfare workers, and about the city's arrangements for staffing the well-baby clinics. All his questions dealt with facts about the system that could easily be discussed openly by the professionals concerned, and that required a minimum of interpretation of underlying motives. The consultant's main task was to fit his findings together into a meaningful pattern in order to form the basis for his intervention.

Of the thirty minutes of interaction, the consultant spent about twenty to twenty-five minutes on his assessment. During that time he not only elicited the facts of the situation but he also learned something about the communication style of his consultees, particularly the pediatrician, to whom his consultation report would have to be delivered. This allowed him to tune in to the consultee's wavelength, so that he could communicate his appraisal of the case and his recommendations in an acceptable way.

The Consultation Report

In client-centered case consultation the consultant writes a report. Wherever possible, this written communication should be supplemented by a face-to-face discussion or by a telephone call, which lets the consultee clarify the consultant's meaning and allows the consultant to make sure that his recommendations are understood and are feasible in the consultee's setting.

It is crucial that the consultant's vocabulary be acceptable to the consultee. Jargon is not appropriate. On the other hand, the consultee should not feel that the consultant is talking down to him. The consultant must be aware not only of the choice of words but also of the nature of the concepts that he communicates. These concepts must fit the culture of the consultee. The golden mean can be found only if the consultant gets to know the communication style of the consultee's profession and the personal communication patterns of the particular consultee, and if he makes a determined effort to talk at the right level.

For instance, a pediatrician or a general practitioner usually feels uncomfortable if a psychologist talks to him about pregenital sexuality, castration fears, latent homosexuality, or incestuous fantasies. Such topics are commonplace among mental health workers, but to many other professionals they are strange and distasteful. They may be important issues in the specialist's own diagnostic formulations. However, since his report is not addressed to himself or to a mental health colleague but to a consultee of another profession, it should contain only material that can be used by its recipient.

For instance, in the example of the head-banging child, the consultant wrote the following report:

I agree that the head banging is probably the result of the child's being deprived of his mother's care and affection. The mother is of normal intelligence but appears dull because she is suffering from a depression that appears to be a reaction to her present unsatisfactory life situation. She left her family and friends in Mississippi when she came to Northville. Her husband lost his job eight months ago and has had no steady employment since then. He is separated from his wife. He has a problem with alcohol, the seriousness of which is hard to determine from the woman's story. She is on ADC and in order to comply with local welfare policy, she took her husband to court for nonsupport. The woman now lives a lonely, isolated life and is grieving for her husband and for her family and friends. Because of her own feelings of deprivation she is not able to give adequate attention to her child.

I recommend that the well-baby clinic workers help the mother explore alternative avenues for dealing with her problems with her husband—the mother knows his address and sees him occasionally. I have the impression that it is the pressure of the court order that is the main factor in keeping them apart. It would be valuable if the man could be induced to come in for an interview with the pediatrician so as to involve the father in the responsibility for the care of his child. The main purpose of such an interview would be to offer him help with his alcohol and employment problems, through referral to the Public Employment Service Office in Northville and possibly to the Alcohol Clinic at Northville Hospital. The public health nurse might contact the welfare worker and explore other avenues than ADC for supporting the family until the father gets back on his feet. The assistance of the neighborhood lawyer at the Oxford Multiservice Center might be needed to disentangle the legal aspects of the nonsupport situation.

From the mother's story, it seems that the trouble between her and her husband is not deep-seated. It was probably precipitated by his not being able to cope with the job at the meat-packing plant for which he was not fitted, and his finding escape in alcohol. If I am correct, superficial support and guidance by the public health nurse should be sufficient to help the couple get back together and readjust their marriage. If not, the social worker at the Alcohol Clinic should be able to help; and if this does not work out, I suggest a referral to the Oxford Family Service worker at the Multiservice Center. The mother's depression is not deep enough to warrant psychiatric treatment. I have every hope that it will lift as soon as her marital problems begin to clear up. If not, she may eventually need antidepressant medication.

I recommend that the pediatrician continue to see the mother and baby at regular intervals at the well-baby clinic in order to supervise the progress of the case and to coordinate the work of the other professionals through the efforts of the public health nurse. I will be interested in the outcome, and I would be pleased to see the woman again in about three months to see how she is doing and to make other suggestions should these be necessary. Please feel free to call on me before then if anything unexpected occurs.

Note that all the consultant's statements are direct and to the point; there is no abstruse discussion of psychopathology. He also spells out concretely the various types of professional intervention needed and differentiates the tasks of the pediatrician and the public health nurse. Note the consultant's offer to see the client again for a reevaluation and to provide further consultation help if things do not turn out as expected. This acceptance of a continuing interest in the case, and a sharing of responsibility for its outcome, is an important source of emotional and cognitive support to the consultees.

This report also offers a good example of a consultant's bridge-building role. His recommendations provide a concrete opportunity for building or rebuilding relationships between the client and her husband, the pediatrician and the public health nurses, the nurses and the welfare workers, and the well-baby clinic staff and several key neighborhood agencies. This consultant happened to have firsthand knowledge of the local caregiving agencies.

Where this is not so, the consultant can often obtain this information from the consultees, who usually can name the appropriate agencies, even though they may not have thought of invoking their aid on the case in question.

Implementation of the Consultant's Recommendations

Implementing the consultant's recommendations is a matter for the consultee. Since he carries the responsibility for the case, he may accept or reject the consultant's suggestions. The recommendations, therefore, should be in line with the consultee's skills. If he decides to accept the suggestions, he should be able to implement them with the resources immediately available in his agency.

Especially with a new consultee, the consultant may not feel confident that this ideal can be attained. For instance, in the case just described, the pediatrician and the public health nurse would need considerable skill to motivate the husband to come to the well-baby clinic, to counsel the couple on their marital difficulties, to persuade the welfare workers to find an alternative to their standard ADC approach, and to refer the couple to the other agencies as well as to interest the busy agency workers in the case. Is this not a tall order for the usual staff of a well-baby clinic? In this case the consultant had reason to believe them capable of carrying out such a plan.

Each consultant must learn for himself the limits of the capacities of his consultees. Many consultees will, however, require some assistance from the consultant in finding out how to go about implementing his recommendations. This is often an essential part of the consultant's contribution and is another reason why he should discuss his written recommendations verbally with the consultees.

In our example, both the pediatrician and the public health nurse had a number of questions about how they should handle the case in conformity with the psychologist's suggestions. He was able to answer many of these questions in quite specific terms, such as how to approach the husband and what to say to the welfare workers. More important, in his expressed attitudes of empathy and understanding for this young couple from a rural background, caught up in a complex of forces beyond their comprehension and control, in a bewildering and frightening metropolis, he was able to present himself as a role model. In this way he once again acted as a bridge and paved the way for the clinic workers to see the tragic human qualities of this family, so that they might be better able to communicate empathically with them and also to interpret the case to the other professionals.

Follow-Up

Whenever possible the consultant should end a consultation by arranging for follow-up information. This is important for two reasons. First, it serves as a rough method of evaluating the efficacy of the consultation. A favorable report on the client three or six months later may not be the result of the consultee's efforts or of the consultant's recommendations, but at least it is consonant with a good result. By discussing the progress of the case, the consultant may also learn more about the consultee's ways of working and how they may have been influenced by his own intervention.

If the report turns out to be negative, the consultant can be more confident in accepting it as an evaluation of his consultation efforts. Since it emphasizes his lack of success, it provides him with a stimulus to review what he did and to try to identify errors in technique. It is likely that the consultee, too, is disappointed with the result and perhaps also with the consultant. A review of the case will give him an opportunity to discuss how he thinks the consultant might be more helpful, which he probably would have been reluctant to initiate spontaneously. In the followup setting, both consultant and consultee can analyze their joint endeavors without either side engaging in recriminations but in a spirit of pooling ideas to improve their future efforts in behalf of clients.

Apart from this, the fact that the consultant wishes to devote time and serious thought to follow-up investigations is likely to have a beneficial effect on the consultation relationship. It consolidates the continuing bond between the consultee and consultant, and it prepares the way for continuing discussion not only of the case in point but of others. Our approach to consultation demands that the consultant not diminish the consultee's autonomy and independence. This involves, however, a hazard: the consultee may perceive the consultant as someone who wishes not to get his own hands dirty. Despite all his attempts to paint an image of himself as a helpful colleague with a nonhierarchical approach, this perception may interfere with the development of an optimal consultation relationship. The consultee's awareness of the consultant's authentic interest in the cases, manifested by the follow-up, serves to counteract such a negative impression.

In the follow-up discussions the consultant should leave no doubt that he is concerned with the fate of the client, not shortcomings in the consultee's operations. The consultant must be sure to convey the impression—which in fact should be his true feeling—that both he and the consultee are equally involved in the client's life, each with his own assigned role and responsibility—the consultant for contributing the specialized evaluation of the problem and recommendations on how to deal with it, and the consultee for translating these recommendations into a feasible plan and taking direct action to implement it.

CHAPTER SEVEN

Consultee-Centered
Case Consultation

In consultee-centered case consultation the consultant's primary focus is on elucidating and remedying the shortcomings in the consultee's professional functioning. The discussion is mainly restricted to clarifying the details of the client's situation to increase the consultee's cognitive grasp and emotional mastery of the issues involved in caring for him. This is likely to lead to an improvement in the consultee's professional planning and action, and hopefully to improvement in the client. But in consultee-centered consultation, improvement in the client is a side effect, welcome though it may be; *like a* the primary goal is to improve the consultee's capacity to function *teaching* effectively in this category of case, in order to benefit many similar *asst* clients in the future.

Because of this educational emphasis, the consultant uses the current case situation not primarily to understand the client but to understand and remedy the consultee's work difficulties. He therefore focuses his attention selectively on certain aspects of the case that provide evidence about the professional work problems of the consultee, rather than on the condition of the client as a person in his own right.

The significant information in this kind of consultation comes from the consultee's subjectively determined story about the client, not from the objective reality of the client's situation. Because of this, there is usually no need for the consultant to investigate the client directly by seeing or interviewing him, and he can restrict his information to what the consultee says about the case.

101

Since the consultee is having cognitive, and often emotional, difficulties in dealing with this client, it is likely that his description of the case will be one-sided, incomplete, or distorted. If the consultant does not examine the client himself, how can he determine the extent of the discrepancies, from which he can pinpoint the consultee's shortcomings? The doubt raised by this question impels some consultants to collect independent objective information about clients. They usually do not conduct as exhaustive an investigation as they would in client-centered case consultation, but they do try to obtain some more objective picture of the client, such as by classroom observation or by asking other observers to describe him, to compare this with the consultee's story.

We do not consider this essential. Our experience teaches us that if we listen carefully to the consultee's statements about his case, we can usually identify his biases and distortions from the internal consistency of his observations; from evidence of exaggeration, confusion, or stereotyping; and from signs of emotional overinvolvement or underinvolvement with one or more of the actors in the client's drama.

This approach has one obvious drawback. Since the consultant's information is restricted to what the consultee *says*, the consultant can never be certain how this is related to what the consultee *does*. The consultation can deal only with the consultee's *capacity* for professional action and not with his actual behavior. This is in keeping with the fact that usually the consultant is not a member of the same profession as the consultee and therefore would not be competent to judge his technical operations, or for that matter to perceive the objective reality of the client in terms of the consultee's professional subculture. This point emphasizes the difference between consultee-centered case consultation and case supervision. The goals of consultation are limited to remedying certain defects in the consultee's professional skills that become salient and visible in specific case situations. Supervision and other forms of professional education have the goal of systematic positive enhancement of knowledge and skills. Supervision also has the goal of protecting the clients of the program and must therefore have access to information from which valid judgments can be made about the professional worker's behavior and its effect on his client.

Types of Consultee-Centered Case Consultation

We have found it valuable to differentiate four types of consultee-centered case consultation: lack of knowledge, lack of skill, lack of self-confidence, and lack of professional objectivity. Each is discussed in this section.

Lack of Knowledge

The consultee's inability to handle the case may be due to his lack of knowledge about the psychosocial factors involved in such situations; he may not see the relevance of theoretical concepts to the realities of his client's problems. Courses in psychology, psychopathology, and community mental health have sometimes been inadequate for such professions as nursing, teaching, medicine, and the law. They are improving, but older practitioners may have some shortcomings in these subjects, and recent graduates may not have learned how to use abstract concepts to analyze particular case situations. Certain topics that are of great importance in understanding the common predicaments of everyday life are even today rarely part of the curriculum in professional training—essential subjects such as crisis theory, drug addiction, alcoholism, suicide, and mental retardation. However much time and effort may be devoted to these subjects in professional schools, advances in the field may not be adequately covered by continuing education and in-service training. Moreover, curriculum content in all these educational programs must necessarily be relatively superficial to allow for the acquisition of the main body of traditional knowledge. It is inevitable that from time to time the professional worker will be confronted by problems that demand specialized knowledge that neither he nor his supervisors possess.

When the consultant recognizes that the difficulties of his consultee are due to such lack of knowledge about mental health, he can obviously remedy the situation by imparting the missing information. In doing so, he should take care not to disturb the role identity of the consultee.

In a well-organized professional institution there will be little need for consultee-centered case consultation occasioned by lack of knowledge. Recruitment and selection will ensure that workers are well trained, and their knowledge will be continually upgraded. Only occasionally will an unusual case overtax these systems and lead to a need for consultation. If a mental health consultant encounters more than a few instances of this type, he should draw to the attention of the appropriate authorities the need to supplement their in-service training efforts. The mental health specialist may himself take a part in this by providing didactic seminars for supervisors or line workers. The former are more appropriate, because they lead to a wider spread in communicating the new information and ensure a more lasting effect—the supervisors are likely to continue working for the organization longer than the line workers. There is also less danger of the consultant's disturbing the role identity of stable senior professionals than of juniors who might identify with him as a role model. In addition, when the specialist filters his knowledge to the line workers through the supervisory group, the supervisors will translate his ideas and concepts into the communication modes acceptable in that setting.

Consultee-centered case consultation is an expensive form of interprofessional operation, especially on an individual basis. It repeatedly takes up the time of a highly trained specialist to disseminate information that could be imparted just as effectively and much more cheaply by straightforward group educational methods. In the absence of an adequate training program in a consultee institution, the consultant should use group consultation to deal with frequent work difficulties that are caused by lack of knowledge. According to the changing demands of the situation, he can modify his method to turn certain sessions into more or less systematic seminars when he comes across areas of ignorance that are common to the majority of the group.

Lack of Skill

In certain cases, the consultant may judge that the consultee's work difficulty is due not to his lack of understanding of the client's situation but to lack of skill in finding a solution to the problem, either by his own direct efforts or by invoking the help of others. The consultant, accordingly, will attempt to help the consultee improve his skills. Since methods are even more idiosyncratically related to professional culture than is basic theoretical knowledge, the safeguards against disturbing the role image of consultees are vital here.

In particular, the consultant must avoid giving straightforward prescriptions for action, unless he has a wide and intimate knowledge of the range of normative behavior in the consultee profession and in the particular consultee institution. Even then, he should not prescribe an answer to the questions in the case but put forward a range of alternative ways of handling the problem, which he has learned to value from previous experience of what has been used in that institution. This is complicated by the fact that the consultee may have unsuccessfully tried many or all of these methods before finally giving up and asking for consultant help.

Rather than listening to the problems presented by the case and then suggesting alternative solutions, the consultant might be better advised to carry out a joint appraisal with the consultee of how he has already tried to deal with them, and by means of this discussion attempt to enlarge the consultee's understanding of the case, which may reveal additional options for action. This is a tricky situation—the consultation can easily slide into a supervisory-type session, with the consultee expecting the consultant to criticize or praise his efforts.

Whenever a consultee institution has a functioning supervisory system, we try to steer clear of this kind of consultation intervention by suggesting that the consultee seek help from his supervisor, or by inviting the supervisor to the consultation interview and shifting from our central consultant role to that of a specialist resource person, while the supervisor takes over the primary task of helping the consultee begin to work out appropriate methods.

In any event, skill development is not a matter that can be dealt with in one or two interviews but demands continued practice. The function of a mental health consultant in this process is first to identify that one or more workers have inadequate skills, and then to energize the agency's training system. Logistically, the most effective role for the mental health specialist is as a resource person to the supervisory group.

We are not advocating that when a consultant discovers that a consultee is having difficulties because of lack of skill he should terminate the session by referral to the supervisor. That would clearly damage his consultation relationship with the line workers, even though it was sincerely meant to avoid infringement on the domain of the supervisors and to prevent waste of expensive consultation time. What we are suggesting is that once the consultant decides that he is dealing with a consultation case of this type, he should focus his efforts for the remainder of that interview on gaining a deeper understanding of the skill difficulties, adding to the consultee's understanding of the issues involved and helping him explore how he might improve his skills within the established framework of his institution.

In consultee organizations that do not have an active system of supervision—for example, a diocese in which the parish priests are relatively independent—a mental health consultant may be the only person available to help consultees improve their skills. Here again, he should try to operate on a group basis rather than on an individual basis. Not only is this logistically sound (spreading the effect of his specialist efforts), it also allows him to restrict himself to the role of a resource person, stimulating group members to share ideas with each other. For instance, in dealing with a case of alcoholism presented to the consultation group, the consultant can contribute specialist information about the difficulties likely to be encountered in dealing with the alcoholic's wife, who may be unconsciously driving him to continue drinking. The consultant leaves to the group the question of how a clergyman could best exploit the potentials of his role and the influence of his congregation in dealing with her. The consultant could also bring home to the group the realistic assets and constraints of the available medical clinics, self-help groups, and community mental health facilities that they might try to involve in their action planning, while encouraging individual group members to recount their experiences in similar cases among their own congregants.

Lack of Self-Confidence

Occasionally the consultee's uncertainty about a case may be caused by generalized lack of confidence, related to such factors as ill health, old age, burnout, or inexperience. The consultant's role is then to provide nonspecific ego support and to smooth the consultee's path to other supportive figures in the consultee organization. If the consultant finds widespread lack of self-confidence among certain classes of workers in the institution—for example, new nurses in a public health unit or new teachers in a school—the chances are that there is some inadequacy in the supervisory or administrative system. If the consultant can stimulate an improvement in this situation he should do so. If not, he might organize a few group sessions, geared mainly to providing peer support among those in the same boat, as well as communicating to the group the solicitude and support of their administrative authorities.

Lack of Objectivity

In a well-organized institution or agency, most cases of consultee-centered case consultation fall into this last category. The consultee's difficulty with his client is caused by a lack of professional objectivity and a loss of normal professional distance. The consultee is either too close or too distant from actors in the client's life drama, and is not able to perceive them accurately enough to carry out his task. Personal subjective factors in the consultee cloud his judgment, so that in this current case he behaves less effectively than is usual for him and thus is not able to use his existing knowledge and skills. By the time he comes for consultation, this situation is usually aggravated by his feelings of frustration at the impasse in the case, by a feeling of professional failure, and consequent lowering of self-esteem, all of which add to his loss of professional poise.

This type of consultation taxes the coordinate relationship of consultant and consultee the most; if the consultee's loss of poise is openly mentioned or discussed, it emphasizes a discrepancy between him and the consultant, who is relaxed and apparently in perfect control of his personal life. It is important for the consultant to deal with the relevant issues by discussing them in relation to some actor in the client's drama, to himself, to some other example, or to a fictitious person in an anecdote or parable—anyone except the consultee. The goal of this "displacement" discussion is to help the consultee regain, without loss of face, his professional poise and objectivity, both in the present case and in connection with the sensitive issue of his personal life or professional functioning of which this case is an example.

There is a vast range of possible causes for lack of professional objectivity, including inadequate professional training and idiosyncratic personality factors, such as low intelligence, poor judgment, insensitivity, and poor motivation. The consultation setting, however, exerts a filtering effect, and most cases fall into five overlapping categories: direct personal involvement, simple identification, transference, characterological distortions, and theme interference.

Direct Personal Involvement. Here the consultee has lost professional objectivity because he deviated from the professional relationship with the client and replaced it with a personal relationship. Examples are the physician who falls in love with a patient, the teacher who builds a maternal relationship with one of her pupils, or the white nurse who reacts to a black patient primarily on the basis of racial prejudice.

In some cases the worker is aware of the deviation from his professional role and is able to resolve the conflict, at the expense of a certain amount of guilt—for instance, the psychoanalyst who falls in love with a patient and interrupts the analysis to get married. Such cases are not likely to come to consultation, although less extreme ones sometimes fall into the domain of the supervisor, part of whose duty it is to protect clients from being exploited to satisfy the personal needs of their supervisees.

In other cases, the worker is more or less unaware of what is happening, or he may consciously deny his awareness of it because of guilt and shame. Such cases not uncommonly come for consultation and are, of course, quite common in supervision and in professional training situations, where a directed effort is made to help young practitioners learn to separate their personal needs from the work setting.

In consultation, the consultee's direct personal involvement with the client can be identified from a variety of verbal and nonverbal cues in his story and behavior. The consultant's intervention is directed to influencing the consultee to replace the satisfaction of his personal need with the satisfaction of professional goals. This may be accomplished, without loss of face, by discussing the client's problems in the same area—that is, his conflict between getting direct personal satisfaction from the consultee and getting the consultee's help in dealing with his problems so that he can satisfy his own needs in normal life situations. The following report by a psychiatric consultant to a school system illustrates how this can be done:

reverse

> The consultee in this case is a female guidance counselor in a junior high school. She is about forty years of age, unmarried, decidedly overweight, and living with her elderly parents. She is regarded by her colleagues as competent and frequently quite effective in her work but as a rather odd person who can make people uncomfortable in social exchange.
>
> The particular case in question involved a thirteen-year-old boy, whose parents were divorced and who had recently come to live with his aunt and uncle. Almost from the beginning the boy had been perceived as a problem at home, around the discipline area. He would not obey his aunt and uncle, nor would he conform to most of their expectations about proper activities and limits for an adolescent boy. While bright enough he had also become something of a discipline problem at school and his grades were suffering accordingly. The guidance counselor further reported that the teachers in the school for the most part "didn't understand him" and that while he was reasonably popular with the students at school, in her view he was "really a very lonely boy." All this foregoing description was presented in a calm professional manner with no evidence of undue emotional participation or sensitivity on the part of the guidance counselor. After some further discussion of this kind, and some attempt to explore the possible meanings of the statement that the boy was really a very lonely boy, it seemed that the case did not involve any significant lack of objectivity and so the consultant dis-

cussed it with the guidance counselor from the point of view of increasing her knowledge and offering some general remarks about the needs of adolescents and the effects of divorce of parents upon the developing adolescent personality. The guidance counselor seemed satisfied with this and the session was terminated.

A week later the guidance counselor called requesting another appointment, and when the consultant arrived at the school he was presented with the problem of this same boy once again. Essentially the picture was presented as previously, but there was a repeat on the theme of the lonely boy who nevertheless was popular with the students. This second time around there was a note of extra intensity in this remark, evidenced by a heightening in color, a speeding of the speech rate, and several occasional deep intakes of breath that almost amounted to sighs. Acting on these cues, I proceeded to ask the guidance counselor for further description of the boy. This time she said that his popularity was not general with the students but seemed to be focused primarily among the girls in the school. She then added, "He's actually a very, very good-looking boy. He's quite tall for his age, very handsome, and very well developed for a thirteen-year-old." This last sentence was delivered with further intensification of autonomic indicators of emotion while the facial expressions remained controlled and calm. In this same way the guidance counselor went on to say that the youngster comes in to see her very often and that he wants to talk about himself. She indicated that the boy has discussed his feelings concerning living with his aunt and uncle and that she herself has been trying "to help him plan for his future. He's a bright boy and he needs to work out his plans and his feelings so he can go on to get an education."

It was apparent here that the guidance counselor was rather intensely involved with this youngster at several levels, some of which from the point of view of her professional role function could serve as appropriate motivators but others of which were obviously too intense and were bound to produce difficulties in her professional relationship with the boy. Her emphasis upon the youngster's physical attractiveness was repeated several different times in different ways, and it is clear that this was a major factor in drawing her to him. It was at this point that I also realized that in several of my past consultations with this guidance counselor, cases with similar features had been presented although the degree of involvement was far less intense than in the present one. The technical problem then was to find a way of indicating to the guidance counselor that the degree of closeness which had developed between herself and the boy had its negative qualities in terms of interfering with the possibility of giving him the kind of professional and objective guidance help he needed. Since it was obvious that this could not be done through referring to the teacher's own feelings about the boy, the situation had to be reversed and the message transmitted exclusively through talking about the boy's reactions. Fortunately, this case gave ample opportunity to do this.

The intervention was formulated after further discussion stimulated by the consultant around the fact that the boy showed a real desire and need to come in for extended conversations with the guidance counselor. When this had been clearly established, I then said to her that it was apparent that this was a youngster who for reasons that were obvious in his past history was a lonely boy, that he did need guidance, and that it was quite possible that the guidance counselor could perform a real service for him. I then added that there was one caution to be observed. Because of his loneliness and because of some of the special areas of sensitivity in a young adolescent, he could easily form much too close an attachment to the guidance counselor and become much too dependent upon her for direction and for companionship. The need was to find a way to let him know that interest in him was high, that he was accepted, but that she, the guidance counselor, felt sure he could also achieve satisfactory emotionally close relationships with others of his own age and with a wide variety of adults. As actually delivered, my message was formulated in a fairly casual confidential tone to the effect that "You and I both know how kids around this age, especially if they've had separations from people who are important to them, can attach themselves to friendly teachers, almost seeing them as people to make up for things they've lost in the past and the things they haven't had out of life. We don't have to be put off by this but just recognize it for what it is, and make it clear to the youngster what he can reasonably expect to get from us and what is beyond reasonable expectation." The emotional atmosphere in which this was delivered is best described as quite *entre nous* and was therefore participated in with some pleasure by this particular individual. She went on to describe several instances in the past in which youngsters had behaved in just this manner until she found it necessary to gently let them know "I wasn't their mother."

A brief outcome observation was available in this instance since upon subsequent consultation about other cases this one was brought up with the information that the youngster still came in from time to time, and was receiving counseling, but that he had "taken the hint pretty well and isn't quite so involved with me now." This last, I feel, is pretty good confirmation that a cognitive statement about the client was also received in a meaningful emotional sense, since it had a lot to say about the emotional participation of the consultee in her relationship with this youngster.

Another technique for cases of direct personal involvement is for the consultant to use himself as a role model. Since he is probably of a different discipline from his consultee, he presents himself as a model of a generalized professional, much as the psychiatrist did with the guidance counselor—"We two professionals are talking together about this lay client." Having set the stage in some such manner, the consultant talks about the client in a way that demonstrates his own professional attitudes of sympathetic empathy coupled with distance. Where racial or religious prejudice interferes with the consultee's capacity to come close to the client, the consultant provides a model of a professional who is able to bridge a cultural gap and, by making a special effort, to succeed in penetrating to the idiosyncratic humanity of the client. If necessary, he can emphasize the special personal difficulty involved for the professional and recount some anecdote of his own experience. In this way, the consultant can reduce the distance between himself and his consultee, and emphasize their coordinate human difficulties in gaining professional mastery over obtrusive personal feelings and biases.

Simple Identification. It is not uncommon for a consultee's work difficulties to be due to his identifying rather than empathizing with the client or with one of the actors in the client's life situation. This identification may be part of a general transference reaction, in which he may be reading into the pattern of the client's drama some aspect of his own life. We will discuss this in the next section. The identification may also be a relatively isolated feature, which we call simple identification. The consultee does not interpret the client's situation or manipulate it to conform to a significant pattern from his own life, but perceives it as something idiosyncratic to the client. On the other hand, his judgment of the situation is disturbed because he identifies with one of the actors in the drama and takes sides in the conflict.

Usually, the identification is fairly easy for the consultant to identify, because it is energized by some obvious similarity between the identification object and the consultee; they may be of the same age, sex, ethnic group, or profession, or have some obvious characteristic in common such as obesity, a stammer, being recently married, having a nagging mother, or having recently had surgery. Another common clue is that the consultee describes the object in very positive and sympathetic terms, while condemning other actors in the client's drama.

For instance, a young unmarried nurse with an Irish name requested consultation about an adolescent female Irish patient, convalescing after tuberculosis. The nurse was obviously quite angry with the patient's parents, whom she described as overbearing and depriving. She was particularly incensed that they would not allow their daughter to go out on dates, and she felt that their hostile overprotectiveness was interfering with the patient's social development. As the nurse's story unfolded, and as the consultant explored the reasons for her opinions, it became clear that her negative judgment about the parents was based not on significant evidence but on the patient's querulous complaints, which she too freely accepted, not realizing that the girl's attitude toward her parents was highly ambivalent. Moreover, the nurse had not listened seriously to what the parents had said; she had already made up her mind that they were not telling the truth.

In a case such as this, the consultant's task is to act as a role model for the consultee and to demonstrate an empathic approach to all the relevant people in the client's situation. In the case in point, the consultant and the consultee jointly examined the details of the patient's behavior and verbalizations; they discussed her probable mixed feelings about her parents and her insecurities about going out again into social situations after returning from the relative isolation of a sanatorium. The discussion also focused on evidence indicating the difficulties of the parents, who had still not recovered from the shock of their daughter's tuberculosis, which had special significance in Irish culture, and who were confused about how to handle the vicissitudes of the girl's adolescent development.

By using the leverage of the consultation relationship, the consultant influenced the consultee to look at the case afresh from the same distance and with the same empathic solicitude as his own. By the end of the first consultation session, the nurse was beginning to weaken her identification with the patient. During the second consultation interview she was able to use her existing knowledge of parent-child relationships during adolescence and of the psychosocial complications of tuberculosis to gain a balanced understanding of the case. She was then able to make some home visits and confirm to her own satisfaction the validity of the interpretations that she and the consultant had developed, and to work out ways of helping the girl and her parents grapple with their problems. It was this personal experience of dealing with the patient and her parents as people with their own idiosyncratic identities, at least as much as the words and attitudes of the consultant, that confirmed to the nurse that the girl was separate from her, and that one needed to collect data and then self-consciously analyze it before one could understand how she felt.

   Transference. Every psychoanalyst knows about patients transferring feelings from past relationships onto him and onto many others in their current life situations, including colleagues at work and clients with whom they have continuing contacts. This is not limited to patients who are quite sick, but also occurs among the fairly healthy analysands in training analysis. It is therefore not surprising to find that professionals frequently encounter difficulties with their clients because of transference distortions.

   In contrast to the simple identifications we have just discussed, these difficulties arise because the consultee imposes onto the client's case a pattern of roles from his own life experience. This leads to a preordained set of attitudes, stereotyped perceptions and expectations, and fixed judgments on the part of the consultee in relation to the people in the client's life situation; and it blocks an objective appraisal of the actual issues in the case. It also prepares the ground for the consultee to act out his own fantasies through the medium of the case instead of planning rational professional action based on an objective analysis of the client's needs.

   Usually, such transference distortions are held in check by reality testing, and in most mental health professionals they are usually temporary phenomena. This is aided by the culturally supported separation of professional and private life that directly buttresses the reality testing and control functions of the mature ego development and strength. This is manifested, among other ways, in a variable propensity for transference and acting out in the work setting.

   This problem, although usually not defined in such terminology, is a significant issue for administrators and supervisors, who maintain surveillance over their subordinates and ensure that they control their irrational impulses. In certain cases the supervisors single out for special attention workers whom they characterize as immature, unstable, or overly dependent, and whose recurrent weakened ego functioning they buttress with appropriate emotional supplies or management controls.

   For instance, a public health nursing supervisor reported to a group of her colleagues at a seminar on supervisory techniques that one of her staff nurses had experienced an emotionally deprived childhood, having been orphaned early in life and brought up in residential institutions. The supervisor said that this nurse had recurrent difficulties with older people, both on the staff and among her patients. She would rapidly build up an overly dependent relationship with them, which was particularly incongruous with patients or with the parents of patients. She would badger the parent figures for attention and then, when this led inevitably to frustration, she would turn against them and accuse them of all kinds of wrongdoing.

The supervisor reported that this nurse was most effective with children, and that she was particularly successful in working in a hostel for crippled children, although she had to be carefully watched lest she slip into her typical pattern in relating to the housemother. The supervisor dealt with this nurse by trying to steer her toward working with young people rather than with potential parent figures, and by giving her extra supervision and emotional support whenever she noticed her beginning to get emotionally embroiled with an older person.

It is the repetitive and stereotyped nature of the transference pattern that makes such individuals recognizable to their supervisors, and these cases often do not come for consultation. Workers with such problems tend to request consultation when supervision is inadequate or when the disfunctioning is not so obvious.

For example, a schoolteacher requested consultation about Jean, a girl in her fifth-grade class who had recently become a disciplinary problem. She described the girl as being immature and given to temper tantrums that were precipitated by emotional scenes in which she obstinately refused to do what she was told. The consultant noted that the teacher talked about her pupil with barely concealed hostility. She was especially upset by Jean's immature and "whining" behavior, and about the fact that she seemed "to imagine she could get away with murder," by which the teacher meant that the child felt she had a privileged position and did not have to conform to the rules of the class. In discussing the case, the teacher said how surprised she had been to find this girl so immature because she distinctly remembered having no trouble at all with

Jean's sister, who had been in her class three years earlier. At that time she had got to know the parents and had thought they were a well-balanced couple who took good care of their children. When she began to have trouble with Jean, she had talked with her mother, and it became "abundantly clear" that Jean had a "privileged position in the household" and was the pampered child who was always preferred, especially in comparison with her older sister. There appeared "to be constant fights between the two sisters, and invariably Jean would be protected by the mother and the other sister punished."

The consultant noted that the teacher discussed certain aspects of the case in a quite stereotyped way, for instance, the remark about the "abundantly clear" evidence that Jean had "a privileged position." At such times she spoke with particular intensity. Moreover, as the consultant tried to get the teacher to give the evidence on which she based her assertions, it appeared that her evidence was very flimsy. The pattern of Jean's family drama seemed preformed in the teacher's mind, and in fact so did her perception of Jean's behavior.

Other information that the teacher gave about Jean, in response to the consultant's questions, did not conform to the main picture she was painting of her. The child's behavior with her classmates seemed trouble-free and her record in previous grades was good. There was no indication of any current family or other environmental predicament that might have precipitated a sudden change in Jean's behavior. She had not been a problem at the beginning of the present school year; in fact, when the parents had come for their routine interviews with the teachers just before Christmas, the teacher had given the mother a good report about Jean. That was when she had realized for the first time that Jean was the younger sister of the child she had taught three years earlier. Jean's family name was quite a common one, and the two sisters did not resemble each other. She remembered her surprise at meeting the mother again, and she was even more surprised that after the Christmas vacation Jean had begun to deteriorate so rapidly.

By this time, the nature of the difficulty began to clarify in the consultant's mind. In addition to the evidence in the current case, he remembered that this teacher had consulted him earlier in the year about another girl in her class, who was suffering from a learning disorder, and in that case too the child had been described as somebody else's younger sister. This had not appeared important at the time, and the consultant had dealt with the case by a somewhat didactic discussion about the nature and causes of learning disorders. That case had not improved but had been "resolved" when the family suddenly moved to another part of town.

The consultant did not know anything about the teacher's personal life, but he hazarded a guess that she probably had a younger sister with whom she had unresolved conflicts similar to those she was now imposing on Jean. It seemed particularly significant that Jean became a problem to the teacher only after she discovered that she was the younger sister. It also seemed that Jean's poor behavior occurred only with that teacher, apparently as a reaction to the teacher's method of handling her.

The consultant dealt with this case in two ways. First he involved the teacher in a discussion of details of Jean's behavior in the classroom, in an attempt to influence the teacher to observe her more closely as a person in her own right, rather than as a stereotyped "younger sister." This appeared to have only a limited effect. Second, the consultant discussed the teacher's relationship to Jean in reverse, as it were. He pointed out that her behavior had regressed after the parents' interview around Christmas. He suggested that after this interview the mother had told Jean that the teacher had been very fond of the older sister and remembered her quite vividly, and had possibly told her that the teacher hoped Jean would be as successful a student. The consultant then involved the teacher in a discussion of what this might have meant to Jean: she might now imagine that the teacher was continually comparing her with her older sister.

The teacher, in this discussion, began to identify with the consultant, reversing roles and empathically imagining how Jean felt as a younger sister, perhaps casting the teacher into a stereotyped role as either the older sister or the mother figure. The consultant then posed the management problem in terms of the teacher needing to convince Jean that her teacher was not a representative of her family constellation, and that Jean was a person in her own right and not just a younger sister.

During the second consultation session, the teacher quite suddenly made a switch in her patterned perceptions of Jean and began to talk about her as a child struggling to overcome in the classroom her misperceptions of her teacher. She then began to plan various ways of dealing with her so that Jean might discover that her teacher was neither a mother figure nor an older sister figure but somebody who was trying to educate her and to help her achieve increasing maturity. During the remainder of the school year this teacher asked for consultation about two other cases, neither one of which was a younger sister. She gave follow-up reports on Jean, whose behavior disorder apparently completely resolved three to four weeks after the second consultation.

Characterological Distortions of Perception and Behavior.
Overt disturbances of work performance due to enduring psychiatric disorders in workers are usually dealt with and kept in check by administrative and supervisory controls. It is not uncommon, however, for covert or minor disturbances to evade the scrutiny of the controlling authorities and then to appear in consultation. For example, a consultant saw a female teacher who invoked his help with a ten-year-old boy whom she described as continually masturbating in her class. He was falling behind in his work and often sat with a withdrawn and dreamy expression on his face. She was sure he was masturbating because he often sat with his hands in his trouser pockets. She also talked about another boy in the same class who was always bothering the girls, one of whom complained that he tried to look up her skirt as she was coming down the staircase.

Further discussion revealed that several other children in the class were apparently also engaging in "harmful sexual behavior." In no case did the consultant find evidence in the teacher's stories to substantiate anything other than normal expectable behavior in children of that age. Moreover, the teacher gave her reports with obvious vicarious satisfaction, and her own behavior during the interview was rather seductive. She was wearing a short skirt, and she kept crossing and uncrossing her legs and drawing attention to them by ostentatiously and ineffectually trying to cover her knees with her skirt. Her handshake was warm and clinging, she spoke in a husky low voice, and she fluttered her eyelashes, like a sexy model in a TV commercial.

Many consultants would be cautious or even pessimistic about the likelihood of success in such a case of apparently long-standing disturbance. How could two or three sessions of consultation, even if repeated several times in connection with successive cases of "sexual behavior" among students, produce any amelioration of this teacher's classroom performance? To improve her professional functioning, would it not be necessary to help her solve her underlying Oedipal conflicts by means of deep psychotherapy or even psychoanalysis? Yet with all her apparent emotional conflicts, this woman was successfully holding down a job. Although her colleagues and superiors felt she was a bit strange and at times irritating, they believed her to be a reasonably steady worker. Her educational results with most of her students were not obviously worse than those of her colleagues. Clearly, despite her emotional problems, she did have sufficient control over herself most of the time to maintain a reasonable degree of task orientation. Although she behaved seductively to the consultant, this was within socially acceptable bounds.

The consultant attempted to handle the case by supporting the teacher's defenses and lowering her anxiety. He discussed each of the children about whom she complained, from the point of view of increasing her intellectual understanding of the nature of their behavior; and, although he had difficulty keeping a straight face, he reassured her most earnestly that for a ten-year-old boy to play absent-mindedly with his genitals while daydreaming in class, or to engage in mild sexual horseplay with a not unwilling girl of the same age, was not unusual or abnormal. He also demonstrated by his manner toward her that he was not upset by her seductive behavior and yet was not impelled by it to deviate from his task-oriented approach to the professional problems she was posing. He was cool and maintained a proper distance, and yet he showed that he was most interested in her work difficulties and willing to spend three interviews seriously discussing them. At the end of the three sessions the teacher reported that the "masturbating boy" was much improved; in fact, she now talked about him with much empathy as a little boy whom she was helping by special tutorial attention to capitalize on his literary interests and talents, rather than being forced into the boredom of going at the slow pace of the rest of the class. Whether there had in fact been some objective change in the boy's behavior, or whether her report was in the nature of a "transference cure," the consultant was not able to determine.

During the remainder of the school year this teacher requested consultation about other cases of the same type. Each time the consultant used a similar approach with apparently identical results. He had the impression that although he was certainly producing no significant change in the personality pattern of the teacher, he was helping her maintain or regain her professional composure in the face of disequilibrating factors about which he had no knowledge, and which every now and again would threaten to disturb her work performance.

Such relatively nonspecific help in controlling transference in the work setting—by opposing regression, increasing professional distance from clients, relieving negative or inhibiting feelings such as of anxiety or anger, and supporting defenses such as intellectualization—can often be better accomplished in group than in individual consultation. As long as the ground rules of the group discussions are clearly defined to exclude the analysis of personal problems of the participants, the consultant can stimulate consensual peer validation of the norms of behavior, both of clients and professionals. The group setting provides for more distance between consultant and consultees and lessens the intensity of transference to him, or at least provides him with more options in managing it. It also provides individual members with the continuing support of their peers in relieving their anxieties and controlling their own impulses.

Theme Interference. Major transference reactions invade the work setting mostly in disturbed individuals or in organizations lacking adequate administrative controls and supervisory supports. Many years of experience in mental health consultation have taught us that minor transference reactions of a special type occasionally complicate professional functioning in most people, whatever their state of mental health. However healthy the workers, and however well organized their institutions, it is not uncommon for unsolved present or past personal problems to be displaced onto task situations and for this to produce temporary ineffectuality with a segment of the work field.

The signs of this process are not difficult to identify. A professional who is usually quite effective and emotionally balanced suddenly encounters a work situation that seems inexplicably confusing and upsetting. If his superiors or peers see what is happening they do not quite understand it, because they know that usually he is able to handle such a problem with his existing knowledge and skills. On this occasion, however, something seems to be blocking him, and he seems unaccountably sensitive to some aspect of the case. This sensitivity is obscured by the fact that the case impasse naturally leads to the professional's increasing concern and frustration, so that it is difficult to know whether he is upset by the recalcitrance of his client or by some sensitizing trigger in the case or in his own life. In fact, it not infrequently happens that the worker is simultaneously upset not only by the case, with which he is having professional difficulties, but also by some disequilibrium in his institution or between it and its surrounding community, and also by some problems in his private life. One sometimes gets the impression of a series of interlocking upsets in the client, in the professional, in the organization, and in the community. And yet as far as the consultee is concerned, all his worry is focused on his difficulties in trying to handle the upsetting complexities of a single problem case.

Prolonged study of these cases has led us to the following formulation: A conflict related to actual life experience or to fantasies that has not been satisfactorily resolved is apt to persist in a consultee's preconscious or unconscious as an emotionally toned cognitive constellation. We call this constellation a "theme."

Since the theme is a continuing representation of an unsolved problem or a defeat, it carries a negative emotional tone of rankling failure. It also has a quality of repetition compulsion. This usually takes a syllogistic form, involving an inevitable link between two items or statements. Statement A denotes a particular situation or condition that was characteristic of the original unsolved problem. Statement B denotes the unpleasant outcome. The syllogism takes the form "All A inevitably leads to B." The implication is that whenever the person finds himself involved in situation or condition A, he is fated to suffer B; also, that this generalization applies universally, that everyone who is involved in A inevitably suffers B.

Normally, the theme is adequately repressed or otherwise defended against, or it is expressed through some stable symptom or inhibition. Sometimes, for a variety of reasons, this equilibrium is upset; then the theme may become salient and threaten to emerge into consciousness. To defend against this, the person displaces the theme into some consonant aspect of the work situation. In particular, he may superimpose it onto a client's predicament that provides appropriate potential transference objects.

A series of cues in the case form a perceived gestalt that is equated by the professional worker with Statement A (the initial category). This arouses the expectation that the client, or other actor in the client's drama, who is involved in this statement will inevitably suffer the fate linked with Statement B (the inevitable outcome). For instance, if Statement A (initial category) is "A person who masturbates excessively" and Statement B (inevitable outcome) is "His nervous system will be damaged and his intelligence will be blunted," the syllogism takes the form of *"All* people who masturbate excessively damage their nervous systems and blunt their intelligence." This theme may be a sequel to guilt-ridden conflicts over masturbation in the professional worker's childhood and adolescence, and represents a foreboding that one day in the future a punishing nemesis will inevitably strike.

When, for whatever reason, the defenses against this old conflict weaken, the situation is ripe for invoking a new defense by displacing onto some appropriate work situation. The consultee unconsciously selects a client from his caseload and fits him into the initial category of "a person who masturbates excessively." This then arouses the expectations that "his nervous system will inevitably be damaged and his intelligence blunted." The worker becomes very upset by this foreboding and attempts to stave off the expected doom; for example, in the case of a child who is not doing well in school, applying pressure to memorize lengthy passages of poetry to prevent deterioration in his memory.

These preventive efforts are usually panicky and inconsistent, and a realization of their obvious ineffectiveness confirms the consultee's certainty that the expected doom cannot be prevented despite all his efforts. Unconsciously, his consolation is that this time the catastrophe will occur to a client and not to himself. At a deeper level, there may also be the reassurance that he stage managed and directed the whole drama by manipulating the actors to conform to his theme and so achieved some measure of mastery of this vicarious experience.

Sometimes, the cues in the client's story are objectively and accurately perceived. In our example, the child may indeed be masturbating excessively, as defined by himself, his parents, and his physician. Sometimes the cues may be misperceived or misinterpreted to force the client into the initial category so that he can be exploited as a displacement object for the theme—the child may be masturbating, but not more so than most. Or cues may be grossly misinterpreted so that the client is stereotyped into the initial category without reasonable evidence; he suffers from acne and appears dreamy and seclusive, and these signs are misinterpreted as bodily and behavioral concomitants of masturbation.

Whether or not the client objectively fits the initial category, once he has been clicked into place in it, he becomes a test case for the inevitability of the theme outcome. There is an absolute expectation of the specified nemesis. If this did not occur, or rather if the consultee perceived it did not occur, the syllogism of the theme would be invalidated—not *all* cases in the initial category would have suffered the inevitable outcome. At some level, that is what the consultee is trying over and over again to prove, to reassure himself that there is some hope in his own case. The repetition compulsion, however, in his own superego, demands that each time the test case should indeed validate the inevitability of the punishment. This is ensured by his manipulation of the actors in the drama and, if this fails, by his misperceptions of what transpires, along the same lines as in traditional "fate neuroses," or repetitive acting-out patterns in hysterical character disorders.

A professional with such a theme interference is apt to have a succession of failure cases conforming to this pattern as long as his conflicts remain salient, or as long as he does not find other ways of defending against them or resolving them.

A mental health consultant may relieve such theme interference in two possible ways, both based on his capacity to influence his consultee's perceptions by the leverage of the consultation relationship. The first approach is to influence the consultee to change his perceptions of the client so as to remove him from the initial category. This could be done by helping him realize that his perceptions of the cues in the client's story were not accurate, or by influencing him to reinterpret the cues so that he concludes that the client does not in fact fit the initial category. For instance, in our case in point, the consultant might help the consultee to realize that acne, dreaminess, and introversion do not necessarily indicate excessive masturbation; he might confirm this by pointing to evidence of hereditary oiliness in their skins leading to acne. In the event that the child, his parents, and even his physician have complained about excessive masturbation, the consultant will have a more difficult task, but he might shake their story by pointing out that they all came from a subculture that was strictly moralistic, especially about sexual matters, and that their outstanding sensitivity made them liable to exaggerate the degree of masturbation. In other words, although it was indeed likely that the boy did masturbate, four or five times a week could hardly be defined as excessive, compared with cases of boys of similar age who are known to masturbate four or five times a day.

The effect of such intervention by the consultant, if it works, is to influence the consultee to give up his displacement onto his client, whom he no longer perceives as fitting the initial category. This therefore frees the client from the inevitable outcome, and the consultee's vicarious interest in him and panicky treatment of him are dissipated. This consultation maneuver is named *unlinking*, because essentially it results in unlinking the client from the consultee's theme. The consequence is that the consultee can now relate to the client without distortion and can deal with him objectively, with his customary professional understanding and skill.

Unfortunately, although the result may be salubrious for the client it is not so for the consultee and for some of his other clients, because the theme has not been weakened by the consultation and may even have been strengthened. The consultee may unconsciously interpret the consultant's eagerness to prove that this client was not an example of the initial category as proof that he shares the consultee's belief that all such cases have the expected bad outcome. Since the theme is left intact or strengthened and the displacement object has been unlinked, the consultee is likely to begin unconsciously searching for another appropriate object. If he has a sufficiently large caseload, it will not be long before he discovers another "excessive masturbator," and the drama will be reenacted.

The second consultation approach is for the consultant to accept, at least for discussion purposes, the consultee's categorization of his client as fitting into his initial category. The consultant, by this agreement, confirms the consultee's judgment that this is a *test case* for his theme. The consultant then proceeds to invalidate the syllogism by persuading the consultee to reexamine the evidence on which he bases his certainty of the inevitable outcome, and influencing him to realize that although such an outcome is indeed one possibility, there are several others, and in fact much of the evidence favors one of the others. When the consultee's certainty about the inevitability of the bad outcome has thus been weakened, his tension begins to fall, and some of the interference of the theme begins to lessen.

This may be sufficient for him to cease his panicky, ineffectual tampering with his client, and he may be able to continue with some return to his normal effectiveness. His subsequent experience with the client then allows him to corroborate firsthand that what he had expected as inevitable outcome did not in fact occur, despite the fact that the client conformed to the initial category. Since the case had continued to be a test case, this one exception to the syllogism is sufficient to invalidate it and to weaken or dissipate the theme. Because the theme applies also to him, the invalidation of the syllogism for his client has an effect of significantly reducing the consultee's tension.

We name this method of consultation "theme interference reduction." If it is satisfactorily accomplished, it should lead not only to an immediate lowering of tension in the consultee and a restoration of his normal objectivity about his current client, but also to a weakening of the theme, a consequent reduction in the pressure of its associated conflict, and a reduced compulsion to displace this and work it out repetitively on future clients.

Two final points are worthy of emphasis. First, although both the mechanism of theme interference and the consultation method of theme interference reduction have been discussed on a cognitive parameter, they clearly have a major affective component. Likewise, although the consultation method handles this material in an apparently superficial manner, what is being dealt with is not really superficial but is a surface derivative with deep psychological implications and leverage possibilities.

Second, because the consultee's displacement is accepted and dealt with within his defensive framework, the theme may be invalidated without the loss of face and major resistance, which would most likely occur if his defenses were undone and the consultee had to confront his underlying conflicts directly. Moreover, the consultant does not have to know the details of these conflicts to invalidate the theme. He can operate quite effectively by dealing with the same projective material in the client's story that the consultee has chosen to act out his conflicts. He can rely on the fact that the consultee has unconsciously chosen the objects and situations to match his own previous life experience and fantasies; as long as the consultant correctly identifies the salient patterns, he obtains a direct leverage on his consultee's unconscious material and processes. This means that the consultant can successfully invalidate the theme without infringing on his consultee's private life.

CHAPTER EIGHT

Techniques for Reducing Theme Interference

There are three steps in the technique of theme interference reduction: assessment of the theme, the consultant's intervention, and ending and follow-up.

Assessment of the Theme

Assessing the theme involves answering certain questions. Is this consultation? Is this consultee-centered case consultation? Is the consultee's work difficulty caused by lack of objectivity? Is the lack of objectivity due to theme interference? What is the initial category? What is the expected inevitable outcome? With which actors in the client's drama does the consultee identify? These questions must be answered in an orderly process involving a sequential narrowing of the field of inquiry accompanied by an increasing magnification from a superficial to a deeper and deeper scrutiny of the details observed or inferred.

Preliminary Phases

The consultant must ask himself whether the approach to him is really for consultation proper, whether it is an episode in contract negotiation or relationship building, or whether it is really a request for collaboration or for referral of a difficult case. If he decides that it is the beginning of a consultation, he must decide, within the framework of the current contract, whether it should be dealt with as case consultation or administrative consultation, and if the

128

former, whether it is to be client-centered or consultee-centered. The work proceeds through a succession of phases.

Phase 1: Superficial Scanning of a Wide Field. In consultee-centered case consultation, the consultant, even before he begins to deal with the case, must be preparing himself for what he might meet. He should continually keep himself up to date about issues inside the organization and in its surrounding community that might have repercussions on his potential consultees. His purpose is to enter a consultation situation prepared to respond quickly to the significance of what a consultee may bring to him. Often, the concern of an individual consultee, as mirrored in his story about his client, is in line with an issue that is preoccupying many people in the community.

For instance, the local newspaper was running editorials about problems of law and order, particularly about out-of-control adolescent rebellion and delinquency. Recent meetings of the Parent-Teacher Association had focused on demands that the school system teach good citizenship and conformity to community norms, while at the same time pressing with equal vehemence for improvements in curriculum and teaching methods to increase the capacity for creative thinking as well as the college entrance examination scores of the students in this middle-class population.

In the particular high school that the consultant was about to visit, a new principal had recently been appointed—a young man with progressive ideas, who was reputed to be inconsistent in his dealing with disciplinary problems, torn between impulse control and encouragement of innovative thinking among the students. The principal appeared to be passing these inconsistent demands on to his teachers, and was having problems maintaining their morale and motivation. This was exacerbated by a clique of teachers rebelling against his authority, led by a senior teacher who had been passed over for the post of principal. Recently there had been trouble at the school involving some teenagers smoking marijuana. At a neighboring high school there had just been an insurrection of the students in opposition to new rules about clothing and haircuts.

As the consultant was removing his coat in the cloakroom, he met the janitor, who greeted him with special emphasis and said he had probably been called in about Jackie, who had attacked a fellow student with a knife the previous day, a real "murderous ruffian" who would undoubtedly "come to a bad end." In fact, when the consultant met with his first consultee, the client did not turn out to be Jackie, but it was not surprising to discover that the case did involve an adolescent who was having problems with impulse control, and that the teacher was particularly ambivalent about his own role as a representative of the repressive establishment.

In this case, the consultant was tuned into the consultation problem even before he entered the school building, and certainly before he sat down with his consultee. Such an expectational set should produce extra alertness and enable the consultant to give a quick answer to the question "Why is this consultee asking me for help with this particular case at this time?" The fact that the consultant was not asked for help with Jackie should serve as a warning: this mental set should not blind him to less obvious aspects of the consultation that might be idiosyncratic to this particular consultee and might not be in tune with the social issues of the moment. In the case in point, the consultant must expect a consultation focused on impulse control versus freedom and also be alert to the need to put this whole complex of expectations aside quickly if he finds early on that something else appears to be bothering his consultee.

The incident with the janitor is of particular significance from the point of view of consultation technique. As the consultant walks through the building on his way to the consultation interview, he should be sensitive to the atmosphere in the corridors and offices, especially to apparently casual remarks and to the verbal and nonverbal cues involved in the way he is greeted. I have learned to ascribe special importance to the way I am received by the secretary of the school principal or the clerk in the front office of a public health unit. They usually have a considerable fund of informally obtained salient information, and their smiles, frowns, welcoming gestures, or attitudes of being too preoccupied to attend immediately to my business tell me a lot about my current standing in their organization and about the relative urgency and system relevance of problems that individual consultees want to discuss.

I also have learned to pay attention to whether a consultee

seems to have come to see me of his own initiative or because he has been persuaded, or even forced, to come in by his supervisor. In the latter case, I am alerted to the possibility that the problem may relate more to some lack of objectivity in the supervisor than in the consultee or that the consultee may be having some idiosyncratic problem that is not related to the salient concern of the rest of the organization.

Once I am in the room with my consultee, I focus all my attention on him, helped and hopefully not hindered by my preliminary scanning of the social systems of which he is a part. My first question to myself, after deciding that I am dealing with an instance of consultee-centered case consultation, is whether my consultee is having work difficulties that impel him to see me, and whether they are based on lack of knowledge, lack of skill, lack of self-confidence, or lack of objectivity.

In answering this, I once again have a preliminary mental set that is based on my previous experience with this consultee and on my knowledge of the traditions and ways of working of his organization. For instance, I may know that in a particular public health nursing agency, recruitment and in-service training, coupled with effective supervision and a clear understanding of the role of consultation, make it almost inevitable that any except the newest nurses will be coming to me because of lack of objectivity. My main evidence, however, comes from the consultee's manner and the way in which he tells the story of his client.

Phase 2: Assessment of the Consultee's Behavior. The consultant must first assess the degree and nature of the consultee's subjective involvement in the case. I find it useful to assume that all consultees at this stage are suffering from theme interference unless I can rule this out. Theme interference will manifest itself by cognitive perplexities and emotional reactions that are found also in personal involvement, simple identification, transference, and characterological distortions, all of which may to some extent be present. Only if I am unable to identify a syllogistic theme with its definable initial category and inevitable outcome, calling for specific consultation intervention to break the link between the two, will I fall back on one of the simpler assessments.

If I find no evidence of subjective involvement or lack of professional objectivity, I will by default put the case into a residual category of lack of knowledge, lack of skill, or lack of self-confidence. Evidence pointing to subjective involvement consists mainly of affective responses of the consultee during the interview, and cognitive distortions such as confusion, stereotyping, and judgments unrelated to the evidence.

Affective Responses. The consultant must be alert to signs of emotional upset in the consultee as he discusses the case. These have to be differentiated from signs of expectable emotional involvement in a professional worker who feels responsible for a difficult case and committed to finding a way out of an impasse. It is only natural that a highly motivated worker should be emotionally aroused in this situation and should express concern for the client's welfare and frustration about his inability to resolve the difficulty. The consultant must also take into account the temperament of the consultee, which will influence his normal emotional expression in such a situation.

These nonspecific types of emotional arousal and upset must be differentiated from those that may be idiosyncratically related to a particular aspect of the client's situation or the work difficulty. Previous knowledge of the consultee and of the norms of behavior in his profession and institution will aid this differentiation; so will his reactions when he is asked to talk about other cases in his current practice or about issues peripheral to the central topic of this case. The consultant is looking for a gradient of emotional arousal or upset that peaks in an exaggerated way as the consultee talks about certain aspects of the consultation case.

Concern about the case must also be differentiated from anxiety about the consultant or the consultation setting, especially in new consultees or new programs. The consultant must be alert to the consultee trying to hide his feelings and to present a façade of relaxed poise. Consultants who are already skilled in psychotherapy, casework, or psychological interviewing will have no difficulty identifying telltale discrepancies between tone of voice, verbal content, and relaxed facial expression on the one hand and strained posture, muscular tension, and unconscious tapping of feet or autonomic manifestations on the other; or between ostensible verbal content and a choice of words, some of which may carry more emotional loading or emphasis than might be necessary to convey the message.

When the consultant identifies some element or actor in the consultee's story about the client that seems linked with increased emotional tension in the consultee, he will be well advised to steer the interview temporarily away from this focus. He does this to ascertain whether the consultee's tension will ease and also to prevent the consultee from becoming too upset. The latter result would endanger his self-control and make him lose face, and would also weaken the stability of a possible displacement; for instance, if the consultee were to get too upset he might himself realize the nature of his subjective involvement.

After a while, the consultant should lead the interview back to the "hot" area and see whether the consultee again becomes upset. By getting the consultee to repeat his story from different points of departure, the consultant can pinpoint those aspects that are regularly associated with an increase in emotional arousal and can confirm his initial assumptions about issues or displacement objects with which the consultee is specifically emotionally involved.

Cognitive Responses. The main evidence for theme interference comes from an assessment of the consultee's cognitive response to the client and his social network. Of particular significance is a lack of clarity or a stereotyping in the consultee's report of particular actors or situations in the client's life drama. Global confusion about the case is not so significant, because it may be the result of lack of knowledge or unfamiliarity with that type of case or inability to understand a complex situation. This should, however, be interpreted in the light of the consultee's usual level of understanding and what is expectable in that institution. More important is the consultant's finding that the consultee tells a clear and understandable story about the client, apart from certain aspects of the case. Sometimes the consultee's patchy confusion is obvious, and sometimes the consultant identifies it because he himself feels confused or unclear about particular actors or incidents.

Missing details in the consultee's case report are useful clues; for instance, a description of a family in which no mention is made of the husband or one of the children. It is advisable for the consultant not to interrupt the consultee to ask for the missing information at that point, because this may endanger the consultee's defenses. Instead, the consultant should record the omission in his own mind, and later casually ask about it. Not unusually, he will then find evidence of confusion or stereotyping. Another possibility is that the consultee will say that he has no information on that point. If it seems appropriate, the consultant can then involve the consultee in a joint project of trying to imagine what the missing information might be by saying, "I wonder what the husband is like." This may sometimes elicit a purely projective story from the consultee that may reveal an important aspect of his theme interference: "He's an unemployed Irish laborer. It's not surprising that he was not present when I visited. Such men usually do not spend much time at home with their wives, except to make them pregnant. I suppose he was out drinking with the boys."

The most characteristic and specific evidence in the cognitive response of the consultee is stereotyping. The consultee perceives some actor or situation in the client's drama, not on the basis of objective appraisal of the gestalt of sensory cues from the world of reality, but on the basis of a preformed image in his mind's eye, possibly stimulated by one or two sensory cues that are then incorporated into a complete pattern.

Stereotyping can be recognized by the following characteristics:

- The outline of the perception is clearer and more consistent than life. It does not vary in response to changes in circumstances.
- The perception has a heroic or villainous character that is larger than life.
- The consultee perceives the actor in exaggerated, oversimplified, global terms—he is all black or all white, all good or all bad.
- The consultee uses emotionally toned words or clichés to express his perceptions. It is as though he were quoting from some widely accepted list of commonly used phrases, rather than using his own normal vocabulary.

Examples of stereotypes, derived from recorded statements of consultees, include:

"He is a poor, crippled creature."
"She is a large, immobile, Buddhalike figure."
"He is a typical, henpecked milquetoast."
"This seven-year-old boy is a real ruffian."
"She is a beautiful, intelligent, competent young woman."
"She is sullen and dull and completely neglects the baby."
"This is a defective baby and will probably never grow up."

When there are superficial indications that the consultee is perceiving some actor in the client's drama in stereotyped terms, the consultant should not directly question the perceptions, but later in the interview he should ask the consultee to shed further light on this aspect of his story. This should elicit the evidence on which the consultee based his perceptions, and the consultant should investigate whether this would be regarded as adequate in the consultee's professional subculture. This exploration should be carried out with delicacy and care. It is counterproductive to confront the consultee with incompatibilities in his story before the consultant has decided on his plan of intervention, for this may unlink the client from the initial category and destroy the test case.

Assessing the Initial Category

In exploring for a possible theme interference, the consultant must look for items in the consultee's story that symbolize or give expression to the two elements of the major premise of the syllogism: initial category and inevitable outcome.

In investigating the initial category, the consultant observes the consultee's behavior and listens to his story about the client in order to identify whether the consultee appears to be perceiving in the case a personally significant pattern. If he demonstrates stereotyping, this may be obvious; the reason for the stereotyped misperception is likely to be that he is imposing a personally meaningful pattern onto the case. More difficult to identify are the instances in which the consultee's perceptions of the case are apparently in line

with objective reality, or with what any other member of his profession would perceive under the existing circumstances, and yet
seem to be given undue weight and to trigger exaggerated affect.

The essential aspect in defining the initial category is delin-
eating the emotionally toned concept that the case portrays for the
consultee. It is also important to identify the situational cues in the
case, for they act as hooks onto which the consultee hangs this
concept. For example, a nurse talked with obvious fascination and
some revulsion about a woman who had three illegitimate children,
all from different fathers. This seemed to be an emotionally significant aspect of the case for her. The consultant wondered to himself
whether the initial category was "a woman who has an illegitimate
baby" or "a woman who has several illegitimate children," or some
similar cognitive element. He involved the nurse in a detailed discussion of her patient from various points of view, and it gradually
became clear that what was upsetting to the nurse was not just the
fact of illegitimacy but her conclusion that the woman was promiscuous. The consultant developed the assumption that the initial
category was "a woman who is promiscuous and has repeated sexual relations with many men." It is important in theme interference
reduction to assess the specific details of the categories. They will
be used to break the obligatory link between categories, while supporting the consultee's use of the client's situation as a test case that
validates or invalidates his personal theme.

In addition to identifying these cues, the consultant should
also be on the alert to detect "preconditions" in the story, extra
elements that are specifically meaningful for the consultee. In our
example, the nurse said that the woman had experienced a deprived
childhood, that her father had been killed while she was a baby, and
that her mother had been a "loose-living woman." The nurse's
evidence for the last assertion seemed flimsy, and alerted the consultant to the possibility that it was a purely projective statement.
From this and other material, the consultant modified his formulation of the initial category to "a woman whose mother was immoral and who, because of being brought up by her, develops into
a promiscuous woman, who has frequent sexual relations, with
many men."

The significance of preconditions is that only clients who fit, or are perceived to fit, them as well as the other elements of the gestalt will constitute a test case that energizes the theme. Thus, a woman who has one or two illegitimate children but shows no other evidence of promiscuity might not stimulate a theme interference in this consultee. Of course, if the consultee was in great need of a displacement object because of some current emotional disequilibrium, she would be apt to select a less than perfect case and fill in the missing details of the initial category from her imagination.

Assessing the Inevitable Outcome

Having identified the consultee's initial category, the consultant must search for the inevitable outcome. It always constitutes some form of doom, and it will always be linked to the person who is the subject of the initial category or to one of his dependents. This assessment is not easy. The consultant must make interpretations while taking an active part in a continuing discussion about the client, a discussion that must flow smoothly and make sense in its own right.

Within this evolving context the consultant will try to identify who the consultee expects to come to a bad end—the person named in the initial category or a dependent—and the exact details of the doom envisaged. The consultant usually accomplishes this in three phases. First, he develops a hypothesis that identifies the victim and the expected catastrophe in general terms. Then he gets the consultee to repeat his story from various points of view to confirm this hypothesis. Last, he explores further to identify the specific details of the expected outcome.

Sometimes the consultation interview reveals evidence about the inevitable outcome before the consultant has assessed the initial category; then the initial category can be identified by tracing backward from the end result. For instance, a teacher talked with considerable feeling about a child in her class who she felt was especially vulnerable to mental disorder and would probably end up in an "asylum." Further discussion revealed that her stereotyped expectation of doom for this child was linked to her perception of the child's mother as "an ineffectual woman with many children, who could not take proper care of them." Similarly, a minister discussed a man in his church who he apparently expected would progressively lose control and behave homosexually. It soon became obvious that he expected this "bad outcome" because the man had been raised in a fatherless family by a mother, a grandmother, and two aunts without any masculine role model.

When such material is freely presented, the consultant should avoid probing for details of the inevitable outcome until he has satisfactorily assessed the initial category. Until this is accomplished, the consultant is constantly in danger of aborting the consultation. For instance, in the case of the child of "the ineffectual mother with many children," the consultant might inadvertently say something about the obvious strengths of the mother despite all her burdens with a household full of children. This reality-based statement, if accepted by the consultee, would weaken the assignment of this mother to the initial category and might interrupt the consultation by unlinking this case from the syllogistic theme.

The third phase of assessing the inevitable outcome—specifying the details of the doom fantasy—is very important. In our example of the promiscuous mother, the question in the consultant's mind was whether the bad outcome focused on the mother or on her children. To begin with, he obtained equivocal evidence. The nurse talked about possible gynecological troubles of the patient. She also was worried about signs of "degeneration" in two of the three children, one of whom had a kidney lesion and the other a harelip and signs of mental retardation. All the family seemed destined for trouble. Further exploration revealed that the nurse's real preoccupation was with the children, whose current problems seemed merely a portent of a much worse fate in store. With absolutely no evidence, the nurse said she felt the child with kidney trouble would very likely develop uremia and die; and a little later she hazarded the guess that the child with the harelip must have multiple congenital abnormalities of his central nervous system and would probably gradually degenerate. She also hinted that although the third child seemed superficially healthy, she was not at all sure that he was as well as he appeared. The consultant then explored to find the nurse's underlying assumptions in these expectations, and she revealed evidence of an irrational belief that this woman had damaged her sexual organs because of her promiscuity, causing prenatal damage to her children. The nurse felt that the woman's lack of adequate mothering in her childhood would inevitably affect her own maternal behavior, so that she would not get adequate medical treatment for the children, thus hastening their bad end.

The damage to the mother's sexual organs was a precondition of the inevitable outcome just as the immoral grandmother had been a precondition of the initial category. The theme could now be formulated as "a woman brought up by an immoral mother (precondition) who is promiscuous and has repeated sexual intercourse with many men (initial category) will damage her sexual organs (precondition) and will not take proper care of her children, who will consequently be born with constitutional defects and will inevitably degenerate and die from a variety of physical illnesses (inevitable outcome)."

As a final note on this case, the consultant recorded after his first interview, "After the nurse and I had come up to the office, at the end of the consultation interview, and she was putting on her coat, I said that this was certainly a complicated case and that I looked forward to continuing the discussion next week. She replied by saying, 'Just wait till next week—they may all be dead!' I looked surprised and she said, 'Oh, I was just kidding!' " Such a doorstep validation of a theme category is not rare. This comment reveals poignantly how a primitive fantasy can maintain its existence in an otherwise professional worker.

Consultant Intervention

The goal of the consultant's intervention is to invalidate the obligatory link between the two categories that express the theme. The consultant accepts and supports the displacement of the theme onto the client's case and the definition of it as a test case by concurring with the initial category in all its details that are personally meaningful to the consultee. The consultant then engages the consultee in a joint examination of the link between the initial category and the outcome category and helps the consultee realize that this outcome is not inevitable. Since the syllogism says that the connection is invariable, if we can demonstrate that on even one occasion *in an authentic test case* that meets all the consultee's unconscious requirements the connection between the categories does not hold, we will dissipate or weaken the theme.

Invalidation of stereotyped expectations is not fundamentally an intellectual process. The leverage comes from the consultation relationship, which makes the consultant an influential figure, someone whose words and behavior have a special meaning. Therefore, it is important for the consultant to make sure that he has fostered the appropriate affective relationship with the consultee before he attempts to reduce the theme interference.

When he is sure of this relationship, and after he has identified the details of the initial category and the inevitable outcome, the consultant then proceeds to weaken the link between them. There are four principal techniques from which the consultant can choose to do this: (1) verbal focus on the client, (2) verbal focus on an alternative object—the parable, (3) nonverbal focus on the client, and (4) nonverbal focus on the relationship.

Verbal Focus on the Client

This is the most usual technique and derives logically from the structure of the method. The consultant discusses the consultee's prediction of the outcome by involving him in a joint examination of the facts of the case. The consultant demonstrates that although the inevitable outcome is one logical possibility, there are other possibilities too; and the evidence indicates that one or more of these is more probable than the doom that the consultee envisages. This examination of the evidence must be sufficiently detailed and the bad possibility sufficiently considered that the consultee cannot escape the confrontation with reality by imagining that the consultant is evading the issues.

The consultant should take care not to communicate to the consultee his own formulation of the theme categories in abstract conceptual terms. If he does so, the consultee may become conscious of the immediate relevance of these abstract categories for his personal life, and the unconscious displacement of his conflicts onto the client will be undone. Such direct confrontation with his own involvement is likely to arouse considerable anxiety and to stimulate immediate defensive maneuvers, and runs the risk of turning the consultation into a psychotherapy session. Because of this, the consultant should take care to focus all his statements on the idiosyncratic details of the client and his social situation.

The following report by a consultant is an example of this type of theme interference reduction.

The nurse introduced this case by saying it had "given her the shock of her life." She went on to say that on the day before Thanksgiving, she had anticipated visiting several families living in a housing project but at the last moment felt somewhat "depressed" at the thought of having to face some of the problems she knew existed in these particular homes. She decided instead to visit a family which she thought of as possessing a nice, healthy, normal home. In this home the parents were people in their early thirties and were quite good-looking. In fact, the nurse described the mother as "attractive enough to be a model." The shock involved finding this ideal family disrupted, with the wife having dyed her hair blond and informing the nurse that she was in the process of getting a divorce from her husband. Then followed a good deal of history, all of which was totally new to the nurse who had been seeing this family for a long time, concerning abusive behavior on the husband's part, drinking, unfaithfulness, and so on. The element which disturbed the nurse the most was what she saw in the wife as a feeling that she was going to start her life over again. "Imagine that, with eight children and the oldest only fifteen!"

At this point the nurse was speaking with considerable intensity and rapidity and other autonomic indicators of emotional involvement. She jumped rather quickly to talking about numbers of divorced people she knew who seem very bitter toward the ex-spouses and implied that a number of these divorcees were leading sexually promiscuous lives. As the nurse talked on it became apparent that she saw an almost inevitable connection between the loss of a mate, either through divorce or through death, followed immediately by the woman involved losing control over her sexual impulses.

As the nurse continued to discuss this case, her degree of involvement became even more obvious, and she stated that she intended to increase the frequency of her visits to the family to see if she could be of any preventive help in this situation. However, at the same time, she expressed very little confidence about her ability to do anything effective, and she also gave real evidence that her professional objectivity in this situation was quite low as a consequence of the rather strong emotional overinvolvement on her part. Indeed, in one sense there was a strong degree of fascinated overidentification on the part of the nurse with this attractive young divorcee who was now free to indulge her impulses. The extent to which real evidence of theme interference existed here was best seen when in response to my questioning about what the wife meant by the phrase "beginning a new life," I was told that she had not actually used these words but that it seemed to the nurse that this is what the woman was thinking about. "She is really quite beautiful and, well, I guess what I'm saying is that she could get involved with someone quite easily."

Consultation approach to this situation involved first accepting as a real possibility the danger that the nurse verbalized. That is, I agreed with her that under these conditions and living in the project environment which the nurse described very graphically it certainly was one thing to consider in the future adjustment of this woman, but I then went on to say that there were a number of other possibilities that I could visualize also. I then used information which the nurse had given me about this woman to point up a number of very definite personality assets and strengths in her which might work toward some other kind of outcome also. The nurse agreed with this, saying that these things were listed as some of the reasons why she "admired this woman so much." I emphasized that it was still much too early to be able to say which way the thing might go but that I felt that we would not go too far wrong if we kept these alternatives open and on the table.

As I was about to leave after this initial consultation, and as so often happens in these situations, while I was walking out the door the nurse gave additional confirming evidence. She began to talk about a young and rather attractive student nurse who was currently in the unit, and to say that this student had been sharing with some of the nurses some of her current social experiences. "She's a very sweet and lovable girl, but I just wonder about the fact that she has an apartment of her own and is really having quite a jolly and wide-open time for herself. She's been telling us something about her weekends and I must say that things have changed since I was a girl." This was said in a tone of voice that did not imply censure or moral indignation; rather, there was a wistful and sad quality present, conveying a definite sense of self-pity.

At the second consultation a week later, I got the nurse to talk further about her knowledge of this young potential divorcee; and as she spoke there came out a mixture of objectively positive information indicating many strong points in her basically healthy personality structure and, on the other hand, evidence of the nurse's identification with this woman, in terms of descriptions of her as having a "bright pleasant personality" and a number of competencies in many areas of life. After this had gone on for some time, I found the opportunity to try to formulate my message in a concise, meaningful way. I said that because of all we knew about Mrs. X, it seemed reasonable to consider the possibility that the situation here, despite the serious disruption in her life which had taken place, might not be so delicately balanced on a thin edge with real trouble looming on either side. I then added, "Besides, even if she did get involved with someone, you and I both know that this wouldn't be the end of the world either." I went on to say that both of us knew of many situations in which people have become involved with all sorts of difficulties and yet have managed to come out of them again and lead successful, responsible lives.

At a subsequent meeting a month or so later, the nurse mentioned this case briefly, describing now her efforts to be of assistance to the young mother in rearranging her life and making sure that the young children were properly cared for. Her manner was much more professional in discussing the case, and there was no intense interest in the details of the sexual and romantic aspects of this mother's life. I believe that the thing that happened here was a weakening of the unconscious automatic connection which the nurse tended to make between loss of a male figure who provided external controls over sexual impulses and the concomitant inevitable breakdown of the woman's own internal controls.

This case illustrates an additional point of technique. The consultant "dosed" his intervention in accordance with his awareness of the consultee's level of identification and emotional arousal. He did not give a simple direct message all in one speech. Instead, he made appropriate comments in the latter part of the first session, once he had defined the two categories for himself; and he continued to give this message in the following session, but always in relation to additional case material that he stimulated the consultee to produce. An experienced consultant learns that the most potent intervention is made when his consultee is within a range of moderate emotional involvement with the identification objects in the case. Below this range the messages are ineffective; when emotional upset is too high, the displacement is endangered and the messages might be taken personally.

Verbal Focus on an Alternative Object—The Parable

When the consultant feels that the displacement is endangered, for whatever reason, and the consultee is close to a conscious awareness of the link between the client and himself and consequently of his underlying conflicts, the consultant must find some way of discussing the theme at a greater distance. As long as he has correctly identified the syllogistic categories, he need not be overly concerned that greater distance will make the discussion merely an intellectual exchange, because he relies on the assumption that the formulated categories are derivatives of unconscious material relatively free from defensive distortion. His goal is to talk directly to the consultee's unconscious, as it were, within the safety of an acceptable defensive framework. This was available when the consultee unconsciously chose to avoid confronting the theme by displacing its core issues onto the client. As this displacement weakens, the consultant must attempt to provide a replacement.

In the previous example, such a weakening of the displacement was seen in the final moments of the first session, when the consultee likened the patient to one of her colleagues who has "having quite a jolly and wide-open time for herself." This type of statement is always a danger signal. In this instance the next association continued the process of reversing the displacement, when the consultee began to talk explicitly about herself. True, she restricted herself to talking about how "things have changed since I was a girl," but her tone of voice revealed a mood of introspective self-pity, and it is easy to imagine that if the consultant had made a suitable response she could fairly easily have moved one step further and begun to talk, or at least to be conscious of, her own sexual pressures and lack of fulfillment, perhaps with regretful memories of past opportunities not grasped. In fact, the consultation session was just on the point of ending, which probably explains why the forbidden material was allowed to come so close to consciousness. The episode confirms the consultant's wisdom in restricting himself to a partial intervention in that interview and leaving it till the following session to drive his message safely home.

By the following session, the consultee's emotional pressure had lessened enough for her to have restabilized her displacement onto her patient, and it was feasible for the consultant to continue with verbal communications focused on the current case. Had there been evidence of continuing or increased instability of the displacement, and had the consultee continued talking about her young colleague or about her own past or present life, the consultant would have had to leave the case and use a more distant object onto whom he would hope the consultee might be influenced to displace her theme. The mechanism for accomplishing this maneuver is for the consultant to direct the discussion away from the current case onto one that is superficially as different as possible but that portrays the same two categories.

This method of communication has been used throughout history to convey emotionally potent messages with minimal arousal of resistance in the listeners. Religious leaders seeking to convey ethical messages that are contrary to current values or that might arouse undue guilt and shame if communicated openly often use this method. They call it a parable. Traditionally, a parable is a story, either fanciful or apparently of an actual happening, whose characters provide widely applicable identification objects. The behavior of the characters and the outcome of the story convey the message or moral. The mutative power of the communication is that the listeners can identify secretly and without loss of face with the characters, and thus vicariously experience the reward or punishment involved in their actions, or can choose not to identify and therefore not to feel pilloried or admonished.

The requirements of the consultation parable are simple. Once the consultant has a clear idea of the initial category and the inevitable outcome, and feels that he can no longer use the consultation case to break the obligatory link between them, he invents an anecdote that portrays the theme. He then discusses its details to show that the inevitable outcome is only one of the possibilities emerging from the initial category, and that in the fictitious case another outcome was in fact experienced. The consultant builds the elements of his anecdote from the details of the consultation case, but he chooses a setting as far removed as possible from the current one and describes the characters as very different in their superficial characteristics. In contrast to the parables of religion or literature, which derive some of their potency from being obviously unreal and mythological, a consultation parable should ring true. Wherever possible, it should be based on some real memory of the consultant, but he should change it and shape it so that it fits neatly into the mold of the theme.

The following report by a consultant with considerable talent for parable making illustrates the technique:

Mrs. Graham said the reason she wanted to talk to me today was because she was so mad about General Hospital. I waited for her to continue and then she said they still had not sent over any evaluation on the child who has repeated first grade twice. It is interesting that Mrs. Graham still does not give this child a name, but always calls the other child by his name, Bob. She again wanted to speak of these two children together but after saying that Bob was to be permitted to stay on at the school and repeat the first grade, she went on to say that the other child couldn't do this because they had a rule that a child could repeat a grade only twice.

She continued by saying she thought General Hospital had really let her down because she felt the mother was not being helped to face up to her child's lack of intellectual ability. I said that this was the child who seemed to be so lovable and had made such a good social adjustment. I was trying to separate out for Mrs. Graham again the lack of intellectual ability from the child's personality. I said that I remembered the case because I had been so impressed with how much the school and the parent had been able to do for this child to make him relate so well to people, and that this was so important for children with limited intellectual ability because they could really get along so well in the world if they knew how to get along with people. Mrs. Graham quite perceptibly straightened up a little bit and said that this was true. Then she said that when she had visited this home the last time, the boy had said, "Come in, Mrs. Graham," and had asked her to sit down . . . and had given her such a sweet smile. She said that kids who were smarter might have stepped all over her and rushed past her and let her find her own way in the house. For the first time I could pick up a real feeling of sensitivity in Mrs. Graham to this child as a person, and I wondered if this accounted for the upsurge of anger at General Hospital, where she thinks they are not giving enough attention to and rather are brushing aside this child.

She went on to say that the mother had called and

called and called and couldn't get an appointment. Now she says that the school will have to make some recommendation to this mother and she knows the mother is going to be disappointed and unprepared to make any plans for next year. Besides this, if the child is referred to a special class, he should be brought to the school so they can do tests and so on, this spring . . . so as to be ready for this fall. I listened to this and then I asked what facilities there were for special classes in this area. This was a lucky question, as Mrs. Graham immediately said this was another worry for her.

She said that she had visited the special class a couple of weeks ago to get an idea of what kind of teacher there was and so that she would know what she was letting this kid in for. Almost immediately I recognized this as something quite unusual for a nurse to do, and it points to a particular involvement with this child and his mother.

She then went on to say she was really worried about whether this would be the right place for this little child because all of the children in primary grades there were "Mongoloids" or very defective children. From this description, I could see that this was worrying Mrs. Graham as much as her anger at the hospital, and possibly there might be some blaming of the hospital because Mrs. Graham is feeling so guilty at putting this "sweet little kid" in with other children who are, to Mrs. Graham, grotesque and undesirable. At the back of my mind, I wondered if perhaps somewhere in Mrs. Graham's family there may be some history of mental retardation or brain damage. I remembered other cases from previous consultations which corroborated this. At one point she said, "I can really understand how the mother feels about sending the kid out of her home."

I thought I would make a try at reducing some of the anxiety about whether these children were really grotesque little monsters or not, so I said I had always had a very warm spot in my own heart for some of these kids because I had had a very close friend in California who had taught a class of children like this. Then I said that in hearing this friend's description of some of these children, and her ability to describe their personalities as very different, and their capabilities—restricted as they were—I had felt almost as if I had known some of these children myself. I said I recalled particularly her description of a child who had a gross hydrocephalic condition. In fact, it was quite unusual that this child should have been able to get around as he did because his head was so large that it made it difficult for him to really balance. (I was making this picture as vivid as I could so that it would have a grotesque element about it, because I wanted to make my message come through . . . that despite this grotesque appearance, this child's personality could shine through.) Then I said that the child had a way of coming over to my friend, and he would rub against her and rest his poor head against her shoulder as if he could get some balance from her. On the other hand, he could be quite naughty and she could also discipline him when he needed it. I put in this matter of disciplining because this is also a sensitive spot for Mrs. Graham and I was trying to bring in the control element here as applying to everyone, thinking that if these kids could be regarded as needing limits they might also be regarded as being human beings like the rest of us . . . at least in Mrs. Graham's perspective.

As I talked, Mrs. Graham started rubbing her eyes and I could see she was close to tears and really that this was quite moving for her. Mrs. Graham herself is a very gruff and sharp-speaking person, with quite a bit of rigidity . . . so that the softness coming through is quite striking when it appears.

I concluded by saying that actually our little friend in the present case might seem to be much out of place because his physical appearance and his personality and adjustment are so very good; again, I said this was a tribute to those who had been helping him but that, actually, these other children, too, could very well have some of the same attractive traits and as we got to know them we might not think this was too bad a placement at all for this little fellow. Mrs. Graham at once responded by saying very firmly that she certainly would see that something was done about this child and that she was going to make an appointment with the school principal the next day to see that some decision was made one way or another. I really feel that her feelings about the child came a little more into perspective through our discussion today.

I asked whether there had been any tests in the school itself which would give more to go on in suggesting such a placement. Mrs. Graham said he had had a number of tests and they were all zero. Here she indicated this not by saying the word but by holding up her hand and making the sign of a circle. Just in case Mrs. Graham might be feeling guilty because she might think it was terribly bad to think of this child as being retarded when he looked so normal, and that she might be wrong, I pointed out the fact that he had made such a good adjustment to his playmates, to the teacher at school, and in his home would make the lack of intellectual proficiency stand out even more. I said this was really a very good diagnostic indication, because if we had been able to discover more in the way of poor relationships with his family, his parents, his teacher, or something in his actions pointing to his being depressed or perhaps acting out, then we might have considerable misgivings because we'd had, in all of our experiences, enough cases in which children who were disturbed were not able to achieve in school. I was really pleased with Mrs. Graham's next remark because I felt this showed a growth in her perception. She immediately said this child was quite different from Bob, who is a disturbed child. In the beginning, Mrs. Graham had held very fast to the feeling that Bob was also retarded and she had denied right down the line that there could be anything at all that could be disturbing in the way he had been getting along with his parents . . . although she had told me of his feeling jealous toward a younger sibling. Mrs. Graham spent the rest of the session talking about Bob. . . .

Summary

It seems clear in this session that Mrs. Graham has some personal involvement with this mentally retarded child and was really in a state of upset because she felt she might be pushing this child into a class situation of grotesque little monsters. I think Mrs. Graham has some horror of grossly mentally defective children or children who may have brain damage. She has real affection for this little boy because of his appealing personality, and she was unable to see that these other children in this class setting also have individual personalities. I have an idea that at the very beginning of this series of consultations, Mrs. Graham equated mental disturbance, emotional difficulties, and possibly other psychiatric difficulties with mental retardation and probably grotesque deformities. I think this is probably why she was upset when the time came near to make some recommendation for placement. I think that at this time there has been some progress in Mrs. Graham's being able to separate out differences between lack of intellectual ability and intellectual ability that is interfered with because of emotional difficulties. There is still a great deal of denial about the role of parents in relation to disturbances in children.

This report is excerpted from a series of interviews. The salient theme appears to be that individuals who have brain damage or are mentally retarded are apt to look grotesque and abnormal and they will be rejected by others as though they were beyond the human pale, so that eventually they will go down the drain. The consultant has not yet specifically defined the inevitable outcome, but meanwhile in the previous session she had obviously been working on reducing the expectation that a diagnosis of mental retardation must inevitably carry the connotation of rejection because the sufferer would appear inhuman. At the beginning of the consultation interview described here, the nurse's outspoken criticism of General Hospital, which seemed like a displacement of a personal feeling, together with the other signs cited in the consultant's report, raised the suspicion that as the tension in the theme was being weakened by the consultation, the need for the consultee to use a defensive displacement onto the client was lessening, and there was some danger that she was about to talk openly, or at least to think consciously, about the person in her own life who was the original object of her worries. This stimulated the consultant to move the discussion away from the client to the anecdotal parable she invented on the spur of the moment, in order to continue the process of reducing the theme interference.

Particularly significant was the consultant's storytelling technique of painting so sensitive and appealing a picture of the fictitious defective that she brought tears to the eyes of the consultee, and then the idea of including the segment about the teacher's having to discipline the child, which implied so graphically that a mentally retarded person was not to be regarded as so fragile and vulnerable as the nurse obviously regarded her own patient, but could be reacted to in many ways like a child of normal intelligence.

Nonverbal Communication

A potent technique for delivering to the consultee the message that he does not have to worry so much about the expected inevitable outcome is to do it through behavioral signs. The consultant discusses the outcome with an obvious lack of anxiety and talks in quite a relaxed manner, for instance, about continuing the discussion at the following consultation session. The consultant used this nonverbal approach to supplement his verbal communications in the case of the about-to-be-divorced woman who might lose control over her sexual impulses. He showed lack of anxiety by postponing the completion of the discussion until the next session and by saying, "We will have to wait and see how events unfold." The implication was clearly that he believed the bad outcome envisaged by the consultee was rather unlikely.

The absence of tension and pressure for quick action by the consultant will have a theme reduction significance for the consultee only if he believes the consultant truly understands the danger in the case. It is therefore essential that the consultant demonstrate his own involvement in elucidating the complexities of the case and indicate his awareness of both the initial category and the inevitable outcome. Only then will his lack of anxiety have an impact. Otherwise, the consultee will believe that the consultant's relaxed behavior means that he does not understand what is likely to happen to the client, or does not care.

Nonverbal Focus on the Consultation Relationship

The fact that the consultee has dealt with a personal problem through theme interference in his professional work indicates two things: first, he must be experiencing a current disequilibrium in a psychosocial conflict that was previously resolved only precariously; and second, he must be prone to using displacement as a defense. It is also likely that the displacement onto the client is recent, and so it is apt to be not very stable.

It is therefore not surprising that a consultee with theme interference transfers his displacement fairly easily to other objects—perhaps characters in a parable, perhaps the consultant himself. The consultant should always be alert to the possibility that the consultee is acting out his theme in the consultation relationship by ascribing a particular role to the consultant and then playing a complementary role himself. When this happens, the consultant should be prepared to divine the inner significance of this charade in which he is being involved and, as with his discussion of the case, accept the initial category and then invalidate the expectation of the inevitable outcome. He should do this nonverbally.

At the same time, the consultant deals in identical manner with the same theme through his verbal and nonverbal reactions to the client's case. He has to discuss with the consultee the manifest content of the case in a way that has meaning in its own right. He must be thinking of the latent content of what is said about the client and formulate his remarks accordingly. He must also be watching what his consultee is doing nonverbally in the transference. And he himself must behave in a way that conveys an invalidating rather than a validating message about the theme outcome.

An example of this technique concerned a nurse who brought a case for consultation that involved a young woman of Italian parentage who had just married a Bulgarian man. The husband, a truck driver, was described as a very powerful man, who was quite taciturn and drank heavily, although he was not an alcoholic. The wife was being followed by the nurse as a prenatal patient with Rh-negative blood. She required careful monitoring through repeated blood tests to make sure her fetus did not develop a blood incompatibility causing brain abnormalities and requiring a massive blood transfusion after birth. Although there was no evidence on which to base this fear, the nurse was quite worried that the husband would be unfaithful to his wife and would eventually leave her, especially if she gave birth to a damaged baby. She also expected that the husband would belittle and exploit his wife.

As the story unfolded, the consultant became aware that the nurse was beginning to behave toward him in a somewhat unusual manner. The nurse was rather small, and the consultant happened to be rather tall. They had previously had several consultations about other cases, in which a variety of themes had emerged and had been satisfactorily dealt with, and the consultation relationship had become fairly warm and relaxed.

On this occasion, however, the consultant noticed that as she talked about her expectations that her patient would be browbeaten and eventually pushed aside by her powerful husband, the nurse began to act with increasing timidity toward him during the interview. As the interview reached its close, she talked about her reluctance to bother the consultant with the case, how busy he was, and how unnecessary he probably felt it was to continue to follow it.

The consultant by then had defined the theme as "A weak and helpless woman who builds a link with a big powerful man and becomes dependent upon him will inevitably be exploited and belittled by him and will be cast aside when her needs increase and she becomes a nuisance to him." This theme was being portrayed both by the case and by the roles that the consultee was manipulating in the consultation. If the nurse could perceive the husband being unfaithful to his wife and rejecting her, she would validate her theme expectation. The same would happen if the powerful consultant were to push her around and if he were to express disinterest in her problems with this case, particularly as she followed it toward the zero hour of the fantasied family debacle.

The consultant dealt with the theme in two parallel ways. He involved the nurse over three interviews in a discussion of the facts of the case, during which he concurred with her perceptions of the power ratio between the huge, rough truck driver and his delicate wife. He then involved the nurse in a discussion of the evidence on which they might predict that the man would infringe on his wife's rights and would leave her in the lurch in her hour of need. He admitted this as a possibility, particularly in view of the truck driver's frequent absences from home. Yet there was plenty of evidence of the man behaving solicitously to his wife, going out of his way to drive her to the hospital for her blood tests, and making arrangements for his older sister to come and live with them at the time of the delivery. From these signs, it appeared likely that the man was, in fact, preparing to support his wife in all possible ways as her time of crisis approached.

In addition to this verbal intervention focused on the case, the consultant also invalidated the link between initial category and inevitable outcome nonverbally, by his reactions to the consultee's manipulations of the consultation interaction. First, he emphasized his own strength and potency by his forthright statements about the case, by allusions to his extensive experience in dealing with prenatal problems, and by reading up and then quoting to the nurse some recent research work on the psychosocial problems of Rh-negative pregnancy. Then he countered every manipulation of the consultee designed to get him to infringe on her rights, by emphasizing his respect for her professional expertness in providing nursing support for this young couple. He took care to communicate his awareness that the nurse was as busy a professional as he was and to arrange interviews to suit her convenience rather than his own. He did not direct further data collection about the case but made it clear that he appreciated the new light she managed to throw on the case by her astute observations during her home visits. He expressed his own intense interest in the case, his initial perplexity about the possible outcome, and his keen desire for a second and third consultation interview (their previous consultations had been completed in one or two interviews). At the end of the third interview he issued a warm invitation to the nurse to come back to see him if the patient's blood sensitivity titer showed a dangerous rise or if her baby turned out to be damaged. In all these ways—by his tone of voice, by his behavior, and by his expressed attitudes toward the consultee and her patient—he conveyed that he was using his power for their benefit and not to push them around, and that he would continue to offer his help as long as it was needed and would not reject them if their demands increased.

The effect of this dual approach on the consultee was quite striking. By the end of the second interview her tension died down; instead of talking about the husband as a huge brute, she began to speak warmly and appreciatively of his efforts to support his wife, and of how she could help him by explaining the nature of the Rh problem. At the same time, the nurse's manner toward the consultant changed. She reverted to her previous role of self-respectful collaboration, and she began to demonstrate autonomy and initiative in her handling of the case. After the woman gave birth three months later, the nurse reported to the consultant that all had gone well, that the baby was healthy, and that the marriage appeared stable and happy. From her description of the way she had supervised the family during the final somewhat anxious weeks of the pregnancy, when the blood sensitivity titer had shown a moderate rise, the consultant judged that the nurse had been operating at her customary level of skill and efficiency and had been a source of considerable support for the young couple.

Ending and Follow-Up

Once the consultant has completed his verbal and nonverbal intervention to break the link between the syllogistic categories, and a satisfactory result has been achieved—the consultee's tension drops and he reverts to his customary level of empathy and professional objectivity—the consultant should terminate the sequence of interviews. He should step back and leave the consultee to continue dealing with the case on his own. It is important that the consultee experience his subsequent success with the case as his own doing and not the consultant's. He must feel that he has personally mastered the previously impossible task. If, in addition, the consultee realizes that he has played an active part in increasing the options and preventing the stereotyped bad outcome, he validates in actual experience what was only a theoretical possibility during the consultation discussions. It is this personal experience with the client that confirms the consultant's messages.

A successful theme interference reduction is usually completed in one to three interviews over a period of three or four weeks. The process as a whole may last several more weeks, as the consultee continues working with the client while he corroborates experientially the breaking of the link between the theme categories.

By the time the consultee really engages himself with the client in line with his new capacity for perceiving him objectively, the consultant has usually left the case. This means that the consultant should not be around to hear about such improvement. It is therefore important to arrange for follow-up reports by the consultee after his tension has subsided and after his behavior in the cases has stabilized.

The consultant should ask for follow-up information somewhat lightly and delicately, so as not to raise doubts about the theme. The best way of accomplishing it is to terminate the series of sessions by saying that the consultant will be pleased to offer help as need arises with other cases and that in future contacts he will be interested to learn what transpired with this client.

A consultant always needs some rough measure of his level of success with his ongoing cases, not only as a yardstick for his own self-respect but also as a guide to improving his professional operations. In addition to the evidence of decreased tension and increased objectivity, there is a second source of evaluative data that the consultant may use. This depends on continuing contact between the consultee and the consultant, contact that provides information that the theme is no longer interfering with the consultee's professional operations. The best evidence for this is that the consultee continues to request help in cases in which a similar theme interference is identified but the degree of interference falls in successive cases, until eventually the consultee appears not to be disturbed by this theme and requests consultation only for cases with other themes.

Such a gradual reduction of intensity of theme interference is more persuasive evidence than a sudden disappearance of that particular theme, and certainly stronger than the fact that the consultee ceases asking for consultation. These situations may just as well be interpreted as signs of a major failure of consultation; the consultant may inadvertently have alerted the consultee to be conscious of the theme and of its significance for his personal life, so that when it emerges again in connection with other cases he consciously or unconsciously avoids the consultant in order to safeguard his vicarious use of the client in handling his own conflicts.

As usual, the most reliable evaluative evidence obtained by follow-up contact with the consultee is negative. If succeeding cases demonstrate the continuation of theme interference at the same level of intensity, the consultant can be confident that either he has not correctly identified the linked categories of the syllogism or that he has not adequately invalidated the consultee's expectations of the inevitable bad outcome. This should stimulate the consultant to renew his efforts and to modify his technique until he finds something that changes the situation.

Theme Interference Reduction in a Group

The techniques of theme interference reduction were developed for use in individual consultation, partly because of historical accident: we accomplished most of this development as part of a research project whose design required that our consultation be carried out with individuals and not with groups. Since that time, however, we have made a number of attempts to adapt the method to the group setting. Consultation in a group has obvious economic advantages in conserving scarce consultant time. By offering peer support, it also reduces the risk of sliding from the consultation into psychotherapy, which usually taxes the skill of even the most experienced consultant.

The main obstacle in trying to use these techniques in a group is that the consultant, however skilled he may be in group dynamics, exerts less control over the content of discussions than he does in an individual interview. In particular, if the group members have any psychological sophistication, someone is likely to see through the defensive displacement of a consultee who has a theme interference. One of the other participants may then make an interpretation that lays bare the displacement—"The emotional way you are talking about the reactions of this girl to her mother makes me suspect that you have a similar problem with your own mother."

One method we have used to overcome this obstacle is to meticulously lay down ground rules that outlaw any comments about the private life of participants. The consultant begins by discussing the differences between group psychotherapy and group consultation, and binds all participants to respect the boundaries of personal privacy as an essential condition for membership and for his willingness to lead the group. Nevertheless, it is difficult for the consultant to prevent interpretive comments by group members toward each other, especially in an emotionally exciting situation; once an interpretation has been made, the leverage of our technique will be dissipated.

Another problem in trying to use the theme interference reduction method in a group is related to the idiosyncratic nature of theme interference. Group consultation has obvious merit when the work problem being discussed is common to all or most members. Occasionally, they may all share a theme interference. For example, a group of nursing supervisors may all have a problem dealing with their nursing director in an authoritarian setting, which may be related to personal tensions each may have had during adolescence in her relationship with her mother. It is the rare girl in our society who emerges from adolescence with stable resolution of her ambivalent feelings toward her mother. The consultant, in this situation, should focus on the pattern of role problems in the work setting, realizing that some of the tension is due to displacement.

More usually, however, one person presents for group discussion a work impasse that is linked to that person's individual experience, which may be unlike that of most other participants. If the group successfully assesses the problem, if the consultant succeeds in preventing anyone from realizing and weakening the displacement, one consultee will be having effective consultation but the rest of the group will only be participant observers. For them, the discussion will be an educational rather than a consultation experience. The specific emotional impact of theme interference reduction will be felt only by one person. In Chapter Ten we will discuss how this problem may be overcome.

CHAPTER NINE

Lessons of an Unsuccessful Case

To illustrate the techniques of consultee-centered case consultation, we present in this and the following chapter an analysis of tape-recorded details of two case examples. They are drawn from a program in which advanced postgraduate students of the Harvard Medical School Laboratory of Community Psychiatry gave consultation once a week over a period of two to three years to groups of fifteen to twenty-five parish priests of the Episcopal Diocese of Massachusetts.

We have chosen as our first example an unsuccessful case. It is often easier to abstract the principles of a technique when it is applied unsuccessfully than to understand its working when it flows smoothly and effortlessly. Let us examine the following case, therefore, in which objectivity was lost all around. Not only was the presenter hampered by subjective involvement in his parishioners' situation, but other clergy in the group and also *the consultant* lost their objectivity, too. Nevertheless, even within the confusion, and despite a host of technical errors that the consultant allowed himself to fall into, the clergyman seeking help did get some support and reassurance, and the group achieved some general increase in understanding.

The Group Session

The case was presented by Joe Waters, a minister in his late fifties, who had always given evidence of sophistication about psychological issues. Because of his competent manner and warm personality, the consultant had special respect for him, and came to regard him as a resource to whom questions about the "proper" functions of a minister in any awkward situation could be referred.

Waters had been troubled recently, he said, by the plight of retired men unable to cope with leisure. "As people approach retirement," he continued, " you get a completely different perspective on time. The only good time is when you are busy or active, and people grow very fearful of time on one's hands. These people don't seem to appreciate this honest freedom. I want to share this problem with you, which I think will grow more prevalent as we go along." The wives of such men, Waters went on, complain that their husbands are forever underfoot, growing dependent on them for suggestions of things to do.

"In our preachments, our own attitudes, our verbalizations, we say one ought to look forward to retirement. This is something that can be rewarding. And yet, when we come to the facing of it, we find that there is a fear that develops in the sphere of reaching this particular age, also the attitude on how to utilize time."

The consultant noted the shifting pronouns and the uncharacterically awkward syntax. He knew that Waters and two other members of the group were nearing retirement age themselves, and he realized that this topic was likely to evoke emotionally charged material close to the surface. So, to prevent the consultee and the other clergy from openly identifying with the problems and being threatened by them, the consultant firmly and wisely declined to deal with this subject in the abstract, and suggested that more fruitful results would emerge if they examined an actual case. In this way, he hoped to keep potentially painful ideas impersonal and distant enough so that those who might be sensitive to them could look at them "out there," with a measure of professional detachment.

In some earlier sessions, the consultant had allowed discussion of delicate subjects to proceed in general terms, with decidedly unsatisfactory results. Discussion was either so abstract that participants were bored, or else these sensitive issues floated ominously over the group with no displacement object to buffer them, until inevitably someone was struck by their application to himself and, warmed by the intimate atmosphere of the group, proceeded to pour out his personal feelings. After each such session, the number of participants in the group dropped.

So in this case, the consultant was wise to suggest that, rather than discussing retirement in the abstract, the group would be better served if Waters could describe an actual case. He readily agreed and launched into a current counseling problem.

The Case

The case concerned a retired man and his resourceful, competent wife. The husband had been an executive in a brokerage firm and had retired a year ago; the wife still worked, writing short stories for women's magazines and performing occasionally in the local community theater. At first, after his retirement, the husband had found little to do, and had "come to the point" of doing a "menial task"—selling magazine subscriptions over the phone for a few hours every morning. In the afternoons, he would return home "with the sense of 'What will I do now?'"

His wife had recently come to Waters in despair; the magazine had stopped its telephone subscription service, and her husband was now idle all day. He was willing to do anything, but he expected his wife to take all the initiative. He was "all thumbs around the house," so he was no help with the chores; and his wife now feared that she had "another child on her hands."

"Did you know the man before?" the consultant asked. "Are you surprised by his reaction to retirement, or would you have predicted this lack of initiative?"

Waters seemed puzzled by the question and answered tentatively, "He has initiative, but no self-confidence." The man, it appeared, had shown no enthusiasm for finding a new job, although Waters had suggested several types of voluntary work. He was not much interested, the minister continued, in the company of men, although he had worked with them all his life. Waters had tried, again unsuccessfully, to prod him into joining a retired men's club, where his fine singing voice and skill in public speaking would have been an asset to the group. But the man did not feel the problem as his wife did, and showed no inclination to do more with his time. She, on the other hand, "feels literally hemmed in," complaining to the minister that her husband does not realize that he is so demanding. Furthermore, whenever she pointed out her discomfort to her husband, he grew hurt and depressed, "almost as though she had spanked him."

Already a pattern was emerging in Waters's presentation. On the whole the husband was described negatively—inexplicably idle, childish, and emasculated. There were significant patches of vagueness in the narrative, as when the minister was unable to describe the parishioner's character before retirement. It was as though Waters saw the man's present state as unconnected to the rest of his life, or that he had never given the man much thought as a person and was now considering him for the first time. In either case, overlooking the parishioner's past was significant. Further, the words he used to describe the case were somewhat exaggerated: he took a "menial job," he acted as though his wife had "spanked him." On the other hand, the wife was described approvingly. The evidence that Waters had lost professional objectivity was strong.

At this point the consultant should have begun to explore the material closely to learn where the minister's main concern lay, where his view of the situation seemed to be constricted. He should have traced, for example, Waters's sources of information. In whose judgment was the man idle, dependent, and at a loss for things to do? Was this the view of the husband, the wife, or Waters?

Instead of continuing to examine the material systematically, however, the psychiatrist launched into a hasty explanation of the case. "This woman's frustration," he said firmly, "doesn't surprise me at all." He then gave examples of how difficult it is when men break into a woman's routine by staying home during the day. He even described his own domestic crisis; he had been confined to the house for four days with flu until his wife "nearly went mad."

Other group members had examples to relate too. How much worse it is, they agreed, when the man is retired, and the woman must adjust to never having the house to herself. One minister commented that the career pattern of a housewife runs opposite to that of her husband. As a woman gets older and her children leave, she finds herself less tied to the house and more involved in community affairs; but retirement brings the man back into the home. Thus a woman is apt to find her newly won freedom snatched away.

The group was now engaged in the fruitless exercise of making judgments about the case before the evidence was gathered. They had little hope of relieving Waters's concern, since they had not listened long enough to find out what that concern might be. The group and the consultant were not only wasting time, but were also practicing a pattern of problem solving that consultation ideally tries to discourage, a pattern in which one jumps to the conclusion, triggered by scanty evidence, that a case fits into a certain category and that categorization determines the treatment of the case. Here, the consultant and the group were reinforcing each other and Waters in a bad habit.

Furthermore, premature interventions of this kind can be hazardous. At this stage of the presentation, we may readily identify areas of sensitivity in the consultee, but we have no way of knowing what the heightened language, the tense manner, and the other signs of concern may mean. Unless restraint is used, therefore, we are apt to find that we have pushed matters in just the wrong direction, raising the consultee's level of concern rather than diminishing it.

In this case, the consultant and the group quickly realized that in Waters's eyes the parishioner's passivity and aimlessness and the wife's irritation at his constant company were of central concern. He presented it as the main feature of the case, and he did so in an emotionally weighted manner. But what was it in this situation that he found so aggravating? Was it the discontent of the wife, whom the minister clearly admired? Was it her rejection of her husband's needs after years of marriage? Was it the retired man's loss of adult initiative and his reversion to childish dependency? Or was a far more subtle cue pressing on Waters at an unconscious level, something that set this case apart from all other superficially similar ones and impelled him to seek the group's help with this particular situation? Unless consultant and group listen patiently to a consultee's exposition, suspending judgment until they have questioned him at length on the details, they will be unlikely to isolate the node of his difficulty, and the force of the entire consultation will be largely blunted.

In this instance, far from enlightening Waters with their comments, the consultant and the group unwittingly strengthened one of his exaggerated concerns arising from the case: that women are indeed trapped and driven to desperation by men who, having lost their proper role through retirement, are made unmanly dependents of their wives. Moreover, the manner of the intervention was subtly belittling. It implied that the situation that the consultee had been agonizing over for days or weeks was in fact so transparent that others could resolve it after a ten-minute hearing. This is a particularly tactless thing to do to someone who might be raising the case out of desperation, having come to doubt his own abilities on this occasion, and whose self-respect might thus be vulnerable.

However, two minor, positive elements in this episode should not be overlooked. First, it developed active participation by most members of the group at an early stage of the session, rather than leaving the consultee in sole possession of the floor. Second, it humanized the consultant. Instead of assuming the stereotyped psychiatric pose of impersonality, distance, and nonreaction, he showed himself by the personal anecdote to be a man among men, a person who could share a seriocomic experience with his friends and equals.

Many clergy have spoken appreciatively of consultants who could set aside their clinical pose to become in this way real members of the group. They also told of their discomfort with other psychiatrists who were unable to shed the aloof manner into which they had been drilled. These people, although nominally coordinate with their consultees, seemed to cling to the vestiges of the hierarchical doctor-patient relationship while they listened to the group sharing stories of their children and grandchildren but never offered similar confidences themselves. One minister said, "We wondered about our consultant for months. He never revealed anything about himself and seemed to brush aside any overtures and attempts to develop a personal relationship. He seemed to want so much to stay objective and clinical. But we were all colleagues, we called each other by our first names, and it was sort of peculiar having this fellow there who remained a consultant to the group, instead of a member of the group, if you see what I mean. Then finally, we got one of the fellows to ask him if he was married and if he had any kids. We wanted to know if his knowledge about relationships was real, or only theoretical."

In the discussion of Waters's case, however, the consultant was already known to the group as a warm and friendly person with whom they all felt at ease, so from the point of view of building and maintaining a relationship, this personal anecdote was really a superfluous interruption: an interruption, moreover, which subtly linked the topic back to "my experiences," how "my wife and I felt when we got in each other's way in the kitchen," rather than stressing that the focus was on Waters's case.

Meanwhile, Waters listened patiently while the group wandered off on its fishing expedition, and he gradually edged his way back into the discussion. He agreed that his retired parishioner tied his wife down, but he insisted that this was a more complex problem than the familiar picture that his colleagues were creating of a woman who had married "for better or for worse, but not for lunch." The problem lay, he insisted, in the man's inexplicable behavior. Even when he had been leaving for his part-time job in the morning, he had expected to find his wife waiting at home when he returned in the middle of the day. If she was out, he was hurt. And although he would gladly accompany her to the rehearsals of plays in which she appeared, he would not move about alone. "He's with her all the time, and she doesn't feel it's wholesome."

"How," asked the consultant, "does the man regard his own retirement? Is it any kind of problem?"

"He's loving it!" snapped Waters. "And that's the awkwardness of the whole situation. He enjoys reading spy stories and sleeping late. He is growing more and more passive and dependent and losing all the interests he used to have."

The consultant asked how the man felt about his wife's state of upset. The minister said that she, unlike other wives, adjusted to the situation on the surface, although she worried underneath, afraid that as her husband clung closer to her, he would usurp more and more of her time. She had urged him to act alone, but, she said, this always precipitated "this hurt feeling," and she no longer dared to work energetically to change the situation.

More elements in the pattern of the case were here emerging. There was obviously a blockage of communication between the husband and wife, although Waters did not seem to formulate it in those terms, since his bias in favor of the wife led him to ascribe the problem exclusively to the husband's wrong-headedness.

"Has the wife noticed any changes over the year of her husband's retirement?" the consultant asked.

"Yes," said Waters. "There's less initiative to reach out, and more of what I call 'usurping' of her time."

"How old are they," asked Mr. Moss, another clergyman, "sixty-fivish?"

"No, he's seventy-one and she's sixty-two."

"That's quite a difference in age," remarked a curate.

"Wasn't it rather a change for the man to sell subscriptions after being an executive?" Mr. Green asked.

"Oh, he gives the impression of not caring about it. He's perfectly happy with his noninvolvement."

"Do they try to travel a bit? Many retired people do."

"No. They have a limited income, only a pension; and their two married children live in this area. They are a closely knit family and visit back and forth, but the man doesn't take much joy in his grandchildren, and can tolerate them for only a short period. The man has no interests and no honest abilities around the house."

"Does the man have a different idea of himself since retirement?" the consultant asked. "Is he showing other signs of change than just having more spare time?"

"He's not senile," Waters answered. "He's not lazy either. To a degree, he has always leaned on his wife; she's always been the resourceful one. But his work gave him prestige."

The curate again said that he was struck by the great difference in the ages of the husband and wife. A woman in her early sixties might have certain expectations of her husband that a man in his early seventies might not be able to meet. "I think," he said, "that someone who is seventy-one is . . . well, is . . ." He was drowned out by nervous laughter from the older men in the room. "Someone of sixty-one may be very young," he continued loudly. "And I know people in their seventies and eighties who are full of vitality; but that's more rare. It's harder for most people to be still expanding their vision at that age."

The issue of age was clearly significant. It was unusual for Waters not to have mentioned the disparate ages of his parishioners when he first described them; most consultees give such vital statistics at once. This was an early clue to the consultee's lack of objectivity. Moreover, when the curate raised the subject twice, it was twice dropped after nervous laughter, indicating the group's sensitivity. This was the first sign of the other ministers' growing embroilment in the case and their difficulty with it.

"Can't they work as a team around the house?" asked Mr. White.

"No," said Waters. "He's completely incompetent. And she's frustrated, because if she tries to talk to him about it, there's that hurt. And he just hangs about, with no hope of being an influence on town politics or anything else."

Waters was here restating the issues that bothered him, signaling that the discussion was off course. This tenacity is characteristic of consultation: if interventions are inappropriate, the consultee will unconsciously reiterate his problem until someone hears him. If nobody strikes to the core of his dilemma in one case, he will be likely to return with another example where he has encountered identical underlying issues, in the unconscious hope that this time he will learn the solution. In this present case, tension mounted as Waters, unsatisfied by peripheral contributions, refused to be deflected from what were for him the salient issues. As he restated his main concerns over and over again, the group became fascinated by the repetition, and were significantly swayed by it, as we will see.

"Is it that your parishioner has no hope of influencing things, or no interest?" the consultant asked.

"Well, that's the funny thing. When you look at him you'd think he was the most happy guy. He probably wasn't that concerned about things when he was working either. She was always the person with depth, with the stronger personality, pushing him."

"The only case of retirement I know really well," Mr. Apple said, "was my uncle, and I think these cases must be similar. I remember that when he had been retired for a while, anyone else might have had a nervous breakdown. In those days, of course, you didn't have such things, you just sweated it out. My uncle got very tense and couldn't sleep till he finally went to the doctor. The doctor saw what was wrong and called my cousins, their children, into this, because, although my aunt and uncle had planned very well for retirement, the one thing they had never considered or discussed was the need for independence; they didn't think that loving, well-bred people should need it. So my uncle's problem was eased when one of his sons suggested that he soundproof his den so that he wouldn't hear the television or my aunt's bridge club, which had been driving him crazy. He also had a greenhouse built at the end of the garden so he could have a life apart from the household. This was best done with more than two people discussing it. The children legitimized the fact that when a man gives up his responsibilities he has a new life, and the wife's life, in a way, continues independent of his."

"But what I hear," said the consultant, "is that while the wife in Joe Waters's case says she wants her husband to be independent, what she really wants is to get him out of her hair, and she doesn't really care what he does, as long as he is out of her way."

This was not a wise remark. First, it ignored Apple's story, which had opened the subject of how to deal with blocked communication. Apple had listened carefully, and had heard Waters allude to this issue three or four times already. He realized its centrality both to the husband and wife and to the minister, who was clearly at a loss over how to restore understanding between the spouses. The consultant not only failed to pick this up, but he took off in another direction that was unwise for two reasons: first, it made a statement about the case, instead of asking questions about the material in order to stimulate Waters to reexamine it; and second, it had a blaming, unprofessional tone. Waters had already shown that he blamed the husband and sympathized with the wife. The consultant was not modeling a professional attitude when he, in turn, condemned the woman.

"No," Waters said, "it's odd you should have this impression. What bothers her is that they can't approach this in discussion so that he can appreciate that he's around *all the time*. He thinks this is just wonderful, and he can't see that she wants an opportunity to do a few things without the sense that she must be home before him, otherwise he'll be hurt."

"How does she present this to him when he seems to get

depressed?'' An excellent question, since it was working around to isolating the communication problem. Waters, however, did not face it.

"He does get depressed; that's the nature of the guy.''

"Are we figuring that it's upsetting him to come back to an empty house?'' the consultant asked.

"That's right.''

"We're figuring that's quite hard on him?''

"That's right.''

"How hard is 'hard'?''

The consultant was now trying to reduce to rational bounds Waters's possibly exaggerated concern that the husband would be devastated by his wife's absence, based on measured experience rather than on fantasy and heightened language. There was a long pause, and then the consultant continued.

"Suppose she said, 'I'll be back by four'; would that satisfy him?''

"With the children, she could do this, but not with this guy. He expects that she be there, and he doesn't appreciate the fact that it's a change for her to be tied like this. And yet, he isn't dictatorial, he isn't a hard person.''

"So he depends on his wife's initiative; and when she takes initiative for herself, and acts on her own, he is hurt because he isn't included,'' the consultant summarized. "He wants to be mothered, and she isn't eager to have another kid.''

"That's it,'' said Waters grimly.

"The question is,'' the consultant continued, "how many of her suggestions to him come from her considering what is best for him, and how many are about what's best for her?'' The consultant was now hovering near the target. "By now, he can probably pick up that there is some self-interest on her part, and each suggestion is a possible rejection. He might not take any suggestions from her because he's getting suspicious of what they mean.''

"This has gotten to be a real hangup for her,'' Waters said.

"That must make any suggestions coming from her very sticky,'' the consultant continued.

"Well,'' the minister said, "they go over his head very neatly.''

"He doesn't want to hear them," said Moss.

"They just go right over, period. It doesn't even knock," said Waters.

"This reminds me," said the consultant, "of a mother who may want the kitchen to herself for a while, and suggests that her kid go try his new coloring book. The kid senses that this means that she wants room to prepare the dinner, so he sticks closer than ever to keep her from succeeding."

Everyone agreed, and laughed uncomfortably.

"This all reminds me," Mr. Gosling said, "of a friend of mine, a minister, who was out of work for a while. His wife told me she used to clean the house in an hour and a half, but with him there, it took her four hours. She couldn't bear having him around the house. They loved each other, of course, but she got really pissed off with him being there all the time."

This is the type of contribution that is likely to arise in a group and against which a consultant must guard. Linking the case to the experiences of a fellow group member facilitates personal identification with the problem. The consultant correctly refused to follow this line of thought, and returned instead to close questioning of Waters's material.

"Are you pretty sure that there is suffering if the man comes back to an empty house?" the consultant asked.

"I'm pretty sure there is. This has always been the pattern."

"I'm wondering, you see, whether this is just his preference, or is he really miserable home alone, feeling neglected."

"This fellow loves reading, so he should be okay alone; but even when his wife goes to the store, he immediately puts on his coat to go too. He even insists on going with her to her needlework club. He sits in the background while the ladies gossip. His wife is terribly embarrassed, and the other women resent him; they can't talk freely with him around."

This produced great hilarity. One curate asked, "How can a tough, go-out-and-kill-'em executive behave like that? He must be crazy! Really masochistic. I mean, how can you believe that this guy has been traveling around for seventy-one years on somebody's apron strings? It sounds absolutely crazy."

"Maybe he wasn't," said the consultant quietly. "Maybe an

equilibrium was held as long as the job was there, and it's now overbalanced.''

"But, what I mean is, I can't believe this can go on forever!"

"Yes," said Waters, "but she is afraid that it will; she's looking into the future."

"Well," said the curate, "how do you see your role? How can you change the situation without taking sides? I'm quite sympathetic, but it looks to me as though nobody's getting the message—they're just breaking into factions."

"The interesting thing is," answered Waters, "that I can communicate with her, but I honestly cannot communicate with him. It's another one of these situations where you are talking, and there seems to be understanding—I even asked his advice about someone else's case that's similar to his own—then out he goes, into the same behavior."

"Perhaps," suggested Apple, "he's locked into his own expectations of what retirement would be. Perhaps his picture has been that he would no longer have to take any orders from anyone, and that he could now really live in the home he has supported for so many years."

"How does this sound to the rest of you?" asked the consultant. "Does this sound like a universal problem that we all share? And in what way? And what can one do?"

This question was a major technical error. The consultant was attempting to deal with a difficulty inherent in group consultation: how to make the discussion of one person's case relevant to the needs of other group members so that they will not become mere observers. But by leaving the specific case and inviting discussion of the issue in the abstract, and by introducing the topic of expectations about retirement as a "problem we all share"—an ambiguous phrase that might refer to counseling problems but might equally be taken in a personal sense—he was inviting the group to leave the safety of the displacement object and to express their own fears and fantasies about retirement. This might be acceptable in psychotherapy, but it is not advisable in consultation, since it violates the rule that discussion must be limited to issues of professional functioning and to details of the client's case. This was a particularly hazardous gambit in this group because the preoccupation of several men with their own impending retirement was so close to the surface of consciousness. Uncovering it would probably have stirred up too much complicated material for any clinician to contain in the remaining time and in that setting, even assuming that this would have been appropriate—which it was not.

The consultant's error was met by utter silence. It was broken by Mr. Philips, a young minister who had participated in the consultation program for two years and who was consequently an experienced consultee. He ignored the psychiatrist's violation of decorum and returned very firmly to the case.

"What bothers me," he said, "is that I see everybody trying to work on the husband, and I've yet to get the feeling that he's at all upset about this. *She's* the one who's upset about it."

"You mean," said the consultant, "that everyone wants to change him to please her?"

"That's right," said Philips. "Here's a guy who has worked for forty-odd years; and now he's got a chance to do what he likes, and nobody's letting him do it!"

"Oh, he is doing it," said Waters, in a rising voice, stammering slightly. "The difficulty is—"

"To correct him!" shouted the curate.

Several people were talking at once, loudly, and there was rising nervous laughter.

"And your counterproposal is what?" the consultant asked the curate.

"Well . . . ," began the young man.

"It would be hard to say," interjected Moss; and the level of laughter kept rising.

"I'm not sure exactly," said the the curate, in a quieter tone. The quips and laughter redoubled.

"The whole thing is crazy!" the young man continued. "I just can't believe it!" Among those now laughing hardest was the consultant.

Here we can see the group reacting, with raucous and inappropriate laughter, to the unbearable tension of finding themselves, like Waters, trapped in the case. They saw no apparent way to move without destroying one of the clients; even if nothing changed, the wife would be smothered. The discussion so far, especially Apple's remark about the possible images a man might have of his own retirement, had intensified discomfort by making the man seem more sympathetic and therefore more vulnerable. Furthermore, the increasing vividness of the dilemma may have been impinging on the private concerns of some of those in the group.

"I'm very surprised at this reaction," broke in Waters. "Perhaps it's my special situation, but I'm surprised that more of you haven't been hearing from the wives."

"Not that way," answered Green. "My men seem to take off like a bat out of hell on all kinds of energetic trips when they retire, dragging protesting wives behind them."

Again the motif was emphasized of retirement as a state when one marriage partner was sacrificed to the needs of the other.

"Well, yes," said Waters, stammering, "but that's a different thing. I've got two or three cases where the husbands are home and the wives are going crazy. Wives want to know what to do with a husband that's retired."

This statement, which now placed the case under discussion into a generally occurring category, marked another danger point. It again diffused the focus of discussion and threatened to make someone think, "Perhaps I'm going to be like that—an unmanly, childlike burden on my wife, who will then resent and reject me." As long as the discussion was tied to the particular plight of Waters's parishioner, that danger was minimized.

"Well," said Moss, "I've certainly seen a good many husbands wear out a good many wives in retirement."

"The problem here seems to be that all this guy needs for happiness is one other person to go along with him. But she's younger, and she isn't about ready to retire herself," Griffin said.

"But she is going along," insisted Waters; "she's been capitulating all along. But she is getting more and more concerned each year about what this will lead to. It looks as though she's going to be *completely* caught in the house."

"If she's saying, 'The older my husband gets, the more I'll have to take care of him,' that's a real concern."

"I don't think she'd be concerned if this were a physical disability. But I think that she feels that she has to wear the pants in the whole situation, and she has no time that she can call her own."

"Then," said the consultant, "perhaps the focus should be on the wife. She is the one with problems, she is the one who's unhappy. He seems contented and to know what he wants."

"Yes," said Waters, "but he's manipulating her; and when she tries to share responsibility, he puts on the hurt or depressed situation, and she doesn't think it fair to shake him."

In this interplay, the consultant was trying to persuade the consultee that what he identified as the problem was not really critical, and that he should address himself instead to a different point; Waters was correctly refusing to be moved. The consultant was saying, the husband is happy, the wife has the problem. The consultee, however, was concerned about the behavior of the husband, which he was determined to understand, and he was not willing to dismiss it.

"She feels she's got another child!"

"But there's no solid evidence yet that his age is a factor in this?"

"No, his health is fine."

"Maybe she's manipulated him into this situation and now doesn't like it," Philips suggested.

"No," Waters insisted, "she isn't that type. I don't think it's a case of a dominant wife who has subjugated her husband."

"Of course," said White, "it's possible that his social life had always been part of his business; and when he retired, he lost all of that."

"Yes," said Apple, "you often hear someone complaining that he doesn't have friends of his own. There are only his wife's friends and business contacts, but no personal attachments."

"It seems to me," said the consultant, "that for either one of these people to get what he wants, it's going to be a loss for the other."

Now the wisecracking and raucous laughter began again and rose higher and higher. Someone, for example, suggested that this man had "retired with a vengeance." Another said, "It's impossible—old dogs, new tricks, you know; it's a charming challenge, Joe, but I'm glad it's *your* case." The consultant had now underlined

and sanctioned the growing fear of the group that this was indeed
a hopeless situation.

"But is it that hopeless?" the consultant wondered.

"From her point of view it could be," Green said.

"It's getting to be a threat to her," Waters said firmly. "She
was in my office a couple of days ago; we talked about this."

"Was he waiting outside?"

"No, as a matter of fact, he was sleeping late that morning."

"So she does get away some," Moss said hopefully.

Waters sighed.

"Looking at it from his point of view," said White, the oldest
member of the group, "I have a feeling that there's a great deal of
sympathy for the wife here, but not too much for him. I can *feel* that
situation in my own retirement that's coming up. The parish is
taken away; you have to move out somewhere else; you have no
friends. Who do you have left? You have nobody but your wife left."

"Yes," said Waters, "clergy retirement is another, most interesting thing, because you are a figure in a community; and when
you retire to another community, where you're not an authority
figure, that puts you in a John Doe situation, to say nothing of
getting reacclimated."

"So," said the consultant, desperately trying to climb back on
the case, "part of his way of acclimatizing was by saying that since
he was somebody before retirement, and nobody now, he can sell
magazine subscriptions, and that's good enough for him."

"We are speaking of clergy," said Waters nervously. "In the
case of that retired man, I don't know if that's the case."

"It could be," said White. "I mean, everyone isn't going to
retire at once. You do it one at a time. It's like dying. And so you're
in a new role, and there's nobody there that you know. The other
people remain on the job, and you . . . you're retired. So you have
nobody but your wife; and if she's not prepared to play that part
with you, you . . . you've got a problem."

"Yes," agreed the consultant, tossing all discretion and disciplined methods to the wind, "an ordinary man only works for
eight hours a day, but you're a clergyman all twenty-four hours. It
must be far worse for clergymen to retire."

This, of course, was a foolish move. Instead of helping a

consultee, who was having difficulty with a case because of some personal link between it and his own life, to gain mastery by learning to treat such cases objectively, by strengthening the boundary between private and professional existence, the consultant was tearing at whatever shreds of a boundary were left. He was encouraging the ministers to look at their own fears of retirement, rather than helping them to manage the case of a retired man in the practice of one of their colleagues. Had the latter task been accomplished successfully, it might have had a secondary benefit in relieving a measure of those very fears in themselves. If this parishioner and his wife could be helped to establish a mutually satisfying rather than a mutually destructive experience, then these clergy in their own retirements might find a similarly happy lot. As soon as the consultant realized that the discussion was veering into dangerous waters, he should have pulled it back to the case, and held it there. Instead, he became so upset by the intimate disclosures and clear identification of some of the men with Waters's parishioner that he contributed to the very situation he knew must be avoided.

Fortunately, there were veteran consultees in the group, and as the consultant broke the rules, they set the situation right. This is one of the advantages of group over individual consultation. Groups are more complicated, but they are safer, since this kind of lapse by the consultant can be absorbed and recovered from relatively easily, as long as the ground rules of consultation have been properly understood and accepted by most of the consultees.

After a stunned silence and then more nervous laughter, Waters said briskly, "Well, come up with some answers, boys. I want help on this."

"I don't know what to do," said Griffin, "but I have the feeling *she's* the one—"

"Sure she is," Waters said. "All right! But the point is, what does she do? Where does she go? She has the problem, but she doesn't want any hurt here."

"Does he think that perhaps you're her mouthpiece?" asked a very perceptive minister.

"I've tried to approach this diplomatically, but he just doesn't seem to realize what a burden he is. I've tried to get this across to him, but . . . I feel for the wife, because I think she's fair, asking for some independence."

"I'm not so sure," Apple said.

"What?"

"I'm not so sure it is a fair thing to ask for."

"But what she wants is almost the same kind of sharing you get in normal life. What he has done is retire from all decision making. He's retired from everything. I've known them for twenty years. They weren't like this before," said Mr. Waters.

"But he doesn't see this as a problem. Only she sees it as a problem."

"But the point is she can't get it across to him that it *is* a problem for her."

"Is this affecting her health?" the consultant asked.

"No. But she is worried about the future, that as he gets older, she'll be more and more tied down."

"If nothing changes, if it gets no better or worse, what will it cost her?" the consultant asked.

"Just the feeling that it's pinning her into a tighter sphere, and that she will be kept from her friends and interests. She realizes that with the age difference, if things don't improve now, they never will. And the way he follows her to her club meetings, that's creating tension in the group that's wearing her down. There's no divisiveness that's apparent between the husband and wife, though, because she holds back on discussing the issues so as not to hurt him."

"Can't she insist that some of her engagements are for women only?"

"No. That would create distrust."

The entire situation was summarized and chewed over twice more, and then, fortunately, the time was up. The consultant noted in a puzzled tone, "You've given us a lot of material. We've checked and rechecked until it's shiny clear, but the group just can't seem to get on top of this one. Let's think about it for another time."

The meeting broke up, amid more inappropriate laughter.

Reasons for the Failure

What happened here? The session floundered mainly because the clergy and the consultant largely failed to isolate the key factors in

Waters's difficulty with the case. They did not deal with the fact that the presenter was regarding the husband not as a real person, with recognizable feelings that could be explored and changed, but as a stereotype, a creature apart, with whom neither his wife nor the clergyman could ever communicate. Here was a man who "has no abilities or interest," "who doesn't enjoy his grandchildren," who was so hurt when his wife left him alone that he accompanied her to the grocery shop and her sewing club like a clinging three-year-old, and who yet remained perversely contented with his lot. The man, Waters insisted, did not see a problem. He sat in the house, like a block of wood, reading novels or sleeping, oblivious to his wife's growing sense of being trapped and to the unseemliness of his own behavior. The act of speaking to him was particularly hazardous, and was regarded with almost superstitious awe. Nobody dared to risk hurting or depressing him, so everyone plotted how to manipulate him into a more acceptable form of behavior without having to face him directly.

The consultation group, with the exception of some isolated remarks from the curate and Apple, simply adopted Waters's stereotype, perhaps convinced of its accuracy by Waters's refusal to be moved from his view of the problem and by his consequent repetition of the elements of the case. The consultant himself was carried away, partly, he later said, because he thought that since Waters was such a wise and intelligent man, his perceptions must be accurate. He forgot that if the minister had been able to bring all his wisdom and intelligence to bear on the case, he would not have needed consultation. The consultant was also preoccupied with the fact that fear of retirement, or of losing their jobs because of parish politics, was close to the surface of group consciousness. Indeed, that fear was manifested on a number of occasions, aided by the consultant's self-fulfilling prophecy, in which he contributed actively to what he feared by linking these issues to personal rather than professional experience.

The only people in the room who seemed at ease with the case were the curate and two or three younger men. The rest of the group, however, consistently rode over their suggestions, which said, "But this man can't be as you describe him." When, for example, the curate roared with laughter at the idea of a man accompanying his wife to a ladies' club meeting and said, "I can't believe that a seventy-year-old executive could really be like that," he was ignored by his colleagues, who were wedded, by then, to Waters's characterization. They were also reacting, incidentally, to a note of discourtesy is the young man's remarks, which the group refused to tolerate. When Apple spoke up on the side of the husband, conveying the possible meaning of retirement as a time when a man no longer has to take orders and when he can at last enjoy the home he has supported over the years, it was never picked up because, by then, the whole current of the meeting was flowing in the opposite direction.

Had the consultant been more objective at this moment, he could have seized on Apple's point to help Waters consider the husband in a more human light; but the consultant was as trapped by the case as were most of the ministers. By this time, he was also relating to it personally rather than professionally, for as he admitted later, "It got me, too. I was thinking about my father's recent retirement."

In the absence of adequate objectivity on the consultant's part, the entire group not only adopted Waters's stereotyped perceptions but began to act out his dilemma. Everyone talked about the retired man just as Waters and the wife had done, trying to find ways of manipulating this inert mass for his own good and his wife's, thereby adopting all the premises that blocked prospects for success. The discussion ran in ever tighter circles, reemphasizing the inherent hopelessness of the case. The consultant tried to extricate himself on two or three occasions, suggesting that present conditions might continue but not deteriorate, and implying that if so, the wife could tolerate them. This, however, was not received with much enthusiasm amid the general gloom of the discussion.

On considering the case later, however, the consultant realized that Waters had unconsciously set up a syllogism in his own mind that was blocking his handling of the problem. This syllogism seemed to say: A man whose relations with people have depended on his role, as does that of an executive (and also that of a clergyman), is likely, after retirement, to grow dependent on his wife. He then becomes like a child, and she must either accept him as a burden, giving up her own independence, or reject him. Either

way, one of the parties must lead an intolerable existence that can
only deteriorate as the years pass.

Since all the participants in the group came to accept Waters's basic premises, the discussion focused on trying to find some
less catastrophic outcome to the situation. And since this was impossible, given the terms of the argument, the tension of the group
rose higher and higher, relieved periodically in high-pitched, nervous laughter, whenever it became particularly clear that however
the minister might turn, either the man or his wife was bound to
be injured. The group found itself obliged either to accept the wife's
position or to attack her. Either they had to contemplate punitive
action against the husband, with whom at least some of the group
identified, or they had to hurt the woman by supporting the husband's hostile dependence. Some, however, may also have identified
with the wife, as the burden carrier who cannot complain openly
but whose independence is sacrificed to the unjustified demands of
others; her plight was especially painful for them to contemplate.

Possible Solutions

One way to break through this impasse would have been to discuss
barriers to communication. Waters might then have been urged to
see that although this man had become socially isolated and idle
because of retirement from his profession, and consequently driven
into exaggerated dependence on his wife, nevertheless, as a mature
person, he must be expected to confront and work through his
difficulties. With the minister's help, the couple might have been
brought to accommodate themselves to each other; but this would
not be likely to occur if the husband were dismissed as an obstinate
child, or regarded as so vulnerable that it would be perilous to talk
to him. Waters might have been helped to consider the case as one
in which marital counseling was required, where he would meet
with both parties together to ease their communication.

Further, it might have been suggested that Waters help the
wife to develop a more realistic appraisal of her husband and his
capabilities so that her expectations of tragedy might have been
modified. Since the husband was so much older than the wife, a fact
whose significance seemed to elude all but the curate, throughout

her married life she might have dreaded the prospect of his one day sinking into helpless dependence. She might have molded his recent behavior unconsciously by this expectation, creating a self-fulfilling prophecy. And she may have actually exaggerated his dependence by her defensive rejection, like a mother who tries to free herself from a child's demands, only to precipitate more whining and clinging.

The consultant might have broadened the discussion to explore certain complexities of interpersonal relations that arose from this case. For example, he might have spoken of the obstacles to the minister's free and trusting relationship with one spouse if he spends most of his time with the other. It was clear in retrospect that Waters was getting almost all his information from the wife and was directing most of his sympathy at her. Consequently, his view of the husband—after knowing him for twenty years—was distorted by the wife's bias. And since in any family conflict there may be discrepancies in the parties' perceptions and expectations of each other, a mediator should not jump to the conclusion that any one story epitomizes objective reality.

That this issue really needed general discussion was borne out some weeks later when a young minister mentioned in passing that he had been told by a female parishioner of her husband's cruelty. The clergyman later learned from a psychologist who was treating another member of the family that the woman's version of the matter was highly distorted. The clergyman said that he then felt betrayed by his parishioner—he thought she had elicited his sympathy under false pretenses—and he concluded that she was far too disturbed for him to help. It did not seem to occur to him to call in the husband to try to resolve some of the contradictions between the two stories. The minister had no doubt been taught in theory what to do in marital counseling, but under the pressure of a complex case, he forgot to apply what he had learned. The consultation session provided an opportunity to make existing theoretical knowledge vital by pinning it to a flesh-and-blood situation.

The ministers might have been warned against the possibility of a coalition developing between one spouse and the clergyman in which they line up against the other spouse. The pastor would then not serve as a communication bridge between the conflicting factions, as he had intended, but would draw them further apart.

Thus, inadvertently, Waters might have been strengthening the wife's conception of her husband as stubborn and hopeless, and may thereby have contributed to her belief that this burden would ruin her life.

Since such inadvertent collusion would be likely to color any contacts between Waters and the husband, the man would probably sense a lack of sympathy in the minister, despite the fact that he was genuinely trying to help. The retired man, therefore, might have dug in his heels further to resist the pressure that he felt was directed toward the exclusive benefit of his wife. In this way, the clergyman might have been creating a self-fulfilling prophecy. Because he was convinced of the man's obduracy, he might have communicated his irritation and pushed too hard, thus rousing further stubbornness in the man, which in turn supported the preconceptions of the wife and Waters. The consultant might have suggested that ministers guard against this by interviewing both spouses together from the early stages of a case. This way they would not only obtain some realistic assessment of the facts and mediate any divergent percep-tions that would emerge, but also demonstrate their own friendly neutrality. In Waters's case, on the other hand, where the minister might already be identified by the husband as the wife's ally, he might have brought in other mediators, whose disinterestedness was ensured, to redress the balance.

In this connection, the consultant might have suggested ex-tending the case's focus, when assessing and treating the problem, to include all the relevant members of the clients' network. Waters had neglected the potential contribution of the couple's grown children. Apple, in his story of his uncle's retirement, recommended precisely this approach: gathering those who are close to the couple, both to dilute the intensity of a situation and to sanction a solution that the couple alone might have thought to be forbidden. This also could have been managed with the help of others in the parishion-ers' lives, such as a family doctor, a neighbor, or any one of a wide group of possible intercessors who can usually be found once the minister realizes the importance of mobilizing them.

Final Outcome

The consultant's performance on this occasion had been well below his usual level of professional activity. Puzzled by this, and feeling foolish, he sought the advice of a colleague, as is customary among psychiatrists when they meet with confusing cases. Now the minister's consultant had himself assumed the role of consultee. In reexamining Waters's account of his parishioners and the course of the group's discussion, the psychiatrist came to realize that his view of the material had been constrained. The second psychiatrist suspected that personal concerns ("I kept thinking of my own father's retirement") had clouded his colleague's professional judgment. He kept his interpretation to himself, however, since his friend had come to him for consultation, not for psychotherapy; instead, he tactfully pointed to data that suggested alternate ways by which the circumstances of Waters's parishioners and the course of the ministers' discussion might have been modified. He helped his consultee to distance himself from the material, to reinforce the boundary between his private and professional lives, with the hope that this renewed objectivity would carry over to other cases of like nature in the future.

Despite the shortcomings of this session, there were some modest gains. Waters showed a certain sardonic satisfaction in the fact that his case had so completely puzzled the group; he may have concluded that he was not, on reflection, as inept as he had thought. Indeed, the discussion seemed to ease his feelings and to suggest some new ideas, for a couple of weeks later, he reported that the husband was not quite such a problem any more. Waters had talked him into attending the church's retired men's club, and he hoped to expand the man's activities even further.

Thus this particular case was eased by the simple fact of sharing it with sympathetic colleagues. Few gains, however, can have been made in educating Waters and the other ministers to human relations issues arising out of it that could be generalized to future cases. It also failed to weaken Waters's subjective involvement with cases of this category in order to strengthen his professional poise or to alleviate the fear of some of the group members about the imagined horrors of their impending retirement. It did, however, teach the consultant that the distorting power of his own subjective reactions should be guarded against as carefully in this type of work as in psychotherapy.

CHAPTER TEN

A Successful
Consultee-Centered
Case Consultation

The failure of the consultation process in Waters's case, summarized in the preceding chapter, was encouraged further by the fact that the psychiatrist and the group attempted to deal with the material in only one session. While it is possible to offer help on some circumscribed matters in a short time, complex cases and deeply rooted blind spots require far more effort. The better a consultant knows his consultee, and the more he learns about the case, the more likely he will be to identify his problem. And since he is not a mind reader, it may take two or three sessions before he has amassed sufficient evidence to see the salient issues and before he can intervene forcefully and directly enough to modify a consultee's settled ways of looking at a particular situation.

The consultee also needs time: first, to build up sufficient confidence in the consultant and the group to reveal the extent of his own perplexity; second, to sort out the details of his case until enough order is established for the few apparently insoluble points to be isolated; and third, to digest and react to the consultant's and the group's suggestions. This third point is of particular significance, since to experience the greatest benefit the consultee must move back and forth between the theoretical formulations of the consultation setting and the untidy realities of his daily work. Only by returning to the actual case to test the wisdom of the group's suggestions, and then analyzing the results in subsequent sessions, can a consultee ensure that these ideas were worth his serious attention; only in this way can he fully assimilate a novel point of view.

Let us examine another case of this consultation group, in which a less hurried approach, coupled with better technique on the part of the psychiatrist, yielded more satisfying results.

The First Session

Mr. Philips, a young minister with a charming manner, was a veteran consultee. In his comments on the cases of others and anecdotes about his own parish, he seemed flexible and imaginative, always revealing a warm, nurturing attitude even toward more conservative or eccentric parishioners. Nevertheless, the consultant had noticed that Philips had a tendency to seek out and react allergically to "castrating bitches," even when evidence for their existence in a particular case was slight. When this minister offered to present a case, therefore, the consultant had these points in mind.

Two weeks earlier, Philips began, a middle-aged parishioner had summoned the minister to his house in the early morning to talk to his wife. When Philips arrived, he had found the woman huddled on her bedroom floor in an acute state of anxiety. This had startled him, since he had known her for some years as an unusually active member of his congregation, a woman who was able to manage capably a house, a part-time job, voluntary activities, and the care of four children, including a seventeen-year-old girl, handicapped by polio since infancy, who was confined to a wheelchair. Philips had seen the woman a week earlier, and he had noticed no sign of strain. He now learned that she had been trying to write a term paper for an extension course at a local college when she had become paralyzed by terror. Philips had spent four hours calming the woman and coaxing her off the floor. He had seen her every day since, first at her house and then at his office, but he felt no improvement in her condition.

"When I just talk to Jane," Philips said, "she immediately thinks of a number of things she cannot do. And I just feel, as I sit in a room with her, and she begins listing the things she can't do, my insides just . . . I almost feel like saying something like, 'Boy, it sure does sound like you can't do a damned thing!' "

The consultant saw that some aspect of the case had struck

Philips on a raw nerve. He jumped to no conclusion, however; he merely asked for more information.

Philips continued: "I can picture dealing with this person for some time, and . . . there's not enough money for psychiatry. My lady did go to the local mental health center, but a neighbor of Jane's saw her going in, and she gossips. Now there's another complication. Jane has an appointment next week with the social worker there about her daughter. The center is trying to involve parents of handicapped children, and she doesn't want to go because she doesn't like the counselor. As far as I can make out, the counselor got impatient with my lady and tried to push her into doing more for her daughter. Then, on Monday, I went to the house and saw the daughter, because the girl had said, 'Can I talk to you, because my mother gives me hell all the time?' I just wondered if any of you guys run into this kind of thing. My long-term concern is, this is something I'm going to have to take care of. I repeat, there's no money for a psychiatrist!"

As the discussion progressed, it appeared that Philips had become so caught in the case than any recital of the parishioner's circumstances only brought him back to his own feelings of worry and perplexity. However the consultant and the group maneuvered, the consultee's level of tension would not come down.

In his daily meetings with Jane, Philips had amassed a vast and dismal array of details about her situation, about her contempt for her own abilities and her resentment of her crippled daughter, about her fear-ridden childhood, dominated by a father who allowed no failures, and about her current existence—obsessed by her struggle to maintain a middle-class, suburban façade with too little money and a husband who could never advance in his job far enough to fulfill her ambitions. Despite his intelligence and psychological sophistication, however, Philips seemed too inhibited, for reasons of his own, to draw this material into a usable pattern; it remained for him a menacing labyrinth in which he felt entangled and trapped.

Waters realized the problem at once. "Do I hear you saying," he asked, "that you are over your head dealing with this person? That you think the case is going to get too much for you to handle?"

Before the consultant could intervene, Philips answered,

"The first time I saw her, her husband was there. The second time, it really was a case of estimating whether this was over my head. I distinctly remember feeling that I couldn't stop her from compounding the kinds of things she could not do. So I suppose part of the difficulty was evaluating whether or not it was over my head. But I think I voted, 'No, it is not.'"

Significantly, the case had not seemed so formidable with someone else present. But when Philips faced Jane and her sense of inadequacy alone, he had an irrational urge to escape. Nevertheless, he persisted, convinced that in the absence of a real psychiatrist, he was obligated to play the psychiatric role. He began to mimic psychotherapeutic techniques, setting himself to uncover and challenge Jane's feelings. He sensed the danger and futility of this, however, for throughout he kept wondering whether he was damaging her.

"What was Jane's major concern?" the consultant asked, drawing the discussion away from a direct review of Philips's own doubts, while opening a path to discovering issues that rendered this case so threatening for him.

"She was taking a night-school course," the minister explained, "which was proving too difficult for her. It is part of a degree program she's been in for three years. She had wanted to take an easier course, but a friend had persuaded her to take this one instead. She didn't like the course, and she had to produce a paper, and she could not write. She was so tense and nervous that she could not apply her mind to the material. She kept insisting that she had to keep on taking the course. She said, 'I'd like to drop out, but if I do, I might not have the determination to continue next spring; then I know I'll be dropped from the program.' Then she said, 'I won't finish! I won't be able to do it!' So I asked her, 'Why is school so important to you?' And she said, 'I don't know; I feel I've got to produce.'

" 'Well, what do you have to produce?'

" 'I don't know, I just have to be in this course!' "

Philips, who was now acting Jane's part by his posture and by the changing inflections of his voice, explained that the woman was afraid that if she were dropped from school for failing to take the prescribed number of courses each term, she would lose all the credits she had earned over the past three years. If she continued, however, she would have to work for nine more years before she got her degree.

"What a depressing prospect!" exclaimed a member of the group.

"I also found out," Philips continued, "that she constantly compares herself with others and thinks she's inferior to them. So she has to take courses that are too hard for her because otherwise she thinks her friends will look down on her."

The minister's attitude was one of exasperation jostling sympathy—exasperation at Jane's apparent determination to persist in an absurd and untenable position. This created a sense of impasse, since all appeals to reason and self-interest were ignored.

"What about her husband?" asked Moss.

"He's an assistant manager in a local plant; nothing spectacular. She says, 'I've always pushed him, and he finally admitted that it was good that I pushed him, because he never would have done so well without being pushed.' "

From this remark and others made throughout the session, the consultant understood that one aspect of Philips's difficulty came from his ambivalence toward Jane. On the one hand, he pitied her suffering; whenever he suspected that she had been attacked, as at the counseling center, he spoke of her as "my lady." But this was counterbalanced by disgust at what he perceived as her bitchiness: her driving of her husband and herself, her grasping after social status, and her "frivolous" complaints about the superficial deprivations of her life. Philips's possible identification with Jane's sense of inadequacy only strengthened his dislike, forming a defense against complaints that might have been unwelcome reminders of problems of his own. The consultant therefore decided that one goal of the session must be to modify Philips's stereotypes, to detach him from identification with the case and thereby reduce his confusion, anxiety, and guilt about his hostility to Jane.

"But the husband hasn't done well," Green pointed out.

"No," Philips agreed. "And this is a constant illustration of the things she has tried to do and has never been able to get any satisfaction from. I began to see pretty clearly that she would *never* see that she was satisfied. She set out to do this twelve-year course because it was impossible to get any satisfaction out of that, and she would have to keep on struggling, and hating the courses, and never achieving anything. This was the kind of hole she began to dig for me. As I speak this, you can all begin to feel, 'What can I say?'—that kind of response."

Philips clearly foresaw an inevitably hopeless outcome for the case, since all its constituent parts were so bleak. This assured him that his own efforts to help Jane would be blocked at every turn.

After further questions, however, Philips did begin to acknowledge, albeit grudgingly, that Jane was functioning remarkably well despite her claims to be weak and incompetent. Her house was immaculate, her children well behaved, and it emerged in an aside that during the past six months she had suffered the deaths of her mother and sister without giving way to the strain. She and her husband were well established in the community.

"They pioneered in this area," Philips said, "and now, as she puts it, 'Everyone has gone by us.' Their friends have moved up and on to higher-class places; and they've been left."

"Is she likable?" Apple asked.

"Very likable—on the surface. I think," Philips continued after a pause, "that she feels that she's always got to be around to take care of the paralyzed child."

"How seriously is the girl disabled?" the consultant asked.

"She's in a wheelchair most of the time. I've just learned that she was living down in the basement, and she's only been upstairs for the last few months."

"Living in the basement?" the consultant asked.

"Yes," said Philips in a strained voice. "I couldn't help the immediate thought that rushed through my mind: 'Boy, you kept her in a hole! You kept her down there!' "

"Sometimes a basement is part of the living area of the house," the consultant said.

Philips quickly agreed. "I'm sure they made plenty of accommodations for her to be comfortable. The mother was telling me about this because she was complaining about the finish being scratched off the furniture all over the house by the wheelchair. I mumbled something like, 'Well, it's good to have Patricia upstairs even if the furniture does get damaged.' I have the feeling that the care of her daughter upsets her very much. There's a constant demand there.''

Here Philips's ambivalence was amplified. The bitch motif was growing stronger, but coexisted with the minister's sympathy for Jane's depression at being tied to the care of a chronic invalid.

"Is it your judgment that this seventeen-year-old doesn't need an adult in the house all the time?'' the consultant asked. Where, in other words, are the realistic boundaries of Jane's burden? This introduced the idea that even such long-term responsibilities may vary in intensity over time, and need not sap the life of the caregiver. This point was explicitly applied to Jane, but it had implicit significance for Philips too, since he perceived a commitment to help this parishioner as all-absorbing.

"It was my feeling that the mother ought to trust the girl more,'' Philips said. "The girl doesn't have friends of her own age. What I learned from the girl was that the deaths of the grandmother and the aunt were catastrophic for her. She prefers older people, and she obviously has a conflict with her mother.''

"What about this counseling service,'' the consultant asked. "How long has Jane been going?''

"She just started.''

"Who got her in? Why did she go?''

"I don't know. It's a good question. I suspect, since it's connected with her daughter, that it was the school.''

"What's the problem with the neighbor seeing her?'' the consultant asked.

"She gossips,'' Philips said.

"So what? What was there to say?'' To this Philips did not seem prepared to answer.

"Some people are ashamed to be seen going through the door of such places,'' White said.

"Jane whispers in my office,'' Philips whispered urgently, as though he were revealing a sinister detail. "There was nobody around on the floor, though you could hear people coming and going downstairs, but she whispered!''

"Was she whispering, no matter what she talked about?'' the consultant asked calmly, restoring a tone of analytical detachment.

"She whispered all the time," Philips answered. "She was just so afraid that somebody else would hear her talk about her problem. Her image of herself is terribly important."

The minister seemed to see Jane's sensitivity as further confirmation that she could not be helped. It proved that defense of her self-image, her "suburban façade," would prevent her from ever exposing the extent of her difficulties even to herself and her pastor. Consequently, she would keep inaccessible the key to a disturbance that was disrupting not only her own life but also those of her husband and children, and thus willfully and absurdly resist measures that might ease her suffering. In accepting the responsibility for her care, Philips saw himself trapped more tightly than ever in a hopeless case; if it were not inherently hopeless, which for some reason he believed it to be, her resistance would make it so.

"It sounds so sad," Apple said. "She sounds like a terribly frustrated woman who has visions of grandeur, and who can't possibly achieve them. She tries to take courses so that she will have a college diploma like other women she knows and be able to get a glamorous job someday; but she's still tied to this family situation, so no amount of effort will do her any good. She's living in your area, which is an on-the-way-up community, full of young executive types. She hasn't much money and probably won't ever have any. She'd do well to move somewhere else if her husband is going to have a low-level job for the rest of his life. She's going to see these things around her till the day she dies."

"What I'd like to do is to help her to see that she's worth something as a person," Philips said without conviction.

The consultant, following Apple's humanizing interpretation of traits that Philips had been describing as perverse, yet trying to minimize the global pessimism of his remarks, said, "It sounds as though something has recently upset Jane's image of herself, and she seems to have a self-image that requires an awful lot of effort to sustain. Could she feel that she's been scolded at the counseling center for failing in her mothering role? Did the counselor get at her about the basement? And then, did all the worries about money, and so on, loom up? If the whispering meant shame and guilt, could it date back to the discovery that her child would be handicapped, and the mother thinking that the girl caught polio because she didn't care for her properly? Are shame and guilt now being stirred up by contact with that center? And then, you've got her father's refusal to tolerate failure, so when things go awry, she feels responsible."

"One thing more," White said, "she's going through menopause. Over the years with this group," he added firmly, "I've learned the importance of menopause." The consultant seemed taken aback. "I mean," White continued, "women feel they're not functioning in that area, so they feel they're not functioning in any other area either."

"Also," Waters said, "as she considers her own resentment against her daughter, who keeps her from doing things, there's a guilt that develops—"

"She said," Philips interrupted, with intense feeling, " 'I don't want to hate my daughter!' "

With the group's help, Philips was able to build the vast tangle of details of the case into a pattern for the first time. When alone, the material had apparently been too confusing and upsetting to examine closely. Since he was convinced, for reasons still not clear, that Jane's situation was hopeless and destructive to those around her, he was afraid of finding these forebodings confirmed. Within the relative safety of the consultation setting, however, even if he were to discover a monster at the heart of the labyrinth, he would have allies to support him. So now he was prepared to consider a factor he found shocking—the full intensity of Jane's hostility toward her child.

"She must think of her daughter as a great big roadblock," said Apple gently.

"A millstone," Philips agreed. "The girl was hospitalized for a long time, and that used up a fantastic amount of money. And now Jane has to pay for counseling. She said to me, 'If I hear my daughter's name again, I think I'm going to scream!' Those were her very words, 'If I hear her name, I'll scream!' To me that meant, 'Everyone's interested in my daughter, but they're not interested in me.' "

"When did she say that?" the consultant asked, taking note of Philips's conflicting identifications, both with the mother and the daughter.

"She said it when I first came in. That was one of the early statements, when she was most distraught."

"I don't know how this fits the experience of the rest of you," the consultant said, "but according to mine, families of handicapped children come to some level of adjustment when the kids are much younger than this girl is now. It may not be a comfortable feeling, but it usually has a steadiness. Either the lady has never acquired this, or something has given the relationship a real shake. It might have been the appointments at the counseling center, or it might be something else."

"You're talking about accommodating to realities," Moss asked, "and admitting, 'This is where we are'?"

"Right," the consultant said. "Acknowledging reality and realizing that the bitter kernel of it isn't going to change."

"You mean," Philips said, "that they learn what she can do, what she can't do, what they'll trust her with, whether she can dress herself, whether she can be left to take care of the younger children? That sort of thing?"

"That sort of thing," the consultant agreed. "They learn it, they learn to accept it, and they weave it into the rest of the family life."

"You know," said Moss, "it strikes me that the thoughts and feelings that she expresses are not all that bad or unusual."

"I agree," the consultant said. "Here's someone who up till two weeks ago seemed in perfectly good shape. She'd come through two funerals, she's been carrying those extension courses for three years, she runs a house well, she participates in church groups, and she handles a handicapped kid plus the little ones more or less adequately. That's quite a record."

"Two weeks ago," Philips agreed, "I would not have suspected that anything was wrong." He still sounded puzzled and unhappy.

"All right," said the consultant, "what happened? What triggered the crisis? Things like this don't come out of the blue; there has to be a reason behind it all."

"I notice," Waters said, "that she's had two babysitters taken from her in the persons of the grandmother and the aunt. That may have taken away some of her feeling of being able to cope."

"That's possible," Philips admitted. "The girl used to stay with her grandmother for weeks at a time."

"We seem to have been exploring two possibilities," the consultant said. "First, that Jane has been accumulating pressures for years until a final straw broke the camel's back; second, that something very particular and new happened recently to upset everything. Taking the first alternative," he continued, "is it possible that she has been carrying that social status business, and the money problem, the handicapped youngster, several other things and the stress of the extension courses, and she could carry the whole lot as long as nothing more was added? Then, a relatively small thing tipped the balance. 'The last straw' is a real phenomenon. People can carry three or four loads, then the fifth, which may be trivial, tips everything over."

"You said something," Philips interrupted, "about being able to accommodate to having a handicapped child?"

"The balance of that might have been upset by something," the consultant explained, "like appointments at the center."

"It's possible that that counseling upset things," Philips mused.

"This business of the guilt," said Green, "and this feeling that if she hears the name of her child once more, she's going to climb the walls—"

"Makes me feel mad at her!" interrupted Moss.

"It doesn't me at all, because I don't see this as being terribly abnormal," Green continued. "I've heard this sort of thing many times. But I think it's crushing to her self-image, the fact that she feels this way."

Here members of the group expressed and answered Philips's unspoken sentiment. He, like Moss, resented the mother's resentment of her daughter. In doing so, he was relinquishing professional objectivity and reacting like an ordinary bystander. Green was reestablishing a professional atmosphere of detached compassion, which allowed for the vagaries of human nature; but he was correcting the atmosphere impersonally, without attacking Philips's position.

"I'm wondering," Green continued, "whether it might be helpful to discuss her feelings with her from the standpoint of

'That's really not so bad, Jane, to feel that way. It's a perfectly normal thing; you mustn't castigate yourself because you have these tremendous guilt feelings. These feelings are the result of some pretty logical thought processes.' "

"Maybe I can explore this whole area of how Jane has adjusted to the girl's illness," Philips agreed, seizing a concrete suggestion that fitted his own taste for psychological exploration so well.

"I'd be rather careful there. I'd keep the idea in my mind that the crisis had something to do with the daughter, but I'm not sure I would say anything about it yet," the consultant said firmly. He was anxious to prevent Philips from engaging in any further explorations of his parishioner's raw feelings where he might rapidly move out of his depth. The psychiatrist was acting as a mental health specialist, watching for forces that might endanger an already unstable personality; he was prepared to veto inappropriate suggestions from the group.

Meanwhile, Philips had built up enough confidence to expose a further measure of his own ambivalence. "I didn't know what to say when she said that about not wanting to hear her daughter's name once more. I instinctively felt like using her name."

There was a shocked silence, and then the group laughed in sympathy.

"I did," Philips continued in a louder voice. "I had the instinctive gut feeling of saying—"

"Patricia!" someone said.

"Patricia!" Philips shouted. The group laughed uncomfortably, but nevertheless, by their understanding reaction, they helped Philips to express his hostility without shame.

"How long before she made that statement had she been to the counseling service?" Waters asked.

"She had *just* seen the counselor who didn't like her," Philips answered in a tone of dawning enlightenment. "And she was supposed to go back to talk about herself and her daughter."

"So, what she got from the session was criticism of herself, rather than the feeling that anyone was trying to help her?" the consultant asked.

"That's right. He gave her the feeling that she wasn't taking the girl out enough, especially to social occasions. Jane says, 'I can't take her. These affairs take place thirty miles away. I have to drive her there, wait for her, and bring her back; and it's one more thing that I have to do for her.' What she's afraid of is that the next session is for the parents, and they will tell her to do more and more."

"The mother may be responding just to the added demands on her time," White said. "I had a case like that recently in which the daughter had to be taken back and forth to the psychiatrist and to group-therapy sessions, and the mother simply didn't have any time."

"Time is a problem for Jane," Philips said. "She's one of those overinvolved suburbanites. She's always rushing off to things, and if anyone asks her to do anything, she takes it on. She never gives herself any breathing space."

"I've got a woman like that in my parish," Moss said. "Whenever she gets into one of these panic states, she goes out and adds something else. It's almost a drive that they have to keep going and load up. This woman complains about not having enough time. She works, but she doesn't have enough time to work full time, so she only works part time; but she stays extra. Then, she has an extra job selling cosmetics in the neighborhood. She's on our parish council; she's doing this, she's doing that. Anyone asks her to do anything, she does it. She just piles herself up the devil of a mess, and all of a sudden, she comes tearing into my office, yelling, 'I can't do any more!' I talk to her for a while. And the next time I see her, she says, 'I just started this new project.'"

"Activity seems to be a high point in many people's lives," Philips said. "It seems to be hard for them to cut out activities. They feel they've failed."

"If people enter into a lot of activity in order to feel better about themselves, to bolster their self-image," the consultant explained, "then it backfires if they can't pull it off. The thing that makes a person load up like that is the same thing that makes her feel bad when she can't carry it all."

Everyone pondered the implications of that idea.

"In my general operations in the church," Philips said, "I have a terrible fear of asking people to do things, because I don't know if they really can handle the load. This is a real problem for me as a parish priest, because there are other people who are so lonely, who really need something like this. Now I never said to Jane, 'You ought to drop your church work.' But if she ever brought up the possibility, I would have said, 'That's all right.' But that would be terribly difficult, because even if the idea had come from her, I feel she would eventually blame me for it. I think churches often do harm to some people under the general philosophy that activity is good for them. Sometimes it just gives them too much to carry."

After the group members had considered that remark in the context of their own parish organization, Waters recalled them to the case at hand. "Would there be any wisdom in supporting the counseling service?"

"One of the things I've thought of doing was calling the counseling service and saying, 'Listen, *I'm* taking care of this deal,' which I could do," Philips said firmly.

"You could, of course," said Apple carefully. "But wouldn't it be good for her to keep on with them? Just because she feels frustrated and afraid with them doesn't necessarily mean that they are not on the right track."

"She might be facing things now," the consultant said, "that another family might have coped with ten or fifteen years earlier. And it's painful; no matter when you do it, it hurts, but the longer you wait, the worse it gets. Now, as I understand it, the counseling center is mainly for Patricia's benefit, isn't it? You are on the side of the mother, but they are working for the child. There might be some benefit in that."

Here, in other words, was a possible way around Philips's conflicting identifications with both Jane and her daughter, which should not be squandered.

"Do you know people at the center well enough to talk to them about this? They may not even realize how shaken she has become after their worker talked to her," Moss said.

"Yes, I do know some of them," Philips answered. "And this has just come to me here and now, which is a very helpful thing. I now plan to approach these people and discuss the case with them without any preconceived notions of my taking the situation over."

"You need all the help you can get in a complicated case like this," Moss said. "There are medical issues to do with the girl. It's highly technical stuff."

"If you were to tell the counseling center that you are taking over, I don't see what that would gain you. It could lose you something," the consultant added.

"I had thought of doing that until today. Now I think I'll just contact them and see what they think."

"There is a question," Waters said quietly, "as to how long you do keep on with the case. You may reach a plateau when you don't feel that much is happening, and then it will be time to hand it on to others."

Philips brushed the suggestion aside, still unable to accept that others could assume a major role in Jane's care.

"How much support does Jane get from her husband?" the consultant asked, following the opening made by Waters. "He doesn't sound very prominent in all this."

"I think she gets a very naive, everything-is-going-to-be-all-right kind of support at the moment. Overall, I think he just goes out to work and provides for his family. Actually, he's the one person I haven't really talked to. I don't know . . . It would keep you busy to be married to a gal like that."

"I look at the basement situation differently," Waters said. "We had a time when our kids loved to live in the basement, and we felt it gave them far more freedom. So it could be looked at in two ways: either as a case of subjugating kids, or a case of releasing them."

"I must confess," Philips said, "I had an automatic response that this girl was being shut away, and I hadn't thought of it from the point of view you've brought up."

"I don't know, of course," Waters added hastily. "It would depend on the child and her own feelings. But it should be taken into account before placing the finger of judgment on the mother."

Philips agreed.

"I wouldn't necessarily think of it as a bad arrangement," White added, "just something different."

"This has been very helpful to me," Philips said emphatically, as the meeting ended.

"Perhaps," said the consultant, "we could discuss this again when you've had a chance to see more of this lady."

Analysis

Besides helping Philips piece the details of the case into some kind of recognizable pattern, the consultant felt that this session had begun to resolve the minister's conflicting feelings toward his parishioner. Since she appeared to him not only as a bitch but as a vulnerable suffering bitch who engaged not only his hostility but also his compassion, Philips found himself in the untenable position of sympathizing both with Jane and with her "victims." This session had begun to chip away at these stereotypes and to create a healthy distance, based on dispassionate reasoning, between the minister and the family. The range of pressures on Jane had been explored, and her apparently petty or harsh demands on herself and her family were now seen to flow logically from poignant experiences.

The fact that Philips was beginning to see Jane as a real, suffering human being, however, *raised* his level of anxiety, for now the cost of failure was increased. If the minister could convince himself that Jane was indeed a bitch, then failing to help her would be painful but endurable. But if she was a likable woman who had been struggling bravely for years to maintain herself and her family despite reverses, then his failure would be unendurable.

The group had only started to tackle the question of whether anyone else shared in Jane's care and thus bore with Philips responsibility for the case. Here the group insisted firmly that the minister not exclude the counseling service, but rather that he join forces with its staff. They also tried to curb his zeal for psychiatric explorations, at least until more was known about Jane's condition. Finally, Philips was encouraged to consider the role of the husband in easing the woman's condition.

Despite an active discussion, in which much material was sifted, the consultant still had only the dimmest idea of what specifically made this case so onerous for Philips and why he felt driven to expend so much time and energy on a situation that appalled him. The help that the group had extended so far had affected only the surface. The core problem would not appear until much later in the consultation process.

Had the discussion of Philips's case ended here, there would have been almost no enduring gains. The next meeting, two weeks later, showed that there had been much backsliding in Philips's attitudes. His tension and despondency had been renewed and strengthened after further contact with the family.

The Second Session

"This, you may remember," Philips said, "is the case of the woman who dropped out of her extension course and needed some hand-holding. Her suburban façade is cracking open. You remember, she has a crippled child, and she alternates between not being able to touch her daughter and feelings of pressure that she has to take her everywhere.

"I asked her about the history of the handicap, and she said that the illness occurred when the girl was two. When she was about ten, she had a series of operations to make her walk, which used up a fantastic amount of money but did not succeed. Pat cried each time she was taken to the hospital, and the mother felt terribly guilty about the whole thing."

Philips had discovered that it was the mother herself who had brought the girl out of the basement.

"She said, 'I had the feeling that she was going down there into a hole, and I couldn't stand it anymore!' But she's still resentful of the fact that the child in the wheelchair is scratching the furniture. I don't know what to do with this woman's conflicting feelings. She feels that all her kids are a drag. She said last week, 'When people ask how Pat is, I feel like throwing up!'

"I see the mother once a week now, and have talked to the counseling center. The social worker there told me that the mother is depressed about not having the energy to go back to school. At the moment, she's upset about their unpainted fence. She says, 'It's an insult to people who come to the house.' I asked who these people are; she says, 'The bridge club.' She's convinced that they are better than she is. She got very angry with me when I asked her what good painting the fence would do. She thought I was making fun of her."

Many of the motifs of the first session were repeated and emphasized in the second. In particular, Philips underlined his impression that everyone connected with the case was becoming exhausted. The husband, he said, "looks *drained* all the time," and worked overtime as often as possible, not primarily to earn more money but to "get away from his family, and who can blame him?" The handicapped child was racked with guilt about the trouble she caused her mother, and was spending her days listlessly staring at television.

The mother was "just on the edge of being able to control herself and I don't detect much improvement." She was barely able to cling to the shreds of her "suburban façade," though she forced herself to "put on a front to my secretary when she walks out of my office door." She felt that "I'll have this kid for the rest of my life," and that she had to give so much to her child that she had no energy left to use elsewhere. She worked part time in her father's photographic studio, where she felt exhausted by the necessity of talking to customers.

"She hates herself, she practically says so," Philips continued. "I suspect she's been this way for years, putting up a front. 'I can do anything; I'm confident; I can juggle all the schedules and take care of everything—house, church, social commitments.' And I think the whole thing was phony; and when the crisis came on, everything began to crash."

Throughout Philips's presentation, it appeared that he himself still felt drained and trapped by Jane's disturbance. "She isn't contented. She *won't* be contented. Am *I* supposed to make her feel contented?" he asked in real anguish.

"She wants to be relieved of the burden of her daughter, but she worries whenever the kid is away. She wants to be emotionally strong enough to go back to school, but the life of the whole family was upset by her studying. She wants all her problems solved at once. She wants her husband to take over. She wants *me* to tell her what to do. I just don't know what I can do for her," Philips continued wearily. "Sometimes I think the only thing I do that is genuinely supportive is to pat her shoulder as she goes through my office door. The counseling service wants more cooperation from her so they can help the daughter. She runs from them, but she will come and talk to me. The counseling people think she's pretty sick. They say that she hasn't grieved properly for the death of her mother."

In an aside, Philips remarked that Jane had told him that she wanted to do away with herself and that, after her mother's funeral, she had chosen a burial plot for herself near her sister's grave. When the group attempted to inquire further into these issues, Philips evaded their questions.

Philips remained caught between contradictory impulses. On the one hand, he felt compelled to shoulder the entire burden of the case, and still insisted that no other sources of help were available to Jane. When Jane's father, however, had asked Philips whether he should offer his daughter money to go to a psychiatrist, Philips had told him not to interfere, because he felt that this would wound the pride of the husband. On the other hand, to protect himself from being drained by what he considered a lost cause, Philips was pulling away from Jane. He denied the seriousness of her suicide threat; and when the consultant asked him to assess the severity of Jane's depression, he insisted, despite the warnings of the counseling center, "I don't think she's terribly badly off." He was decreasing the frequency of his contacts, now seeing her only once a week. He reported with perplexity that while she had canceled one appointment—which had cheered him—she seemed disturbed when he did not offer her another.

The consultant and the group helped Philips to realize that he was, in fact, giving much support to his parishioner and her daughter despite his despondent thoughts to the contrary. He had, for example, found a job for the girl in the church school, which got her out of the house for a few hours a week, thus raising her spirits and relieving the mother's sense of pressure. Nevertheless, the group urged him to see that the burden of Jane's care was best shared by a number of different people and agencies. The consultant, for example, suggested that the woman might be helped by joining a support group of parents of handicapped youngsters.

"She wouldn't have to be ashamed in front of people who shared the same problem as herself," he explained. "They would accept her contradictory feelings about her child without being shocked by them; and in that group, she wouldn't have to worry about being inferior to the others. It's a big step to join a group like that; but once in, I've known people to stay for years."

"She won't associate with groups for the handicapped," Philips insisted.

"You should encourage her," Waters said. "I always try to move people out of a one-to-one relationship with me into a wider social context as soon as possible where there are people more competent to deal with the situation."

"Often, you know," the consultant continued, "another mother can do more for someone like that than a doctor or anyone else. Another mother can *feel* the pain; and they are the *real* authorities on the problem of living with a handicapped youngster."

"You may be right," Philips said doubtfully. "But she's caught in this great isolation of suburbia. She doesn't know people like that. She didn't even know there was another kid at Patricia's school in a wheelchair. But you may be right; maybe I should pursue this a little further than I have."

"You realize, I'm sure," said the consultant, that when you suggest to her that she join this group, she will balk. That's only to be expected. You might ease the way a bit if you could get some information about these groups first, like where and how often they meet, and the names of some of the persons involved. That might take some of the strangeness out of it for her."

Philips was pleased as the idea began to seem more practicable. "I will make some inquiries," he said. "This is something I can offer to her."

"And you might also make things easier," Moss suggested, "if you could get someone to take her to the first meeting. I've found that that makes a difference, when they don't have to walk in as strangers."

"The odds are," said the consultant, "that you'll be trying a number of things before one of them works. But I think this is worth a fair amount of effort because I would guess that if she would join, the other women will tell her that they have feelings about their own youngsters, or have had such feelings in the past, that are like what she's going through. And if some of that can be legitimized, she'll have one less heavy weight on her."

These suggestions not only gave Philips a way of getting his parishioner to an effective, outside source of support; they also encouraged him to explore a resource that might prove useful in other cases.

The counseling service had reported that Jane refused to discuss her feelings about her daughter, but Philips had been able to introduce the topic successfully. It may be remembered that the consultant had warned Philips not to explore this area; but the consultee, as was his prerogative, had chosen to ignore this advice, and had apparently been proved right. Throughout this case, despite severe inhibitions, Philips nevertheless continued to act with considerable autonomy, picking and choosing among ideas offered by the group according to how he perceived the needs of the situation.

"Is she worrying about appearances and putting up a front with you, too?" White asked.

"No," Philips admitted with some surprise.

"So she is developing a real trust with you at least." Philips looked somewhat more cheerful.

"Let me get this straight," the consultant said. "Recently, when you said, 'Let's meet next week,' she put it off. Now, I agree, to meet once a week has a natural feel; it's repetitive and you can schedule it. But it may not match her needs. It might be good to listen for what she wants. It might be something less formal than what you are offering. Maybe what you think you are giving is time, but what she's getting is a sense of your concern."

"The demands on me are such," Philips said, "that I'm scared to death that if I don't set an hour with her, I'm not going to give her the time she needs."

"It might not take an hour, though," the consultant said. "Her needs might be such that it won't necessarily take sixty minutes to deliver it."

"True," said Philips.

"She might want to decide that, and not have you decide it," added White.

"Suppose I let her call me when she wants an appointment? But then I'd have to gauge whether she *would* call."

The group agreed emphatically that this was a risky business.

"Let's think about this, and discuss it again," the consultant said, "since *we* have now run out of time."

Analysis

In considering this session, the consultant felt that many of the points of the previous meeting had been reinforced, and that Philips now seemed somewhat more receptive to the notion of sharing Jane's care with others who might have competence more specialized than his own. A serious problem, however, had now been introduced—the safety of the parishioner. It was clear that Philips feared that the woman was highly disturbed and possibly suicidal. With almost superstitious awe he described the cracking of her "suburban façade" and the draining of energy from Jane and her family. Although there was evidence of exaggeration in Philips's assessment of the case, nevertheless, it was possible that reality and illusion were indeed very close. The evidence supported the assumption that the woman really was in acute difficulties, and in fact might commit suicide. The social worker had said that Jane had not mourned her mother in a healthy way. She was menopausal. She was feeling unworthy and panicky about the future. All this tended to make the picture look ominous.

One of the more fascinating and complicating features of this case, and one that posed the greatest challenge to the consultant's technique, was the fact that Philips's fears and actual circumstances lay so close together. It appeared that Jane did indeed need a psychiatrist, that Philips by himself was unequal to the situation; and that in the absence of fairly prompt medical intervention, the danger of further deterioration was real. But despite these facts, Philips was reacting inappropriately. Instead of meeting the emergency in an orderly, disciplined way, he was thrown into panic and despondency himself by issues that confused and frightened him.

He felt that it rested on him alone to avert an outcome he was convinced was inevitable. So he fought on, singlehanded, while at the same time he tried to safeguard himself from the guilt of failing by denying that danger existed, by mentioning suicide as though it were not a serious threat. The consultant in reviewing the data decided that if Jane's condition did not improve by the next session, he would insist that she be sent for a psychiatric evaluation.

The Third Session

The next session found Philips looking more unhappy than ever, but persistent in his search for help.

"Well, fellows," he began, "are you ready for the next exciting chapter of my lady?"

"Give me a one-sentence synopsis," said Griffin, who had missed the previous meeting.

"This lady is depressed," Philips said heavily.

"Oh?" asked Griffin.

"There's been no change. This lady is *still* depressed, I'm not able to get her undepressed. I'm not sure if God really cares anymore."

"Is that your thought or hers?" Griffin asked.

The consultant moved at once to divert the discussion from Philips's feelings, since it was clear not only that he was indeed depressed, but also that he had built up sufficient trust in the group to expose his emotional links to the case at the least opportunity. This is one of the technical difficulties associated with multiple sessions on the same case. Inevitably, as the deeper issues of the client's situation are dwelt on, the intimate links of the consultee with the material rise to the surface; hence, there are greater demands than ever on the consultant to safeguard the consultee's privacy.

Once attention had been drawn away from this inadvertently tactless remark, Philips continued: "I now wonder whether I should put her in the category of another lady who contacted me the week after I arrived in my present parish. She was very depressed, and she said to me, 'Have you ever heard of anyone coming out of a depression like mine?' Then, last month, I talked to the chaplain at the local mental hospital. He asked me if I knew this lady from my area who had just been admitted. It was the same one. I said I had seen her a week earlier, when she had again asked me the very same question, 'Have you ever known anyone to come out of a depression like mine?' The chaplain said, 'Is that so? That's what she asked me seven years ago, when she was hospitalized for several months in another hospital that I was associated with!' ".

The consultant felt that a highly important problem had now emerged. For some reason beyond the purview of consultation, Philips seemed to have particular difficulty with cases of depression, since he evidently shared the second woman's pessimism about her prognosis. When his parishioner had asked her question, Philips had not been able to reassure her; now, in a thinly disguised manner, he was referring the question to the group. Apparently it was not only Jane's problem that inhibited him, but an entire category of cases that is far from rare in the population. If Philips were helped to cope with Jane's depression, he might use the experience to deal with many other parishioners as well.

"More specifically," Philips continued, "my lady is really no further along, and I'm no further along with her."

Questioning by the group, however, revealed that some progress was discernible, at least in Philips's approach to the family.

"It was very helpful to me when you people suggested that I see the husband. After the meeting here, I phoned the husband and asked him to come with her for a joint meeting. This will be the first time I'll be sitting down with the two of them together, and I don't really know if this is a step in the right direction or not. He is rather . . . unsure of himself, but a good man. She would like him to be stronger, and yet she dominates him on every occasion when he tries to be strong. I don't know exactly what I'm going to do with whatever we talk about on Monday. Another thing is, her meetings with me are very painful. She gets no quick relief. All I do is bring up painful subjects and we discuss them. She feels no better upon leaving than coming. That's my distinct feeling."

"And she expects to feel better?" Green asked.

"Yes!"

"Why would she still be coming if she gets nothing from it?"

"Because *I* want her to. I feel like I'm getting into a box!"

The consultant shifted the discussion to another topic to lower tension and to explore a key factor in the case.

"How does this lady talk about the future?" he asked.

"She says, 'I don't know what's going to happen to me. I don't know what's going to happen to my children.'"

With this additional reminder that Jane might be contemplating suicide, the consultant prepared to make a major intervention. He wanted to convince Philips to enlarge the range of supports available to his parishioner and, if possible, to make a serious attempt to get her to see a psychiatrist. To do this, the consultant had to break through the minister's defensive denial, to convince him of the realistic danger to Jane's life, while on the other hand helping him accept the equally realistic possibilities of the situation. The consultant wanted Philips to realize that with effective, flexible management not only could a catastrophe be averted, but the depression itself could be cured.

"No matter who does anything," Philips went on, "you lose. And her husband, he walks with hunched shoulders. He's a beaten man."

"What's the status of the counseling service?" the consultant asked.

"I went to a staff conference on the case," Philips answered, "and we discussed the whole thing and agreed that for the time being, I would substitute for the person working directly with the mother." Jane, it appeared, was becoming more isolated than ever from mental health supervision.

The consultant now prepared to act. He had waited, with an eye on the clock, for an opening in the discussion. He determined to stress the risk to the parishioner, while keeping a matter-of-fact atmosphere that would dampen alarm.

"I don't get the impression," the consultant began, "that this lady is getting enough support. It sounds to me as though she is having a pretty tough time. I winced a bit when you told us that she said, 'I wonder what will become of the children.' When depressed parents talk like that, I lean forward to see what that might mean."

Philips argued hotly.

"Wait a bit," the consultant said; "you said that she was expressing concern about the younger children at that point, not the handicapped youngster?" Philips agreed. "Is there anything wrong with them?" Philips admitted that they were all right. "But if there's no reason to worry about the kids because of something happening in their lives, there's more reason to assume that she may be talking about herself, which makes me a bit uncomfortable."

"I wonder, though," Philips said, still denying that matters could indeed be so serious. "The younger kids are boys. Perhaps she wants the father to do more for them. Do you think he could be more involved? To give them a stronger father image?"

"Well," said the consultant, "you did tell us that she wanted her husband to be more dominating; and if he could be helped to be stronger, it might be very beneficial for the whole family." The consultant was determined to increase Philips's interest in the role of the husband wherever possible.

"This depression might be caused by menopause," White suggested. "And it might go on and get worse."

"If it is menopause," said the consultant, "that weighs things even more toward the chance of critical things happening. I think this woman would use a fair amount of her strength to cover up as long as she could in order to safeguard her self-image. The fact that she has now come out into the open with you at least may be a measure of the strain she's under."

Several members of the group sighed and made despondent remarks. Philips gradually joined in. This was what the consultant wanted, an acknowledgment of the seriousness of the woman's plight by the entire group so that Philips would be supported in accepting the unpalatable fact.

"How much is known of how the husband sees his wife's problem?" the consultant asked.

"I think he feels completely helpless and a little impatient with it," Philips said. "He just walks around with this hangdog expression all the time."

"What I'm really wondering is, does he think things are worse than they've been?"

"Good question. I haven't really asked him. I see him around now and again. He's in one of the church clubs. But I haven't really known how to approach him. He comes to his club because he's getting away from the family for a bit, so I really hesitate to get into discussion with him about all the problems at home. I'm not sure he's *capable* of understanding emotional intricacies.''

The consultant wondered how much of Philips's assessment of the husband's attitude was based on real knowledge, and how much was a projection of the minister's own sense of futility and desire to escape. The psychiatrist felt that Philips should be brought to recognize the husband as a potential ally in caring for Jane and in relieving the minister's own sense of lonely responsibility.

"Is it your impression that he is worried about her safety?'' the consultant asked.

"He stayed home that first morning,'' Moss said.

Philips seemed shaken. "She won't hear of him staying home usually because they need the money. She must have been feeling *really* bad to let him stay home that first day!''

"Now it seems to me,'' the consultant continued, "that the first time you described this family, the possibility of a psychiatric evaluation was mentioned.''

"She said,'' Philips answered quickly, " 'I'm not as sick as that, am I?' and there was the lack of money. I didn't recommend it because I didn't see how they would pay for it. I guess there *are* clinics, but I don't know what they are or where they are.''

"The family might have assumed that contact with a psychiatrist is necessarily a long-term venture,'' the consultant said. "They might not, for example, have differentiated treatment from evaluation.''

"That's interesting,'' said Philips after a pause. Apparently he had not considered the point either.

"Perhaps the family counseling service has someone who does the evaluation,'' Apple suggested.

"Yes, I could ask them,'' Philips agreed.

"Up till now,'' the consultant continued, "we haven't established whether there is a psychiatrist in this center at all. I'm thinking of her seeing someone who is thoroughly familiar with psychiatric medication, who would know whether prescribing antidepressants would be a good idea.''

"To keep her from killing herself?'' Philips asked timidly. Now that an avenue to help was opening, the consultee was able to acknowledge the existence of the risk.

"I am much impressed by this picture of a depressed mother under so much stress talking about her children's future in these particular terms," the consultant explained.

"She's certainly worrying about the future. She said, 'Am I going to feel in the spring, when the next night-school course starts, the way I feel now? Then all the work that I've done up till now will be wiped out.' I keep trying to bring back things to right now, but she always brings us back to this point."

"So here's a lady who's saying in December, 'Am I going to be this depressed in March?' " Waters asked.

"It's exactly what the other woman was saying," Philips said eagerly. " 'Have you ever heard of someone pulling out of a depression like mine?' "

"If she were to seriously think of suicide," Apple said, "how would she go about it? Pills? Slashed wrists?"

Philips looked horrified and shook his head.

"How is she with firearms?" Moss asked. "Are there any around the house?"

"I don't know," Philips admitted, still shaken. Then, after a pause, "She works in her father's photography shop. She might swallow developing chemicals."

"I think," said Griffin in a decided tone, "that would make her horribly sick, but I doubt it would kill her."

"People generally signal before they harm themselves," Moss added. Everyone murmured agreement.

"This whole case really intrigues me," said the consultant, catching the group's attention, "because it sounds so similar to what happened recently to one of my kid brother's closest friends. They were both working for Ph.D.s in economics, and this fellow was scheduled to take his orals. Twice he froze at the last minute and couldn't go through with them. The second time, when he canceled a day before the exam, he phoned my brother in a panic and said, 'Get me to a psychiatrist! I can't go on! I'll never get my Ph.D.!' So my brother called me, and we fixed him up with a colleague of mine; and every now and then, this young man would phone up and say, 'I can't go on with this!' My brother would answer, 'Nonsense, of course you can do it. You're perfectly competent,' which I then told him was the classic mistake, since the

answer always came back, 'I'm not! I never carry things through!'
So my brother decided that the answer for this particular boy was,
'Then it's time you did!'

"About a month before his orals were scheduled for the third
time, he said to my brother, 'You know, it's a funny thing. Nothing
much has changed in the last three months, but I don't feel the same
way I did before. I've got the orals coming up; nothing's changed;
and yet, I know I'm going to take them.' A week ago yesterday, he
took them and passed. Toward the end, the depression manifested
itself as a terrifically bad temper. He bit my brother's head off a few
days before the exam, but he pulled through."

"He was able to take the anger and direct it out, not inward
at himself," mused Philips.

"Was he having continued psychiatric help?"

"Yes," said the consultant. "He was depressed and he felt
inadequate. He, I suspect, like your parishioner, had the unfortunate habit of putting very high stakes on everything he did. His
whole identity rested on every single throw of the dice, until all the
A's in his courses didn't count any more, but the B+'s were a
tragedy. One of the things he had to learn was to have mercy on
himself. But the point was that he felt, especially the second time
he panicked so badly, that he would never, ever be able to face that
exam and that would be the end of his career. A few months later,
he just took his orals."

"Without the external factors changing?" asked Philips.

"Nothing changed, except that he was now getting a lot of
support to tide him over a difficult period. There was the psychiatrist, and all the people around him were ready to help. His girl-
friend was very firm with him, and said, 'Cut it out! You are
brilliant but you can't accept that, so sit down and work!' She was
very intelligent about this, and actually gave him assignments. He
said, 'I can't pick up a book. I can't study. My mind goes blank at
the sight of a book.' She said, 'I don't care. You sit in front of that
book and turn the pages.'"

"They're still together?" Moss asked.

"They just got engaged. One's first impulse with such a person is to be terribly gentle and to go along with his gambits. But
here, a good shove from people who obviously cared really worked."

"Yes," said Philips briskly, "I do think the attitude of my parishioner's husband is the worst possible thing for her. That's one reason I want to work with him at once, to see if he can be more supportive. At the moment, when she says, 'I feel terrible,' he says, 'Yes, I know, dear.' "

The consultee's manner had now become energetic and less anxious as he came to realize that Jane's depression might improve. Philips had found proof of her inevitable deterioration in the case of the second depressed parishioner who had never recovered despite years of treatment. The consultant opposed this gloomy view not by direct, cognitive arguments, but by offering the counterweight of another case, where the outcome had been quite different. By answering Philips's fears in the terms that he had chosen, the consultant achieved faster results.

"Maybe the husband would do more if he could see some clear-cut alternative," the consultant continued. "Maybe he's doing so little because he doesn't see what he *might* do."

"I think I'd better take all this advice down," said Philips suddenly, pulling out pen and notebook and making notes hurriedly.

"This man has been in this situation quite a while," the consultant added. "He might have a pretty restricted view of what the situation is really like."

"You're absolutely right," said Philips. "Especially since there is such a hopeless tone about so much of what she says. I'll try and get this solved by next time so I don't have to bring this up again," he added in some embarrassment.

"I'd like to hear what happens," said the consultant firmly, and the group agreed. "I'd like to know what the husband's views are of the whole situation. And one shouldn't discount a psychiatric evaluation. Treatment was a great help to my brother's friend and it might work here too. I think you mentioned at one point that Jane's father was willing to pay for her to see someone?"

"But would she be willing to go?" asked White.

"It seems to me," the consultant said, "that she might wonder whether psychiatric evaluation might imply that she had to give up her contacts with her minister. She might think that this was a substitution, a replacement, while it need only be the *addition* of another point of view." Implicitly, this was reassurance for Philips that he would not be shouldered out of the case, since he so clearly wanted to remain the primary caregiver.

"Well," said Apple, "it's hard to predict people's reactions to suggestions like this. For all we know, she might welcome it as a great relief. Perhaps if you raised the question with her, you'd get an answer."

"Yes," Philips agreed uncertainly.

"Does the husband think of this possibility?" the consultant asked.

"I don't know," Philips admitted.

"He sounds like someone who keeps his shoulder to the wheel and doesn't look up as often as he might."

"I think I could help him," said Philips, "by asking him what he'd like to see, what possibilities he sees for this entire situation. I think I could really listen to what he has to say."

"You'd have to be very careful," White advised, "when you brought up the possibility of a psychiatrist that Jane didn't get the idea that you wanted to get rid of her."

The group agreed.

"You'd have to define things," the consultant said. "An evaluation doesn't presuppose an outcome of long-term treatment."

"Perhaps you could find a psychiatrist who could explain this to her with whom you could discuss the matter afterward," Griffin suggested.

"Man, I'd like to know that psychiatrist," Philips remarked. The group then spent a quarter of an hour exploring the various possible sources of psychiatric care in Philips's area and suggesting ways of contacting them.

As the session ended, the consultant said, "After all, Jane is suffering from a depression. That is not some vague discomfort of the spirit. It's a medical condition, a real disease, and doctors have ways of treating it. Why should this woman suffer so much when she might be helped?"

Philips looked immeasurably relieved to have the condition that he had been regarding fearfully reduced to a relatively comprehensible medical category.

Analysis

One might legitimately ask why the consultant had spent so much time urging Philips to get his parishioner to a psychiatrist instead of simply offering to see Jane himself. Had he done so, he would have disrupted the consultation relationship by becoming an active agent, relieving the minister of a measure of direct responsibility for his case, and hence depriving him of the opportunity to expand his own skills. It would also have been subtly belittling, since it would have confirmed for a man who was already unsure of his competence in a particular category of cases that he was indeed beyond his depth, and that the consultant was now coming in to rescue the situation. This loss of self-esteem would not occur if the consultee were himself to decide that mental health care was indicated for a parishioner after weighing the ideas of the group. He would then retain his autonomy and self-respect.

By not offering to intervene, the consultant was ensuring that his own role in the minister's work would be temporary. Consultation, after all, is designed to be time-limited. Direct intervention in the case would imply that in future the minister could again refer people to the consultant, who would then become an indispensable, continuing part of the clergyman's network of resources.

In consultation, the case at issue is used as a pattern for similar ones in the future so that the minister will learn to manage such situations on his own; but this increased self-reliance means that he must also learn to identify specialized needs that do require referral elsewhere. Therefore, one of the goals of the consultant is to teach the consultee the importance and the method of establishing and maintaining links with a range of resources in his own community. This end would hardly be served if the consultant were simply to give the clergyman an easy alternative to forming such contacts by himself entering into competition with local specialists. That might seem cheaper in the short run, though it would turn the consultant into a traditional clinician, whose professional activities were perforce limited to his own caseload, which, however it grew, could never satisfy the needs of all the mentally ill in the community. But in the long run, it would be self-defeating, since it would leave the minister stranded if he or the consultant were ever to move from that area. The clergyman would then be no better equipped than before to find another psychiatrist. Consequently, this consultant pressed Philips on a number of occasions to discover and use various facilities in this community rather than to muddle through on his own or to rely on the consultant. And it is significant that Philips, as an experienced consultee, never asked the psychiatrist to see Jane, since he knew that this was inappropriate.

Having said this, we must add a proviso. In cases where there is a clear and immediate danger to the client, such as risk of suicide, the consultant, by virtue of his psychiatric training and the fact that he is a clinician licensed by the community, does have responsibility if there should be a catastrophe. He must use his judgment, therefore, to assess, albeit on the basis of hearsay evidence, how acute and imminent the danger might be. If he decides that it is too great, he may have to push the consultee aside and step into the case to protect the client's life or sanity.

The consultee, having told the consultant of a possible risk, can rely on the fact that the consultant will bear basic professional responsibility for the outcome, even though the consultee might have ignored advice from the specialist that could have averted tragedy. In practice, consultants are rarely forced to intervene in this way, since professionals of the level of sophistication to become consultees in the first place by and large know when the danger level is rising. Then, rather than asking for consultation, they refer the case at once to local hospitals or agencies. Nevertheless, the possibility of such a situation has to be borne in mind.

In this case, the psychiatrist judged that the risk of Jane attempting suicide was high but not high enough that he need personally intervene. He knew that she was being watched by her father and husband and by a family doctor who was currently treating her for a chronic respiratory condition. He could also rely on Philips, who, despite his perplexity, was completely adequate in any real crisis. At the moment, the minister was inhibited by his own emotional links to the abstract issues of the case; but his view of Jane's plight was clear enough for the consultant to have no doubt that if real and immediate danger threatened, Philips would act appropriately. What the consultant wanted to ensure was that matters need never approach so near a crisis—that Jane would be helped long before she was driven to desperation.

Outcome

Philips left the meeting in an energetic and hopeful mood. The following week, he still looked cheerful and relaxed.

"Well?" everyone asked.

"I saw them both the other night. I think one of the most helpful ideas that came out of last week was that the husband had to be helped to get some clear notions of how he might handle the situation. So we all met, and it was very, very good. She was more animated; she actually yelled a few times, which was fine, since every other time I'd seen her, she'd whispered. This time she was much more relaxed.

"I brought up the whole question of how her depression affected Patricia and her husband—how they felt about it, and how she felt about it herself. It was very constructive and helpful. He relaxed, because I was able to challenge her position, as he had not been able to do, while at the same time supporting her but not always going along with her. I intend to see them together again."

"What did the husband feel that this had done for him?" the consultant asked.

"I think he felt relaxed from the burden of taking care of Jane's problem all by himself. I think he felt ever so much better that I was there with him and Jane. I can't put my finger on it more clearly. I think he expressed his confusion about her; I don't know if he'd done so before."

"And their interaction was about as you'd understood?" the consultant asked.

"It was better than I thought. Somehow, I felt that both of them were more open to each other than I'd expected. And she was so much more relaxed. It could be she was discovering things."

"What one might hope for," the consultant said, "is that with your backing, he might feel stronger and be more supportive to her, while his own anxiety about the situation is reduced. That would be an ideal combination; and at this point, it doesn't look impossible."

"My impression was that he was just beginning to get a glimmer that there might be some possibility of improvement," Philips continued. "I think that over the years, he'd sort of turned off, and had hidden from the fact of her emotional upset. I thought that he was now beginning to be willing to look again."

"He might feel that he could afford to notice more, if he feels less alone," the consultant said.

"That's a good way to put it," Philips agreed. "I think this was what was beginning to happen to him. He made some self-deprecating remarks about his work, and I didn't accept them. I just felt that I could infuse a little more confidence in him about himself. The first time I talked to him alone, the more he talked, the more depressed he became, and I just terminated. I didn't know what to do with it. He didn't understand her, he didn't understand himself. This time, there wasn't any of that; he was less hopeless."

"I wonder if a couple of months from now," the consultant said, "it will turn out that the fact that you and the husband established contact with each other has helped both of you to support her; that it will produce greater results than would have come if each of you had worked separately."

"I had been completely unaware until this session that he had the feeling that he had to bear this thing all by himself, and he just didn't know what to do with this woman," Philips went on. "Now he has found somebody else who understands the situation and who was giving some alternatives to just sinking into a morass of misery that he saw himself falling into. There are enough strengths in him that there can be a change; and I have the feeling that she wants him to be stronger. Because although she basically runs everything, she'd prefer it if he ran things."

"I think you're telling us more than that," Waters said. "I think you're answering the question you quoted last week: can a depressed woman get better? It seems that you're now saying, there *are* possibilities here."

"That's true," Philips said quietly.

Here was evidence of success. Philips was now talking of Jane's and her husband's future and of his own work with the family in a hopeful, energetic tone. He no longer saw himself carrying the weight of the case alone, since he had discovered that the

husband could be helped to assume part of the burden. Philips was
no longer so ambivalent about Jane; he could accept her
domineering manner with more tolerance and detachment.

Half an hour later, an even more hopeful sign appeared.
After a review of a case presented by another group member, Philips
interrupted: "Can I ask a question about a depressed person? I referred last time to a woman who asked me, 'Does a depression like
mine ever get better?' She called me again last night and sounded
better than I've ever heard her before; but she said, 'I've got such an
awful depression and I don't think it will ever go away. They did
shock treatment on me and it didn't work.' At this point in the past
I had listened. Last night I didn't listen, I talked—and I wouldn't
let her continue her story. Would you say this was a good way to
deal with a person like this? Her husband was going away for three
weeks and she wanted someone to be with her at suppertime, which
is the toughest part of the day for her. I said I'd try to find someone
in the congregation to come and visit her at that time. I think this
came to me because of your story about your brother's friend, when
your brother didn't go along with him when he said, 'Oh, I can't
take that exam.' And your brother said, 'Yes, you *can* do it'; and that
was a way of approaching the whole situation."

Here was a noticeable reversal of Philips's earlier attitude
and manner. When he heard again from his chronically depressed
parishioner whose plight had so upset him the week before, he no
longer reacted with undue sensitivity. When he felt that "she
sounded much better than I've ever heard her before," he was hearing her through his own greater self-confidence. *She* had not
changed, *he* had. Instead of responding to her stereotyped gambit,
in which she made a bid for his sympathy and both felt helpless,
he now interrupted the sterile pattern with an offer of real help. The
woman was suffering in the absence of her husband. The minister
could send her company to tide her over the worst period of her day.
Instead of entering into collusion to confirm her in her identity as
a case of hopeless depression, he acted positively to reduce her
suffering.

What fascinated the consultant was the disappearance of inhibition from Philips's manner—of the stiff, literal grasping after
any concrete suggestion from the group to rescue him from confu-

sion. On this occasion, the consultee had assimilated a new point of view so well that he was able to use it selectively and to abstract from it to apply its principle to a quite different situation. He was acting once again like a fully independent, mature professional whose confidence and initiative were renewed.

It was clear that this process could not have taken place in one or two sessions. It required at least four meetings for Philips to work though his deep perplexity. What may seem surprising at first is that the group did not resent so much time and attention being given to one case. On the contrary, there was active participation throughout in helping Philips explore the material and in considering the implications for their own work. As the entire group came to share Philips's concern for Jane, so they participated in his relief and renewal of energy when they succeeded in helping him to find a way out.

Group Aspects of Consultee-Centered Consultation

We are now in a position to address the question posed at the end of Chapter Eight: Even though group consultation may be an effective vehicle for conducting consultee-centered consultation, is it not unduly time consuming for consultees and costly for their institution? Members of the group must wait their turn, sometimes for many weeks, to ask for help with a current case; most of the time are they not merely participant observers while the consultant is helping a colleague? Perhaps this setting offers an excellent seminar educational opportunity, because their colleague's case provides a living example of a professional predicament. But is it not likely that the unique leverage of the consultation method in influencing attitudes and feelings in personally meaningful cases will be restricted to the presenter, and possibly to a few of his colleagues who may by chance be disturbed by similar themes?

What emerges, however, from our analysis of the examples discussed in this and the preceding three chapters points in a different direction. Our consultants conducted the group sessions in such a way that they catalyzed an additional set of important influences. They stimulated group members to play an active part alongside the consultant in helping the presenter work his way through the complexities of his problem case. Group members did not just sit back and listen to the interchanges between the consultant and the presenter. In fact, over time they repeatedly alternated in the roles of *consultee* and *co-consultant*. In the latter role they were able to use freely and objectively their professional experience and rational judgment in analyzing the case and grappling with its complexities, and to appreciate how the presenter's perceptions and expectations were being constricted and distorted by his subjective involvement. They had repeated opportunities to experience the normality of the latter phenomenon, as they moved in successive meetings back and forth between the two roles. This enabled them to discover systematic ways of overcoming the expectable distortions without being inhibited by feeling that these were in any way shameful or reprehensible.

Our case examples demonstrate that group consultation conducted in this way results in many members learning to operate effectively, both when they seek support from others and when they offer support and tactful guidance. The consequence over time of such group experience is the acquisition not only of consultee and consultant skills but also of increased tolerance for the burdensome feelings and cognitive distortions in oneself and others that are energized when a person is involved in a sensitive case. This increased tolerance provides the freedom to operate in an orderly manner in overcoming these obstacles to effective planning and action. It is well worth the time and money that must be expended to acquire it.

CHAPTER ELEVEN

Program-Centered
Administrative Consultation

In program-centered administrative consultation, the consultant is invited by an administrator to help with a current problem of program development or organizational policies. He is expected to come into the organization, study its problems, assess the significance of the relevant factors, and then report his appraisal of the problem and his recommendations for dealing with it. This type of consultation is usually requested on an ad hoc basis, and the consultant is expected to present his report in writing after a fairly short period of study, ranging from a few hours to a few weeks.

Preliminary Considerations

In many respects program-centered administrative consultation resembles client-centered consultation, except that instead of a client the consultant focuses on an organization and instead of recommendations for case management he presents a plan for administrative action. In both types of consultation, the consultant is personally responsible for correctly assessing the problem and for giving a specific action prescription or range of alternatives to be carried out by the consultees. In both it is therefore essential that the consultant is working with accurate information and that he has the expert knowledge to deliver a wise plan. He does not have the leeway of the consultee-centered case consultant or administrative consultant, whose contract calls for him only to improve the consultees' understanding and operational effectiveness.

In client-centered mental health case consultation this situation is relatively simple. The mental health specialist's background in psychiatry, psychology, psychiatric nursing, or psychiatric social work is probably more than adequate to enable him to make a correct clinical assessment of the client's condition and to develop a valid recommendation for remedial action. In administrative mental health consultation, on the other hand, the nature of the program or policy problem is likely to require knowledge in organizational theory and practice, planning, fiscal and personnel management, and the ramifications of general administration, in addition to the clinical area.

Should the Administrative Consultant
Be a Mental Health Specialist?

When a human services organization seeks administrative help, should it call in a management consultant or a mental health specialist with administrative competence? Many problems could be dealt with equally well by either. There are generic aspects of the operations of all organizations, irrespective of their specific goals, so that many problems of planning, budgeting, personnel policies, and managerial controls in, say, a program dealing with the rehabilitation of mental disorders could be competently handled by an organizational specialist who has a modest knowledge of psychiatric issues. On the other hand, a mental health specialist may be in a better position than a generic consultant to suggest an approach when the problem lies in the content area of the program.

For instance, a traditional management consultant might give as good advice as a mental health consultant to a state mental health department on how to organize a statewide program of decentralized community mental health center facilities through contracts with general hospitals. The community mental health specialist, however, may be more likely to question some of the basic premises, such as the likelihood that such a system would reduce community rates of mental disorder.

A similar problem is not infrequently encountered in reverse. An organization that has little or no explicit mental health "product," such as an army unit or an industrial firm, may seek consultation for problems of productivity, program development, or personnel management. Such problems may involve a significant human relations factor—poor leadership, lowered morale, or communication blocks. All organizational consultants deal with such issues in their everyday work, but when these issues are particularly obtrusive, there may be special merit in invoking the aid of an administrative consultant who is a mental health specialist. Some administrators think so, and increasingly over the last few years community mental health specialists have been called in to give advice on human relations aspects of administration. As someone who has had experience in such cases, I have sometimes asked myself whether there was any difference between what I did and what would have been done by a management consultant.

I have not yet been able to answer this question to my own satisfaction, except to say that perhaps my image as a physician competent in mental health makes it easier for me to penetrate the social system quickly and to develop relationships of trust with informants at different levels. My clinical background in differential diagnosis allows me to focus quickly on salient issues without losing the implications of the whole complex of factors in which they are embedded. My psychiatric knowledge allows me to place interpersonal issues into perspective against the backdrop of organizational matters. And my community mental health practice skills enable me to collect and analyze data at the population level to complement what I pick up from individual and group interviews.

What emerges is a style of working and of communicating that may differ qualitatively from that of many consultants drawn from business management or organizational sociology, although I suspect that those whose personal talents are comparable to mine would probably focus on similar issues and make roughly similar recommendations.

Who Determines Relations with Staff of Consultee Institution?

In case consultation it is usually possible for the consultant to collect most of his data himself by conducting an appropriate clinical investigation of the client. In most examples of administrative consultation, on the other hand, the consultant must rely for much of his data on the staff of the consultee institution. He gets some of his information directly from individual and group interviews in which he taps their opinions, but additional information about the internal and external affairs of the organization comes from data that others assemble for him.

This means that administrative consultation often requires much staff time, and also that information usually not available to outsiders must be released to the consultant. These aspects must be specifically sanctioned by an appropriate authority in the organization, and this sanction must be clearly communicated to all concerned. One of the consultant's first tasks must be to appraise the area of the organization that is likely to be covered by his investigation and ensure that he has been called in by someone in a position to grant this sanction.

The assistant director of a state department of public health, who was in charge of the mental health unit, called in a consultant to advise on the reorganization of this unit in the light of developments in federal funding and state planning. A preliminary telephone discussion alerted the consultant to the fact that the reorganization problems were much affected by current plans involving the alcoholism and the crippled children's programs, which fell outside the jurisdiction of this assistant director. The consultant then stipulated that he would come only if he was called in by the director of the whole department, so that he could be assured that all relevant operations of the organization would be open to his investigation, and so that the person to whom his recommendations would be addressed would have the necessary authority to implement them if they were found acceptable.

Collaborating with wide sections of the staff involves two issues that sometimes lead to methodological difficulty. First, the program-centered consultant must realize that he is ultimately responsible for collecting and analyzing the information about the organization and developing the recommendations. He should not be misled, by the format of group discussions and his own group dynamics skills, into believing that his role is to catalyze the staff to collect only the information they think relevant and work out their own solutions.

No doubt the consultant will be interested in the staff's spontaneous suggestions and recommendations. But he must usually go beyond this, both in fact finding and in problem solving, because he will be held responsible for the assessment and recommendations. Moreover, because program-centered administrative consultation is usually a relatively short process, a few days to a few weeks, the consultant is operating under considerable time pressure, and he cannot afford to move at the slow speed that is comfortable for a staff hampered by communication blocks or morale problems. The approach is much different in consultee-centered administrative consultation, where the consultant's primary goal is helping the staff improve their own capacity to understand and master their problems.

The second, and related, issue is the consultant's use of authority with the staff. Remember that his consultee is not the staff group but the administrator who called him in. Their relationship must be coordinate and noncoercive, and the administrator must feel free to accept or reject part or all of the consultant's recommendations.

On the other hand, the consultant's relationship to the administrator's subordinates is not coordinate. To accomplish his mission he must have authority to move freely within the organization, to obtain information, and to require the participation of its staff, whether or not they agree with his plans and methods. Of course, in most instances he will be well advised not to throw his weight around and behave in an authoritarian manner. Moreover, he cannot use more power than the administrator has given him; and the authority of his consultee may be limited. But everyone must understand that the consultant's friendly appeals for staff collaboration are underpinned by the authority vested in him by the chief; and occasionally this power must be clearly and quickly invoked to overcome an obstruction and get the job done.

A consultant was called in by the head of a governmental department to advise on the reorganization of a certain division. On his arrival, he had a short conference with his consultee, who told him that all the technical arrangements for his seven-day stay would be handled by the division chief, who was not available that afternoon but who would meet with him the following day. The next morning the consultant was surprised when, instead of the division chief, his secretary came around to his hotel to welcome him. She brought a schedule of his appointments over the next five days that the division chief had prepared for him with exemplary efficiency. This program scheduled him in two-hour blocks to meet with most of the unit heads of the entire department but few line workers or supervisory staff. The consultant asked whether he could first meet with the division chief and discuss the schedule, because at first sight it did not seem to be the best way of using his time. The secretary replied that her chief was busy on urgent business that morning and would not be available till later that day.

This situation presented the consultant with a dilemma. Apparently, the division chief was defensive about his visit and was possibly avoiding him. There was nothing obviously wrong with the schedule except that it filled his time completely, leaving him little room to maneuver, and led him mainly into the general field of forces in the department rather than into the internal affairs of the division that he had been called in to investigate. It seemed rude to question the arrangements that had been so efficiently made on his behalf and that were being so obligingly presented by the charming woman who had been sent to guide him. To accept the arrangements graciously would calm the fears of the division chief, and perhaps there would be time later that day to discuss the program and negotiate its modification. On the other hand, the absent division chief might persist in being otherwise engaged; his name did not appear on the interviewing schedule until the fourth day! By then it might be too late to collect enough information to make a valid assessment.

The consultant asked the secretary where her chief was at that moment. With some reluctance, she divulged that he was chairing a meeting of his unit chiefs at a divisional office building on the outskirts of the city, several miles away from the headquarters building where the scheduled interviewees were awaiting him. The consultant told her that he was sorry that he could not accept the schedule of interviews and asked her to drive him to the divisional office and then to inform his interviewees at headquarters that he would see them at a later date. He dealt in a friendly but firm manner with her protests, and she took him to the divisional office.

Once there, he found out where the meeting was being held and marched into the room. To the consternation of the division chief, he interrupted the meeting, introduced himself to the assembled group, and told them about his mission and about his mandate from the head of the department. He said that their meeting provided him with an unexpected and marvelous opportunity to meet immediately with the principal people whose views he was eager to obtain. He then said that if the division chief had no objection, he would like to preempt the meeting time to discuss these matters, since he had traveled several thousand miles to get there and had very little time available to reach the core of the situation. The division chief was obviously furious but could do nothing but meekly go along. The consultant then engineered two hours of explosive and illuminating discussion, which laid bare the fundamental problems of the division.

Such high-handed and defense-attacking coercive behavior should be used infrequently in this type of consultation, but occasionally the situation demands strong action. More frequent is the need to influence the staff to realize that although the consultant carries the authority of the director, who may be perceived as authoritarian and coercive, the consultant normally holds his power in reserve and conducts his business on the basis of a free interchange with staff, to whose needs he is sensitive and on whose personal and professional rights he takes pains not to infringe. Only if there is an obvious attempt to obstruct him or to manipulate him too far off course must he invoke his power.

Consultation Procedure

Consultants should organize their interventions into the following series of steps.

Preliminary Contacts and the Initial Agreement

The first contact is usually by telephone, sometimes by letter, which is usually short and vague and best followed up by a direct telephone conversation.

The representative of the potential consultee institution who first writes or speaks to the consultant is rarely its director but usually a staff member who has been deputed to explore arranging consultation.

It is always worth trying to find out how the consultant's name came up for consideration, because it throws light on the administrators' expectations. Often they say they heard of him through some personal contact, that they have read some of his contributions to the mental health literature, or that they have heard of his successful consultation to a similar institution or with a comparable problem.

Occasionally, the initial contact may not be explicitly about a consultation but a vague request to give a lecture or conduct a seminar; only as this request is clarified does it transpire that what the administrators really want is to get to know him and to find out whether he is competent to help with their administrative problems. The consultant may agree to come out to give some lectures, but he would be well advised to suggest first exploring the situation to discover how his visit can be useful and what he should cover in his lecture. This often rapidly leads to a reformulation in which the need for consultation begins to take precedence.

The exploratory telephone discussions are usually helped by the consultant's very free admission of his ignorance about the problems posed. His posture should be the realistic one that although he is a specialist in mental health and in consultation, he cannot initially judge to what extent his knowledge and experience may be helpful in the situation. He must therefore find out more about it; and even if he agrees to come on a visit, he cannot guarantee to do more than explore the problems and be as helpful with as many of them as time will permit.

If the organization is one of a type that he has not yet worked in, he should frankly say so. He should indicate his hope that his experience with roughly similar organizations may be of help in this situation, but that he will need quickly to learn some of the elementary information about the institution and its program elements. He should emphasize, and in this he should be sincere, that he has no pat formula into which he can fit the problems of an unfamiliar organization.

This reality-based modesty begins to mold the administrators' expectations about the kind of assistance they can get from him. It also sets the stage for a series of exploratory telephone conversations, during which the rough outlines of the consultation problems are mapped out.

One initial goal of the consultant is to identify the authority level from which he should draw his consultee. Whenever he is in doubt, he should go for the person at the top, at least in the locality from which the call is coming. This is usually the person who made or authorized the decision to contact him. For instance, when I was phoned by the head of professional services of the Indian Health Area in Arizona, I suggested that I would consider coming as the consultant to the director of that area, who I discovered had considerable local autonomy over his program; I did not feel that my consultee should be the head of the Division of Indian Health in Washington, his immediate superior.

The person making the initial contact with the consultant is usually not upset by the suggestion that the primary consultee be his administrative superior. On the contrary, this is usually welcomed, since it shows that the consultant recognizes the need for direct contact with someone empowered to sanction his entry and carry out his recommendations.

If the initiative for the first contact did not come from the director of a service but from one of his subordinates, and if there is reluctance in involving the director, the consultant should think twice before accepting the invitation. He will almost certainly encounter insurmountable opposition from other unit heads at the same level. In such a situation the most the consultant should promise is to come for an exploratory visit. It will then be necessary to identify on the spot the person with power to sanction his fact finding and to implement his recommendations and then to find out whether this person wishes to accept him as consultant.

Two other issues must be settled during the preliminary telephone negotiations. The first concerns the length of the consultation visit and whether the consultant will come alone or with a team of assistants. This depends on the amount of ground to be covered in the assessment, the availability of consultant resources, and the financial constraints, which should be very frankly discussed and decided. The second point is to set up arrangements, so that the consultant may learn as much as possible ahead of time about the organization and its current predicament, and so that relevant staff members can begin to think systematically about the nature and boundaries of the problems.

I have found it useful during the preliminary telephone negotiations to have a talk with the director to begin to formalize the consultant-consultee relationship. During this discussion, I usually suggest that he appoint a task force, drawn from different units and administrative levels of his organization, to work with me in clarifying the nature of the problems. I say that I will eventually discuss my recommendations with this task force, so that they may be evaluated in light of day-to-day operations. I then ask the director to send me as much written material as possible, so that I can brief myself on the structure, history, traditions, and problems of his organization. I ask particularly for organization charts, with the names of current officeholders, and copies of recent internal memoranda that deal with relevant issues. I also ask the director and his staff to send me a rank-ordered list of the administrative problems on which they want my consultant help; and I make it clear that the relatively short duration of my consulting visit, which is all that we can afford in the light of mutual time and financial constraints, is not likely to permit us to work on more than a few of the problems at the top of the list.

Following these telephone discussions, there should be an exchange of letters between consultant and consultees, so that the details of agreements can be recorded and specifically ratified by both sides. This ensures that when the visit takes place there is a maximum opportunity for consensus to develop on what each side should expect to give to and receive from the other, and so that the time can be most productively used to solve the mutually agreed upon tasks.

Preparation for the Consultation Visit

Once the consultant has agreed to visit the consultee organization, he should use the intervening time to learn as much as possible about the setting and the problems, to anticipate the predictable issues, and to consider how to deal with them.

He will be helped by studying the documents the consultees sent. They provide not only a factual account of the organization but also a preliminary view of the value system, operating style, and preoccupations of its staff.

If the organization deals with a content area with which the consultant is unfamiliar, he should also use the lead time to do some library research. For instance, before my consultation visit to Arizona, I read a number of books about Indians; and while preparing for a consultation visit to Alaska, I read some books about Eskimos and an ethnographic account of one of the Eskimo villages I was being asked to visit. The knowledge I had gleaned, though superficial, was of great value in orienting me to what I should look for.

The more ignorant a consultant is about the content area or about the social, cultural, political, or geographical setting in which the institution operates, the bigger the potential return from reading a few books ahead of time. Not only can he tune in more quickly to the realities of the setting, but he can impress the consultees with his serious approach to understanding their situation and his awareness that he has a lot to learn from them. He can capitalize on his initial naiveté to arouse their trust, but by doing his homework he shows that this naiveté is not synonymous with simple-mindedness and so he also stimulates the building of respect.

The consultant should also try to use collateral informants. He can often find others in his city with a specialized knowledge about the institution or profession, or about the sociocultural and ecological setting in which it operates. They may also be able to suggest others he might talk with. Naturally, he will preserve the confidentiality of his assignment; but this is not difficult, because all he need divulge is that he is going out to study the local situation or give some lectures. Especially if the institution is in some distant place or unusual setting, I have found it very easy to get a lot of information from others who have been there before me; they are usually delighted to talk about their travels and to share their ideas on local customs. They may also provide the names of their own contacts in the area. Sometimes these can be useful, but I have often found that when I arrive it may not be politically expedient to look up these friends of my home contacts, because they are outside the circle of my consultee group or sometimes are members of opposition groups.

In addition to these general informants, an experienced consultant usually develops a network of specialized informants, some of whom can give him confidential background information about the field of forces in the consultee agency and possibly about recent events that led up to the consultation request. The telephone is a useful device for getting such information, and my long-distance telephone bill always rises steeply during the weeks before I travel to a program-centered administrative consultation. Confidentiality is still an issue in such communication, although the nature of the relationship between the consultant and his specialized key informants may permit him to go into more detail because he can trust them not to divulge the information. Even with close friends, however, I make it a practice to be explicit, to them and to myself, about the boundaries of confidentiality. Such self-discipline is valuable in preventing the little slips of the tongue that can have major negative consequences to a consultant's reputation.

During the preparatory period the consultant should also try to initiate meaningful communication with some staff members of the consultee institution, either by writing or telephoning individuals to clarify specific issues, or by starting a dialogue with the advisory committee that the director has set up. In my experience, these attempts usually do not get very far. The staff is busy at its day-to-day activities, and the consultant becomes a reality to them only after he has appeared on site. Apart from the liaison person with whom the initial negotiations were carried out, few others can be significantly involved in building up relationships at a distance. But some effort along these lines is worthwhile, if only to improve the consonance of expectations on both sides, so that when the consultant arrives he can as soon as possible begin to work collaboratively. I like to think of this as getting on the same wavelength, which implies recognizing the issues that seem significant to the others and learning something about values and semantic barriers that will have to be surmounted. In administrative consultation, time is usually of the essence, and anything that can be done, however slight, to accelerate this process before the consultant arrives is of potential value.

Initial Process on Site

After consultants enter the consultee organization, they should organize their initial interactions in the following series of steps.

Negotiating the Contract. The first goal of the consultant on arrival in the consultee organization is to confirm the identity of his consultee and to negotiate the final agreement, based on the earlier provisional contract. The length of the visit, the remuneration, and the nature of the consultation report will probably already have been fixed, but within this framework much still has to be decided.

The consultant must confirm the direct line of communication between himself and the authority figure with whom he is consulting. The goal is to ensure that this communication will not take place through intermediaries, important as it will be for the consultee to delegate staff members to help.

I have found it valuable to meet alone with the director as soon as possible after my arrival in his organization, and to have a confidential chat about his view of the problem and my possible contribution to its solution. This is also an important step in building the consultation relationship.

In this initial conversation, the consultant must ascertain what problems are most important to the administrator and must quickly judge which of these he can handle in the time limits. He should share with the administrator the predictable limitations of his contribution and should involve him in a joint decision about priorities.

The consultant should be alert to avoid a commitment for help with problems outside the administrator's jurisdiction, where it would be difficult to get information quickly and to implement recommendations. On the other hand, it is important for the consultant to allot some of his time and energy for independently assessing, if only superficially, the external field problems the organization faces in fulfilling its mission. In his initial conversation with the administrator, as they are planning how the consultant will spend his time during the visit, he should emphasize the necessity for this.

For example, during a ten-day consultation visit to the Alaska Native Health Area to advise its director on interpersonal aspects of administration, I felt that, despite my prior reading, I knew so little about the realities of Eskimo and Indian life and health problems that I could not make sense of the staff's internal predicaments. To understand the morale, communications, and personnel problems, I felt I needed firsthand experience of conditions in native villages and small towns, and I had communicated this view during preliminary telephone discussions before my visit. After I arrived, we discussed specifics of allocating my time, and we decided that after half a day's meeting with the core staff in Anchorage I should spend three days at a field health station about eight hundred miles away and go by boat up a nearby river to visit four Eskimo villages and fishing camps.

Another goal of this initial discussion with the administrator is to achieve consensus on the ground rules of the consultation process, especially the consultant's way of working with the staff. The consultant should ask the administrator to sanction his obtaining relevant information from them, and they should discuss how best to communicate this sanction to ensure their collaboration. But the consultant must also emphasize that he can operate effectively only if he can encourage staff to talk freely without fear that incriminating details will be divulged to their superiors. The administrator must explicitly sanction the consultant to withhold from him material that may reflect on personalities in his organization—at least information communicated in confidence—and he must also let his staff know that he has guaranteed this privilege.

Another point that should be clarified in the initial interview is that the consultant will probably arrive at his formulations by progressive approximations. He will collect some data and develop a preliminary formulation of a problem and some possible solutions. He will share these ideas with relevant staff members, to get their reactions and suggestions for modifications. This will then lead them to collect further information to refine his formulations, which will again lead to feedback and modification.

The consultant should ask the administrator to what degree

he personally wishes to be involved in this process. If possible, the consultant should encourage him to make himself available from time to time during the process, so that his own reactions to the unfolding pattern can mold the consultant's ideas. In many of my consultations I have arranged to meet the administrator for lunch or dinner intermittently during my visit; and I have found these opportunities for informal interchanges invaluable, both in keeping him informed and maintaining my sanction, as well as in checking out my hunches and involving him in shaping my plans.

It is also advisable at this initial meeting to set up some formal channels for presentation of the consultation report. The consultant will usually be asked for a written report, and this will be included and paid for in the contract. Preferably, it should be submitted within a couple of weeks after the visit, so that it can capitalize on the interest aroused by the consultant's personal interventions. The consultant should let the administrator know that all the points raised in the written report will have been discussed with him before the consultant leaves. The administrator should decide on a private reporting session and also on a formal presentation to key staff.

Getting a Bird's-Eye View of the Problem. To plan the consultation program, the consultant must be prepared to make a rapid initial assessment of the organization and the particular predicament. He will already have some vague ideas on this before he arrives, and his confidential talk with the administrator will have firmed up the picture. He should, however, be particularly alert, in his first formal and informal contacts with everyone connected with the organization, to modify and then reformulate the main outlines of this picture.

At this stage he should not be particularly interested in details but in a general pattern, which will guide him in regard to the people and units that he should explore. The consultant should not be afraid to play his hunches in formulating this initial gestalt, even on flimsy evidence; but he should be equally quick and confident in modifying the pattern in response to discrepant information.

Because of the time pressure, and because of the inevitable confusion in a newcomer entering a social system that generates numerous and complex stimuli on many different levels, the fate of the whole consultation may hinge on a valid initial formulation that will guide the consultant in choosing avenues to explore. More than any other aspect of consultation, I have found this to be most demanding on the consultant's native talent. I believe that consultation is an art, and that the basic asset which enables a person to be an excellent consultant is an elusive fundamental attribute of his total personality. It is this that molds his perceptions and enables him to react intuitively to his initial impressions.

I am aware that my approach to this issue is that of a clinician, who is trained to make a differential diagnosis by a process of successive approximations; and that a consultant who comes into this field from social science may use a different approach, collecting data and suspending judgment until they are analyzed. It would be interesting to explore this issue but, as elsewhere in this book, I am presenting principles derived from my own experience and that of like-minded colleagues, which therefore are consonant with our own style. Many students have validated that this is not entirely idiosyncratic, but I do not claim that these principles are universal; and I am confident that other styles of consulting are likely to achieve results as good or, in certain situations, better.

Fact Finding

Once the consultant has a clear idea of the principal problems, he must collect the information needed to understand them and to clarify the possible solutions. He does this mainly by talking to individuals and groups both formally and informally, and by observing the behavior of the staff as they go about their daily work and as they interact socially outside the job setting.

Some consultants supplement relatively unstructured individual and group interviews by developing interview schedules and questionnaires for use by auxiliary field interviewers, especially when they are assessing the attitudes and opinions of a large organization. I make little or no use of such survey techniques, and rely on a more clinical approach based on data collected by personal interview or direct observation.

I begin my interviewing by working through a list of key

people and groups that I have drawn up in collaboration with the director or his assistant. My first interviews are usually rather long and full, but as I learn more about the situation they become shorter, and I search only for supplementary information or for items that validate my hunches about particular patterns or issues. I often ask interviewees to recommend other informants, and once a pattern clarifies I cross check by a kind of triangulation process—I try to get perceptions of it from people with different points of view.

The process of fact finding usually goes through three phases. Initially, I have a relatively clear idea of what I am looking for, such as information about the causes of low morale in a certain unit, or about poor communication and collaboration between two divisions, or about ineffective performance in a particular department. This clarity emerges from the stated perceptions of my consultee or from my reformulation of his problem.

The second phase begins as I collect information from various people about their perceptions of the issue and their explanations of the factors involved. Characteristically, these stories conflict, and each interview brings to light fresh dimensions. My initial clarity gives way to confusion. It is important that I accept this confusion and do not try too early to resolve it by accepting any one ready explanation. The confusion is cognitively and affectively burdensome, but I have learned to allow it to continue until it resolves spontaneously when further information comes to light and is intuitively organized into a meaningful gestalt. The pressure for premature clarification is aggravated by the need to produce a quick answer to the consultation questions. Much experience has taught me a practical time perspective in this regard, which I use to maintain my equanimity during the phase of confusion.

I have found that, leaving aside the period of preliminary exploration and fact finding, I can safely allow one-third to one-half of the remainder of my consultation time to be spent in a state of greater or lesser confusion. During this phase I purposefully do not attempt to pin down a conceptual pattern or to tie ends together or to reconcile apparent incompatibilities in the data. Nor do I focus too narrowly on the lines of inquiry that I originally set up; instead I allow myself to roam the field in response to whatever cues appear of intrinsic interest. This is a process not unlike the unfocused attentiveness of an analyst to the free associations of his analysand. And as in that situation, I rely on my unconscious or my intuition to produce the integrating pattern.

The third phase is that of the gestalt closure. Suddenly or gradually, the pattern takes shape. I begin to see what appears to be happening and how different strands of factors on a variety of parameters are meshing to produce the present situation. In phase three, which can be called the phase of cognitive organization, the whole picture in all its ramifications is rarely seen immediately. Most often, part of the picture becomes visible and then in successive insights additional facets clarify and articulate with the rest, often as a result of looking for and finding supplementary information.

The list of informants varies with the three phases. In the first phase, a logical list is drawn up that mirrors the formal organization chart, people and groups who would be expected to relate to the problem. It is rare for a consultant to interview everyone on this original list, so he should make it clear that it represents only a tentative plan or else some sensitive members of staff will be insulted if they are bypassed.

The consultant does not complete these scheduled appointments because he soon moves into the second phase, and then he no longer is certain that he understands the focus of the problem. It is important that he not waste time by perseverating with his initial list, because this will probably lead to redundant data. In fact, it is this redundancy that usually alerts the consultant that his original choice of interviewees is ceasing to be productive. At this stage, the consultant should begin to work on an ad hoc basis, and he should choose his next couple of informants on the basis of leads suggested by his current interviewee.

When he reaches the third phase, the consultant will once again develop a clear idea of the relevant people to interview, because he will know who can be expected to validate his thesis or what new avenues he must explore to enrich or round out the picture. Some of these will be people he has previously seen and from whom he requires specific additional information or opinions.

During the second phase of confusion, some consultants maintain their composure by systematically exploring issues, such as the quality of morale, the nature of the leadership, how power is allotted and used, and communication process within the unit and between it and its surroundings. I feel that any system of this type, while supportive to the consultant, is often rather a waste of effort. I rely instead on my hunches and on cues of the moment to determine pragmatically what to do next.

In all phases of data collection, chance informal contacts often reveal valuable information. At social gatherings after working hours the consultant's presence usually catalyzes discussions that overtly or covertly deal with the salient issues. The consultant need feel no guilt about receiving information informally from the families and friends of the staff, or from workers in other branches of the organization, as long as he introduces himself clearly as someone who has been invited to study local organizational problems. On consultation visits a consultant is on duty twenty-four hours a day. This is quite fatiguing, but just as patients often make their most significant remarks as they are leaving the office, so the informal comments of a peripheral person at a social gathering may be the key to the consultation puzzle. The consultant's professional alertness on all such occasions may reap important harvests.

A consultant invited by the administrator of a large public health department to advise on improving morale and productivity was visiting the home of a senior staff member. She was introduced to another staff member who had just returned from vacation and so had not been on the list of interviewees. This individual, who had not heard about the consultant, was told briefly about the purpose of the visit and immediately launched into a list of the many administrative problems he was encountering in his communications with the specialists at headquarters. Among his complaints was his anger at being forbidden to use the telephone to consult with his senior colleagues about difficult cases. Instead, allegedly to reduce telephone expenses, he had been instructed to make such communications in writing. But the overworked specialists at headquarters usually did not reply for several weeks, and this often meant that his patients were ineffectively treated in the meantime, and some of them were kept in the hospital unnecessarily, which represented a much greater waste of money than the cost of a telephone call.

When the consultant returned to headquarters she asked the director of the department, without revealing the identity of her informant, why there needed to be such tight control over telephone expenses in an organization with a far-flung system of field stations. The director was amazed at the question and maintained stoutly that he actually encouraged telephone communication as a way of reducing travel costs. It emerged that the director had some months earlier been interested in analyzing the pattern of telephone communication and had asked field units for information about their use of telephone communication compared to written communication. He was amazed that this innocent request had become garbled as an authoritarian message prohibiting telephone communication.

This incident led the consultant to realize that the director, who was a quiet, nonauthoritarian person, was being misperceived by many of his staff, especially those in distant field stations, as "a behind the scenes manipulator" who was exercising an iron control over their every activity. This finding illuminated other aspects of the administrative climate, and the consultant began to understand that the image of the director was being molded, not by his actual personality, but by some of his subordinates who were creating a rigid, authoritarian atmosphere.

This example raises another issue. A mental health consultant who is called in to help deal with human relations problems in administration is expected to examine the influence of the administrators' personality, particularly personality disorders, on the problems of the organization. Information relevant to this factor is often pressed upon the consultant, and sometimes it is sufficiently dramatic and diagnostically intriguing to persuade the consultant to see it as the focal point of the predicament. This is usually an oversimplification and often leads to missing the main point.

The key person may in fact have a personality disorder, and this may be one factor in the situation, but usually there are also many other factors operating, and it is the constellation as a whole that determines the sequence of events, including why the administrator's idiosyncratic quirks are being currently stimulated and why he is being allowed or encouraged to distort his role functioning. The special merit of having an administrative consultant who is a mental health specialist is that his expert knowledge should enable him to see a personality idiosyncrasy in proper perspective, not as a stereotyped fixed "thing" but as a function of a person in a field of forces. The consultant must not be so impressed by the dramatic or peculiar aspects of one person's behavior that he fails to search for the interpersonal, intergroup, and system factors that are also operating.

For example, in a social welfare agency the morale in a particular department was very low, as evidenced by a high turnover rate among the junior staff. When the consultant interviewed the agency director and a number of the caseworkers, the consensus appeared to be that the prime cause of the low morale was the rigidly obsessional personality of the chief supervisor of that unit. This was apparently confirmed by her behavior and statements when she was interviewed. On the other hand, whether or not she had personality difficulties, it seemed clear from her account of the predicament of her unit that she was confronted by an extremely complex and difficult set of reality factors, related to the attitudes and problems of her client population, which was in a state of violent upheaval.

The consultant was not satisfied that the supervisor's personality disorder was the main cause of the low morale, and he asked the director to obtain the figures for staff turnover in that unit over the previous ten years. These revealed that the attrition rate of line workers had started rising five years previously; and even though it was higher now than in units dealing with other parts of the city, it had fallen significantly during the two years since the supervisor had taken over the unit.

Moreover, it appeared that the supervisor's personality difficulties were well known in the agency, and she had been transferred to this difficult unit as a kind of punishment. The headquarters staff were frustrated because they could not fire her on account of civil service protection, and they were expecting that she would make trouble wherever she was placed.

In addition, the consultant felt that the advisory board of the agency was ambivalent about its service to the client population served by that unit. This mirrored a major conflict in the community, and it had resulted in allocating a smaller slice of the agency's resources than might be considered optimal for that population— including appointing a supervisor with a poor reputation. Also, the supervisor was given less administrative support by headquarters staff than other supervisors in grappling with current difficulties.

By widening the focus of his data collection beyond the supervisor's personality disorder, the consultant was able to understand the richer complexity of the agency system and community supersystem problems, and within this framework to assess the significance of the various factors in developing suggestions.

During the third phase, of cognitive organization, and while the consultant is beginning to develop recommendations for solving the administrative problems, it is often valuable to assemble an ad hoc group from the various units of the organization that have a bearing on the issue. Such horizontal communication cuts across the usual boundary lines of vertically organized units. As these representatives talk about their perceptions of the problem and their suggestions for a solution, the consultant receives rich information with which to validate his hunches and to understand more clearly why certain "logical" remedies may not work.

The consultant must use such ad hoc groups sparingly. These meetings interrupt the usual routine of the organization, especially as they have to be convened at short notice and primarily at the consultant's convenience. Moreover, it is not unusual for such meetings to endanger the participants' defenses, which have been maintained by selective inattention to certain aspects of the problem and by lack of communication between particular units. The meetings may therefore be burdensome both for task-oriented and for affective reasons. It is a good idea to delay such meetings till the final stages, by which time the consultant has built up a good relationship with the staff and has begun to demonstrate that they can expect some concrete benefits in return for the burdens he is causing them.

A small but important practical issue in regard to fact finding is record keeping. A vast amount of data in the form of verbal and nonverbal communications, as well as documents and statistical tables, is usually rapidly accumulated. The consultant will be expected to keep the relevant issues constantly in focus and to have various details and facts readily available.

An excellent memory is a useful asset for an administrative consultant. Since I, unfortunately, have a poor memory, I have had to develop ways of compensating. Taking notes is the obvious answer, but this interferes with the spontaneity of the consultation process and adds a special burden to the consultant who wishes to focus his attention on the many complicated issues of an interview or a group discussion. I have sometimes been lucky enough to have an assistant who acts as a recorder, and this has been invaluable, although apart from information about names and titles of interviewees, I must admit that I really use them only to check my memory for a few details. Their value is mainly psychological—I do not have to be concerned that I won't remember some detail, because it is being recorded. This frees me to remember what I need. Interestingly enough, I do seem to remember the important things. The reason probably is that I immerse myself experientially so completely in the consultation situation and in the current life of the organization that for a while it is my life; the details do not have to be remembered as an explicit act.

When I have no recorder I take notes myself at the time. These are usually quite rough and consist mainly of cue phrases about topics or personalities. The only specific information I record meticulously is the name and title of individual interviewees and group participants. When I write my report, this information is essential, and it is quite frustrating not to have it readily available.

Another practice I have found useful is to spend a little time at the end of each day, or occasionally during a rest period while waiting for an interviewee, to summarize in writing the main points of the day's events. The time is mainly taken up in thinking; the writing usually involves merely jotting down a series of rough notes to remind me subsequently of the points. They are in no sense a narrative that would be understandable to anybody else.

Developing the Recommendations: Feedback and Modifications

As we have seen, the consultant's recommendations are developed and refined as a series of progressive approximations. He should discipline himself not to start this process until phase three of his fact finding, when he begins to get a clear idea of the dimensions and etiological constellation of particular problems. Suggestions for action during the phase of confusion are usually attempts at premature closure to escape the frustration; and ideas for solution that emerge during the first phase of initial clarity should be studiously inhibited, because almost inevitably they will be based on oversimplifications and preconceptions that miss the main obstacles of the situation.

If the predicament were so simple that an outsider could arrive at a sensible plan from a cursory review of superficial information, it would usually have been handled by the administrators without his help. In fact, the quick *tour de force* of a visiting expert, even if occasionally sensible, will have a noxious effect on the development of the consultation relationship, because the consultees will feel that the consultant does not have a proper respect for their intelligence and commitment to their task if he believes that he can immediately produce an answer to the problems that perplex them. This is complicated by the fact that consultees often test out the consultant by demanding just such an immediate answer from him. Their ambivalence will become apparent if he falls into the trap of accepting the gambit.

On the other hand, initial formulation of recommendations can also be delayed too long, with negative consequences. The consultant must continually pace himself in relation to the trajectory of his site visit. He must leave adequate time to refine his recommendations by discussing them with the staff. Under all circumstances he should try to avoid developing a plan and including it in his report without giving the staff a chance to discuss it. This is not merely a relationship-building issue but is based on our experience that unless people personally collaborate in developing a plan, they are less likely to accept it and work toward its implementation.

The main issue is that in the short time at his disposal the consultant cannot possibly obtain more than a superficial view of the life of the organization; although this may be sufficient to enable him to foresee the main impact of a recommendation, it will not be enough to tell him about its side effects and the consequences of reactive reverberations within the system. Only those who have a living experience of the organization are likely to be able to predict in detail the practical implications of the changes the consultant is recommending.

The seductive aspect of the undiscussed recommendation is that it usually seems clear-cut and logical, precisely because the ideas do not get confused and obscured by discordant facts and probabilities.

Having regard to all these considerations, consultants should aim to begin formulating their recommendations piecemeal and in tentative terms shortly after the third phase of fact finding begins— that is, as soon as they begin to understand clearly what some of the problems are and which etiological factors are involved. I make it a practice to open most of my interviews and group meetings from that stage on with a brief description of how the situation seems to me and what I think might be done about it, and then I ask the staff to react to my ideas, correct or modify them in the light of their more intimate knowledge of the local situation, and provide more information to broaden and deepen my understanding.

The consultant must not hide the tentative and exploratory nature of his ideas; he must be completely sincere and frank in soliciting divergent opinions. Many people are concerned lest a consultant, especially a mental health consultant, who is often stereotyped in Machiavellian terms, manipulate them by forcing his ideas onto them. They will be particularly alert to evidence that although he solicits their reactions, he is not really interested in any ideas that negate his own. Because of this, the consultant should be perfectly open about what he is doing and about the degree of his own commitment to any of the ideas he puts forward. And he should let people know whether or not he accepts their suggested modifications.

The consultant should not modify his plans merely because they disturb or arouse opposition among the organization staff. His recommendations almost inevitably will imply changes from accustomed patterns of thought and practice, and such changes often make some people uncomfortable. It is important that the consultant neither accept nor reject discordant ideas merely because of this factor. Instead, he should pay careful attention to both the emotional and cognitive responses to his tentative recommendations and in the light of this added information decide whether and in what ways to modify his recommendations.

A consultant's recommendation develops by accretion, like a snowball, getting progressively richer, more detailed, and more complicated, as he discusses it with different staff members. It is useful to conduct these discussions systematically at as many levels of the administrative structure as possible, and to feed back and forth between them.

The consultant might identify a problem at the level of a unit chief and explore it by talking to the chiefs of other units. He shares his tentative formulations and suggestions with them and then with the division and department heads and with the staff of the director's office. At each higher level of the structure he discovers new constraints and demands and modifies his plan to conform with them. Then he takes it back to the unit chiefs to see how it looks to them in its revised form and whether it is generalizable across units with different clienteles and working conditions. Eventually the consultant presents the latest revision of the plan to ad hoc groups composed of representatives of different levels of the structure and in which its horizontal and vertical reverberations can be assessed.

For instance, in my consultation with the Alaska Native Health Area, I was asked to advise on the recruitment and training of village health aides. I discussed this issue with the head of the area office of training services, who told me of his plans to establish a training program at the Native Medical Center in Anchorage, where Eskimos and Indians would be trained in elementary medical and surgical procedures and in practical nursing and then deployed in native villages, where they would be the local representatives of the doctors and nurses of the health service units.

When I visited a health service unit in the field and some Eskimo villages, I discussed the problem as seen from those levels; what had started as a simple matter of curriculum development and training techniques began to take on a different shape. It became clear that because of the vast distances involved and the transportation difficulties, the village representative of the health service should be more than a technical assistant to the doctors and nurses but should have considerable capacity for independent judgment.

Optimally, his duties should extend beyond first aid and simple nursing and doctoring in acute illness and accidents, to the important area of health education and disease prevention. This was all the more necessary because of major cultural barriers between the villagers and the staff of the health services, who were not succeeding too well in communicating the most elementary notions of personal hygiene and communal sanitation.

It further became clear that since the health aides were either volunteers or poorly paid, they were mainly recruited from low-status people in the villages. This meant that they had little influence among the villagers and achieved little effect in modifying the conditions of village life that were associated with high morbidity and mortality rates.

By the time I returned to Anchorage, I had developed the idea that the village health workers should not be relatively low-level, poorly paid medical and nursing auxiliaries but high-level and high-status village officials who would be members of, and responsible to, the village councils, the governing bodies of the villages.

Both in the field and in Anchorage I then discovered that my simple plan would be complicated by lack of funds to pay such village workers, by difficulties in gaining the collaboration of the village councils, by difficulties in deciding how the workers should be supervised, and by the fact that a number of other federal and state departments, such as the Bureau of Indian Affairs and the state health and welfare departments, were also currently planning the development of a network of village representatives. There was already a budgetary allotment for training village health aides, and this money had to be spent within the budget year or it would have to be returned.

The problem now seemed to extend beyond the domain of the office of training services and into the domains of other units of the Anchorage staff, such as health education, environmental sanitation, public health nursing, professional services, and the office of the director, including his native affairs officer. It also involved issues of the relationships between the Alaska Native Health Area and the Alaska branch of the Bureau of Indian Affairs, the Alaska state health and welfare departments, and a variety of other federal and state agencies, including a special federal field commission established to coordinate economic and social planning for the state, and a task force of the Office of Economic Opportunity and other federal agencies within the framework of the President's Economic Advisory Council. The dimensions and implications of the issue seemed to be rapidly escalating.

Since by this time I had only about four more consultation days left, and a variety of other problems also on my agenda, I rapidly initiated a series of exploratory and feedback sessions with relevant members of the Anchorage staff. I requested a meeting of all the unit and division chiefs most immediately involved and started a discussion of my evolving plan. I then discussed with the native affairs officer how statewide native organizations and village councils might best be involved, and how the plan might be modified to secure their collaboration. With his cooperation, I met the leaders of statewide native associations. I talked with the director about possibilities of collaboration between his agency and the other major federal service agency involved, the Bureau of Indian Affairs; and he arranged for me to discuss the plan with its director in Alaska. He also arranged for me to talk to an appropriate representative of the Federal Field Commission for Alaska.

In the light of these discussions I then met again with the director of the office of training services and suggested that whatever the outcome of my ambitious plans for village workers, he should, as an interim measure, move his upcoming training program for health aides from Anchorage to one of the health service units in the field, and if possible organize some of the training sessions in native villages; and that he should enlarge the focus of this training from first aid and practical nursing to health promotion and maintenance through community development and health education. I also suggested the advisability of involving health educators and native leaders, as well as Bureau of Indian Affairs community development personnel, in planning and implementing the training program, as a step toward the eventual goal.

As I moved among the individuals and groups at the different levels of the health agency and in the client population and contiguous agencies, I was doing more than gathering information about their individual, group, and organization needs and resources and their criticisms of my formulations of the problem and my successively more sophisticated suggestions for solving it. I was also being stimulated to bring to bear on this issue my background knowledge of psychosocial and sociocultural processes. What eventually emerged in my mind, and was discussed and then committed to paper, was not only a series of concrete suggestions but also a statement of some philosophical principles that I felt were relevant guides to planning. The following excerpt from my report illustrates this.

> A fundamental problem will be how to pool the agency contributions in order to pay the salaries of Village Workers and how to involve Village Councils in their selection and supervision so as to provide Councils with the real power that is indispensable for full involvement, and yet protect the program from the changing winds of local politics and ensure that the governmental agencies fulfill their several goals. The local people must be given sufficient power so that they can control the type and rate of delivery of our professional offerings, and tailor them to the currently perceived needs of the village population. We must provide them with the community organization skills so that they can effectively resist those of our well-meaning efforts which they realize are not in the best interests of their people. In the 1890's the Moravian missionaries made very effective use of village "helpers" who were recruited and trained along similar lines to those which I am advocating. They used these workers, however, to destroy the essential basis of the village cultural system. They did much good, but they have left us and the villagers with a legacy of demoralization because of their indiscriminate attack on the cornerstone of Native life. We must avoid their mistakes even though we make use of social techniques similar to the ones which they proved to be so effective.
>
>   The only people who have a deep enough understanding of the essential needs and conditions of indigenous life to know how far and how fast to go in supporting and supplementing indigenous strengths by means of the professional resources and knowledge of our modern civil-

ization are the native Americans themselves and their leaders. We must therefore develop such a system that protects them against our enthusiasm and drive and against our professional and bureaucratic blind spots—even though this will inevitably frustrate some of our most cherished schemes and timetables. Paradoxically, true and lasting progress with a minimum of unexpected bad side effects will be quicker and surer that way.

We must be prepared for the villages to move at widely differing speeds in their capacity to make proper use of our assistance. I believe that of the more than 300 villages in Alaska we will find at the present time no more than about 50 in which the Village Councils are already well enough organized and led to be able to collaborate effectively in the Village Worker program. I feel that we should restrict our initial efforts to this sub-group. At the same time, the regional community development workers should begin to work with the most promising of the remainder in order to help the villagers identify their natural leaders and to organize their community life under their direction. Only when a Village Council achieves an appropriate level of development and power should the village be admitted to the program.

Continuing Contact with the Director

As already indicated, the consultant should arrange to have as much contact as possible with his principal consultee while he is assessing the problems and developing recommendations for solution. This is partly to ensure that in the rapidly expanding field of his interest in a particular problem, he remains in touch with the practical realities of his consultee's preoccupations. He must be in a position to receive the guidance of someone whose role encompasses an overview of subsections of the organization and also its connections and overlaps with other systems. The director's reactions also allow the consultant to assess the short-term and long-term acceptability of his recommendations.

In Alaska, for example, my daily contacts with the director

of the health agency not only helped me decide quickly whom I should interview and smoothed my path, but also reassured me that my broad and innovative approach was in line with the task demands. Whether or not my ambitious suggestions will ever be accepted or implemented, I was convinced from my discussions with the director that they fitted within the framework of his own conception of his mission and that envisaged by his superiors in Washington. In fact, he urged me to feel free to reappraise the policies of his agency in the light of whatever fundamental principles my own past experience and basic philosophy made relevant. I was able to validate that he meant what he said by his reactions of interest and his practical suggestions during our daily informal discussions.

In other cases, a consultant may not be so fortunate in gaining such frequent access to the head of the consultee organization, who usually has many pressing demands on his time besides the consultation. In such instances, the consultant should make a determined effort at least to touch base with him now and again during the consultation visits. This will ensure that at the formal reporting sessions before his departure there will be consonance between the focus of consultant and consultees. At that advanced hour it is too late for the consultant to make a major readjustment in his views to make his appraisal and recommendations seem feasible to the consultee group.

The Consultant's Recommendations

It must already be clear that the consultant's final recommendations are developed collaboratively between him and various people within and outside the organization. Some of the ideas may be taken directly from them, but they are likely to have a different impact when they are reformulated and enunciated by an outside specialist.

The consultant should acknowledge privately his indebtedness to individuals whose ideas he incorporates in his recommendations, but as always he should preserve the confidentiality of these communications. He might embarrass both the staff member and himself by publicly announcing that of all ideas he had heard, he favored those of Mr. X. Moreover, he will almost certainly have changed the content or emphasis; and in any case, he must accept the entire responsibility for anything he recommends.

The best way for the consultant to deal with the question of acknowledgment is to make a blanket admission of his debt to various collaborators and his other interviewees as an introduction to his remarks at the reporting sessions and in his final report.

No consultant worth his salt will merely sift the suggestions of the consultee group and piece together those that seem most sensible into a set of recommendations. This may be useful, but it is not sufficient. The consultant is expected to add ideas of his own, by bringing into focus forces from hitherto unrecognized relationships within and outside the organization, and by suggesting novel avenues of exploration or remedial action.

In formulating recommendations for action, the consultant should usually have a double focus. First, he should recommend what should be done immediately, or in the near future, with resources currently available. Such action should be sensible in regard to achieving a specified goal; it should also be acceptable within the framework of existing assets, liabilities, and values of the organization.

Usually this type of recommendation will involve additions to the existing duties of the staff, or modifications of role that make their work more complicated. The consultant should ensure that he is not asking more than they are able to accomplish, and that he has also suggested how they can be supported in their additional or new responsibilities.

Not infrequently this type of recommendation will be unpopular in certain quarters. Change is often painful. Addition or redistribution of responsibilities to one segment of the organization may involve reducing the status of another segment. Some people may be demoted or even lose their jobs as an immediate or eventual result of the recommendation.

A mental health consultant will be particularly sensitive to the possibility of infringing on the rights or well-being of individuals as a consequence of his recommendations for organizational change. He will try to prevent this as much as possible; or if it is inevitable, he will try to suggest ways of remedying the damage by discussing with the administrators ways of finding a new job inside or outside the organization. Wherever possible, he should give those whose status may be diminished an opportunity to confront him and express their feelings and ideas. If they do not persuade him to modify his recommendation, he should frankly say so and explain his stand. He should, however, not change his position merely because it is not acceptable to certain parties. They will have their chance after he has gone to protect their rights and values as the institution decides to accept or modify his plans.

It is not part of the role of an administrative mental health consultant to allot blame for an administrative impasse or failure, but he should objectively and honestly analyze difficulties and recommend remedies that replace areas of organizational weakness by opportunities for strength.

A consultant who was called in to advise on the reorganization of a state mental health department developed a series of recommendations focused on decentralizing many activities. He suggested changing two line positions, chief psychologist and chief social worker, each administering a large division, to the staff positions of senior psychologist and senior social worker. Most of the workers would be incorporated under the line authority of the heads of individual units such as hospitals, clinics, and rehabilitation centers. The staff specialists at headquarters would, in the new plan, provide their colleagues with technical guidance and consultation and in-service training. They would also help directors of peripheral units recruit and select workers in their discipline.

The chief psychologist was quite upset about these ideas. He argued that to put psychologists under the direction of heads of units who were mostly psychiatrists would stifle their professional creativity. He pointed with pride to his division's record of growth and published research. He felt that maintaining a compact reference group improved morale and increased recruitment possibilities. When none of these arguments swayed the consultant, he raised a personal matter. He reported that the state government was about to reorganize its civil service rating system, and under the proposed scheme he would be recategorized to a lower grade. The consultant said that this would be most regrettable and that he would raise this matter with the director, who might be able to help, but that this did not alter his basic advice. The consultant made his recommen-

dation, which was accepted by the director and by the state authorities. Unfortunately, the psychologist did not wait to see whether his
civil service grade would be reduced. He resigned shortly and took
another job with higher pay and increased responsibilities. Neither
his career nor the interests of the department were apparently
harmed by the changes.

The second focus of a consultant's recommendations goes
beyond the immediately feasible changes to an eventual, long-range
situation. His freedom from the institution's day-to-day concerns,
together with his breadth of vision, frees him to look to the future.
The consultant should make it clear that he is taking a distant view,
envisaging long-term goals that can be attained only with different
resources of staff, finances, and administrative structure. This aspect
of his functioning is usually much valued by the consultees, as long
as his long-term recommendations have some practical feasibility
and as long as they supplement a series of down-to-earth recommendations for achieving short-term goals. I have found that most consultees appreciate a consultant with his head in the clouds as long
as his feet are firmly on the ground.

The Consultation Report

The report should communicate in writing material that has already been discussed with the key people involved. In this written
form, it can be disseminated widely and can be shared with authorities who may be involved in implementing the changes. Because
of this, the report should be rather formal and should contain
enough information that it can be understood by those who have
had no personal contact with the consultant. It may become part of
the organization's archives and be consulted for years to come.

Each consultant will undoubtedly develop his own style of
reporting. Over the years, my reports have begun to take on a consistent structure.

Introduction. I begin with an introductory section that
briefly describes the setting, the reasons for my being invited in, and
an outline of my activities during the consultation visit. I usually
end this introduction with some personal remarks of appreciation

to those whose hospitality I enjoyed. In my report on a consultation visit to the Indian Health Area in Phoenix, I mentioned the "general atmosphere of warm welcome extended" to me and my family by its director and his staff and also said, "We were especially impressed by their solicitude for our religious dietary requirements, a sensitivity to our cultural idiosyncrasies which I feel is an indication of their basic respect for others with different ways of life. This must be a significant element in fostering good relationships with the Indian population." In an appendix to the introduction, I list the individuals and groups with whom I had contact.

In the introduction to my report on my Alaska consultation, I wrote:

> During my stay I was happy to be invited to participate in some of the recreational activities of the staff of the Service Unit. I attended a farewell party for the Deputy Nursing Director, at which I watched a fascinating demonstration of Eskimo dancing. One morning I went out fishing for salmon on the Kuskokwim with Dr. _____ and his family. We fished Eskimo style on the incoming tide with a drifting gill net, and had what I was told was a moderately successful catch for the time of the year—10 silver salmon. I took the prize of the catch, a 17 lb. fish, back to Boston as a memento of my visit.
>
> We returned to Anchorage on August 28th carrying a severely ill infant complete with intravenous drip on the plane with us. This I was told was frequent practice in order to conserve travel costs of accompanying staff.

Such personal items are not only a sincere expression of appreciation for the human interchanges during the visit but serve to introduce the consultant and the staff as understandable people with whom the readers of the report can empathize.

Philosophy. Following the introductory section, I occasionally include a short theoretical section, presenting my point of view about a central theme of the consultation. For instance, in one consultation, where I was called in to advise on methods of in-service training in consultation, I wrote a short section titled "Definitions," in which I summarized my approach to consultation and differentiated this process from administrative direction, administrative supervision, technical supervision, and educational programs. This systematic approach set the stage for me to use the terms throughout the report without repeated explanation. Even when such conceptual expositions are not necessary for the whole report, communicating my philosophy may be significant in particular sections. The quotation earlier in this chapter from my Alaska report about my views on safeguarding the power of dissent among villagers is a good example.

An administrative consultation report is not a literary endeavor but a business document. On the other hand, many of the consultant's recommendations are heavily value-laden, and his personal assumptions and beliefs should be made explicit wherever possible, so that consultees can take them into account in deciding whether to accept his ideas. All communications by the consultant should be designed to maximize the consultees' freedom of choice and to reduce their tendency to accept suggestions because of dependence on higher authority.

Body. The body of the report is a systematic statement of problems and short- and long-term suggestions for grappling with them. I usually classify the problems according to, for example, organizational level or geographical location. In my Alaska report, for example, I dealt successively with problems at the village level, the service unit level, the Native Medical Center in Anchorage, and the area office. Since any organization is a reverberating system of interdependent parts, any such classification makes for difficulties, and there must be constant cross reference and not a little repetition; but I find that the alternative approach of systemwide exposition usually leads to greater confusion.

I follow my exposition of each problem or subproblem with a list of suggestions and recommendations, rather than dealing first with all the problems and then discussing all my recommendations. I also have found it useful to enumerate the problems and suggestions systematically, with appropriate headings and subheadings, so that the consultees can use my report more easily in their follow-up discussions. For example: "Problem 2.2. Low Morale of Social Workers." Then reasons for low morale are listed successively, *a* to *e*. "Recommendations 2.2. Practical Steps to Raise Morale." Steps are listed successively, *a* to *g*.

Whenever I see no clear way of dealing with a problem, I do not hesitate to confess my uncertainty and to provide a series of alternative suggestions for further exploration. When I am a little more sure of myself, I give a list of tentative suggestions. When I am confident that I have some workable ideas, I offer firm and detailed recommendations. If I see alternatives, I say so. If not, I express a definite opinion. I do not believe in pretending to be uncertain in order to preserve a coordinate relationship with my consultees. On the other hand, my style and the whole tone of my report are explicitly nonauthoritarian and calculated to open questions rather than to close them off. For example, in a consultation report about a county health department I wrote:

Problem 2.4. Difficulties of Communication Among Specialists and Across Administrative Boundaries

A problem perceived by most of the specialists with whom I talked is that of promoting better communication among specialists and across administrative boundaries. In particular, there was dissatisfaction with the amount of communication among the four chief units in Centerville— the Offices of Program Services, Environmental Health, and Administration, and the group of department heads of the County General Hospital. Each of these units encompasses specialists who could be making more of a contribution to the work of the others, and each seems to be operating in too self-contained a manner. Some specialists felt that they were not being called in often enough by those in other units. Some felt that other units did not respond adequately when asked for assistance. An example of the former is the feeling among staff of the Office of Administration that they usually become involved with other units only to communicate the constraints of State policy. They are thus often seen negatively as opposing and limiting the plans of their colleagues, and as exercising undue control over professional decisions because of their fiscal knowledge and power. Since they are not health professionals, they feel that they are often perceived as non-professionals, that their expertise in such fields as systems organization, program planning, and personnel management is not respected, and that consequently their guidance in such matters is not sought.

Suggestions 2.4.

(a). This problem is common to all organizations, and is no more marked in Centerville than elsewhere. I know of no ideal way of dealing with it. Differentiation of function and bounded units are essential in the structure of complex organizations; and lower communication across boundaries than within them is an inevitable aspect of the operations of a sub-system.

It might be useful for Dr. Jones [the health officer] to devote special attention to counteracting this difficulty in his organization. He might develop formal ways of ensuring that people from different units worked together on specific tasks so that they would have to learn to talk to each other, and thus discover each other's specialist capacities. This might be done by establishing *ad hoc* task forces whose members are drawn by design from each of the four main units, as was done in preparation for my visit. Such groups should be given a concrete short-term task to accomplish, and should then disband, in order both to prevent the erection of new ingroup boundaries, and to provide an opportunity for involving others in this kind of activity.

(b). One type of task force which has special relevance for my theme is that of a group of colleagues from Centerville who travel together to a District Office. At present such joint trips are encouraged, but are left to individual initiative, and they occur less often than they might. Such joint trips do not necessarily involve a saving in staff time, because if three specialists all want to talk to the same person at a District Office they may block each other in the field. Team consultation in group meetings is expensive in staff time and should be used only when specifically indicated. No person should attend a consultation or supervisory session whose presence is not absolutely necessary—spectators waste the agency's money.

Despite these cautions, I believe that Dr. Jones might well consider convening task-forces of specialists to make joint trips to District Offices—either as part of a long-term plan or in reaction to a current crisis.

(c). It might also be worth exploring a team approach to consultation with an appropriate District Office on a demonstration basis. In this case a core group of consultants could be assembled from the four main units, and given the long-term task of systematically exploring and handling the problems of the District Unit and its catchment area. This would involve both group and individual contacts with its staff, as well as planning and evaluation meetings which could take place in the car travelling to and from the site. Such a project would have both the goal of helping the staff of the District Office and also the function of promoting communication among Centerville specialists.

Follow-Up

In this, as in other types of consultation, efforts should be made to get follow-up information to assess the impact of the intervention. This assessment is somewhat easier here because it is likely that formal administrative action will be taken to implement the consultant's recommendations, and this will be a matter of record.

The consultant should discuss, during his last conference with the head of the organization, his interest in learning what transpires. His request will probably be received positively, since it will be seen as evidence that he has become committed to the organization and its future welfare. I feel that the highly cathected relationship between the consultees and myself should continue after my departure, and should remain a significant bond during the writing of my report and its consideration by the consultee group. Their communication to me of their reactions to the report and their plans to deal with the issues I have raised brings the consultation to a close; after that, the vividness of the emotional encounter begins to fade into memory.

In some instances, I have been called back as a program-centered administrative consultant for a second and third visit, sometimes for continued consultation on the original problems but more often for fresh problems several years later. The staff by then had usually changed; and apart from some familiar figures, the consultation relationship had to be rebuilt from the beginning. Such experience confirms my feeling that this type of consultation should usually be considered a circumscribed encounter, in which consultant and consultees rapidly develop an emotionally charged working relationship for a specific task, and then bring this relationship to a close when the task is accomplished.

As in other types of consultation, evaluation of success is very difficult. Administrative changes in line with the recommendations may be a sign of success, especially if long-term follow-up indicates that the underlying problems seem to have been resolved. Unfortunately, such long-term follow-up is rarely possible, because once the consultation report has been acted on, communication with the consultant drops and it is hard for him to get valid information. Moreover, he can never be sure that the same changes might not have occurred even without his intervention, especially if the staff also changed in the meantime.

It is, however, possible to be fairly confident about negative results. If the consultation report is quickly shelved and few of the suggestions accepted, this should be obvious, although it may sometimes be difficult for the consultant to obtain this information from people with whom he has built up a friendly relationship and who may wish to protect his self-respect. It is important for consultants to try to get this knowledge, because they can use evidence of lack of success in certain aspects of a consultation to learn what to avoid in the future. By and large, we learn more from our failures than from our successes, if we have the courage to confront them and try to analyze why things went wrong.

Finally, it must be admitted that many administrative consultants do not have a good record either in adequately following up or in trying to evaluate their consultations. Yet somehow they develop a good reputation, which convinces them that they have been successful. Presumably, satisfied consultees talk about them to their friends, and this leads to new consultation requests. This is a less than perfect basis for professional development, and I hope that eventually we will develop more systematic follow-up procedures and better evaluative techniques.

CHAPTER TWELVE

Consultee-Centered
Administrative Consultation

Consultee-centered administrative consultation is probably the most demanding type of mental health consultation. The consultant is called in by the administrative staff of an organization to help them develop on their own new ways of working so that they may more effectively deal with current problems in organizational planning, program development, personnel management, and other aspects of policy implementation. The consultant is interested in collecting information about the organization, its goals, programs, policies, and administrative structure and functioning, as a way of assessing the problems that impede the operations of the consultees and as a vehicle for helping them overcome their work difficulties.

A consultant who is asked for this type of help may be invited to consult with a single administrator or part or all of the staff. Unlike program-centered administrative consultation, his work is usually expected to continue for a substantial period—months or years.

If the consultant is asked to work with part or all of the staff, rather than just a single administrator, he will work with individual consultees and various established groups, and possibly the general population of administrators. The number of administrators in the organization may be too big for him to talk to all of them directly. The possible multiplicity of consultee individuals and groups is one of the factors that make this type of consultation so complicated.

The knowledge and skills demanded from the consultant include not only individual and group methods but also a specialized

264

understanding of social systems and of administration and organization theory and practice, especially their implications for the organization's contribution to the mental health of its community and to the staff's psychological needs.

Over the years we have engaged in many examples of consultee-centered administrative consultation, and it is largely on this experience that this chapter is based. In some of these programs, single consultants have been involved. In others, consultants have operated in teams, either to increase the range of knowledge about the subject matter of the problems or simply to cover ground more quickly.

The general principles of consultee-centered case consultation apply also to consultee-centered administrative consultation. An administrative consultant is usually asked also for help in dealing with individual cases, so his operations usually include consultee-centered consultation as well as occasional client-centered consultation. At times he may be asked to make specific recommendations for planning a circumscribed program in the mental health field, and if he feels the change of role is appropriate, he may temporarily engage in program-centered administrative consultation or in administrative collaboration.

Choosing Consultees

The most important characteristic aspect of this kind of consultation is the need to be flexible in the choice of consultees. Occasionally, this choice may be predetermined, as when the consultant is restricted to helping an individual administrator. He may then have little contact with other members of the organization staff, and his operations would be similar to those of individual consultee-centered case consultation, except that instead of focusing on a client he would be dealing with a current administrative problem. On the other hand, the administrator may ask the consultant to talk with some of his subordinates, to gain a deeper understanding of the organization. This would be analogous to interviewing the client in consultee-centered case consultation. In administrative consultation such action may be more helpful than in case consultation, because the consultant is not likely to know as much about the content area of the discussion as if this centered on the psychological aspects of an individual or family, the field in which he has had years of professional experience.

If he does agree to see the administrator's subordinates, the consultant should beware of the trap of thinking they too are his consultees. If he has been invited to offer consultation only to the director, rather than to the total administrative staff, this should have been made explicit to the rest of the organization; and his contacts with other workers should be clearly structured as a way for him to collect information for the purpose of advising the director.

Another example of predetermined choice of consultees was the invitation to offer consultation to the directors and assistant directors of the nursing division of a general hospital. This group had a regular three-hour meeting every Wednesday morning, and the mental health consultant was asked to meet with them for half of this time every other week. In the same hospital, the consultant was invited by the nursing directors to offer consultation to twenty-five nursing supervisors. Since this group had no regularly scheduled meetings of its own, a time was chosen that was most convenient for the day, evening, and night shifts, and all the supervisors were invited to attend a special group consultation meeting at two-week intervals. Over a seven-year period the attendance varied from ten to twenty.

The usual pattern encountered by administrative consultants in large organizations, such as large mental hospitals, school systems, and industrial firms, is quite different. Here the consultant may be invited to offer help to the entire organization, and he may be expected to play an active part in deciding which members of its staff he will engage in consultation discussions. Usually, the director of the organization and his senior staff will have specific ideas on this subject and may wish to be seen individually, as part of regularly scheduled meetings, or in specially convened consultee groups. They may suggest that the consultant attend regularly scheduled meetings of various work units, interdepartmental task forces, or layers of the administrative hierarchy; and they may also convene special consultation groups, such as the nursing supervisors in the previous example.

As the consultant collects information about the organization, he might suggest that other individuals and groups be involved in the consultation. This means that during his period of consulting, there will be changes in the roster of his consultees.

Whenever he moves to a new group of consultees, the consultant must carefully build up relationships of trust and respect and must negotiate an agreement on mutual goals and rules of procedure. He can never rely on their effective cooperation merely on the basis of sanction from their supervisors.

Making Initial Contacts

Many programs of consultee-centered administrative consultation have developed logically out of earlier mental health programs that have gone through stages of collaboration, education, client-centered case consultation, and consultee-centered case consultation. More and more, however, as the achievements of mental health consultants in large organizations have been publicized, organizations are beginning to ask for this type of consultation from the beginning, either on its own or, more usually, as part of a general program that includes mental health education and other types of consultation. For example, the director of a Job Corps camp asked a mental health center for a program of consultee-centered administrative consultation for himself and his staff; many senior staff members had had satisfactory experiences with mental health consultants during earlier service in the Peace Corps. He also wanted case consultation on problems among his students and assistance with the in-service training program of his instructors and counselors. In this, as in a number of recent instances, we have been impressed by the sophistication of administrators; they understand just what kind of consultant help they want and put their highest priority on consultee-centered administrative consultation, rather than seeing the community mental health agency or other clinical facility only as a place to refer individual problem cases.

In negotiations with such knowledgeable and highly motivated administrators, each side must first learn as quickly as possible what the other wants and has to offer, and what is its basic approach to organizational problems and to community mental health. They will no doubt amplify and corroborate their personal impressions of each other with additional data from other informants.

If these preliminary explorations are satisfactory, and if the needs, capacities, and philosophies of the two sides seem compatible, there is no point in prolonging the initial negotiations. The consultants should pay a quick visit to the organization and then agree to a contract for a trial period. This contract need not be a particularly formal document, although in the case of a governmental or other public organization, services and fees may have to be stated. The agreement should be written in general terms, to allow the details of the operations to evolve collaboratively in the light of joint experience.

One detail of the initial agreement is important. The consultants must have direct access to the top administrator of that part of the organization in which they will be working. In offering consultation to the nursing division of the general hospital, for example, the consultant related primarily to the nursing director and not to the director of staff education, who made the original arrangements; in the Job Corps camp the basic relationship was with the camp director, not the program coordinator or head counselor, who had been sent by the director to conduct the initial negotiations. This ensures that the consultant has the backing of the top person and can move freely across intraorganizational boundaries and make contacts with all the staff. One of his next tasks is to negotiate sanction through all grades of the hierarchy, down to and including the various levels at which he intends to consult.

It is essential, during the initial negotiations with the director, to obtain explicit assurance that he will not ask the consultant to act as his agent in either giving or receiving communications. This does not mean that the consultant will withhold observations of staff problems, but it does mean that he will be empowered to maintain confidentiality and that the director will not expect him to divulge details that may reflect on the behavior of particular individuals and groups.

The initial negotiation of sanction to operate is part of the first two tasks of the consultant in the consultee organization: (1) building his relationships with its staff and (2) learning about its social system, including its organizational structure and functioning and the values and traditions that bind its members together.

Building Relationships

The consultant's fundamental goal is to stimulate a coordinate relationship of mutual trust and respect. The consultees must perceive him as a reliable professional who has specialized knowledge and skills that he is prepared to put at their disposal without endangering their occupational status and personal self-respect.

The main technical problems, in addition to those already discussed in Chapter Five, are related to the administrative consultant's role as a change agent who is empowered to cross boundaries between individuals and groups and across levels of the organizational structure. This may interfere with the orderly patterns of communication that people use to maintain equilibrium in their daily work. The entry of an administrative mental health consultant, who is authorized to question accepted values and traditions and customary patterns of communication and perceptual distortions, may be particularly threatening.

Besides this, there are three other dangers. One is the possibility that the consultant may be seen as a spy for the director. A second is that he may be perceived as the director's agent, using specialized psychological techniques to exert undue influence on the staff. People may fear that the consultant will use his power to side with certain factions and against those who, for their own good reasons, oppose current policies. Third, the consultant may indeed have his own axe to grind. He may have his own ideas and values about organizational structure and functioning. He is interested in promoting mental health. Perhaps he has some blueprint of an ideal organization at the back of his mind and wants to manipulate the organization to conform to his pattern. His lack of experience with this particular organization, and the unproven and possibly fallacious value-laden premises upon which he bases his ideal pattern, may make his plan unworkable.

These are all significant reasons for reservation in welcoming an administrative consultant; they supplement many less rational suspicions and stereotyped expectations that have been discussed in previous chapters. It is clear, therefore, that it will not be easy for the consultant to establish himself as someone whose help may be accepted without danger. He should intervene cautiously, lest he indeed do more harm than good.

The fundamental method of building relationships is the same as for other types of consultation: the consultant establishes proximity and promotes a process of mutual exploration so that the consultees can get to know him as he really is and not as they imagine him to be. In a large organization, especially one where the consultant has been invited because of current turmoil, rumors start easily and the stereotyped expectations they produce are hard to undo. It is therefore important for the consultant and his team to move about to all levels of the social system as quickly as possible after the start of the program, so that most of the staff see them personally.

In these early contacts, it is advisable for the consultant to move along established channels of communication, at least in relation to group meetings. He should sit in at meetings that are convened for regular organizational purposes, and make as little use as possible of groups called by the authorities expressly for the purpose of consultation. When such a special meeting is convened, the consultant should give people an early opportunity to define some of their own needs that might be satisfied by this discussion, rather than taking it for granted that they have assembled only so he can see them and their work. In this way he can show his respect for them and his realization that, whatever advantage they may eventually derive from his efforts, his entry into their system is an interference with their work day.

In all his initial contacts, the consultant should emphasize his wish to be helpful and his interest in learning more about the organization. He should stress also that he still has no clear idea how the consultees can best use his knowledge and skills. On the other hand, he should not hide the fact that he has a store of expertise that he is willing to place at their disposal. This message is best communicated by the kinds of questions he asks as the discussion progresses. In previous chapters we have referred to the special style of consultation questioning: aligning oneself with the consultees in facing the issue of the moment and then raising questions that widen or deepen the focus of the discussion. One consultant has referred to this as "complicating the thinking of the consultees." This is a safer method of presenting credentials than giving premature answers to questions when knowledge of the organization's realities is yet inadequate.

A relationship-building problem that occurs in most types of consultation, but is particularly obtrusive in consultee-centered administrative consultation, is how to maintain a coordinate relationship with consultees in the lower echelons. This is especially problematic in institutions where status differentials are marked, such as in the military or in a traditional mental hospital or public health agency. It is hard for the staff to see the consultant as having only the authority of ideas; it is hard for the consultant to divest himself of the mantle of power handed over to him by the director, as well as invested in him by social evaluation of his professional status. Experience shows, however, that a coordinate status can be achieved by an informal, modest, sympathetic, and friendly manner, combined with meticulous avoidance of authoritarian formulations. The consultant must also show in the privacy of the interview setting that he sets aside his mantle of status and power while retaining his potency as an expert colleague.

Relationship building in an organization is a never-ending process. Apart from the continual addition of new groups of consultees as the consultant moves from level to level and unit to unit, the staff is usually changing. Gradually, the consultant's reputation becomes part of the culture of the place, and it is easier for new consultees to perceive him in his true colors; but the consultant must never rely on this. Each time he begins with a new individual or group of consultees, he must start again on the process of mutual exploration, role definition, and relationship building.

Studying the Social System

In consultee-centered case consultation it is important to learn a great deal about the institution and to keep abreast of current issues, in order to understand the institutional implications of the individual case the consultee brings for discussion. In consultee-centered administrative consultation this knowledge is even more important, because it forms an integral part of the content of the intervention.

It might be argued that a skilled consultant should be able to pick up enough information from his interviews with his consultees to assess the nature of their work problem and to plan how to help them. This might be true if the consultant limited himself to theme interference reduction with a regular group of consultees; but the essence of consultee-centered administrative consultation is that it may have a wider focus and may include intervention beyond the limits of specified consultees. It is this need to obtain a view of the total organization, in order to identify issues that are *not* brought to the consultant's attention by his consultees and that he might deal with by encouraging other members of the organization to ask for help, that sets its stamp on this type of consultation.

This is vital to the administrative consultant. By widening his range of data collection and by accepting responsibility for problems beyond those brought to his immediate attention, he faces the question of how far to go in initiating action to achieve organizational change. The more specific he is in planning solutions for the difficulties he sees, the more he is likely, consciously or unconsciously, to manipulate his consultees to carry out his plans. An administrative consultant who develops his own plans for changes in the organizational structure should state these recommendations openly—in which case he will be engaging in *program*-centered consultation. It is then up to the consultees to accept or reject his recommendations.

After identifying organizational problems, the consultee-centered administrative consultant should intervene to increase the range and depth of consultees' understanding of the issues and to augment their emotional capacity to use such knowledge productively. It is then up to them to work out solutions in the light of their own personal and role-related choices.

From these considerations emerges the principle, common to all consultation but most salient in consultee-centered administrative consultation, that in the consultant's mind he must separate the three phases: (1) collecting information, (2) making a consultation plan, and (3) implementing the plan in his specific consultation intervention. This conceptual differentiation, which helps him control what he does in a disciplined way, is obscured by the fact that in practice all these mental operations overlap, and any of his actions may include elements of all of them, so that an outside observer may have difficulty separating them. This is particularly true, for example, in the consultant's choice of the kind of data he collects and his methods of collection.

In *program-centered* administrative consultation, the consultant collects data that he considers relevant to the problem he has been invited to solve; when he reaches the stage of tentatively formulating solutions, he collects further data that will illuminate the possible effectiveness and feasibility of his alternative plans. He uses normal tact and good manners in encouraging staff members to collect some of the needed information for him, but in the final analysis he relies on the authority vested in him by the director to ensure their cooperation.

In *consultee-centered* administrative consultation, on the other hand, the data collection has many more constraints. First, the consultant has accepted no coercive authority from the director, and so collaboration of the staff, although authorized, must be freely volunteered and is more likely in certain issues than others. Second, the consultant is continually aware that while he is collecting information he is also building relationships that will form the vehicle for eventual consultation intervention. In fact, his intervention usually starts at the moment of his first contact with his potential consultees, who may from the beginning be watching such things as his way of asking questions and the areas of his major interest; this process of identifying with him is one of the major ways they are influenced. Third, although the area of his inquiry has not been predetermined by a request to deal with a particular administrative predicament, and so is apparently wide open to include any or every aspect of the organization, the consultant realizes that the resources at his disposal are necessarily limited. He must therefore narrow his focus to those issues that the consultees feel to be currently most pressing, and which they are thus likely to want to discuss.

With experience, consultants develop a special skill, similar to a psychotherapist's intuition in following productive leads: superficially scanning the entire field of the organization and then making quick judgments of the "hottest" areas for deepening his inquiries, choosing topics that provide leverage points of salience and feasibility for the consultees. An ongoing systematic examination of such statistics as staff turnover, client movement, or staff absenteeism should form the background of data collection and may suggest leads for further exploration. But the consultant's main method of scanning will probably be moving about as a participant observer within the life space of the organization and chatting with as many people as possible at different administrative levels, to find evidence of unusual behavior or preoccupation that may indicate administrative difficulty.

Increasing knowledge of the culture of certain types of institutions and increasing experience with a particular organization may alert the consultant to repetitive sources of difficulty. He will thus be prepared to identify minor clues that should be followed up, such as communication blocks or interdisciplinary rivalries.

When the consultant does identify a salient problem, or when it is brought to his attention, he is faced, in this type of consultation, by an interesting technical dilemma. The more active he becomes in searching, himself, for more data from additional informants, the more accurate a picture he will obtain but the less influence he will have on his consultees during the process. On the other hand, the more he sees himself as a catalyst, stimulating consultees to obtain additional information, the more likely is his picture to be lacking in clarity and fullness, because of the very limitations and blocks in the consultees that his consultation is designed to remedy.

The consultant must judge in each case at what point on that parameter to pivot his approach. If he is working on a regular basis with one consultee, he will probably operate closer to the catalyst end of the parameter, along the same lines as in consultee-centered case consultation. He will rely mainly on his ability to identify distortions in the consultees' story for evidences of theme interference, and on trying to reduce that interference with the hope that increased objectivity will enable the consultees to get, and to transmit to him, a more realistic picture. He will also attempt to increase their knowledge of additional sources of useful data. If the consultees do not manage to use this knowledge and professional objectivity with greatest effectiveness in analyzing the current administrative predicament, he will rely on continuing contacts with them on future problems to lead to progressive improvement, and he will be satisfied to move forward at their pace.

What makes consultee-centered administrative consultation so interesting—and also so demanding—is the wide range of possible factors and levels that the consultant must be prepared to handle. He must appraise individual personality characteristics and problems among the key administrators, intragroup and intergroup relations in and among the various units of the enterprise, organizational patterns of role assignment and lines of communication and authority, leadership patterns and styles, vertical and horizontal communication, and traditions of participation in decision making. These encompass the full range of individual psychology, group processes, and organizational structure and functioning. Of particular importance are changes induced by intraorganizational dynamics, such as those related to movements of individuals among positions, and by alterations in the relationship between the organization and its external community, from which it derives its resources and to which it delivers its products.

A mental health consultant cannot be expected to be equally expert in all these areas—psychology, psychiatry, small-group processes, sociology, anthropology, administration, and economics. He must, however, develop some generalist working competence in each. He must also study the traditions, values, and customary practices of the organizations with which he consults. His own expertise consists in a specialized knowledge of certain aspects of the field and in his ability to help his consultees strengthen their mastery of those aspects in a balanced relation to the other factors. In this regard, his operations resemble those of a lawyer, who has to learn enough about the details of a wide variety of fields in successive cases so that in each one he can focus his legal knowledge in a meaningful way.

The following list of issues raised in successive consultations with general hospital nursing directors and supervisors may illustrate the width of this range of factors: The question of maintaining discipline among ward nurses in procedures relating to the poison cupboards. Relations of the nursing division and hospital security in controlling illicit drug use among nurses and aides. How to reduce nursing staff equitably and effectively because of low patient census. Emotional difficulty of the nurse who resigns or is fired. How to prevent medication errors—how to study their causes by epidemiological methods, and how to deal with nurses who have made serious mistakes. How to encourage nurses to become more productive in a culture that is in transition between authoritarian and participant leadership styles. How to increase information feedback to central policy makers from line workers. The problem of controlling rumors, and their relation to low morale due to poor nursing leadership on a particular unit. How to support the head nurses so that they can maintain nursing policies and withstand the pressures of resident physicians who want their own way. The difficult status of the nursing supervisor—her negative image as a "snoopervisor" on the prowl to identify policy infringements and as someone called in only when there is trouble; how to increase her sources of professional gratification and her feelings of self-respect. How to deal with a medical resident who loses his temper with a ward nurse and shouts at her in front of her patients; relations between the nursing division and the medical department concerned. How to promote communication among supervisors on the three shifts who work in a particular department. How to handle depressed, possibly suicidal, patients on general wards. Tensions between nursing service and nursing education in relation to nursing students working on the wards. Effect on the nurses of low morale on a medical unit caused by the impending retirement of a chief of service. Problems of recruitment of new nurses, and relations with the hospital personnel department. How to increase the participation of the nursing division in deciding hospital policy on such matters as increasing bed capacity and census when the number of nurses is thought inadequate.

Planning the Intervention

Although in practice an experienced consultant usually moves smoothly and quickly from his assessment of the problem to his helpful intervention, it is useful if he teaches himself to pause while he reviews the situation and explicitly chooses his goals and his methods of reaching them. This pause for planning should not show as any perceptible interruption in the flow of an interview. As in all other forms of consultation, the consultant must learn to continue talking at the manifest level while cogitating about the latent content and the process of his operations.

The consultant may intervene at an individual, group, or organization level. His interventions are time limited and circumscribed; and whether they are prompted by his own awareness of an issue or initiated by a staff member, they must be limited by the boundaries of what the consultees feel are salient current predicaments. This means that although the consultant may be visiting the organization on a regular weekly basis for several years, and having continuing contacts with particular individuals and groups with whom he develops stable relationships of a gradually evolving character, his consultation interventions continue to be an ad hoc type, focused on temporary intercurrent episodes.

This is so even though the consultant may recognize in his own mind that certain repetitive issues are linked to major continuing difficulties in the organizational structure. From time to time he may choose an opportunity for focusing discussion on these major problems; but on the whole, his strategy is to help the consultees handle them piecemeal in relation to the crises they produce. This allows him to capitalize on the increased leverage of the crisis, which motivates participants to ask for help and temporarily increases their susceptibility to outside influence.

The details, timing, and speed of change in structure and culture are thus molded by the staff through their intimate living knowledge of the organization and their own capacity to cope with change. This provides an optimal opportunity to deal with reverberations and undesirable side effects occasioned by the possible weakening of institutional defenses against individual and group anxiety, and permits the staff the time to work out alternative systems of cooperative defenses.

Ending and Follow-Up

The consultee-centered administrative consultant, whether he meets with an individual consultee, an ongoing group of consultees, or with a variety of consultees on an issue he has uncovered in the general life of the organization, will complete his intervention on a particular problem within a short series of visits—usually one to three. He will then take up some other problem. The regularity of his continuing visits to the organization should not obscure this pattern, or his work will be in danger of sliding insensibly into general emotional support, education, or administrative collaboration, that is, sharing responsibility for program development.

Each short series of consultations focused on a particular problem should be terminated by the consultant when he feels he has made his contribution. He then leaves it to the consultees to make whatever use of his contribution they wish. As he closes each episode, the consultant should express interest in learning the outcome of the problem and should arrange for the consultees to tell him of further developments when it is convenient for them to do so. The timing of this follow-up may well be left vague. This will allow both sides to use the follow-up discussion, if they wish, as a way of initiating future consultation contact.

PART II

Mental Health Collaboration

CHAPTER THIRTEEN

The Nature and Purpose
of Collaboration

In this chapter, we focus on the work of a mental health collaborator—a specialist inside the institutional framework of other caregiving professionals, whose domain he penetrates in order to implement his own mission of preventing mental disorders or improving the care of those served by other community institutions, such as schools, hospitals, courts, or welfare agencies.

The essential difference between this type of reaching out and mental health consultation is that in collaboration, the mental health specialist *accepts responsibility* for the mental health outcome of the client, and plays an active part in diagnosing and treating the client as a member of the professional team inside the host institution. What the specialist says and does must improve the care of, and the outcome for, the *client*, not merely improve the attitudes and performance of the staff.

In mental health collaboration, the partnership agreement stipulates that the staff members of the host institution will enable the mental health specialist to collect data not only about the client but also about the program, as a basis for assessing the client's mental health needs and developing a plan for his care. This plan will be implemented as a team effort, by the specialist and by members of the institution's staff. This effort involves allocation of diagnostic and treatment tasks, supervision and follow-up to ensure that the tasks have been carried out, and evaluation, which may lead to replanning the case management program.

A mental health *consultant* is free to choose the topics to focus on, according to his own judgment of what he believes will

281

contribute to improving the operations of his consultees; they in turn are quite free to accept or reject whatever he says. The only constraints in this situation derive from the consultee's belief that what the consultant says seems relevant and helpful, and the consultant's belief that the consultees make enough use of his contributions that it is worth his while to continue.

In *collaboration*, on the other hand, both parties are compelled by their shared responsibility for the outcome of the case to focus their communications on issues relevant to the current case, and to planning and implementing actions that will improve the client's condition. Neither party is free. Each is equally tied to the well-being of a particular client.

Establishing a Framework for Collaboration

For a mental health specialist whose home base is an autonomous institution, such as a psychiatric clinic or mental hospital, or a relatively independent department inside a human services agency, and who wishes to reach out into another community agency or institutional department, the guidelines for establishing a collaboration program are similar to those discussed earlier for developing a program of mental health consultation.

Choice of the target institution or department will depend on evaluating *salience* and *feasability;* that is, estimating likely benefits of the partnership in improving the mental health of significant numbers of clients, and also the probability that the staff of the other unit will be amenable to developing a working partnership with mental health specialists.

Preparing the ground is also similar, and uses the same techniques: creating proximity, gaining entry into the other unit, getting to know each other, developing mutual trust and respect, overcoming obstacles to communication rooted in mutually disparaging stereotypes, negotiating sanction at different levels of the power hierarchy of each unit, maintaining sanction to continue and develop the partnership in line with a series of agreements that will define and legitimize joint activities, leaning each other's semantic system, and developing a joint language.

In mental health consultation, the specialist should ideally investigate the social system of the host institution, the patterns of communication, leadership, authority, and decision making. He needs to study all this so that he can understand his consultees' work problems and their resources, and thus know which issues to focus on and how best to communicate. His formulations will have value only if they make sense to his consultees and as long as they have the skills to improve their care of the client. Otherwise the consultant will be wasting his time.

In collaboration, these issues are not just desirable but *essential,* because the mental health specialist has undertaken personal responsibility for improving the client's mental health. If he fails because he has not evoked the cooperation of the other staff, he can be criticized or condemned by his own superiors and by those of the host institution, and he can feel that he has not achieved goals he had set for himself.

The effectiveness of the host institution is not of primary importance to a mental health consultant, because he is not responsible for the mental health outcome, unless he gives incorrect guidance that distorts the functioning of a consultee who accepts his formulations. The consultant is, apart from this, responsible only for enhancing the mental health attitudes and competences of his consultees, irrespective of their current level of functioning, by improving their knowledge, skills, personal security, and professional objectivity. If the consultee system turns out to be too ineffective, the consultant will probably not be willing to spend his time with it; but this is a matter of personal choice for himself and his supervisors. Likewise, salience and feasability are significant in choosing institutions to work with, in line with the limited resources of the consultant agency.

In contrast, the effectiveness and efficiency of the host institution are central to mental health collaboration, because the mental health specialist must rely not only on an adequate level of partnership but also on the ability of his partners to carry out their segment of the joint program to help the client.

Status Issues

In mental health collaboration the status situation is more complicated than in consultation. The fact that the collaborating professionals share joint responsibility for the mental health outcome of the client imposes a hierarchical element on their status relationship, which must be geared to facilitating a correct evaluation and an effective treatment plan. For their partnership to succeed, his colleagues must accept the dominance of the mental health worker's specialized opinion. Although he must pay proper attention to their opinions, for they know more than he does about the complicating factors in the setting, in the final analysis, the decisions on how to handle the case must be most influenced by judgment of the mental health specialist.

On the other hand, the mental health worker has accepted membership in the staff team. The mandate of this team is not merely to deal with mental health matters but to carry out the general mission of the host institution. The leader of the team will therefore be a senior member of its staff; all members of the team, including the mental health specialist, must be subordinate to his authority. The team leader must have the ultimate power to decide how to handle the case, after taking into account, one hopes, the possibly discrepant specialized opinions of the team members of different disciplines.

The mental health specialist must often make a fine judgment, weighing the relative importance of the mental health issue against the larger mission of the host institution. He must decide how far to claim precedence for his point of view against those of other team members, particularly the team leader. If he feels that his own view of the case is crucial for the client's well-being, he must try to persuade his colleagues to give it precedence; if necessary, he must apply whatever moral and administrative pressure might be needed to mold their decision. If he fails, and the client should in consequence be harmed, the mental health specialist will be culpable.

A senior child psychiatrist in the child psychiatry department of a general hospital was assigned to work in collaborative partnership with the doctors, nurses, social workers, nutritionists, and other staff on the pediatric ward. After several months, she felt that she had satisfactorily established her role on a ward unit directed by a senior pediatrician, with whom she developed a relationship of mutual respect. On daily ward rounds, which she often attended, and at a weekly "psychosocial conference" where cases were reviewed, her contributions were usually taken seriously by the unit chief. She had free access to all the patients on the ward unit, and she could initiate diagnostic or counseling service on her own or as a staff decision.

She became involved in the case of Esther, a five-month-old infant, who had been born at six and a half months' gestation, weighing nine hundred grams. Esther had spent her first four months on the ward's intensive care unit for prematures. She had needed surgery for an inguinal hernia and had been in a respirator because of airway obstruction and occasional apnea (cessation of breathing). She had been transferred to the general pediatric unit a week before the psychiatrist first saw her. The infant at times suffered from pneumonia.

The parents, both twenty-five, had immigrated to Israel from Turkey six years previously, and now worked together in their small neighborhood grocery shop. The father worked long hours and was rarely available to help in the home. There were two other children, a girl of six and a boy of two and a half. They had had an older son, who two years earlier had been run over and killed in a street accident when he was six. The parents had married in Turkey when they were fifteen, and in the ten years since then, the mother had undergone six planned abortions for socioeconomic reasons. There was a suspicion that the mother had tried to abort herself when she became pregnant with this baby but had failed. She had apparently become reconciled to the pregnancy in hope that she would have a son to replace the one who had been killed.

The paternal grandmother lived with the parents and took care of the home and the children while both parents worked. The father had hardly ever visited the baby in hospital, in part because he did not get home from work till late every night. The mother had not visited the child in the intensive care unit, and she visited only occasionally after the transfer to the pediatric ward. She rarely looked directly at the child, and she never spontaneously made an attempt to touch her.

The psychiatrist felt that the mother was not bonded at all to the baby. She had apparently rejected the pregnancy, as she had at least six other pregnancies. The absence of bodily contact during the five months since birth had prevented maternal attachment. The psychiatrist recommended that the mother be urged to visit frequently and that an attempt be made to get her to hold and care for the baby on the ward, with the direction and supervision of the nursing staff. Over the next few weeks, this was attempted but without much success.

The situation was complicated by the fact that the grandmother became ill with diabetes, chronic nephritis, and eventually pneumonia, for which she was hospitalized three weeks after the psychiatrist had first been called in. The mother was forced to stop work to care for the home. This preoccupied her, and prevented her focusing her interest on the baby and spending much time with her.

Nevertheless, the baby's physical condition improved. She got a good deal of stimulation from the nursing staff. She recovered from her pneumonia, but she suffered from intermittent attacks of apnea at night, which usually responded quickly to a short period of forced respiration with an oxygen mask.

An older Turkish woman was brought into the home as a housekeeper while the grandmother was hospitalized. This worked out well, and the mother began to visit the baby in hospital more frequently. All attempts to involve the father in the care of this baby or his other children were unsuccessful. He continued to devote most of his time to his business, apart from occasionally visiting his sick mother. A joint meeting was arranged with the pediatrician, both parents, and the psychiatrist to discuss the problems of the baby and to develop mutual support of father and mother in caring for her after discharge from the hospital. The father did not appear.

Despite efforts to initiate bonding by instruction and role modeling, the mother continued to hold the baby awkwardly and at arm's length, sometimes with her head down, as though she were afraid of her, and as though she had no awareness of her needs. On one occasion she was described as "holding the child like a tray and not like a baby at all."

The child's physical condition continued to improve, and the pediatricians felt that she was well enough to be discharged. The danger of nocturnal apnea persisted, but they felt that this could be handled by providing an apnea-alarm instrument and an oxygen mask, which the parents could be taught to use whenever necessary.

However, the psychiatrist warned that because the mother was not yet bonded, she could not be relied upon to protect the child adequately or to give her essential care. The psychiatrist recommended that a nonprofessional child-care worker be recruited to care for the baby in the home full time for several weeks, and to continue training the mother by acting as a role model to help her bond to the baby.

The ward social worker attempted to implement this plan, but could not mobilize the necessary budget from welfare funds. The parents said they could not afford to pay for private child care in the home. Eventually the pediatricians disregarded the psychiatrist's warnings. They felt that the grandmother (who by then had returned home) and the housekeeper between them could manage the care of the home and the children, and they arranged for a public health nurse from the local well-baby clinic to visit the home at intervals to supervise the baby's care.

The baby was discharged in good health. The parents were given the apnea monitor and told how to use it. Six days later the grandmother died, and ten days later the baby was rehospitalized with a respiratory tract infection. The mother's handling of her baby in the hospital showed that she was still not bonded.

Ten days later the baby had recovered from her chest infection, and she was discharged. The psychiatrist once again opposed this disposition, on grounds that the absence of a bonded mother in a case of nocturnal apnea and vulnerability to respiratory infection was life threatening.

Once again the psychiatrist was overridden by the pediatrician, who felt that it was not in the best interests of the child to prolong her hospital stay, and that the apnea alarm plus surveillance in the home by the public health nurse was sufficient safeguard.

Five days later, on a routine follow-up home visit, the ward social worker discovered that the apnea alarm was not working. Instead of dealing with this as a dangerous emergency and demanding that the parents immediately bring the baby into the hospital until the instrument could be repaired, she told the mother to bring the alarm to the hospital electrician for attention. At 4:00 the next morning, the parents found the baby dead in her crib, apparently as a result of an apnea attack.

During a process of painful soul-searching after Esther's death, the psychiatrist tried to reduce her own feelings of guilt by asking herself the following questions: What could I have done differently that might have prevented the death of this baby? Could I have argued more strongly in order to persuade my colleagues? Should I not have emphasized more than I did the many hazardous factors in the home, in addition to the lack of mother-infant bonding? Should I have refused to acquiesce when the pediatricians brushed aside my reservations? Could I have brought more pressure to bear on the unit chief to accept the validity of my objections?

She discussed the matter with the head of her own department of child psychiatry, and asked him to arrange a confidential meeting between them and the head of the department of pediatrics, with whom the contract for the collaboration program had been negotiated. At this behind-the-scenes meeting, the chief pediatrician made it clear that he had full confidence in his unit head, saying he was an excellent and well-balanced pediatrician properly fulfilling his responsibilities in exercising his authority to decide on the infant's discharge from hospital, even though advised against it. The chief pediatrician said that if he had been in the unit head's place he might easily have come to the same conclusion in the light of the other factors in the case: the baby's physical recovery from her pneumonia, the danger to her of reinfection in a ward full of very sick children, the pressure on beds, and his feeling that they had to reeducate this mother to take on more responsibility for the care of her child and to stop her continually trying to dump the baby onto the hospital. What happened in this case was the result of bad luck. The breakdown of the apnea alarm instrument was unpredictable, as was the chance occurrence of an attack of apnea just that night, before the instrument could be repaired.

Eventually, it was decided that in the future the psychiatrist should feel free to appeal to the chief pediatrician for a review of any case in which she felt that a child might be endangered by a difference of opinion between her and the unit head. And in an exceptional case in which the psychiatrist might feel that there was actual danger to the life of a patient because both the unit head and the chief pediatrician decided to disregard her opinion, she should feel free to make a formal declaration that she was withdrawing from collaboration on that case. This would certainly bring maximum pressure to bear on the pediatricians and would absolve the psychiatrist of her partial responsibility if a tragedy were to occur. After the meeting, these decisions were communicated to the unit head, and he accepted them as valid additions to the collaboration contract.

This example shows vividly the potential predicaments faced by a collaborating specialist because of subordinate status and decision-making power in relation to the team leader. It also illustrates a valid mechanism available for the specialist: appeal to a higher authority in the hierarchy of his home base, who in turn may communicate with an administrative superior of the team leader. This maneuver avoids an open confrontation between the specialist and the team leader, which might damage their professional relationship.

This maneuver is not available to a specialist such as a school psychologist who has been hired as an individual to work in an institution. If he appeals personally to higher authority against a decision of his team leader, he may damage his relationships both with the team leader and with administrators higher in the line of command, who may resent his not going through channels.

Decision Making and Sanctioned Roles

On the pediatric ward, the psychiatrist had negotiated a contract that allowed her to play a full part, in collaboration with other staff, subject to the overriding authority of the unit leader, in making decisions about diagnosis, treatment, management, discharge, and follow-up of patients. Many of these decisions were made during the weekly psychosocial conferences. But day-to-day decisions were mainly made during once- or twice-daily ward rounds. The psychiatrist made an effort to attend rounds on a regular basis, but since she also had other important assignments in her home department, she had to develop procedures to update her information about decisions that were made in her absence. She also had to negotiate sanction by the unit head and her colleagues to ask for clarifications and give her an opportunity to question these decisions at subsequent meetings, without them seeing this as a waste of their time. Clearly, she had to take care not to overdo her requests for review of past decisions, but it was important that her right be recognized to initiate such a review if, in her judgment, important mental health issues had not been adequately considered in her absence.

A general principle emerges that is important in mental health collaboration: the specialist status of the mental health worker must be recognized and respected by colleagues in the host institution, and the practical implications of this must be covered in the basic collaboration contract or be negotiated in the early stages of the program.

Also, the mental health specialist should be permitted to move freely through the institution with the power to initiate contact at will with the clients and their family, unless an exception is requested by the decision-making body. Exceptions may occur where the local culture ascribes stigma to mental health workers, or where particular clients may feel that contact with mental health workers might endanger them. For instance, on a pediatric ward, parents of a patient admitted for an ostensibly bodily complaint may resist relabeling the illness as "psychosomatic" and focusing attention on psychosocial problems in the family. In such situations, a wise mental health worker may agree that diagnostic data are best collected by pediatricians and nurses and remedial action best undertaken by them.

Many mental health collaborators have grappled with this difficulty by arranging to be seen publicly, such as on ward rounds in a hospital or in classroom situations in a school, as integrated members of the institution's staff team. In such a routine public setting, it is less likely that their initiating contact with a particular patient or client will be felt to be stigmatizing.

Fearful fantasies about the dangers of contact with a mental health worker may not be confined to clients, but may to some extent also be shared by some members of the professional staff of human services institutions. Therefore, professional respect shown to the specialist by authoritative figures in the institution is particularly important. This respect may be expressed through the serious consideration given to his opinions; this may be particularly influential in reshaping attitudes to him and overcoming negative stereotypes. This is not a one-way affair. The mental health specialist may find that his own disparaging stereotypes about colleagues of certain other disciplines, particularly in regard to their sensitivity and sophistication in human relations, may be radically modified as he sees the respect accorded their contributions and as he experiences the actual merit of their ideas and actions.

Choice of Case

In mental health consultation, the consultee chooses which of his cases to discuss. The consultant strictly restricts his intervention to these cases, even though he may become aware of other cases in which the consultee may be having difficulty and even though, in consultee-centered consultation, the consultant may choose to discuss issues that the consultee may not have thought to be salient. In contrast, in a collaboration program it is the mental health specialist who, by mutual consent, basically decides which cases to discuss, even though he also accepts cases on which his partners ask for help.

In the collaboration on the pediatric ward, the staff at the weekly psychosocial conference, in line with the suggestion of the psychiatrist, decided that at the start of each meeting a pediatric resident would distribute a list of all patients on the ward, including a brief summary of the medical problems of patients who had been admitted since the previous meeting. Any participant, but especially the psychiatrist, would then be free to focus discussion on any case. This procedure was worked out to conserve discussion time in a conference restricted to an hour and a half, while making sure not to overlook any case that might include obscure psychosocial issues. At the beginning of the program, the psychiatrist initiated consideration of many cases that the pediatricians and nurses had not perceived as problematic from a mental health point of view. As they became more sophisticated, the number of such unrecognized cases gradually decreased.

A special benefit of the psychiatrist attending general ward rounds was the opportunity this gave her to screen all patients and to draw the attention of her colleagues to significant covert psychosocial factors. But she had to be careful not to hold up the progress of the round by initiating time-consuming discussions, so she usually asked for such cases to be put on the agenda of the weekly psychosocial conference, unless she detected an urgent matter.

Implementing Decisions and Replanning

The specialist in collaboration programs must press for staff who have been allotted particular assignments to report back about the complications they may encounter and their ways of overcoming them. This applies as much to the specialist as to other members of staff.

For instance, after Esther died, the psychiatrist reviewed her actions in the case and then consulted her department head. Although she wanted his help in setting up the meeting with the chief pediatrician, her discussion with her own supervisor provided an opportunity to evaluate how she herself had handled the case. Her department head focused on the psychiatrist's criticism of the actions of the social worker, who might have prevented the baby's death if she had treated the breakdown of the apnea alarm as a major emergency. The department head pointed out to the psychiatrist that blaming the social worker might reduce her own feelings of guilt but was not particularly productive. He recommended that she not raise this issue in the interview with the chief pediatrician.

He also pointed out that he knew from discussions of previous cases that the social worker was unskilled and inexperienced. If there was a reasonable chance of having her transferred from the ward, that might be useful, except that she would then endanger patients on other wards where countervailing mental health supports were less available. He pointed out that there was a shortage of experienced social workers in the hospital, including casework supervisors.

An added problem was that this particular worker was a middle-aged woman, who had only recently graduated as a social worker. She made an initial impression on people as a senior worker; but after they discovered that she was inexperienced, they tended to disparage her, and this made her more insecure. However, her chronological age made it more difficult for her to admit her need for supervisory help.

Perhaps more important than her poor judgment about the alarm was the social worker's failure to implement the decision to arrange child care in the home. The social worker's excuse had been that the neighborhood welfare agency had said that funds were not available. In fact, although funds were certainly in short supply, nonprofessional home helps were being provided by that agency in other cases. Could it be that the negative response in this case was linked with the social worker's perceived low status in the welfare agency as an inexperienced professional? Perhaps the psychiatrist had not adequately evaluated this possibility at the time, and had not considered how she might have collaborated with the social worker to overcome this obstacle.

This raised a related issue. When the programs of mental health collaboration started in the hospital, the involvement of mental health specialists on the wards had been warmly welcomed by the head of the hospital social work department and her senior colleagues. But when the program was implemented, many of the junior social work staff were ambivalent. Previously, irrespective of their seniority in their profession, they themselves had functioned as the specialists in mental health matters on the wards. When the psychiatrist began to attend the weekly psychosocial conferences, the social worker may well have felt supplanted. This was especially burdensome for this worker, with her conflict of image caused by the discrepancy between her age and her experience level. She had reacted by becoming more dominating and opinionated, earning the resentment of her colleagues.

The head of her department raised the possibility that this resentment might have influenced the psychiatrist to be less active than she might otherwise have been in developing a collaborative partnership with the social worker, difficult as that might have been to achieve. Had she done so earlier, the psychiatrist might have joined forces with the social worker in her campaign to persuade the welfare agency to send the child-care worker.

The two psychiatrists came to the conclusion that one important lesson to be drawn from this case was that the ward psychiatrist should reach out and develop an active partnership with her social work colleague. She should enroll her in a subunit that would meet regularly to plan and coordinate activities in their joint mission.

In this example, the process of evaluation and replanning focused not on management of a case, because unfortunately the death of the patient ruled this out, but on improving the collaboration program. The principles illustrated by the example, however, apply equally to both.

The Collaborating Specialist as Organizational Change Agent

Although it was quickly discarded, the suggestion that the psychiatrist might attempt to have the social worker removed from her post on the ward is an indication that the mental health specialist had accepted a mandate to improve the unit's effectiveness through organizational change. This is in line with a basic element in the mission and role of a mental health worker in a program of collaboration: personally to initiate appropriate action to effect organizational change in the host setting, if needed to ensure the mental health of its clients. The greater the shortcomings of the host setting, the more active the specialist must be to energize organizational change.

The mental health worker's mission will be to improve leadership, authority systems, communication patterns, decision making, planning, implementing of plans, monitoring, evaluating, replanning, personnel practices, and the like, if they are relevant to the mental health of clients and staff, as well as to educate supervisers and line workers about mental health matters. The sanction for such activities should be covered explicitly or implicitly by the terms of the original collaboration contract, or should be negotiated as soon as feasible once the program is under way.

Techniques of organizational change vary in different host institutions; specific examples are discussed in the following two chapters.

Characteristics of Mental Health Collaboration: A Summary

The main characteristics of mental health collaboration that have been raised in this chapter can be summarized as follows:

Mental health collaboration is an interprofessional method in which a mental health specialist establishes a partnership with another professional worker, network, group, or team of professionals in a community field or a human services institution. The mental health specialist, by agreement with his colleagues, becomes an integrated part of their evaluation and remedial operations, and accepts responsibility for contributing his specialized knowledge and for personally using his specialized diagnostic and remedial skills in dealing with their cases. He takes part in the process of making decisions about the diagnosis, management, and treatment of the clients. He is professionally responsible for the mental health outcome. He may himself play a direct role in investigation or treatment, or he may act as an adviser to other workers who share assessment or remedial assignments.

Because he accepts personal professional accountability for the mental health outcome of the cases, he is, by agreement with his staff colleagues, expected to direct their attention to relevant aspects of their evaluation and remedial efforts to ensure effective action on their part, or to supplement this by his own efforts to achieve optimal results, subject to the overall authority of the individual or group directing the host institution's program. He will also seek to foster appropriate changes in the organization and administration of the host institution that will improve the mental health outcome of the clients for whom he has accepted responsibility.

In line with these functions, the mental health worker has a range of status relationships with his collaborating colleagues: *coordinate* with other collaborating staff who have specialized knowledge and experience in their own specialties—he and each of them must recognize and respect the other's superior status in their own field; *hierarchical* in regard to authority to determine case decisions in their own professional domains, but subject to his acceptance of the overriding authority of the director of the host institution.

In addition to improving their handling of the current caseload or programs, the mental health specialist helps his colleagues increase their understanding and skills so that they will be better able in the future on their own to handle such issues or to decide to invoke interaction with a mental health specialist. At the same time, it is expected that the other staff will help him to learn more about their own specialized professional domains and about the ways of working of the host institution, so that in the future the mental health specialist will be more competent to understand and deal with relevant issues on his own or by realizing the value of invoking the help of others.

CHAPTER FOURTEEN

Collaboration
in an Effective Organization

Techniques of collaboration must be geared to the host institution's level of effectiveness, since the outcome of action is dependent on it. This chapter describes how a collaborating mental health worker deals with the problems and opportunities he is likely to encounter in a well-organized institution, using as an example the experience of a child psychiatrist working in a pediatric surgery department of a general hospital.

An effective and well-organized human services institution can be recognized by an effective and respected leader or leadership group; clear and accepted lines of authority; a good communication system that ensures that understandable messages pass and are received without delay; good procedures for identifying and appraising problems, developing remedial plans, alloting responsibilities and tasks, implementing plans, reporting back, monitoring progress, evaluating, and replanning; low levels of interunit and interpersonal tensions; high staff morale; and good personnel policies, recruitment, in-service training, supervision, and consultation. All these characteristics were found in the pediatric surgery department.

The collaboration program was initiated at a meeting between the chief pediatric surgeon and the chief child psychiatrist. The psychiatrist had previously been invited onto the pediatric surgery ward for occasional client-centered consultations, and he had been impressed by its excellent organization as well as by the ubiquity of mental health problems among its very sick patients and their families. He suggested the two meet to explore whether the surgeon was satisfied with the consultation service provided by the department of child psychiatry. The surgeon said that the service had been satisfactory as far as it went, but he raised the possibility of getting a more intense type of service that would better meet his needs.

The psychiatrist welcomed the surgeon's suggestion but said that because of prior commitments, he personally would not be able to devote much time to working on a regular basis with pediatric surgery. This clearly disappointed the surgeon. However, the psychiatrist promised to assign his senior assistant, a mature and a very experienced child psychiatrist, to the project if a viable plan could be developed. They decided to meet again to explore the matter further and to invite the senior psychiatrist to participate.

During two further meetings, they worked out a plan that provided a mutually acceptable framework for a collaboration program. The senior child psychiatrist would join the surgical team and participate in as many ward rounds as possible, during which she would take a full part in discussions and decision making. She would move about the ward and initiate contact with a patient, family member, or staff member whenever she saw the need. She would also be expected to undertake remedial interventions with patients and families in line with decisions made at ward rounds or in discussions with senior members of the ward staff, as long as they did not interfere with surgical treatment plans.

The surgeon noted that it would take the psychiatrist time to learn about the complicated realities of modern pediatric surgery and emphasized that he himself would guide her in this, as well as smooth her path in developing the relationships of mutual trust and respect with the other members of his team that he believed essential for a productive partnership. He also made it clear that he expected her to help him and his colleagues increase their skills in dealing with the psychological complications of their daily work.

The surgeon then went on to describe his department and how it was organized. It was a very busy department of forty beds, divided into three wards. The first was an intensive-care unit for newborns, where many of the patients were infants in highly sophisticated incubators, often premature with major congenital anomalies that required emergency surgery, followed by complicated postoperative care. Another unit on this ward gave initial postoperative care to older children. The two other wards housed children who were being treated surgically for the sequelae of trauma or burns, or for malignancies, gastrointestinal obstructions, respiratory blockages, or genitourinary problems that had required obligatory surgery, or else they were undergoing investigation to decide on appropriate surgical treatment.

The wards were often overcrowded, since the department had to admit for immediate emergency treatment acutely sick children from the city and the surrounding region. Crowding was also aggravated because parents were encouraged to stay with their children, and wherever possible help to nurse them. Parents slept at their children's bedside or in the dayroom or corridors. They would be immediately available for the informal treatment of family issues.

To cope with the pressure for admission, the department was geared to a rapid turnover of cases. Important decisions about case management were made during morning ward rounds attended by the entire staff and at a more leisurely weekly case conference. The psychiatrist was invited to attend and participate in these meetings; she tried to do so at least four days a week.

The surgeon then described the makeup of his interdisciplinary team and its interlocking functions. The group consisted of senior and junior surgeons, surgical residents, nurses, medical students, a social worker, a nutritionist, and part-time medical and scientific consultants, physiotherapists, occupational therapists, and play therapists. The chief surgeon emphasized that because of the complexity of their work, often involving the need for life-and-death decisions, the team was bound together by tight discipline and a set of close professional relationships, with clear and unambiguous allocation of tasks. The system required regular reporting back to the decision-making meetings, subject to his overall authority and to authority delegated by him, as needed, to his representatives. He had personally selected and recruited his senior surgical and nursing colleagues over several years, and had trained them.

Already, in these preliminary planning meetings the child psychiatrist began to appreciate that she was entering a new and very complicated professional world. This realization deepened as she became involved on a daily basis. She had to quickly give up her oversimplified stereotypes about surgery as a technical field involving mainly "cutting and sewing," and to discover that modern surgery, particularly pediatric surgery, involves a knowledge not only of anatomy, physiology, embryology, pathology, and operating room techniques, but also of internal medicine, pediatrics, biochemistry, pharmacology, microbiology, immunology, child development, nutrition, and the like, all of which were essential in understanding the problems confronting her surgical and nursing colleagues, and their dilemmas in making decisions about treatment and aftercare.

Another decision made during the preliminary planning meetings, which later turned out to be crucial in ensuring the success of the program, was that the two department heads and the child psychiatrist would meet regularly to monitor the progress of the new program and to deal quickly at top executive level with whatever unexpected difficulties might emerge as the program unfolded. These meetings were first held every two weeks, later extended to one month and then two months. It was agreed that any of the three could convene an additional meeting in the interim if an urgent problem demanded immediate attention. In fact, over a four-year period, this never happened, mainly because the relationship of mutual trust and respect and the freedom to communicate become so solid during the first year that the child psychiatrist and the pediatric surgeon were able to deal with emergent problems effectively on their own.

This relationship became personalized; when the child psychiatrist was forced by hospital rules to take compulsory retirement on account of age, the collaboration program never recovered. A very well-trained and gifted child psychiatrist was appointed to replace her, and the chief of child psychiatry attempted to provide support to help the new worker take over the role, but without much success.

Then the chief child psychiatrist himself was forced to retire on account of age, and the hospital administration decided for reasons of economy to close the separate department of child psychiatry and to integrate its functions into the hospital's department of general psychiatry. This effectively terminated the program of collaboration with pediatric surgery. Involvement of child psychiatry in this department reverted to intermittent on-demand case consultation. The pediatric surgical staff felt that they had learned so much about the diagnosis and management of psychosocial issues during the collaboration program that they could handle most of the mental health complications of their daily practice on their own, and that only in unusual instances was there a need for calling in a specialist in psychiatry.

Let us examine the issues encountered and the ways they were handled; this example of collaboration may provide guidance in other similar situations.

Developing the Collaboration

The following are issues addressed by the psychiatrist that have generic significance.

Establishing the Framework

Before they even met, the heads of both departments were interested in building up a partnership, and both used "creation of proximity" as their technique to move in this direction.

The head of the department of child psychiatry became aware that the surgeons were reaching out as the number of requests for case consultation multiplied, and he guessed that he was being tested, even though he had never met the chief surgeon, who kept in the background during these exploratory contacts. However, even superficial experience with the pediatric surgery department convinced the psychiatrist that it was a tightly controlled unit and that little took place in it without the knowledge and approval of its chief. Because the psychiatrist was interested in possibly developing a collaboration program, he conducted the consultations himself rather than delegating them to a more junior member of his staff. And when he invited the chief surgeon for an "evaluation meeting," it was a stratagem for getting to know him personally, to explore the possibility of collaboration.

He purposely allowed the initiative for moving the partnership in the direction of collaboration rather than consultation to remain in the hands of the surgeon, and he was very pleased when he moved so quickly in this direction. He later learned that quick decisive action following a careful assessment of the field of forces was a dominant characteristic of this surgeon. The psychiatrist, by design, allowed the surgeon to determine the speed with which the initial contract was worked out. Had the surgeon been more hesitant, the psychiatrist would have adapted to this. The basic principle is that from the start the leader of the host institution must be allowed to mold the program to satisfy his felt needs and to avoid endangering the preferred patterns of operation of his unit.

Nevertheless, it was the psychiatrist who convened the first meeting; and he did so as soon as he felt that the other party had had sufficient opportunity to monitor his professional competence and willingness to reach out beyond the boundaries of his own department. The correct timing for this first overt step is important, and depends on a subjective judgment based on necessarily incomplete information. If it is taken too early, the other side will feel they are being sucked into a situation before they have a chance to explore its implications safely. If it is taken too late, it will carry the message that the mental health group is too preoccupied with traditional intradepartment activities to wholeheartedly participate in a joint program. When four years later a junior psychiatrist was assigned to take over the collaboration program, her relatively low status may have been perceived as a signal of flagging motivation and may well have been an additional factor in determining the ending of the partnership.

As it turned out, the timing of the initial meeting was just right. In addition, both department heads discovered that they were equally highly motivated to move forward quickly and equally sensitive and sophisticated in satisfying the needs of the other side. The only hesitation showed by the surgeon was related to his discovery that the chief psychiatrist, who had himself conducted all the consultations in pediatric surgery, was not able to become the specialist who would implement the collaboration program; this disappointment was relieved when he was told that the assigned representative was a senior psychoanalyst and a child psychiatrist of many years' experience, who had for many years directed an important child psychiatry program in another state. When the surgeon met her a week later, his doubts were further relieved, and were quite dispelled when the continued active involvement of the chief psychiatrist was ensured by establishing the executive steering committee under his chairmanship.

Both sides ascribed great importance to this steering committee, and in fact it proved to be a crucial mechanism in ensuring the success of the project. It was continuously available as a forum for systematic analysis of complications encountered during the daily operations of the program, for working out solutions for unexpected problems as they emerged, and for developing new policies to master such problems routinely in the future. Particularly in a busy hierarchical organization, it provided an important safety valve to ensure that possible differences of professional opinion between the chief surgeon and the collaborating psychiatrist could be worked out in a task-oriented way, free from personalized hierarchical tensions and undistorted by interdisciplinary stereotypes. Once a strong personal relationship of mutual trust and respect developed between the two, this steering committee became less important.

Conforming to the Structure of the Host Institution

Because the host institution in this case was so effective and efficient an organization, with a dominant philosophy of sensitivity to the human relations aspects of its operations, the collaborating psychiatrist did not need to be much of a change agent. Instead, she could concentrate on fitting herself into the current structure and becoming accepted as someone who would help the department implement its policies and assist other staff to do likewise. Because of the hierarchical nature of the departmental organization, the nature of its mission, and the personality of its leader, her efforts could be concentrated on building her relationship with the chief surgeon and using him to help her build good working relationships with the other staff.

The attitudes of trust and respect in which she was held depended on her being perceived as a professional of high status, whose opinions were of value and whose performance could be depended upon, not only to benefit patients with whom she would interact but also to guarantee that she would not inadvertently endanger their surgical program with seriously ill patients. Part of this status was what social scientists define as "ascribed"—derived from her age (she was the oldest professional on the ward), her professional qualifications, and her reputation as a former head of an important child psychiatry program—and part of her status was "achieved"; namely, it derived from her proving her value by the observed results of her interactions with patients, members of their families, and other staff on the wards, and very much also by her devoting the effort to learning the elements of pediatric surgery and acquiring fluency in the language of the department. Her regular participation in ward rounds and the staff conference was most important in this regard. Her learning was also facilitated by the fact that on many of these occasions the chief surgeon was functioning also as a medical school professor and was teaching medical students and residents the elements of his specialty. She became, as it were, part of the class, and she spent much time afterward reading the professional literature assignments, until she had learned the fundamental concepts of pediatric surgery.

It is of interest that the head of her own department, who clearly outranked her in ascribed status but who had not acquired her knowledge of the professional lore of the host department or of its language, was treated with considerable reserve whenever he replaced her on the ward. He was treated with respect but was rarely invited to function as more than an outside consultant.

The building up of her working relationships with the rest of the staff was mediated at the beginning by the chief surgeon. He made a point of asking for her opinion during ward rounds and of explaining routines and abstruse issues to her, and his remarks were always couched in terms of great respect in a way that invited the other staff to identify with him.

On her part, it was easy for her to express her admiration for the way the department was organized, for the crucial, life-saving work of the surgeon and his staff, and for their sensitivity in supporting the parents as they coped with the ordeal of the child's illness. She also took pains to conduct her own diagnostic, supportive, and remedial operations on the actual ward and its corridors, so that she demystified her actions and allowed all to see what she was doing. Even though the department was often overcrowded and it might have been easier to take patients up to the privacy of her own office in an adjoining part of the hospital, she chose wherever possible to talk to them in full view, and often within the hearing of their fellows, in the crowded ward corridors. She usually conducted her clinical interventions in informal small groups of patients or family members, whom she convened whenever she wished to deal with an issue of general significance or to energize mutual support among them. In all such activities, she invited the participation of staff who might be in the vicinity and who were not otherwise engaged.

This informal, open social network type of operation fitted the culture of the department, but the psychiatrist specifically used it to let everyone know what she was doing and to combat the stigma attached to being signaled out by a psychiatrist for treatment. Even in talking with staff members about case-related issues, the psychiatrist almost never took them off to her own office, but conformed to the customary department practice of talking with them in the nursing station or in one of the ward treatment rooms, whenever possible with the door left open, unless privacy was really essential.

Psychiatrists are physicians, which probably facilitated her acceptance by the pediatric surgery staff. Her perceived status and her medical approach to problems of diagnosis and treatment probably made it easier for her to be accepted in this quintessential medical setting than if she had been a nonmedical psychologist of equal knowledge, skills, and experience. But once the factor of *achieved* status becomes dominant, the original disciplinary identity of the specialist probably becomes less significant, because the relationships will have become idiosyncratically personalized.

Role Overlap

Early in the program, the psychiatrist alerted the staff to the necessity of safeguarding the traditional boundaries of their professional identities. As each side learned the other's ways of thinking, she said, they should try to avoid falling into the trap of becoming "proxy psychiatrists" or "proxy pediatric surgeons." In a lighter vein she quoted as a cautionary tale the story (probably fictional)

of the actor who had become famous portraying the role of a court-
room lawyer in a TV series, and who later made a fool of himself
by trying to represent himself in court proceedings in real life. On
occasion, the psychiatrist had to pull herself up sharp when during
a ward round she found herself arguing for a particular type of
surgical intervention based on her own elementary knowledge. And
she had to dissuade one of the surgeons from opposing a plan that
every four hours a mother should catheterize her teenage daughter
because he feared the possible psychological trauma this might
cause the girl. The psychiatrist had to tell him tactfully to leave the
mental health pleading on this issue to her, and to focus on arguing
the case for the life-saving importance of regular catherization.

Menachem, Lipton, and Caplan (1981) have written about
the difficulties that arise when a psychologically oriented pediatrician overly identifies with the psychoanalytic therapeutic role and
insensibly drifts beyond the disciplinary boundaries of his culturally expected domain. What is apt to happen in such a case is that
parents who, for instance, had brought their child to see the pediatrician because the child was suffering from what they considered
bodily illness would become upset and angry with the doctor when
the pediatrician began overtly to uncover psychosocial conflicts in
the family; they would break off contact and take the case to a more
traditional physician. They may have been unconsciously defending against seeing any conflict themselves, and they become upset
when, without their prior sanction, the pediatrician begins to act
like a psychotherapist by making interpretations of unconscious
processes rather than like a traditional physician who ostensibly
accepts the situation as they have defined it. It takes long and specialized training, which the psychiatrist has and the pediatrician
has not, to appreciate the significance of powerful defense mechanisms against unacceptable unconscious impulses and fantasies,
and the practical implications of stirring up intolerable anxiety in
"making the unconscious conscious." It demands expert judgment
by a specialist before deciding on making such an interpretation in
the absence of a therapeutic contract.

It is difficult for a pediatric surgeon, or a pediatrician, or for
that matter a schoolteacher, to define abstractly the difference between functioning as a psychologically sensitized member of his

own discipline and functioning as a professional who has crossed the boundaries into the other discipline. Learning the difference comes from experience and self-awareness, helped either by the reactions of the collaborating specialist or by the discomfort shown by clients who feel they are being treated very differently from what they had expected.

Types of Intervention

The collaborating specialist makes his contributions in the host department in four main ways:

1. He takes part in staff meetings to provide mental health input.
2. He intervenes with patients and their families, modeling new diagnostic and remedial operations for the nonspecialist staff.
3. He provides psychosocial and emotional support to the other staff members as they grapple with the mental health aspects of their work.
4. He helps to diagnose, treat, and manage those problems of patients and families that demand specialized intervention, and he explains these to the other staff, to help them understand the nature of his discipline and to differentiate his specialized roles from theirs.

Staff Meetings

The collaborating specialist's contributions to staff meetings are geared to identifying cases where psychosocial aspects are especially significant. Whenever he identifies such a case, he adds his voice to staff discussions that focus on exploring the implications for team action within the overall planning of the case. Clearly the other staff are mainly preoccupied in dealing with the biological issues involved, and the mental health specialist must understand what they are doing in order to integrate an appropriate consideration of the psychosocial dimension.

In our example, despite the staff leader's strong interest in exploring to the fullest the specialist contributions of the psychiatrist, she moved slowly and cautiously in the initial months. She did not want to arouse undue anxieties in the staff by provoking them in discussion of potentially emotionally burdensome material that is commonplace in mental health staff meetings but is usually excluded from nonspecialist discussions, such as unconscious fantasies and sexual and aggressive instincts. Gradually, however, as time passed and the psychiatrist became more accepted as a supportive figure, and as she was better able to gauge the increasing psychological sophistication of the staff members, she allowed herself more freedom in raising issues of deeper psychological significance, although always with a sensitive awareness of possible signs of anxiety and defensiveness in their reactions. She took care not to use psychological jargon, restricting herself to the vocabulary of everyday life until she had learned the language of the pediatric surgery department.

The psychiatrist was also sensitive to safe topics for the families of the ward patients, topics that would not upset them and arouse resistance that would prevent them from accepting her professional recommendations. For instance, until she became an integral part of the culture of the ward and her specialized role was accepted as helpful and nonthreatening by new patients and their parents, the psychiatrist paid much attention to the stigmatizing and weakening effect of talking directly to parents and to the likelihood that they would disregard many of her recommendations. She talked openly about this issue in case conferences whenever it was relevant, and helped the staff plan how to overcome the difficulty of communicating needed mental health messages to parents who were unlikely to pay attention to what a psychiatrist would say. It proved feasible to overcome this difficulty by using the chief surgeon as team spokesperson instead of the psychiatrist. He was usually held in very high regard by the patient and the parents, who saw in him an all-powerful figure who was saving the life of the child and whose words were completely trusted.

One such case involved a four-year-old girl who was discharged from the hospital after surgical removal of a low-grade malignant tumor. The diagnosis and the treatment had been profoundly upsetting for the parents, and they focused a lot of attention on the child in the home. This aroused the envy and resentment of a seven-year-old brother, who began to behave aggressively toward her. The parents became overprotective and came down heavily on the brother, which upset the family constellation still further. The child psychiatrist helped the staff realize that the family was over-emphasizing the little girl's fragility, and that she herself might incorporate this view and begin to view herself as a chronic invalid, thus impeding her recovery. Coached by the psychiatrist, the surgeon organized a special meeting with the parents. He told them that the girl had made an excellent recovery from her surgical operation and that while in due course chemotherapy and possibly radiation therapy might be necessary, meanwhile, the program of rehabilitation demanded that the child return as quickly as possible to her preillness state of functioning. She was currently healthy and not at all fragile. She could defend herself just as well as ever before against her brother's attacks. They might try to reduce these attacks by giving the boy more attention; his resentful envy was a natural reaction that they should be able to understand. Whenever it really became excessive, they might curb it, but on the whole they should let the relationships of the children resolve themselves spontaneously, which could be expected to happen within a few weeks or a month or two, as long as the parents did not get too tense about it.

The message delivered by the surgeon was completely accepted, and the family problem speedily resolved. The surgeon had given the remedial message in his own words, but he deeply appreciated the specialist contribution of the child psychiatrist in alerting him to the need to intervene and in helping him plan what to say.

Modeling to Nonspecialists

The collaborating specialist uses two sets of techniques that he demonstrates and teaches to the other staff colleagues as an addition to their traditional professional tools. The techniques are generic and can be used with mentally healthy clients (G. Caplan, 1986b). They do not need psychotherapeutic skill, but they do require interpersonal sensitivity and human caring attitudes. Many workers of different professions have these attributes; certainly they are not the unique province of mental health professionals. The child psychiatrist on the pediatric surgery wards had ample opportunity in her daily work to demonstrate these techniques and to discuss their rationale in staff meetings.

The first set of techniques are those of *crisis intervention,* namely, anticipatory guidance and preventive intervention.

Anticipatory Guidance. This method is employed, if possible, immediately after admission, or whenever time is available before an operation or a planned painful investigation. Wherever feasible, the intervention should take place in a group setting of patients (if they are old enough to understand) or of parents; parents should be present when their children are receiving guidance so they may reinforce the messages afterward and so they may support each other.

The method consists of arousing anticipatory distress by describing the expectable stressful events or procedures in evocative detail, while at the same time providing the reassurance that the distress, which is a natural phenomenon, will usually be limited and can be mastered by appropriate activity. The boundaries and duration of likely pain and discomfort are predicted, to counteract feelings of the child and the parents that the pain will be never-ending and will be completely intolerable and destructive. The child and his parents are urged to use techniques of relaxation and diversion, such as by focusing on pleasant memories, which are likely to make the discomfort easier to bear. They are told that the nurses are always willing to give them medicine or injections to dull the pain; they are not expected to be great heroes and to suffer unnecessarily, and whenever they feel the need they should ask the nurse or the doctor for such help. (Empirical studies have shown that patients who have been given this message ahead of time usually require less analgesics because they know that they can get them as soon as they ask.)

A crucial element in this method is that the professional conveys the hopeful expectation that although unfortunately the situation may be unpleasant, it can be kept under control by these activities and that the patient will be able to master it rather than be a completely passive and helpless victim. The intervenor also guides family members in helping and supporting the patient and each other, and stimulates them to ask for and to give support to others on the ward who are in the same boat.

The final and not least important message to the family members and to older children is that the expectable expressions of pain and emotional upset during the experience are normal reactions; they are not to be ashamed of, and are not signs of psychological illness or weakness of character. The anticipatory guidance also demonstrates to the patients and their family members that the staff do care for them and will provide whatever support is needed to ensure mastery of an admittedly unpleasant and stressful experience.

Preventive Intervention. In this method, the professional operates during the stressful experience by providing information about what is happening to promote a feeling of cognitive mastery in place of the weakening effect of confusion and of confronting the unknown; he helps lower negative emotional arousal; and he provides the family with guidance and material assistance in dealing positively with their predicament. The essential techniques include the following:

1. Make repeated short contacts during crisis to satisfy increased dependency needs.
2. Support strategic withdrawal at height of crisis.
3. Then support active confrontation of problems. Impart information. Help find meanings. Help focus on the present. Help plan what to do.
4. Help family members communicate with each other.
5. Help plan activities to solve crisis problems. Take part in implementing plans.
6. Help them bear the frustration of the unknown outcome and urge perseverance despite confusion.
7. Warn them about the danger of expectable fatigue. Encourage division of labor to prevent fatigue. Organize monitoring of fatigue level and rest periods for recuperation.
8. Maintain hope. Encourage activity to achieve mastery.
9. Encourage invoking outside help and counteract shame that this means weakness.

10. Remind them of their precrisis identity. Do not validate the crisis-eroded identity of weak helplessness.
11. Urge family members to express negative feelings and help each other master them. Emphasize normality of expectable upset.
12. Counteract blaming of self or others to relieve tension.

These techniques focus on the here and now. They do not involve identifying past reasons why individuals may not be grappling effectively with the crisis problems. Rather, they use the personal influence of the intervenor to modify current behavior. Therefore, no specialized psychological training or sophistication is necessary, and this approach may be quite adequately used by laypersons in the form of offering an ordinary human helping hand to individuals in crisis.

Support Methods

The child psychiatrist focused many of her efforts on support systems methods (G. Caplan, 1989), and she communicated by modeling and by explicit verbal teaching to the other staff, who quickly appreciated their importance and were very keen to learn them.

The techniques included acting toward the patients and their families in an explicitly nurturing and caring way that was concerned, warm, and personalized. The family members were made to feel that staff were interested in them as individuals and were eager to guide and support them in grappling with the trauma of the child's illness.

Central to the supportive approach was *information mediation;* the child psychiatrist collected and funneled current relevant information about the case from the staff to the patient and vice versa, and interpreted its meaning in both directions. Even in a small, closely knit unit like pediatric surgery, the activities of so many professionals and consultants of different disciplines are often confusing to patients and relatives, who pick up half-understood and sometimes discrepant information from a variety of team members. It is difficult for the family to maintain a coherent picture of the case, particularly as they may be so anxious that they may distort what they hear.

In theory, the daily ward rounds that clarify the current situation to the staff, and certainly to the chief pediatric surgeon, should provide the opportunity for communicating an up-to-date picture to the family; but they are usually kept away from the bedside and parents have to eavesdrop on discussions from the corridor. Apart from specific important decisions that are communicated by the surgeon or one of his assistants, the doctors are usually too busy to devote adequate time and effort to telling the parents what is happening. And hospital tradition does not encourage the nurses giving information about the case to the family. To be sure, it would not have been helpful to communicate *all* the details to the family, but incomplete or patchy communication serves usually to stimulate fearful fantasies that weaken the coping capacity of the family members. And facile reassurance that "everything will be all right" or "all is going well" often have a paradoxically negative effect.

The child psychiatrist often raised this issue in staff meetings and obtained sanction to act routinely as spokesperson, funneling suitably edited information to the family, with the proviso that in certain instances particular items would be withheld pending staff meeting clarification and an overt decision. Information was not simply baldly communicated, but was interpreted in a way that emphasized positive and hopeful elements. Fostering hope, even in situations of great danger and privation, is an essential ingredient in providing psychosocial support to people in adversity.

Another element in the supportive approach, the importance of which has been appreciated only in recent years, is to encourage people in crisis to avoid confronting overwhelmingly painful issues at peaks of stress. Defenses such as distraction of attention, denial, emotional blunting or isolation, or cognitive confusion can be extremely valuable in helping people, little by little, come to terms with the inescapable realities. Only then can they be helped to deal with what is happening.

In the past, psychiatrists often were so committed to the importance of people facing their burdens openly, and so concerned about defense mechanisms that characterized established cases of psychiatric illness, that they pushed normal persons under stress to face reality more quickly than was desirable. The results were often traumatic. Nowadays, we have learned to temper our confrontational zeal by respecting the need of stressed people to defend themselves by temporary "strategic withdrawal" against unfaceable calamity, until they have had an opportunity to mobilize their intrapsychic and social resources. The professionals then offer their support and guidance in a "return to the fray," but at a pace that keeps the emotional distress within bearable limits.

A number of empirical studies have recently validated the hypothesis that individuals exposed to major stress are less likely to be damaged by the experience if they concurrently receive psychosocial support that enables them to master their difficulties without breakdown in their mental health (G. Caplan, 1986b). It has therefore become a primary goal of sophisticated professionals to foster and validate such support among family members and to influence them to put aside possible family tensions during periods of stress so they can help those who are experiencing most strain. The setting on the pediatric surgery wards where family members were continuously present was conducive to such a mission, and indeed the child psychiatrist worked hard influencing family members to support the patients and each other and guiding the other staff to do likewise. Similarly, she mobilized psychological support for the patients and their families by relatives, friends, community professionals, and natural helpers, whom she helped to convene and whom she encouraged by pointing out to them that their supportive activities would contribute significantly to a positive outcome in the treatment of the child (G. Caplan, 1989).

Another very important contribution of the psychiatrist was to monitor the level of fatigue of family members, and to urge them to rest whenever this seemed necessary. Left to themselves, their sense of urgency would often lead them to wear themselves out, and to put off resting because they would feel guilty about leaving the scene of the struggle. Only when they were told authoritatively that they would be more helpful to the child if they replenished their strength could this guilt be relieved.

Other support systems methods included organizing a mutual help partnership between the child (if he was old enough) and his parents with another similar case on the ward. The more experienced child or parents could offer guidance and support to others, and at the same time gain a greater sense of mastering their own stress, rather than being passive victims.

The ward setting provided the psychiatrist and the other staff with an excellent opportunity to organize informal support systems among children and parents who could offer each other nonprofessional help as people who share a common suffering. There is particularly valuable benefit in the natural mix of "oldtimers" and those who are experiencing this stress for the first time. The psychiatrist modeled for her staff colleagues the way professionals convene such mutual help networks and provide them with backing, without distorting the more spontaneous, close, and personalized style of this overtly nonprofessional support.

A central role of the child psychiatrist, which she shared in this instance with the chief pediatric surgeon, was to offer support to the other staff and to help them support each other in overcoming the cognitive and emotional burdens arising out of their roles in supporting children and their parents confronting death, suffering, and crippling, and their own human reactions to these sufferings. The mission was to influence the staff to remain empathically sensitive to patients and their families, without becoming personally overinvolved, or without defensively turning off their own feelings and becoming insensitive. The psychiatrist focused on these issues, whenever relevant, in the weekly staff meetings and in frequent contacts with staff members. She met regularly with the head nurse, who was in the most precarious position, since she represented the staff in many daily contacts with patients and family members and also had the task of monitoring the reactions of the other nurses and of supporting them.

The child psychiatrist had to make it clear from the outset that her discussion of staff members' feelings was purely to assist them to deal with the expectable reactions of sensitive professionals, and was in no way intended as an attempt to diagnose or treat them psychiatrically. She used techniques of relationship building similar to those used in mental health consultation. In this aspect of her work it was important to emphasize that she was coordinate with other staff: all were in the same boat. The psychiatrist showed that she too was often emotionally aroused by close contact with the sufferings of children and family members, and was in as much need for support from colleagues as they were.

Many very sick children died on the ward. Obviously this was always very burdensome for all concerned; but, by and large, experienced staff soon learned to maintain their professional poise despite real empathy for the family. But in certain cases, when a child to whom they had become attached died after a long fight to save the child's life, their mourning often threatened their customary emotional equilibrium. When this happened, the psychiatrist participated actively in the mourning process. She wept along with the family and with her colleagues, demonstrating that she was not afraid that her tears would erode her capacity to carry on with her professional mission once she had expressed her anguish and recovered her poise.

Without such explicit support, the twin dangers of staff burnout and dehumanizing insensitivity would be considerable.

Specialized Activities

On her own, the child psychiatrist investigated and treated cases in which she detected significant psychopathology in a child or one of the parents, or in which the relationships within the family were idiosyncratically disordered. In these cases she reported in general at staff meetings, but she did not go into detail, apart from pointing out the external manifestations of the problems so that staff members might learn how to identify deviant cases.

Occasionally it was possible to offer short family therapy to resolve a current impasse produced when the child's illness had triggered long-standing conflicts. Mostly, however, the psychiatrist's therapeutic interventions were geared to helping the family accept the need for longer-term psychotherapy for themselves or for the child after discharge from the hospital. The trauma of the illness generally made them more amenable to the psychiatrist's recommendations. Her daily presence on the ward with them, and the opportunity to see the various family members in a concentrated way, also increased her influence.

Special Concerns

As her program unfolded, the psychiatrist had to deal with a number of significant problems.

Conflicts of Interest

At times, the child psychiatrist had to deal with real conflicts of interest between her mission to protect the mental health of patients and family members and the dominant mission of the department. When this happened, it was important that she should identify the existential reality of the conflict and take steps to resolve it by open negotiation, either in the weekly staff meeting or in the executive steering committee.

For instance, it occasionally happened that the psychiatrist needed more time to complete her diagnostic investigations of potential psychopathology or her treatment of family disorders, in order to work through with parents a plan to have specialist therapy for themselves or their child after the hospitalization. The question would then arise whether to delay the discharge of the patient until the psychiatrist could complete her work, especially if the family did not live close enough or were not motivated enough to collaborate in this process after discharge. The mission of the department might require that the bed be vacated to make room for another patient. Moreover, the cost of inpatient hospitalization in pediatric surgery was very high. Was it justifiable to prolong a patient's stay just to allow for continuation of psychiatric investigation, particularly as it could at best usually result only in preparing the family for long-term treatment elsewhere?

Eventually the policy was crystallized to make no blanket rule, but to have all the staff become reconciled to the reality of this dilemma, to weigh up the balance of factors in the case, and to decide on a case-by-case basis whether the benefit to the patient by prolonging the hospitalization was worth the cost. It was also decided that a decision to discharge a patient, in cases that had been flagged by the psychiatrist, should be made only after she had been given the opportunity to express her considered opinion, which would be carefully evaluated by the surgeon and the other staff.

Adjusting to Changes of Staff

The final development in this program has already been described as an example of what tends to happen if a key staff member is temporarily absent or leaves the team. It appears that the partnership is interrupted and previous steps in development have to be repeated and relationships built up afresh, with the negotiation of new agreements conducted, if necessary, in the steering committee.

An example of this process, this time in adjusting to a change of staff in the host department, occurred three months after the start of the program, and after the relationships between the child psychiatrist and the rest of the staff had been worked out and consolidated by generally accepted procedures. Suddenly, the head nurse was forced to leave for family reasons; she was replaced by a senior nurse from an internal medicine ward. The psychiatrist realized that she would have to build up a working relationship with her, but although the pediatric surgeon introduced them and explained the nature of the psychiatrist's role, the new head nurse behaved as though the psychiatrist was a visitor on the ward. She seemed to regard the psychiatrist's attempts to engage her in conversation about cases as a distraction from her own concentration on urgent ward business. She also showed reluctance to divulge information about patients, and she never asked the psychiatrist for an opinion about a patient or a family.

After a couple of weeks of increasing frustration, the psychiatrist raised the problem in the steering committee. (She had not yet built up a close enough relationship with the pediatric surgeon that would have encouraged her to raise the matter directly with him.) At the committee meeting, the surgeon said that he was well aware of the difficulty and welcomed a discussion of the issue. Apart from the need to solve this problem, the discussion gave him an opportunity to provide further information about his pattern of organizing his ward. He said that he had purposely recruited a nurse from an internal medicine department so that he could personally train her in surgical nursing; he wanted to avoid someone having to unlearn techniques of adult surgical nursing that might be different from those needed in caring for child patients. "It is easier to get someone to learn a quite different role than one which is similar but subtly different from your old accustomed style of working."

He emphasized that she was a very competent nurse, with great organizational potential, and that in her past position she had demonstrated leadership capacity and professional flexibility. "But you have to realize that she feels overwhelmed by the demands of her new job, particularly by having to react so immediately to very sick patients. Internal medicine has a much slower pace. It will take her a few more weeks to adjust to the pace of her new position, and I am carefully dosing the demands I make on her. I know that she has no real idea of what is involved in our mental health partnership, and that what I said to her about it went in one ear and out the other. But I promise that if you will have the patience and wait until she feels less overwhelmed, I will show her how to deal with you and help her see the benefit."

Indeed, three weeks later the surgeon began to build the necessary attitudinal and communication bridges between the head nurse and the child psychiatrist; in the meantime, the psychiatrist relaxed her pressure on the nurse. When the relationship building did start, it followed a similar pattern of development as with her predecessor, but it progressed more quickly because of the atmosphere of acceptance of the psychiatrist by the other staff, which the new head nurse rapidly began to appreciate once the surgeon opened her eyes to the significance and ways of working in the collaboration program.

CHAPTER FIFTEEN

Collaboration in a Poorly Organized Institution

A children's rehabilitation hospital on the outskirts of a large American city requested mental health consultation from a community mental health center. The request was made by the medical director, a senior orthopedic surgeon who was a friend of the chief psychiatrist. The psychiatrist agreed to conduct a preliminary study of the rehabilitation institution and discuss how her center might develop a program. The medical director obtained the sanction of his board of directors for this study, which was carried out over a period of three months as a program-centered administrative consultation by the psychiatrist and her staff.

The institution dealt with children who were chronically crippled by congenital anomalies. Most of these severely disabled children and adolescents spent several months in the institution, and some stayed for many years in custodial care. The institution had eighty beds, divided into four wards that catered to infants, school-age children, adolescents, and young adults. In the fourth ward were several young adults who had been there for many years and for whom discharge to other community custodial facilities had not proved feasible.

The institution was staffed by a multidisciplinary group of surgeons, pediatricians, urologists, nurses, social workers, teachers, physiotherapists, and occupational therapists. The physical plant and housekeeping were managed by a nonmedical administrative director. The professional program was organized in a number of disciplinary units, including surgery, pediatrics, rehabilitation, nursing, social work, and counseling. The whole professional program

320

was administered by the medical director, who spent only three to four hours a week in the institution and had little personal contact with its day-to-day operations.

The study revealed that apart from efficient management by the nonmedical administrator and his staff, including public relations and fund raising units, there was little supervision and control of the program. Lines of authority and communication were vague. Unit chiefs administered their own units and recruited their own staffs with the formal agreement of the medical director and the board. The institution had grown in an unplanned way over the years, and there had apparently never been a clear definition of its policy. The professional level of the staff was mixed. Some workers were highly trained and dedicated; others were not—they gave the impression of continuing to work in the institution because it satisfied their personal needs, without much apparent commitment to serving the patients or fulfilling a professional mission. Each unit was a law unto itself, with varied morale and cohesion according to the competence of its director. Despite lip service to the idea of a coordinated multidisciplinary rehabilitation program, there was no effective communication or joint action among separate units; in fact, rivalries and professional and personal tensions separated them.

The result was absent or inadequate planning of individual cases, ineffective implementation of treatment that required joint action among units, low morale of patients, much waste of staff time in interminable general meetings that led to no productive action, much bickering and feuding between individuals and between groups of staff, and undue and hopeless passivity among long-stay patients.

The picture was not all bleak. There were many devoted workers, and some of the units were effective in carrying out their own service functions. A few attractive patients did receive adequate care if they stayed for a relatively short time. To a superficial visitor, the place gave the impression of an institution that catered well to a very deprived population of chronic cases, who were well housed, well fed, and treated with modern equipment.

The conclusion of the study team was that the mental health salience of the institution was high but that, apart from individual and perhaps group psychotherapy for some of the patients to help them cope with the effects of their crippling disease, any attempt to better the lives of patients by psychiatric intervention was doomed. A systematic program to improve their lot would demand the coordinated activity of several different units, and it seemed highly unlikely that this would be feasible, since central professional authority was lacking.

The results were reported in a tactful way to the medical director and to his board, who received them with no surprise. The team's main recommendation for remedying the administrative problems was to establish a clear line of authority by recruiting an active clinical director or a new medical director who would devote full time to the job. The psychiatrist said that if this recommendation were carried out, she and her staff would be willing to participate in building a mental health service in the institution and helping actively to improve the human relations aspect of its functioning.

Over a two-year period, the psychiatrists provided occasional case consultation on request, and they accepted referrals of a few difficult cases to their clinic. Then the medical director retired. He was replaced by a highly competent orthopedic surgeon who was willing to become the institution's full-time medical director and to reorganize it along rational lines. One of his first acts was to invite the community mental health center to set up a mental health program in his institution. This invitation was fully backed by the board of directors, and the psychiatrists accepted it.

History of the Collaboration

They established a mental health unit based on collaboration rather than consultation. The board allotted one full-time salary for a senior psychiatrist, and this money was used to pay for the part-time work of several junior and senior psychiatrists who operated as a team in the four wards. The unit was managed by the chief psychiatrist, who coordinated the program with the medical director, with whom the team met once a week to plan activities and to obtain his sanction.

It was arranged that all new patients admitted to the institution would be seen by members of the team; within a few months the team had become involved with about half the patients on the four wards. In each case, a diagnostic and management plan was made, including individual or group psychotherapy whenever indicated. Case responsibility was allotted to one member of the team, which included four junior psychiatrists (one to each ward), the chief psychiatrist, and another senior psychiatrist. The staff member responsible for a patient was expected to contact all relevant personnel involved in the case and to coordinate joint activities. System issues were discussed at the weekly unit conference, attended by the medical director, and the two senior psychiatrists supervised the junior psychiatrists in their diagnostic and remedial activities. Representatives of the unit were also supposed to attend all institution ward rounds and general staff meetings.

This plan was based on the expectation that the institution's preexisting organizational structure might lead to problems if certain aspects of case management required coordination with other units. It was hoped that the authority of the medical director would help to obtain the concurrence of workers of other units. It was also expected that at institution ward rounds the mental health workers would get information about diagnostic, treatment, and rehabilitation plans for all patients, so that they could participate in ongoing management programs for each patient.

But it soon became clear that the medical director, though a competent orthopedic surgeon and an affable, open-minded man who was sensitive to the human relations aspects of patient care and highly motivated to develop an effective partnership with the mental health unit, was not by nature a forceful person. He had no previous experience in institutional administration. He chose not to act as a "new brush sweeping clean" but instead tried to be a friendly, understanding leader. He hoped to achieve his goals by slow and gradual methods of persuasion, rather than by cutting through some of the obvious organizational tangles with which he was confronted.

For instance, he allowed the chief of the rehabilitation unit to continue to run the hospital ward rounds and staff meetings, despite evidence that this surgeon, although competent in patient care, was held in low regard by most of the staff. The hospital ward rounds were held each week on a different ward, and were attended by all the staff of the rehabilitation unit and by line workers of other units, but not by their seniors. These meetings tended to involve long discussions of technical issues relating to physiotherapy, occupational therapy, and physical medicine. The meeting produced what seemed like ideal plans for psychosocial rehabilitation, requiring coordinated activity by nursing, counseling, and social work personnel, but there was no precise formulation of treatment plans, no allocation of tasks or responsibility, and no monitoring of implementation. Three weeks later, when the same case was again discussed, a similar plan was usually proposed, often without evidence that the surgeon remembered that he had gone over this ground before. The mental health staff felt that attending these ward rounds was a waste of their time, and, like the senior workers of other units, they stopped coming. Only the junior psychiatrist assigned to the particular ward whose patients were being surveyed felt obliged to be present to answer questions about a patient, and even such questions were rare.

Admission and discharge of patients and their possible transfer from ward to ward were determined informally by the chief social worker, sometimes with the participation of the head counselor, countersigned by the rubber-stamp signature of one of the physicians, usually a junior resident. The chief psychiatrist asked the medical director to take over these decisions, which she felt were crucially important in the reorganization. The medical director appreciated the significance of this issue and agreed to make the decisions himself, but he did nothing about it, possibly because he wished to avoid an open conflict that he expected to lose—the chief social worker had great informal power. She had been there longer than most other senior staff, and had close links with the public relations and fundraising program and with several influential members of the board. She effectively controlled many patient discharges because she was responsible for finding community placements and sheltered jobs for chronically disturbed patients.

The chief social worker had ostensibly welcomed the mental health program, but it did not take long for her underlying negative attitudes to become manifest. She seemed to feel that the psychiatrists had invaded what had previously been her exclusive domain of being responsible for the psychosocial aspects of patient care. She felt that her ideas about the human relations dimension of rehabilitation of crippled children and their families, ideas based on many years of practical experience, were more valid than the new-fangled concepts of the psychiatrists.

When the chief social worker learned of any precise case plan that involved a specific decision to discharge a patient to an outside agency or institution, she intentionally sabotaged it. A fourteen-year-old boy with a chronic orthopedic leg problem had been involved in delinquency before admission and had been brought in from a residential correctional institution. He was investigated by the staff of the mental health unit, who found that the boy suffered from a neurotic personality disorder based on long-standing problems in his relationships with his mother. It was judged that his delinquent behavior was the result of undue dependency that had led to his being drawn into an antisocial street gang and was not a consequence of a delinquent personality. It was decided that at the conclusion of his orthopedic treatment the boy should therefore not go home or to the residential correctional institution, where he might be trained to be a criminal, but to a nearby residential psychotherapeutic institution that specialized in treating by milieu therapy boys with his type of ego disorder.

The psychiatrists negotiated with this therapeutic institution, which agreed to take the boy. This fact was communicated to the boy's social worker, who had participated in the case discussions, at which the medical director had also been present. After discussing the case with the chief social worker, her supervisor, the boy's social worker, without informing the psychiatrist, arranged for the boy to go home to his parents' house. Four days later the boy quarreled with his mother, and she contacted the probation officer and arranged for his readmission to the correctional institution. The medical director, who had wholeheartedly supported the staff conference plan, was furious but did nothing about it. The psychiatrists chose not to remind him of the likely consequence of his passivity, since the damage to the boy had already been done; they felt that the medical director was by nature not tough enough to control the chief social worker, and that exerting pressure on him would probably be counterproductive.

Another case was even more serious, since it not only harmed a patient but also aggravated a significant social system problem. A highly intelligent seventeen-year-old from an underworld family, suffering from traumatic paraplegia following a spinal cord injury after a fight between rival gangs, was a great behavior problem on the senior ward. He smoked marijuana brought in by members of his family. He continually invited visits by his underworld friends, who came and went at will and who regularly helped him break the rules of the institution. He was the leader of a gang of older boys on the ward, who terrorized the other patients. He did not participate in studies or in occupational therapy, he stayed late in bed, and he bribed or terrorized staff to let him do as he liked. The psychiatrists felt that he was suffering from an antisocial personality disorder; he was living out omnipotent fantasies to mask an underlying depression linked with the terrible consequences of his injury.

It was felt that this boy must be removed from the institution and be given a chance to understand his fantasies and the negative consequences of his refusing to participate in the rehabilitation program. He was offered the chance to be admitted to the open psychiatric ward of a university general teaching hospital, and, after three days' thought, he agreed to go there rather than return home. One day before he was due to be transferred, the chief social worker put him in an ambulance and sent him home on a week's leave, getting a new pediatric resident who had no knowledge of the case to sign the papers while the medical director was away. On his return, the boy did go to the psychiatric ward, but later that day he made a "dramatic escape" in his wheelchair and was readmitted by the chief social worker to the rehabilitation institution, despite the medical director's standing instructions to the contrary. The medical director expressed his anger at the chief social worker's manipulations, but she persuaded him to agree to her alternative plans: to arrange an apartment in town for this boy and another patient, who would be encouraged to get jobs and become partially independent, plans that would take her months to implement.

Six months after the collaborative program began, it was decided to try to reduce the opposition of the chief social worker by inviting her and the chief counselor to attend the weekly psychosocial case conferences. The counselor attended regularly, but the social worker came only intermittently, claiming that she was too busy. When she participated and took part personally in decision making instead of hearing about case plans from her subordinates, she sabotaged them less, at least by conscious design. But she expressed her antagonism to the approach of the mental health workers more openly in the conference discussions.

The original program of the mental health unit was based on the expectation that the medical director would use his authority to ensure compliance with jointly developed plans. As it became clear that this was not succeeding, a new approach was tried. The program was decentralized: four task forces were organized, one for each ward. Each task force met regularly with the other staff of its ward to discuss patients and to coordinate staff activities on a case. This fostered the development of partnerships between individual line workers with less involvement of their seniors. When dissonance at higher levels was encountered, the case was discussed at a central psychosocial conference, chaired by the medical director, to which the chiefs of the other divisions were specially invited. Mental health education meetings were organized by the psychiatrists on each ward for nurses and for patients who were old enough to participate.

An attempt was also made to build personal relationships with the relevant groups by reducing the number of mental health staff working on a daily basis inside the institution. One of the junior psychiatrists began to spend several hours a day in the institution and was available to interact on a regular basis with many levels of staff. He spent much time working on cases with the chief social worker, who felt less threatened by him. He also spent an hour each week discussing cases with the chief counselor. The medical director's help was invoked on a case-by-case basis by psychiatrists when they encountered difficulties, and the chief psychiatrist offered him administrative consultation.

The entire program was less than optimally effective; in complicated cases, particularly those involving chronic patients, it proved impossible to implement case plans proposed by the mental health workers because of poor coordination. But in many other respects, this decentralized pattern of organization did succeed; personal influence by the mental health staff on line workers was not interfered with by their seniors, often because of the inadequate supervision and control within their own division.

Finally, it is worth emphasizing that even though the medical director was not forceful enough to exercise the leadership that would have permitted maximum collaboration, he did exert sufficient influence to foster a decentralized pattern of collaboration. He protected the mental health unit from being completely extruded by the vested interest groups and their leaders. Without him the situation would have been quite impossible; in fact, when he resigned several months later, the mental health program was terminated. It had, however, left its mark: the new medical director, a younger and very forceful orthopedic surgeon, recruited the junior psychiatrist who had been the central member of the mental health team to reestablish the mental health collaboration program.

Principles of Technique

The overriding principle is that the way a collaboration program is organized must conform to the realities of the host institution, and must not be based on a preplanned blueprint. Our example shows that a centralized model, originally designed to articulate with the pyramidal authority and communications system of a well-organized institution, does not work in a poorly organized institution that lacks an effective central authority. Moreover, it must be recognized that, as in our example, such a poorly organized institution may be quite stable and enduring. The board members, although they were aware of certain shortcomings in the care of patients, were proud of their fundraising success, their modern facilities and equipment, and the high quality of the housekeeping and maintenance. A number of the units were also quite happy with the status quo, and probably felt that their personal and professional needs were being satisfied by the success of their own specialized service operations.

The fact that many of the patients, particularly the long-stay patients, were depressed, apathetic, and passive could be interpreted as an expectable consequence of their major chronic disablements. And some patients, such as the seventeen-year-old paraplegic, could get compensatory, if perverted, satisfaction from being allowed to live the way they wished in the shelter of the institution that catered to their needs for board, lodging, and recreation. Similarly, some of the tenured staff could feel that they had occupational security in a job that was not too demanding and in a setting that conferred on them the social status of meritorious service.

Any attempt by mental health intervenors to engage in a head-on confrontation with entrenched division heads would be doomed to failure; even the signs that they might make the attempt would probably stimulate defensively hostile operations, as in the case of the chief social worker. The only way that such staff might be brought into line with a rational plan of reorganization would be through determined action by a strong central leader, who would have the full backing of the board of directors.

In the absence of such centralized authority, a viable collaboration program requires that central figures should be effectively bypassed with a *decentralized* system that focuses on cooperating closely with line workers and attempting to influence them through individual personal relationships. This may succeed if there is ineffective supervisory control by those division heads who feel threatened by the mental health workers, as with the chief nurse in our example.

The other approach is to use a mental health specialist who is sufficiently senior to arouse the respect of line workers but not of high enough status to make a unit head, such as the chief social worker, unduly defensive. In a well-organized institution, by contrast, success depends on using high-status psychiatrists and is endangered when a junior psychiatrist is assigned to the daily operations. The pediatric surgeon and his representatives were themselves sufficiently secure and had enough control of their field that they could not be threatened by a high-status collaborator from outside their discipline.

Focusing a collaboration program on personal influence at the line level may lead to successful results in caring for individual patients, but it will necessarily have a less enduring impact on institutional policies than a focus on the total hierarchical system. Moreover, after a great deal of effort is invested in increasing the sensitivity and skills of such line workers, they may become dissatisfied with the system and leave, or may rebel against their supervisors and be fired. They may carry their skills to other workplaces, but this institution and its future clients will receive no enduring benefit from them.

The mental health specialist may feel impelled to weigh the profit to be derived from his operations in terms of achieving his population-oriented goals against the cost of expending time and effort in this setting. If his achievements mainly involve benefit to particular clients and have little or no enduring effect on the institution's program, he may be better off treating clients as an autonomous specialist in his own clinic or hospital, or in seeking to work in some other host institution that may be equally salient but more feasible.

The final consideration is the actual power and influence wielded by the central authority figures in the host institution. They may not spend enough time there or may not be sufficiently steadfast to impose their influence on the institution, but they may still be strong enough to sponsor, support, and protect the mental health intervenors.

In our example the original leader, the very high-status and forceful chief orthopedic surgeon, spent so little time and was so uninvolved in daily activities that his sponsorship was considered very unlikely, and it was felt that it was not worth even trying to establish a collaboration program. The next medical director was strong enough to provide sponsorship but not powerful enough to reorganize the system. When he was eventually replaced by a person more junior but more forceful, who was given stronger backing by a board that had by then come to realize the essential need to reorganize the institution, the situation began to change radically. Interestingly, the third medical director, instead of requesting the mental health center to send another team into the institution, recruited the young psychiatrist who by then had become well known and had built up personal relationships of trust and respect with many of the personnel. He asked him to join the staff and establish a mental health unit that from the beginning would be an integral part of the institution and would work in close partnership with him to reorganize the institution.

This raises an interesting question: What are the advantages and disadvantages of sending specialists from another organization into a host institution to establish a collaboration program, versus the institution's recruiting a specialist to join its own staff and become an integrated member of its work force? The first alternative provides the possibility of deploying a more senior specialist, who will initially satisfy his career needs by membership in an established clinical facility, and provides outside support and guidance for a junior specialist attempting to steer his way among the complicated forces operating inside a poorly organized institution. But once the initial hurdles have been overcome, a specialist who is an insider, who builds personal relationships with fellow staff members, who more fully identifies with the institution, who is perceived as "one of us," and who has been forced to develop his own patronage and support base within the institution may be better able to exert a continuing influence on the institution's atmosphere, policies, and program. It remains for future practice explorations to help us answer this question. Until then it is advisable to keep an open mind.

PART III

Methodological
and Technical Issues

CHAPTER SIXTEEN

When School Psychologists Use Mental Health Consultation and Collaboration

Three factors must be taken into account in considering the practical implications for school psychologists of the concepts and techniques of this book: First, the school psychologist is an in-house member of staff and as such has an assigned role, governed by the policies of the school department and its administrators. This role usually includes promoting the psychological well-being of students, in addition to helping teachers and other specialist staff cater to the particular needs and personal idiosyncrasies of individual children.

Second, schools in Western countries in the 1990s usually have been entrusted by community leaders with an expanded social mission in addition to their traditional function of teaching "the three R's." They are expected to prepare children to become responsible family members and citizens, to inculcate moral values, to educate them in methods of healthy living and avoidance of socially unacceptable practices, and to help them survive psychologically such major stressors as war, terrorism, and natural disasters. In the past, these types of education were largely the responsibility of the church and community agencies, or the private domain of the family. Nowadays, the school psychologist, as the in-house mental health authority, must participate in and advise on all these issues.

The third element is that most schools have added to their staffs a range of specialized workers to share the responsibility for their expanded socioeducational mission. These specialized support staff often include doctors, nurses, social workers, nutritionists, speech therapists, and health educators. They have their own areas

335

of expertise. But there is considerable overlap in their competences and their mission both in regard to which students and which problems they are trained to handle. They can accomplish their goals primarily by direct interaction with students and parents or indirectly through the intermediation of teachers, school administrators, or other staff, on either a case-by-case basis or by molding school practices and curriculum. The allotment of specific tasks and responsibilities and the division of function among various staff members will be worked out in detail over time in each school on the basis of administrative policies, local traditions, and the personality, skills, and status of each staff member. Thus, in various schools, sex education may be entrusted to the school nurse, the school psychologist, the health educator, the guidance counselor, the social worker, or selected classroom teachers.

A school psychologist will usually have a variety of different roles in relation to different student problems and to how the pie has been divided in his particular school. He quickly learns that although his job title may be the only one in the school that explicitly includes the term *psychologist,* most of the other school staff are likely to have professional knowledge and skills in the field, even though they may use a different vocabulary.

The Mandate of Collaboration

In the light of these considerations, it is clear that whenever he is part of a task force dealing with a particular case, a school psychologist in his daily work is most likely to use mental health *collaboration.* (Of course, in direct interaction with students, he uses traditional methods of psychological testing, diagnosis, and counseling or therapy.) In each problem situation he must supplement the techniques of collaboration discussed in Part Two by identifying the pattern of responsibilities he shares with the other specialist support staff and determining his own contribution and his need to initiate direct or indirect action. He may also need to negotiate or to clarify how he and the other specialists will work together, and how they will keep teachers and administrators informed and involved.

In this aspect of his work he should find valuable the principles of assessing social system issues and negotiating acceptance of his chosen role that are discussed in earlier chapters of this book, even though he will not be required to use the specific techniques of community exploration, building relationships with a consultee institution, and negotiating and maintaining a consultation contract, which a mental health consultant coming in from the outside would need; such issues are already covered by the terms of his employment as an in-house staff member.

The school psychologist's division of his time between direct action and partially indirect action in partnership with other specialists and with teachers and administrators will depend on the terms of his service. For instance, he may have been hired to investigate children who are considered deviant or problematic by their teachers, to test the children, to diagnose them, to counsel them, to treat them by psychotherapy, perhaps to recommend transfer to another class, and perhaps also to advise teachers on better ways of handling them. He usually spends a significant part of his time and effort as a specialized member of those school teams that deal with problem children on a case-by-case basis or in group or classroom settings.

The basic mandate of the school psychologist naturally includes mental health collaboration in partnerships with other staff members, in addition to carrying out specialized testing and therapeutic duties in his own office, where indicated. He usually does not need to *initiate* a program of collaboration, since this is likely to be one of the functions for which he was originally hired. He is already an integral member of the school staff, with a mandate to undertake partial responsibility for improving the mental health care of children who may be referred to him by his educational colleagues.

In some schools, he may have been hired to fulfill an additional preventive function, in which case his job description may include organizing programs to screen the student population to identify children who may have future difficulties, even though teachers may not currently consider them problematic. Here too it is likely that the psychologist will automatically involve other members of staff in developing such a program. This provides a natural framework for what we have called *mental health collaboration.*

What is likely to vary from school to school and from person to person is the ratio of time that the psychologist devotes to work inside his office, in testing or psychotherapy, compared to the time spent collaborating with or advising other staff in joint plans. This ratio will be influenced by the policies of the school authorities and also by the psychologist's own philosophy and training. He may, for instance, be oriented to individual clients and therefore may wish to spend more of his time using his own specialized techniques. If he is population-oriented, he may wish to spend more of his time in collaborative activities because by doing so he will not only benefit the index cases but he will also be adding to his colleagues' mental health sensitivities and skills and improving the mental health aspects of school policies and practices, and thus he may hope to affect the lives of many children with whom he himself will never deal. It may be that the school authorities share this philosophical approach, in which case they may have recruited him for the job with the intention that he will devote much of his time to collaboration and consultation. If, however, they were more traditionally oriented, he will have to influence them to sanction his operating according to his population orientation.

Whether or not the school psychologist has to devote special effort to develop his program of mental health collaboration, he will need to pay attention to similar issues as those faced by a mental health specialist who penetrated the school from an outside base, issues we have discussed in the previous three chapters.

Consultation: Constraints and Opportunities

Finally, we may turn our attention to the techniques of mental health *consultation*. It is again worth emphasizing that we are referring here to the types of technique described in this book and not to just any kind of work carried out by a specialist psychologist, even if he is referred to in the school as a "psychological consultant" or "consulted" about a case by another member of staff, meaning that he has been asked for some kind of help.

On a parameter of direct versus indirect action, mental health consultation is at the opposite end from the traditional techniques of diagnostic testing and therapy conducted in the psychologist's office, where he controls the field of forces himself so as to operate with maximum efficiency and professional effectiveness. Mental health collaboration is in the middle of such a parameter, since it combines elements of direct action with the student as well as indirect action through influencing the operations of other staff. In client-centered consultation, a relatively small part of the psychologist's time and effort is spent on classroom observation or testing the child, to provide data for the consultee. Consultee-centered consultation is the purest form of indirect action and is located at the extreme end of the parameter, since all the psychologist's time is devoted to interacting with the consultee. If successful, this type of professional operation offers the hope of maximum efficiency in terms of widespread benefit from minimum expenditure of time and effort, and is thus the preferred action for a population-oriented psychologist.

Unfortunately, the school psychologist's role and the school setting make consultee-centered consultation technically more difficult to carry out than it is when used by a consultant coming in from outside. A school psychologist must overcome two outstanding obstacles: (1) achieving a coordinate, nonhierarchical consultation relationship that leaves the consultee free to accept or reject what he says, and (2) preserving confidentiality about what takes place during the consultation. If the psychologist believes that his responsibility for the child's welfare demands a certain type of behavior by the teacher, he will not feel free to allow the teacher to do something else. Moreover, the psychologist's own hierarchical rank in the school may give him the power to coerce the teacher to do what he prescribes. The teacher will probably be guarded and defensive, which will make the consultation assessment of his shortcomings very difficult. Rebelling against pressure from a superior, he may resist taking as his own those ideas that are proposed by the psychologist. This situation will be further aggravated if there is no credible guarantee of confidentiality; thus the teacher may legitimately feel that the psychologist may report derogatively about his professional behavior to a staff supervisor who has line authority over him.

Over the years many school psychologists have worked out ways of overcoming these obstacles so that they may effectively use techniques of consultee-centered consultation. They say that the crucial issue is that the psychologist be in a position to make an explicit judgment that the child's apparent difficulties do not absolutely demand the psychologist's personal intervention to prevent an immediate danger, and that a few weeks are available to allow the teacher to try to work things out on his own, with the support of his consultant. Since this initial judgment must be made without the psychologist observing or interviewing the child, which would itself be an obstacle to continuing the case as a consultee-centered consultation, it presupposes that the psychologist has had previous experience with that teacher and can rely on his description of the case, or that no major danger signals are apparent.

Other factors that might influence the psychologist to feel free to use a consultee-centered approach would include sanction by the school authorities to operate in this way and the existence of other staff whose immediate help with a hazardous problem is available.

Having decided to use consultee-centered consultation in a case, the psychologist must make another explicit decision: he must somehow make it clear to his consultee that he is setting aside his superior rank and is freeing the consultee to reject anything he may say. He must formulate his contributions to confirm this message, by studiously avoiding directive prescriptions, by not indicating what he himself would do, and by talking in terms of a range of alternatives that he has seen used by other teachers. He must also make sure that he counteracts testing-out "one-downsmanship" manipulations by the teacher, and above all, he must, literally or figuratively, "sit at the side" of the teacher so that they jointly share ideas about the *child's problem*. The discussion must explicitly focus on the child, even though the data are all coming from the teacher's statements.

An advantage that the traditional mental health consultant has in establishing a coordinate relationship is usually that he can readily feel respect for the consultee, who has a body of professional knowledge that the consultant does not have and who knows more than the consultant about the real-life situation. The school psychologist offering consultation to a teacher does not usually have this advantage. The psychologist may himself have some background experience in classroom teaching; his expertise in *educational* psychology includes sophistication in the process of classroom teaching; and he may know more about the inner workings of the school in which he works than the teacher-consultee. He must therefore go out of his way to feel and to communicate his respect for the teacher as a professional peer, who in his everyday operations is grappling with a range and intensity of problems that are no less challenging and demanding than those the psychologist faces in his own role.

The issue of confidentiality must also be dealt with seriously, not lightly dismissed by general statements such as "Of course, everything we say will be kept confidential." The psychologist must negotiate a clear decision on this issue with the school authorities, based on differentiating between reports about the child and reports about the teacher. If he wishes to conduct consultee-centered consultation, he and the school must pay the price of his never divulging details about his consultees to the school authorities; he must assure his consultees that he will not do so, and that he has negotiated the essential sanction to maintain such a practice. In any case, psychologists have learned that they need be under no pressure to convey to the school authorities detailed information about possible harmful behavior by a teacher that they may have identified during consultation, because in the relatively intimate social system of a school there are very few secrets.

In summary, mental health consultation, although not the main technique of a population-oriented school psychologist, can be developed as a significant part of his professional operations, and the special technical obstacles can be overcome by attention to the details discussed here.

Most Frequent Techniques

A number of school psychologists have reported that group consultation is particularly useful in schools. The active participation of peers provides an opportunity to review a range of options that others have found effective in overcoming the shortcomings of lack of knowledge or skill; the support of the group makes it easier for the consultant to maintain his coordinate relationship with the consultees than if he is alone in the room with a single consultee.

When a psychologist first starts helping teachers in a school, the type of mental health consultation most likely to be requested, whether in an individual or group setting, will probably be client-centered case consultation. As the program develops, the psychologist, if committed to an ecological population orientation, will often be able to foster in teachers and school authorities an appreciation of the merits of consultee-centered consultation. When this occurs, it is likely that teachers will demand consultation to remedy shortcomings in knowledge, skills, and confidence, unless those issues are effectively handled in that school by a supervisory and in-service training system.

Eventually, consultee-centered consultation to overcome lack of professional objectivity may be required and theme interference reduction may be indicated, although many school psychologists may not feel comfortable using the complicated techniques described in Chapter Eight. Instead, they may restrict themselves to providing focused psychosocial support to their consultees to help them overcome their subjectively distorted perceptions. The results may not be as generalizable as techniques that break the link with syllogistic expectations in a test case, but they do lower the consultee's tension in the current predicament and provide immediate benefit to the client. In consequence, they also improve the consultee's professional self-image.

School Psychologist Consultation Training

Specialized training programs are needed to train school psychologists to use the consultation approach advocated in this book. These programs must take account of the unique features of the daily work of school psychologists, particularly the assets derived from their accepted roles as in-house members of modern multidisciplinary school teams. Many schools customarily sanction a preventive, population-oriented approach as an integral part of the psychologist's expected workday without the need for the psychologist to do the preparatory organizational work usually demanded from specialists who come into a potential consultee institution from an outside home base, such as a community mental health center or child guidance clinic. Moreover, the traditional concepts and skills of educational psychologists and their intimate knowledge of the social system of the school that is acquired by their daily work and by regular interactions with teaching staff provide them with spontaneous opportunities to obtain a deep understanding of what is happening in their institution and of its implications to fellow staff. They have no need to laboriously acquire this understanding, as outsider consultants do. But the school setting also faces the school psychologists with particular liabilities and obstacles when they use our techniques; overcoming these difficulties demands from them the acquisition of special skills, in addition to those which outsider consultants have to learn. This means that specialized programs must be used to train school psychologists in our methods of mental health collaboration and mental health consultation. These are in important respects different from those which we have developed in community mental health settings for training mental health specialists to act as outsider consultants. For instance, school psychologist consultation training programs must concentrate on the detailed content of psychologically sophisticated methods to be used by teachers in dealing with problem students inside and outside the classroom, in addition to the focus on the social system forces of the school setting and the process of consultant-consultee communication that is needed by all consultants who use our methods. These specialized aspects of a training program for school psychologists usually require a practicum different from the kind we developed, for example, in training programs for psychiatrists and other clinicians at our Harvard Laboratory of Community Psychiatry. School psychologist training requires an intensive practicum sequence inside a single school, and possibly inside only one or two classrooms; it must provide an opportunity to learn in depth the complications of the daily work of a small number of teachers and how to use this understanding to help them enrich psychologically their classroom and extracurricular teaching activities. This training is different from the supervised experience of a trainee offering a few consultation sessions to a number of teachers who intermittently request consultation, the dominant pattern of practicum in training programs for outsider consultants. The mental health content of what these consultants communicate to their consultees has been learned during their original professional specialization.

Promoting Our Approach

Let us now consider how the approach to consultation advocated in this book can be spread among school psychologists and made acceptable to school administrations. Reviews in professional journals (Medway and Updike, 1985) of research that validates the efficacy of this type of consultation may have some effect, as may our book and those of other authorities who support similar ideas (Alpert and Associates, 1982; Brown, Pryzwansky, and Schultz, 1991; Conoley and Conoley, 1982). But the major impetus for change will continue to come from the efforts of those professors of educational psychology who stimulated the publication of our book and guided us in writing this chapter. They and like-minded colleagues form a network of influential advocates who promote approaches to mental health consultation such as ours.

Through their academic training programs they have raised a new generation of school psychologists who not only put these ideas into practice but spread them through many progressive school systems, and thus provide models to be emulated by psychologists in other schools. If this development leads to a demand for postgraduate training programs in mental health consultation organized by the university departments of school psychology, the ripple effect will be further enhanced.

CHAPTER SEVENTEEN

The Significance
of Manipulation

Is mental health consultation *manipulative* or *Machiavellian?*
These terms carry the generally negative implication that a cunning
person is underhandedly motivating another, more ignorant or
naive than himself, into acting against his own interests for the
benefit of the manipulator. Let us examine a case involving explicitly manipulative activities by a psychiatrist, to see how they differ
from those of a mental health consultant.

A Case of Manipulation

A child psychiatrist who was an experienced mental health consultant was called in by a family to extract it from a confrontation with
a school. The family had recently and temporarily been relocated
by the husband's firm to an upper-middle-class suburb of Chicago,
and their adolescent son, Frank, was resentful and depressed about
leaving his friends in Boston. He developed insomnia, and started
waking David, a younger brother, in the middle of the night to
watch films on TV. The younger boy's teacher noticed his fatigue
and questioned him closely. She elicited accounts of his anger at
being awakened, and his fears at witnessing nightime confronta-
tions between his parents and the adolescent brother that were noisy
and emotionally charged. She took David to the school counselor.
Under the counselor's questioning, David's tale grew ever more
vivid and alarming. The principal, much excited when told the
story, summoned and warned the mother that this was a case of
psychological abuse, that the welfare department and the police

would have to be informed, that social workers would be sent into the home, and that Frank might be removed by the police and taken to an institution to be taught the error of his ways, since the parents were clearly unable to control the situation.

When the mother pointed out that the family was trying to deal with the problem, but that Frank was also a vulnerable child whose welfare had to be considered, the principal shouted, "No, he's a monster!"

"You wouldn't think so if you met him," the mother protested.

"Oh, I would. I would be terrified of him, a child who is not under the control of his parents!"

At the end of the meeting, the classroom teacher came to the shaken mother and said, "I was so upset when I heard Davey's story! I had tears in my eyes. I had to pull myself together really hard because I had to face my class again that day. I can't bear to think of such things happening to my Davey."

When the mother subsequently contacted the principal to inform him that the situation was now under control, it only intensified his apparent hostility and threats. The teacher and the principal questioned David and his younger sister every day about what was happening at home. When the children reported that everything was back to normal, they were accused of lying. Both children began to show signs of incipient school phobia. The parents asked the child psychiatrist to resolve the predicament.

The psychiatrist went to the school to talk to the principal, the teacher, and the counselor. At the meeting, the psychiatrist, as an experienced consultant, quickly identified lapses in the professional objectivity of the staff, and also problems in skill and in the administration of the system. The principal, a talented teacher who had recently been elevated to an administrative position, was terrified by specters of lost control.

The teacher, a warm and caring woman with no children of her own, had developed a passionately protective attachment to the child, whom she repeatedly called "my Davey." As she described his academic progress, which she had fostered, she mentioned that he was less successful socially. The child complained, the teacher said, that his classmates disliked him. "We discussed this in a class meeting," she said. "The other kids say he is teacher's pet, and they resent it that he gets extra time with me and on the class computer. I try not to have favorites, but I feel that this child really needs the extra care and attention. So I keep him close to me. And look at the fine work he is doing as a result!" As the teacher described the boy, it became clear to the psychiatrist that she was directly and personally involved with the child and that this was distorting her view of the case. Her description of an enthusiastic, achieving child who could "stand up for himself" and complain about his classmates slighting him, for example, did not coincide with her fantasies of an abused, defenseless victim at home.

In addition to evidence of theme interference in the principal, and overinvolvement in the teacher, the psychiatrist suspected that a lack of judgment and skill was also at work. The staff were convinced of their own sophistication in psychological matters, but like many who see themselves as a vanguard against mental distress, they were not able to titrate their intervention. They could see that there was a problem, and they felt that they had to take some role in solving it, but they were selectively insensitive to the effects of their actions. This was all the more interesting because the school, the psychiatrist knew, had elaborate mental health backup services available, which had obviously not been invoked in this case. The psychiatrist could only guess what administrative and supervisory functions had failed to spot this inappropriate staff behavior, but it was clear that the monitoring safeguards had for some reason failed to catch the problem.

The psychiatrist had no mandate to conduct consultation, but years of experience in the field had endowed him with the ability to observe, plan, and act on various levels simultaneously. As he identified the tangle of problems revealed by the staff's discussion, he never lost sight of his main priority—to relieve the pressure on the family as fast as possible. He accomplished this by using selected mental health consultation techniques.

First, because he came on behalf of the family and was of higher seniority than the school staff, he had to actively create an atmosphere of trust and coordinate status. He did this by expressing great respect for the teacher's professional competence and, by extension, for the school's standards, and by frequently interrupting the teacher's descriptions of the child's progress with comments of warm agreement and praise. The staff were not left wondering what the outside specialist thought of them, and an atmosphere was quickly created of fellow professionals sitting side by side, looking at a case together.

Having symbolically aligned himself with the staff in examining the case, rather than arguing about the validity of their view and their actions, the psychiatrist studiously avoided drawing attention to any of the nonobjective material flowing past him. He never mentioned the teacher's explicitly expressed overidentification with the child, or the inconsistencies between her picture of the active, resilient boy in the classroom and her fantasies of a depressed victim at home. He never challenged the principal's statements about a "monster," or his fears about loss of control. Though he was fully aware of their lapses in professional judgment and skill and the failure of the supervisory system around them, he never drew attention to any of this.

As in consultation, the psychiatrist used a parable. He said that he had learned from his own frequent appearances as an expert witness in law courts that even the most experienced psychiatrists have difficulty evaluating the truth or falsehood of a small child's account of an incident. The more a child is questioned, the more tendency there is for imagination to flower and for the child to tailor his story to satisfy what he thinks the adult questioner wants to hear. He remembered, the psychiatrist said, a particularly difficult case that might have led to the wrongful arrest of some young construction workers when a seven-year-old boy said that they had dragged him onto their construction site as he walked past it. Before they had a chance to harm him, he had wriggled free and run away. The police eventually concluded that there was insufficient evidence for a trial. The psychiatrist had himself questioned the child, and still was not fully certain in his own mind whether the story was true or false, though he tended to suspect the latter.

At the end of this possibly fictitious narrative, the young counselor suddenly found evidence in her notes that Davey's story had escalated in the telling. The psychiatrist made no mention of her failure to notice this earlier, nor did he suggest any motives she might have had, preconsciously, to overlook facts when the principal was eager for a crusade and to find them now, when a higher-status professional was taking the opposite view. There was merely an understanding nod exchanged on all sides and a shaking of heads over the difficulties "we professionals" have dealing with children.

Since this was not consultation, the psychiatrist made no attempt to resolve the various themes; instead, he rendered them irrelevant. The psychiatrist said that, according to his own observations, Frank was a caring child, with deep attachments to his absent friends and to Davey, his favorite sibling. He had intended no harm to the younger boy by dragging him out of bed in the middle of the night, though it was true that by so doing he was exploiting Davey to ease his own loneliness. But Frank honestly thought that the younger child would enjoy these films and he was surprised to learn that his little brother preferred a night's sleep. Hearing this extraordinary fact from the mouth of Davey in the presence of the psychiatrist, rather than from irate parents he thought were only trying to deny Davey a thrill, Frank was prepared to accept the situation and to leave Davey alone.

Furthermore, the parents had, in any case, decided to send Frank back to live with a married sister and her family in Boston so that he could rejoin the class and the friends he missed so badly. The school staff were palpably let down—none of their nonrational concerns had been addressed—but they were obliged to accept the assurances of a senior child psychiatrist that Davey was in no danger now, if he had ever been.

We should notice that while techniques of consultation were used in this case, consultation itself did not take place. The underlying themes were never fully explored, their syllogistic terms were not elucidated except in the most general way, and the expectations of doom were not invalidated by focusing on real circumstances. We have only to look at what followed the meeting to realize that the expectable gains of a successful consultation were not achieved. Davey reported, with considerable puzzlement, that his teacher had turned against him. She no longer allowed him to monopolize the computer when he wanted it, and she brusquely sent him off to play with the other children at recess. Other ears at the meeting besides the psychiatrist's had apparently heard "my Davey" and "teacher's pet," and had perhaps ordered her to act more impartially. Formally she did so, but the overidentification remained in place, still manifested as a display of professionally inappropriate affect that impinged on her relationship with the child.

The principal's unresolved theme interference still drew him obsessively back to the family. He questioned Davey's younger sister whether Frank had actually left town, as the psychiatrist and the parents had promised. Then, when he was reassured that the "frightening monster" was indeed removed, he asked merrily, "Aren't you happy that Frank has gone?" The question, of course, reflected the principal's feelings, not the child's. The girl was upset by a question that exposed her own ambivalence, since like the rest of the family she missed her brother. She spent the afternoon crying and uncharacteristically wet her bed that night.

The Difference Between Manipulation and Consultation

At the meeting with the school staff, insights gained by experience with consultation enabled the psychiatrist to effect a rapid and surgically precise extraction. He knew what points to press and which to ignore to achieve maximum leverage. He addressed the teacher's concern that "her Davey" was safe. He assured the principal that the "monster" was leaving town and, incidentally, leaving the jurisdiction within which the school might have a legal obligation to act on mere suspicion of child abuse. He circumvented the issue of parental control and rendered it irrelevant. The counselor was neutralized by invoking higher status. Everyone's weaknesses were exploited to effect an escape from an uncomfortable situation, and the staff was left with no further ground for continuing the struggle. They were, in other words, manipulated into giving up the case.

It would have been far neater, of course, for the psychiatrist to have finished the job properly by following through with mental health consultation, but that would have been wholly inappropriate. The school personnel had not asked for any help, nor did they appear to think that they needed any. Had they felt any such need, mental health services were already in the system with a mandate to act. The psychiatrist knew better than to trespass on his colleagues' turf by using the meeting to offer his own services. He restricted himself to his brief to help the family, and he resisted any urge to intervene in the school "for their own good."

One point to be borne in mind here is that the methods, sensitivities, and tact of an experienced consultant are flexible elements in his general professional repertoire. They can be used in isolation from the rest of the consultation system to achieve other professional goals.

But a second question remains, that of ethics. When is such a pure manipulation approach legitimate, and when does it lapse into impropriety? Unlike consultation, manipulation requires in each case an explicit calculation of whether the ends justify the means. At what point does it become improper to sacrifice the object to the objective—here, the school for Frank and his family?

For mental health workers who make use of pure manipulation, this calculation must be informal and individual, because this technique has not been professionalized in their discipline, as it has in such other professions as diplomacy. There are no clear guidelines or institutionalized controls for its use, as there are, for instance, for the techniques of mental health consultation.

A consultant may personally like or dislike a consultee, but he must develop nurturing concern for the consultee's autonomy and professional growth. The consultant will actively seek to build a relationship with his consultee that will conform to professional standards of propriety and warm solicitude, for just as a consultee must over time develop trust in his consultant for the process to succeed, so too must the consultant develop respect and authentic caring for his consultee. When, as is possible, personal feelings of the consultant obtrude on this process, they will be controlled by guild prescriptions, supervision by colleagues, and the consultant's internalization of these influences during his training and professionalization.

The situation of the manipulator is very different. A purely manipulative relationship is by its nature colder, more detached, even adversarial. A sustained personalized concern like that felt by a mental health consultant may be absent or fabricated. The psychiatrist in our example made warm, positive comments to the teacher and principal. He may have approved certain of their contributions to David's education, but he also had definite reservations about their behavior, and those reservations reduced the sincerity of his comments, which were made mainly to exert leverage on the school staff to drop the case. His behavior was guided by his individual judgment and feelings, not by professional prescriptions. He was free to decide, for instance, whether he should punish them for causing suffering to his clients. That he did not try to do so was a purely personal decision.

One of the points of contrast between consultation and manipulation, and one that helps us to evaluate their respective ethical standing, is the expectable reaction of the recipients of the intervention if they should be fully informed about what is happening. A consultee, even when he understands that consultation requires his consultant to covertly evaluate and consciously, if silently, take into account any manifestations of private, unresolved problems, would usually still be willing to engage in consultation. His awareness of acceptable gains from the process outweighs and supersedes any qualms he may have about revealing weakness. He would give informed consent, believing that whatever he exposes will help him, and that the consultant will take no unfair advantage of his insights nor reveal private shortcomings.

On the other hand, the object of manipulation would give no consent and would feel furious and betrayed if he discovered that his private and unconscious sensitivities or problems had been noted and used, because he would feel that he stood to gain nothing in return. On the contrary, he stands to lose, because the case that has served as an irrational displacement, the case whose existence he seized on unconsciously to fit his irrational needs, has now been snatched from him by harnessing his own weaknesses. This process is potentially weakening, since the person being manipulated is being sacrificed for the benefit of another's needs.

In summary, both the mental health consultant and the pure manipulator seek to identify the weaknesses of the person with whom they are dealing. But whereas the manipulator seeks to use this understanding to undermine the person's opposition to being influenced in order to subjugate him, the mental health consultant's mission is to help his consultee overcome his weaknesses and remedy his shortcomings.

In our case example the psychiatrist, in fact, did no damage to the school staff. They were prevented from causing further harm to David's family, which was what the psychiatrist was trying to achieve. He used manipulation as a tool to resolve the predicament quickly, quietly, and without loss of face to anyone involved. Similar techniques, however, could be used to inflict actual damage, for instance by covertly collecting information that might be transmitted to their superiors, which might result in loss of status or salary. In that event we would be crossing the ethical boundary.

Manipulation as a covert method of influence can thus be used in a range of ways. Some would be judged by the person being manipulated as negative, since that person might feel that his interests were being subordinated to those of the manipulator; and some would be positive, since all would be likely to agree that they had benefited. The use of manipulation techniques as part of consultee-centered mental health consultation would therefore probably be judged by most consultees to be positive. But the question still arises as to whether some people might not feel upset that a person engaged in helping them, particularly a fellow professional who makes such a show of egalitarianism, is keeping hidden from them the details of his thinking about them during the encounter and the mechanisms he is using to influence them.

They might feel that by asking for mental health consultation to help them deal with a work problem, they did not give permission for the consultant to scrutinize their personal sensitivities and to use the results to influence them, even if it does benefit them and their client. By what right does the consultant decide what is in the consultee's interest? The situation is not identical with that of patients asking for treatment from a physician, whom they would expect to keep his thoughts about possible causes of their symptoms to himself until he has decided which of these causes is relevant and how best to communicate this knowledge to his patient. It is also not the same as going for an evaluation interview with an administrative superior or for guidance by a counselor. In those cases, they will expect that the other person will not reveal to them all his thoughts about them; the difference is that they are free to choose whether to be interviewed.

In such cases there is tacit or explicit consent. We maintain that this level of consent is also involved in a consultee asking for consultation with a work problem. What interests him is what the consultant says and does, not what he thinks. As in all polite inter-actions, one expects to be treated with tact. This implies that the other person will be selective in what he says and how he says it, so that one's self-respect will not be affronted.

Nevertheless, it must be admitted that, particularly in cases where the consultee's handling of a work problem has become in-tertwined with his own personal life, even if he has no conscious awareness of the nature and meaning of the links, he should have the right to decide whether to seek consultee-centered mental health consultation from a consultant who uses our techniques. We have made it clear earlier in this book that he will only do so if he has developed a certain level of trust and respect for the consultant, and believes that he will not be manipulated in a negative way. We have also emphasized that the issue of the consultant's expertise and sensitivity in tactfully helping consultees master the emotional as-pects of their work problems must be emphasized in negotiating the consultation contract. If the framework has been adequately built this way, we feel that consultees have been adequately prepared for what is involved. There is surely no reason to make the issues more explicit during a consultation, forcing consultees to give up psycho-logical defenses that they have erected. To do so would be tactless as well as unproductive. In our experience potential consultees who have been fully informed about the mechanics of mental health consultation have never raised objections about being manipulated. Reservations on this issue have been expressed only by potential consultants who may not feel comfortable using techniques of ma-nipulation because they have not learned how only to do so in a positive and ethical way.

But we must also face the possibility that potential consultees whose sensitivity to privacy issues is so great that they would be unwilling to expose themselves to our consultee-centered tech-niques might also be reluctant to tell us about their reservations. So in the final analysis we must admit that not everyone is a suitable subject for our consultee-centered method. This we do freely and without in any way disparaging such people. They have the right to opt out of this aspect of our program in that institution. If they should nevertheless be coerced by their superiors to meet with us, we should be prepared quickly to realize their reluctance, and to move the level of our consultation from a consultee-centered to a client-centered or program-centered approach that entails no more manipulation than that inevitable in ordinary polite human interactions.

Experience in our culture has convinced us that if the issues of preparing and negotiating the consultation contract, discussed in Chapters Four and Five, have been adequately handled, only a small minority of potential consultees may feel this reluctance. But the situation in other cultures that have other values and sensitivities about loss of face may be different. We are reminded of an experience I had in a Copenhagen restaurant, to which I was taken one evening by my Danish hosts. I discovered a piece of dirt stuck to my fork, called the waiter over, and quietly asked for a clean fork. The hostess, a close friend as well as a colleague, told me that she was terribly embarrassed by this rudeness to the waiter. When I asked her how I should have behaved, she replied, "You should have used the dirty fork. It had probably been through the restaurant dishwasher anyway, so it would not have killed you. The only bad thing that might have happened to you if you have an oversensitive stomach would be that you would suffer a few abdominal pains. If you are as sensitive as all that, you could have eaten with your dessert fork or your spoon!"

If we take into account variations in culture and in individual personality sensitivities, it becomes clear that no techniques as potent as those used in our consultee-centered mental health consultation can be expected to be universally acceptable. As long as we build in safeguards to ensure sensitivity to the possible legitimate pyschocultural idiosyncrasies of a small minority of our potential consultees, and as long as we avoid using manipulative techniques with those few, we can operate with equanimity with the vast majority. This apparently still leaves to us the onus of decision making about whether to use manipulation, which may not satisfy the purists. But in fact, we can be confident that since we have developed an institutional framework for consultation that allows most consultees voluntary choice about invoking our help, we can safely leave it to them to keep away from us if they so desire.

CHAPTER EIGHTEEN

Basic Principles
and Key Modifications

Mental health consultation, as a technical method of interprofessional partnership, has stood the tests of time. In the last few years recognition of the limitations of the method has led, as we have seen, to the development of complementary techniques of mental health collaboration, which are fast also becoming accepted, as they are being refined in the light of practical experience.

Basic Principles

Here we summarize the basic principles of our approach.

Consultation must be guided by understanding its ecological field. A mental health consultant must guide the development of the consultation program by exploring and monitoring the interconnected field of forces: the community, the consultee and consultant organizations, the consultant and consultee individuals, and the client and his family. Understanding the ecological interplay of the historical, sociocultural, and psychosocial forces is a prerequisite for effective consultation.

Consultation contracts must be explicated. We have repeatedly confirmed the importance of making explicit and formalizing the successive agreements between the consultee and the consultant institutions. These agreements provide the matrix for developing the individual consultant-consultee relationships. A consultant is not merely a person of good will who is offering his help to a colleague. He is the representative of his agency, which has worked

356

out a partnership agreement that seeks to fulfill the professional missions of both institutions. This implies that much of a consultant's work must be devoted to exploring feelings of need in the consultee organization, preparing the ground, and negotiating and maintaining sanction, as well as periodically involving the consultees in assessing results and changing needs, so that the contract may be renegotiated.

The consultation relationship must be noncoercive. In the approach we propose, the consultant has a *coordinate, nonhierarchical power relationship* with the consultee. The consultant expresses this relationship by not accepting administrative authority over the consultee's actions or professional responsibility for the client's welfare. The consultee's professional autonomy is fully maintained throughout the consultation, and he is free to accept or reject anything the consultant advises about the client, the program, or the organizational structure of the consultee institution.

The noncoercive relationship enables the consultant to exert maximum influence quickly. The consultee must choose from the consultant's ideas the ones he can use in his own work. To leave his consultee free to reject what he says, the consultant must have no professional responsibility for the client or for the actions of the consultee. He is responsible only for doing his best to express a sensible opinion about the case. After twenty years, we remain convinced that this approach is valid.

Promote consultee-centered consultation. Our 1970 and 1972 books divide consultation into *client-centered consultation* and *consultee-centered consultation.* We have continued to appreciate the value of this division. In consultee-centered consultation, the consultant must focus his investigation on analyzing the consultee's report about the case or program, as though it were a projective test protocol that reveals his attitudes and perceptions. He must discover whether the consultee's difficulties are due to his lack of knowledge about the issues involved, lack of skill in dealing with them, or lack of professional objectivity. Our books conceptualized lack of professional objectivity as being the result of the distortion of the consultee's judgment because certain elements in the case have subjective implications to him—the so-called theme interference.

Helping the consultee overcome this theme interference was a cornerstone of our consultation method, and it remains so.

Avoid uncovering types of psychotherapy. We are as committed today as we were twenty years ago to the principle of keeping the consultee's professional role separate in our minds and in our formulations from his private life. We are just as opposed now as we were then to using techniques of psychotherapy in consultation. Our experience has convinced us that we should avoid even drawing attention to the specific personal source of a work difficulty. Consultants must maintain their status as a professional objectively discussing a case with a colleague, even when they are working hard to understand what elements are triggering his loss of objectivity, and how they can help him overcome them without endangering his professional confidence and poise.

Use the displacement object. A consultee may become emotionally involved and may express his own inner conflicts by identifying personally with certain elements in his client's drama. The consultant can also exploit these same elements, by discussing them in ways that send potent messages to the consultee, without making the process explicit and without the consultee having to become aware of what is happening. He thus avoids arousing the resistance that would inevitably appear if he were to weaken the consultee's defenses by uncovering the nature of his unconscious displacements. It is safe for the consultee to feel and express intense feelings about an issue, as long as he consciously believes that he is talking about the client and not about himself. And although the consultant's tact in not drawing explicit attention to this makes some people uncomfortable—they label it "manipulation"—we ourselves see this aspect of our technique as entirely positive and supportive.

Foster orderly reflection. Increasing experience has emphasized the value of orderly and unhurried reflection during consultation discussions. It increases the consultee's awareness of the range of options and counteracts premature, emotionally based closure. Emotional arousal usually distorts cognitive operations, narrows perceptual focus, and prevents rational problem solving. Consultation combats stereotyping and "complicates the thinking" of consultees, because the consultant, as it were, supplements the consultee's ego strength with his own.

Widen frames of reference. A consultant, using our approach, guides his consultee in collecting information about the case and analyzing his work problem within the interpenetrating institutional systems of client, consultee, and consultant. The consultee is encouraged to widen his own frame of reference and his cognitive focus because the consultant supports him in feeling safe while dealing with emotionally sensitive issues.

Consultants must be trained. Our original books gave a precise description of a body of concepts and techniques that should be an accepted part of the discipline of the traditional mental health professions. It must be learned as a separate method and as an addition to the usual professional curriculum. A professional may be a competent psychologist, but unless he has systematically studied this method or some analogue, he will not be an effective consultant.

Consultation is not modified counseling, or modified psychotherapy, or watered-down psychoanalysis; its skills do not come naturally because a person has specialized knowledge of those other methods or just "understands human nature." In this connection we should avoid semantic ambiguity. We do not use the term *mental health consultation* to denote *all types* of extramural interaction of a specialist with another professional, but as *one defined and circumscribed type* of intervention that conforms to certain specifications.

Modifications of the Mental Health Consultation Model

The principles of mental health consultation are not sacrosanct and immutable. They are not based on theory or ideology, apart from incorporating our philosophical commitment to a population orientation and the importance of supporting other people by a human relations approach. Each item was developed pragmatically, as a result of evaluating our own work experiences, and was refined in the light of our conclusions about what seemed to get good results. The list as a whole represents a set of guidelines that has accumulated over several years. Each item can be conceptualized as a building block that may be used to develop a program that must be tailored to the demands of a particular setting and to the capacities and style of specialists.

We therefore envision that our list of basic principles will help us and others conceptualize a variety of models of service delivery in response to the needs of each setting. Within each model our principles should enable us to work out a consistent pattern of operation that can be precisely specified and that can be communicated to other experts and to students. In this way we hope to retain flexibility, avoiding on the one hand the incoherence and ineffectual lack of focus of an eclectic approach, and on the other hand a rigid prepatterned system, into whose procrustean bed we may be tempted to force information and people, a process that will inevitably lead to the dehumanization we oppose.

Described below are some of the service delivery models that have emerged from this approach, in addition to the major model of mental health collaboration described in Part Three and the mixture of mental health collaboration and modified mental health consultation that we developed for use by school psychologists, as described in Chapter Sixteen.

Bishop-to-Bishop Coordinate Status Consultation

This model emerged from our mental health consultation program for Episcopal parish priests in Massachusetts, which we described in Part Two. Gerald Caplan was asked to provide mental health consultation to a group of Episcopal bishops, who wanted to explore whether they could have a similar experience to the parish priests of Massachusetts. Since the bishops came from all over the country, and since it was necessary to conserve travel time, it was decided to invite the bishops for a three-day residential "seminar" in a hotel in Cambridge, Massachusetts.

This group consultation took place as planned, and proved quite attractive to the participants. But the closing request was somewhat unusual: not for further, similar consultation groups but for educational seminars to teach bishops consultation techniques so they could offer consultation themselves to individual parish priests or to groups of clergy in their own dioceses.

After much discussion, the participants concluded that although it might be possible to train bishops in consultation techniques—they had, after all, considerable understanding of human nature and experience counseling both clergy and parishioners in personal and family problems—the hierarchical social system and professional culture of their church would make it almost impossible for a bishop to operate as a mental health consultant to his subordinates, whom he was responsible for supervising. If he did so he would inevitably mimic the role of a clinician, which was alien to his own institutional mission.

This led the bishops to propose a new model. They might learn mental health consultation techniques, but they would use them to offer consultation not to the clergy of their own diocese but to fellow bishops of *other* dioceses. One bishop might help his colleague deal with human relations complications of his diocesan role, and then the two would switch roles, so that each in turn would receive consultation from the other.

This proposal emerged after Gerald Caplan had described how he and Eric Lindemann had developed a similar pattern of offering each other consultation about their current predicaments in the Harvard School of Public Health and Harvard Medical School respectively, where each was directing a population-oriented mental health program. The two psychiatrists met once a week for lunch, and at each meeting they alternated the roles of consultant and consultee.

Gerald Caplan agreed to meet two to three times a year for three-day seminars with groups of bishops, training them in those elements of mental health consultation techniques that would enable them to offer consultation to each other. The bishops chose the rather unwieldy name of "coordinate status bishop-to-bishop consultation" for the method they developed, since they felt that it demanded a radical departure from the hierarchical relationships traditional in their church. Even if one bishop in a consultation was significantly senior to another, both would explicitly set aside their relative rank in operating alternately as consultant and consultee.

Each bishop attended three or four seminars to learn the techniques, consolidated by occasional follow-up sessions where problems encountered in operating the program were discussed. Bishops paired off during seminars and in the interim; each couple arranged face-to-face meetings, often in airport restaurants, as their customary frequent travel schedules intersected, or else they got together in a planned way at regional church meetings or in annual meetings of the House of Bishops. Consultations about urgent problems were also conducted by telephone, but these tended to be one-sided, without much alternation of roles; role switching proved feasible mainly in the less hurried atmosphere of personal encounters.

Over a period of five years, Gerald Caplan trained some fifty bishops (they represented a significant part of the membership of the House of Bishops). This led to an interesting development in this institution, which is the supreme governing body of the Episcopal church in the United States. Its plenary sessions continued to focus on issues of church policy and programming, but on a parallel basis outside the formal plenary meetings, pairs of bishops spent considerable time consulting with each other about the human relations complications of their daily work. This gradually led to a system of mutual support, which often was conducted in small ad hoc groups of bishops. Most of them had been trained in the consultation seminars, but they often recruited others who had not been trained, and involved them, too, in their mutually supportive interactions.

As the program developed, the role of the bishop when he was acting as consultant to his colleague ceased to be that of an expert. Instead he became a peer, whose role of the moment allowed him to be more objective and clear-sighted in coming to understand a problem and how to deal with it than was possible for his colleague, who was personally involved in his professional predicament both cognitively and emotionally, and whose judgment was therefore likely to be impaired. Bishops who participated in the program came to recognize this change in the consultant's objectivity and professional distance as similar to what they experienced when they were called on to act as chairman of a committee of which they had previously been a working member.

Mediation in Community Conflict Management

Mediators use many different systems of technique, influenced by their varied professional backgrounds and disciplines. We too have developed and explored our own approach to mediation between parties involved in communal conflicts that we described in the book *Arab and Jew in Jerusalem* (G. Caplan and R. Caplan, 1980). The subtitle of that book was *Explorations in Community Mental Health*, because it analyzed the mental health implications of living in prolonged situations of community conflict and cultural dissonance, and ways a population-oriented psychiatrist or psychologist might intervene to ameliorate the harmful forces.

Although our intervention was based on our previous experience with mental health consultation, the techniques of mediation were in essential ways different. Some aspects were similar—paying attention to the ecological field of forces, negotiating successive contracts to intervene, avoiding "uncovering" types of interpretation, using the displacement object, and widening frames of reference by orderly reflection. But the central focus of our mediation techniques was the development of nonpartisan relationships with representatives of the conflicted subpopulations of Arabs and Jews as a basis for exploring their current needs and for communicating them to the other side.

In Jerusalem at that period, the degree of hostility and mutual suspicion was so great that it was not feasible for the two sides to meet personally for a productive discussion. We developed techniques for helping each side identify those aspects of need that were existentially important, and that were as little as possible colored by their feelings of anger and bitterness; as we moved back and forth between them, we helped the parties identify those elements that would be acceptable also to the other side, since they were not felt to infringe on their own interests. For instance, a superordinate goal that we identified in this way was that of organizing ambulatory health services for the Arab population. These services were badly needed by the Arabs to combat disease and personal misery in their community. They were also regarded as valuable by the Israelis, not just on humanitarian grounds, but also to enable the Arabs to live productive lives within the framework of Israeli governmental control.

Of significance is that Gerald Caplan, as a mediator between Arabs and Jews in Jerusalem, was not operating as an "expert" in community mental health, but as a knowledgeable person of good will who had become accepted as a trustworthy nonpartisan by both sides. The Arabs knew that he was a Zionist American Jew who was a professor at Harvard University, but few of them understood or were impressed by his psychiatric credentials. His perceived status was "achieved" because he passed a series of covert, manipulative, informal tests of his apparent influence with key Israelis and did nothing to damage Arab psychosocial rights, and because he kept his promise to operate entirely outside the political field, including never allowing his work to be reported in the media, where it might be used by others to undermine Arab political campaigns. The Arabs therefore felt they could use him to pass messages to the Israeli power figures. The Israelis, on their side, felt that he was valuable in identifying specific Arab needs and ways they might be safely satisfied without interfering with the political status quo.

Caplan's personal problem was how to set aside his own political bias in order truly and credibly to operate with equal sensitivity to each side. In maintaining professional self-control in this regard, he was helped by his training and experience as a clinician, but he was probably not more effective in this than mediators coming from many varied backgrounds, such as lawyers, jurists, and organizational specialists, who have also learned how to use techniques of professional self-awareness to remain nonpartisan in conflict situations. In this instance, as with the bishops' consultation program, we realize that many of the techniques of mental health consultation can, with some modification, be used effectively in other settings by professionals who are not specialists in psychiatry and psychology.

Conciliation for Divorcing Parents

Over the past eight years Gerald Caplan has been directing in Jerusalem a program to prevent psychological and social disorder in children of divorcing parents. He has been using our customary techniques of mental health consultation and collaboration to stimulate and facilitate partnerships with such other caregiving professionals as teachers, school guidance counselors, welfare workers, doctors, public health nurses, lawyers, and judges. Together they work to support parents and children in mastering the stresses of the divorce process and living in a divided family. In addition, he has been using techniques of *conciliation* with couples contemplating divorce, to help them work out a mutually acceptable divorce agreement that will deal with such matters as custody of children, contacts of the children with the noncustodial parent, and division of property. The goal is to safeguard the rights of the children and form a basis for future collaboration of the parents as a parental couple after they are no longer man and wife.

The techniques that have developed are modifications of those of mental health consultation and resemble the techniques of mediation that were developed in Jerusalem. There are three main differences: (1) the intervenor convenes a short series of face-to-face meetings between himself and the parents, occasionally with the participation of the children; (2) the process is often obligatory for the parties, since it may be carried out by order of the divorce courts, and even if not is "in the shadow of the courts"; and (3) the intervenor's role is complicated by his also operating as an expert in child development who will at appropriate stages express his own specialist opinion as to whether the terms of the agreement being worked out are beneficial to the children, whose rights he is safeguarding.

In the recent book *Population-Oriented Psychiatry* (G. Caplan, 1989) these techniques are described in detail, and there is no reason to discuss them further here, apart from drawing attention to the fact that while certain basic principles of mental health consultation and collaboration apply in this work, conciliation requires modifications in technique because it is not an *interprofessional* method. Like counseling or psychotherapy, it is used by a professional to help laypeople with their personal problems. Thus the major emphasis of our consultation and collaboration techniques—safeguard and strengthen the boundaries between professional persona and the complications of private personal life—does not apply. On the other hand, such techniques as avoiding "uncovering" interpretations and using the displacement object may at times be of great value, as the specialist attempts to help the parents to control and set aside emotionally toned reactions that may be interfering with rational judgment in the service of their children.

Other Modifications

It is likely that over the coming years psychologists and psychiatrists will continue to develop modifications of our basic consultation and collaboration techniques for use in new service settings in
health, welfare, education, and legal programs.

In addition, the main use of our basic principles and techniques may be by professionals working outside the mental health
field, most likely in business, industrial, and management consultation. Understanding, sensitivity, and skills in dealing with human nature are not confined to the mental health professions. In a
variety of organizational settings, such as the military, industry, and
public administration, workers emerge who develop roles that call
on them to promote the human needs of staff in ways that also
further the mission of the organization. Most elements of the techniques discussed in this book may well be incorporated by such
workers within their own professional operations, or by consultants
who in turn support them.

Wherever there are people whose role calls for them to help
others, there will also be the need to "help the helpers to help" (R.
Caplan, 1972). In such settings the concepts and skills of interprofessional communication and influence discussed in this book may
find new application.

CHAPTER NINETEEN

Avoiding Distortion
in Dissemination

Before ending this book we feel impelled to raise certain issues that
have recently begun to concern us, lest our efforts may lead paradoxically to negative rather than positive influences.

The rationale of mental health consultation and other methods of population-oriented psychology, particularly those geared to
models of primary prevention, demands wide dissemination of
helpful ideas and practices if they are to affect the lives of large
numbers of people. The specialists who promulgate the ideas initiate this dissemination process, but their influence then spreads via
their colleagues, their students, and their publications to many
other people with whom they themselves will have no direct contact. The relative success of their efforts depends on how their ideas
will be interpreted and implemented in practice, as well as on the
intrinsic merit of these ideas.

A major goal of mental health consultation and collaboration is to improve human relations in community institutions and
services by increasing the sensitivity, knowledge, skill, and objectivity of other professionals. But we must face the possibility, unfortunately empirically validated in many settings, that our humane
messages may not be properly understood or adequately implemented by our colleagues, who may in an excess of zeal exaggerate
and distort them, or who may develop programs that while ostensibly promoting mental health may actually unduly infringe on
family privacy, foster regressive overdependency on professionals,
or in other ways dehumanize their clients.

There is a covert message in much of contemporary mental health practice that may not be optimally beneficial for the mental well-being of the population—the insidious and all-enveloping idea that any challenge is unmanageable without professional guidance. It implies to the layman that all stress is bad, and that the ideal of mental health is a lotus-eaters' land of placid moods patroled by vigilant and wise mental health professionals. The ideas of community mental health—preventive intervention, anticipatory guidance, support systems, and so on—when universalized and mechanically applied have given rise in many places to intrusive assaults on the autonomous problem solving of people who would often be quite capable of coping on their own. Such messages ignore or downgrade self-developed mastery in favor of professional intervention.

There appears to be, in the eyes of many well-meaning caregivers, an analogue to Politically Correct Expression, and that is a Psychologically Correct Attitude. This attitude demands that members of the public acquiese to professional guidance and always be available to join support groups or submit to counseling for any stress or change in life, or for any attitude or action that current psychological fashion deems undesirable. Gone is the adult ideal of a person who can stand alone with internalized moral standards and psychological strength that can withstand the tests of life. Nowadays, it is apparently felt that everyone needs help at some point; if they think they do not, they are repressing or denying, or inhibited, and they need it more than ever. As a school announcement for a lecture on stress put it, "If you feel under too much stress to attend, it proves that you should be there."

There is a tendency, not shared by all mental health workers, of course, to take a pessimistic and cautionary view of any experiences that are psychologically demanding and not entirely conventional, gratuitously identifying them as mental health hazards. They thereby denigrate and weaken, rather than support, those who have such experiences, for example widows, stepmothers, and immigrants.

So misused have many ideas of community mental health become—such as support systems—that sometimes we feel reluctant to even mention these concepts that we used to consider progressive and enlightened, so denatured and absurdly transformed have they become. People who are afflicted with the most serious or the most trivial of problems are all pressed to join some form of therapy. Sometimes the results are refreshingly comic. A suburban American paper reported that local ladies had formed a support group for "mothers of boys." At their first meeting, they sought guidance for the stress of forever having to clean bathrooms in which small boys had missed their aim. In other instances, the tendency has grown more sinister. Those who refuse to conform may be coerced into accepting the patient role by professionals in positions of power. The family in the "psychological abuse" case discussed in Chapter Seventeen, for example, was told that they could escape some of the pressure of the school by submitting to counseling from one of the in-house mental health staff. The family felt no inclination to expose itself to such doubtful ministrations; moreover, they considered themselves reasonably healthy and capable of managing their own affairs as long as the violations of their privacy and autonomy stopped.

Let us examine a situation in which mental health ideas ran wild and were inappropriately applied. We refer to the quivering concern that rippled through the media and through professional circles in the United States during the war in Kuwait whenever the subject of stress was raised, especially when it related to children. News broadcasters, newspaper articles, and even children's entertainment programs became obsessed by the need to protect children from the supposed danger to mental health that would occur if they were left psychologically unguided to watch and hear about the war, to suffer separation from relatives bound for the Gulf, and to deal with fantasies of invasion and bombing at home.

Schools sent home articles and directives on how to cope with a child's questions and anxieties. The children's section of public libraries prominently displayed such materials. Children's TV programs were interrupted by exhortations to young viewers, "Are you afraid about the war? Talk to your parents and teachers." A large metropolitan school system announced that it was readying psychologists and counselors to cope with the children when the dreaded and potentially casualty-filled land war would begin. More reprehensibly, news broadcasts transmitted classroom discussions in which young children were questioned in front of the camera about their fears, and then admitted, with trembling voices and glistening eyes, to being terrified of bombs, of dying, or of losing their relatives. Similarly, adults were shown in support groups, confessing to anxieties and doubts, and holding hands in mutual sympathy, and perhaps in mutually induced fears.

So concerned were people about the stresses of war and the need to engage in anticipatory guidance and crisis intervention, that teams of mental health workers traveled to Israel, to teach the local professionals how to manage populations enduring the Scud attacks. They found their Israeli colleagues already well versed in this, although some media workers did behave like their fellows in the United States. In an Israeli TV interview with some passersby in the wake of a missile raid, the people expressed no particular fear. "We've survived it before, we'll survive it now," was the ordinary person's view. "Do you hear that?" asked the commentator in the studio. "People are so terrified, they can't even bring themselves to express their terror."

War was being portrayed as the latest mental health hazard, a psychic pollutant. Yet nobody seemed to remember that, historically, war has been experienced precisely as a mentally *healthy* phenomenon, so much so that its seductions had to be countered and minimized. War has long been observed to suspend smaller, purely personal worries and despairs as individuals are swept up into identifying with and working for their own country, so that suicidal tendencies and social withdrawal, for instance, are reduced. War has always been seen as exciting not only for combatants, but also for those who stand and wait and cheer from the sidelines. Since it seems to stimulate the best as well as the worst in people, educators and philosophers bent on creating systems of character building have long sought a "moral equivalent to war."

In this recent conflict, the psychologically health-inducing aspects of the crisis were ignored, perhaps because such an idea is neither politically nor psychologically acceptable. Few if any spokesmen reassured people that their reactions, even the disturbing ones of excitement, preoccupation, and difficulty in sleeping, were probably normal and time limited. Few, if any, reassured the population that they were strong enough to master separations and worry, and would come out of the experience perhaps more resilient and mature.

Instead, many zealous caregivers, particularly those associated with children, *recruited* cases; preexisting fears and problems were focused on rather than eclipsed by the situation; and other tensions were suggested. Treatment and management were offered for situations that people might have otherwise mastered on their own, such as separation anxiety, or philosophic scruples about their revised attitudes to violence, which seems to have particularly troubled liberals, driving them, before the TV cameras, into support groups to resolve their ambivalences.

One example of a radically different approach can be cited. During the Gulf War the mayor of Jerusalem asked Gerald Caplan to organize a team of experts to advise him on measures to support the civilian population. Among other tasks, this team addressed the difficulties produced by misguided clinicians who were appearing on radio and television and stimulating feelings of insecurity among the public by telling them they might be suffering from pathological anxieties and phobias caused by the threats of possible poison gas attacks, and by then offering to give them appropriate diagnosis and therapy in their clinics, whose services were being mobilized and augmented to handle the extra load of patients produced by the war. Caplan prepared a statement that was incorporated in a message the team prepared for the mayor to disseminate to the public. Exhibit 19.1 is an English translation of Gerald Caplan's memorandum.

Let us now focus on a second issue. It is axiomatic to most mental health clinicians that their treatment interventions should be precisely based on a diagnostic assessment of the current situation and needs of their patients. Those professionals who extend their operations into the field of prevention surely do not intend to change this approach. But once they leave their clinics and their focus on particular patients, many of them insensibly abandon their habits of prescribing specific treatments on the basis of diagnostic assessments, and instead develop standardized interventions that they recommend for widespread use. When their methods are adapted for even wider use by caregivers of other professions who do not come from a therapeutic background geared to diagnosis,

Exhibit 19.1. Message to the Public.

How to Overcome:
Practical Measures for Every Citizen

1. Recognize the signs that you are successfully mobilizing yourselves to master the current danger situation. The central element is psychological and bodily arousal shown by anxiety, fear, anger, and increased alertness and vigilance, and the associated bodily manifestations of increased heart rate, muscle tension and trembling, sweating, dry mouth, changes in appetite, nausea, and sleep disturbance. These are signs that your mind and body are prepared for emergency action. They are signs of positive biological adaptation to a danger situation, even though many people may feel uncomfortable. Others may feel excited and exhilarated. *These reactions are not symptoms of illness and should not be labeled or treated as such.*

2. During the air raid alert in the sealed room, the personal upset may be reduced by the following well-known steps:
    a. Be active in preparing the room, taping the door, putting on the gas mask, helping the children, etc.
    b. Listen to the information on the radio. Uncertainty and surprise weaken you.
    c. Talk to other family members and reassure children and old people.
    d. Sing together. If religious, pray together. If the alert lasts more than 30 minutes play games together or watch a video film.
    e. Relax by breathing slowly and deeply.
    f. Relax your muscles one limb after another.
    g. Focus your attention in a planned way on pleasurable memories or fantasies.

3. Between alerts, expect the psychological arousal to continue for several weeks. It will lessen as you become accustomed to the situation. Talk to other people about your reactions and compare notes. Give and receive emotional support by expressing solidarity.

4. Psychological arousal during an emergency is a sign of *coping strength*, and is not a sign of weakness or a psychiatric illness. Respect these manifestations in others. Do not belittle or blame others in order to reduce your own tension if they withdraw temporarily at the height of the crisis by seeking places of refuge and relative safety.

5. Bind members of your family together to share the burdens and to increase your strength. If there are family conflicts, try to put them temporarily aside so that you can all support each other during the emergency. Help each other and your neighbors in practical ways, e.g. sharing shopping and caring for children and old people. Increase your interaction with other people, with neighbors, people in the supermarket and others in your neighborhood.

Exhibit 19.1. Message to the Public, Cont'd.

6. Because the situation is complicated and routines of life have been upset, it is quite likely that you may need guidance or special help. Do not hesitate to contact wise neighbors, community leaders, professionals of the municipality or the school system, or nonprofessional volunteer organizations through telephone open lines. *But do not go to clinics or hospitals,* unless you have had a preexisting illness for which you were getting medical treatment. Do not try to calm yourself with tranquilizing drugs or alcohol; all these will weaken you.

7. As soon as your family commitments allow, return to your regular job, and also spend some of your spare time in volunteer activities to help others master the emergency. The more you become involved with others in meaningful activity the stronger you will be.

8. Watch for signs of fatigue in yourselves and others. Take rests to replenish your strength. Encourage relatives and friends to take time off to rest by undertaking some of their duties on a temporary basis. If you are not able to sleep at night do not toss and turn in bed and do not take sleeping pills which will reduce your alertness and efficiency. Get up and read, listen to the radio or watch TV. Next day take short naps or an afternoon siesta. No harm will come to you from occasional loss of sleep.

9. Strengthen other people who may feel weak or helpless because they believe that they have lost control over their life, and perhaps because they misinterpret their discomforts as signs of impending nervous breakdown. Remind them that in the past all of you succeeded in overcoming such tribulations, and that by closing ranks we will overcome on this occasion too, particularly as we have a powerful army and very powerful allies, and our leaders are quite effectively guarding our personal as well as our national interests.

10. Remind others that our present discomforts will lessen in a few weeks as we all get adjusted to our new routines in dealing with the danger situation. Our discomforts will end two to three weeks after the war is over; we will all have been strengthened from having overcome this crisis, as has happened repeatedly on past occasions.

---

this slide toward stereotyped all-purpose measures is apt to be exaggerated: what is valuable in one situation is expected to be equally useful in other situations that are rather similar. In this development, interest in the idiosyncratic needs of the individual tends to be lost. With no ill will, the interventive procedures may nevertheless become quite dehumanized and potentially harmful to mental health.

For example, a freak accident on a school playground killed a number of small children and injured others. Because of the nature of the catastrophe, the event was intensively covered by the local media. The school district sent in a mental health team to counsel the witnesses and survivors, and there was widespread sympathy and support for all involved.

In a nearby town, another school reacted to the tragedy in an interesting way. The mental health staff sent out a notice: "Children and adults need time to work out their feelings or responses to sudden grief and shock, and we must respect the time needed for individuals to deal with the trauma." The notice went on to recount how, in the days following the accident, a staff meeting had been held, so that the teachers could discuss "their own feelings," and so as "to plan approaches to deal with the impact of this disaster on our students." The teachers were told to begin their day with class meetings, "establishing a safe environment for the children to express their perceptions and feelings." Recommendations of the American Academy of Child and Adolescent Psychiatry were summarized for the benefit of parents. These included such formulations as "children can be expected to have greater difficulty with times of separation, so extra reassurance is important"; and "allow the child to discuss the tragedy, but do not force it"; and "be aware that delayed reactions to this tragedy may occur"; and "professional advice, consultation and perhaps treatment for children affected by a disaster, can help prevent or minimize further problems." The mental health worker who sent the notice concluded by inviting the parents "to drop by my office if you wish to talk."

The directives listed and the advice given were undeniably appropriate to a population undergoing trauma. But in this instance there was the fortunate *absence* of trauma. The target of all the good intentions was simply not involved. The event slipped away from the attention of most children in a short time; and it would have done so sooner, no doubt, if their teachers had not been told to "work it through" by dwelling on the event in class meetings and creative writing assignments.

The fact that a psychological idea or practice may not be applicable in a particular instance is no guarantee that it will not be used. The reaction of this institution was not, moreover, the aberration of an individual. The entire staff were invested in the idea that they were engaged in crisis intervention and preventive mental health. Actually, they were involved in a one-sided experience that fulfilled their own image of professional functioning, but had little relevance to the needs of their client population.

We have already drawn attention to another potentially harmful practice, namely intrusion by professionals into the private domain of individuals and families. This is more serious than an infringement on privacy. If the resistance of the clients is broken down by moral pressure or by psychological blackmail by the caregivers, this may weaken the clients' autonomy and the strength that comes from mastering a predicament through self-initiated mobilization of their inner resources.

On the other hand, all primary prevention involves intervening in a population of currently healthy individuals, or at least individuals who are unaware that they are currently exposed to potentially harmful circumstances that have not yet led to explicit pathology, the discomfort of which might arouse in them a need for invoking outside help. So paradoxically, all programs of primary prevention that aim to increase personal autonomy require that the preventive agents reach out and influence their targets to become dependent on expert knowledge, guidance, and help. If we were to sit back and wait for the pathogenic factors or for the lack of psychosocial supports to begin to take their toll, we might expect that the target individuals would be motivated to ask for our help, but by then we would have missed the opportunity to preempt the beginnings of the pathological development.

So some uninvited contact between primary prevention workers and their potential clients is inevitable. How can we draw the line between this and the kind of invasion of privacy that we deem undesirable and potentially harmful? Moreover, the barriers of privacy may not be merely those of people who just do not want others to meddle in their affairs. They may have dynamic meaning as part of a system of psychological defenses to hide from awareness certain unacceptable impulses or irrational resolutions to emotional conflicts; in the family, for example, the unconscious exploitation of children to solve psychosocial problems of their parents. This leads people to actively resist intervention by other people who might weaken or upset such defenses. Privacy in such cases is essential to preserve the equilibrium of the system. And by what right does an outsider break down such resistance in pursuit of his own definition of what is good for others?

Yet experience teaches us that it is often feasible to find the golden mean in such matters, to intervene uninvited in ways that the target individual does not resent now, or will not in retrospect, once he understands what has been involved. This is more likely when the privacy barrier was high mainly because of the person's lack of knowledge and insight about the hazardous nature of his current situation. If he were aware of this, he himself might well enlist the help of the intervenor, and issue the necessary invitation.

Important also is the degree of the person's fear that the outsider will harm him or override his interests and take over control of important aspects of his life; in other words, the amount of trust that the outsider will not infringe by design on his interests, and the level of his respect that the outsider will be capable of dealing wisely with him and not inadvertently damage him. As we have seen earlier in this book, the development of a personal relationship, for instance between consultee and consultant, takes time to shape, and as it deepens so does the individual's freedom to open up his life to scrutiny by another. By specifically restricting the universe of discourse to the bounded professional domain, we facilitate the most rapid development of a person's freedom to talk openly and frankly about his case.

A trained mental health consultant actively manages the growth of the relationship with his consultee by sensitive interpretation of successive feedback cues. In this way he keeps his interventions in line with the progressive voluntary relaxation of privacy boundaries by the consultee. Caregivers who lack such training may nevertheless gauge how far and how fast to extend their interventions in the lives of their clients by empathic awareness of their clients' willingness to relax privacy boundaries.

It is also possible to develop guidelines that help us plan uninvited interventions that will be least likely to be resented. For instance, in our Family Center in Jerusalem we have worked out, at the request of the Rabbinical Court that handles divorces, a one-page guide for parents that aims to help them minimize the psychosocial harm to their children that might be caused by their divorce. This guide is systematically transmitted by court officials to all parents who open a file for divorce. We had to consider with care what content to include and how to express our ideas to avoid upsetting parents who had not requested such an intervention, even one restricted to a routine one-page handout. Exhibit 19.2 presents a translation of the guide from the Hebrew.

Examination of Exhibit 19.2 reveals that its content is restricted to simple messages that few parents would be likely to resent, even though they may not themselves have previously taken them into consideration. Basic information is provided about the expectable reactions of children to parental divorce and about uncontroversial possibilities of dealing with them, which aim to reduce stress and increase support. The information is given special status as deserving of attention by all parents by virtue of the imprimatur of the Rabbinical Court. Suggestions about the possible advisability of seeking further information, guidance, or mediation are presented in a low-key, noncoercive style, and are explicitly left open for individual parents to decide entirely on their own. In fact, most parents do not take the matter further, and it is generally understood that this is quite in order. But meanwhile, the entire population of divorcing parents has been offered the essential information in an acceptable form in their period of crisis, and those who choose to do so may use it in their own ways.

The three principles that governed this intervention are (1) it identifies crucial items of information that have widespread applicability; (2) this information is validated as worthy of being seriously considered because it has been transmitted by a public body that protects the interests of children; and (3) the parents are given free choice of how they will make use, if at all, of the information, and are not subjected to any form of coercion or persuasion.

Similar elements characterized Gerald Caplan's Jerusalem memorandum during the Gulf War. In fact, these elements perhaps may be considered a basis for guiding caregivers in keeping their uninvited messages to the public in line with the privacy constraints of ordinary people. To this we add the advisability of paying empathic attention to and respecting feedback cues in situations of personal interaction. If this were done, much of the potential unintended harm by caregivers who seek to fulfill the precepts of community mental health would be avoided.

Exhibit 19.2. Information for Divorcing Parents.

It is important for the good of your children to pay attention to the following points:

1. Breakup of a family is a source of serious stress for most children. This is so despite the benefits to parents from the interruption of their quarrels and the pain of their marital conflicts. Children need continuing positive and stable relationships with both parents to promote their healthy psychological and social development.

2. Parents should make a special effort to arrange appropriate conditions to reduce the stress and suffering of their children and also to provide the psychosocial support that will help the children master their unavoidable privations caused by the breakup of their family. This is so, despite the likelihood that the parents will themselves currently be preoccupied and burdened by their own personal tribulations.

3. Immediately after decisions have been taken about divorce, custody of children and contacts of children with the other parent, *the two parents should meet jointly with their children* and should together inform them of these decisions. They should emphasize that their love for the children will continue even though the parents may have stopped loving each other, that each parent wishes the other parent to continue to maintain good relationships with the children, and that each will try to help the children overcome the unavoidable separation problems caused by the family living in divided homes.

4. Parents should allow their children to express freely and openly their possible opposition to the divorce and their negative feelings about it: their sadness and pain, their rage, their insecurity. The parents should support their children in coping with their turmoil during the coming months.

5. Parents should work out a divorce agreement that protects the interests of their children. If necessary, the parents should seek the help of a mutually accepted mediator. This mediator will help them discover the least harmful arrangements for the children, which will not be unduly influenced by the difficulties the parents may currently be having in collaborating in their planning because of their mutual antagonism exacerbated by the upsets of the divorce conflicts. Although they have not succeeded as a *married couple*, the mediator will help them work out how to collaborate successfully as a *parental couple* who are jointly responsible for the care of their children whom both of them love. Such a program should include arrangements to guarantee the continuation of close contacts between the children and the noncustodial parent, in order that he or she may continue to function as an authentic parent, who feeds, educates, nurtures, and puts the children to bed, for example, and not just as a host or hostess to whom the children pay social visits only for purposes of recreation.

How can mental health consultants and mental health collaborating specialists ensure that caregivers with whom they work do not distort preventive messages and actions by the dehumanization, stereotyping, inappropriate use, infringements of personal privacy, and fostering of undue dependency that appear to be so widespread?

First, the very awareness of these possibilities by the mental health specialist will alert him to the need to speak and act carefully to avoid giving caregivers wrong impressions. Inadvertence is the supreme danger, and good intentions are not an adequate insurance against harm.

Second, the mental health consultant must be continually aware of himself as a role model, and must explicitly and overtly demonstrate his own humanism and his respect and caution in relating to his consultees and in talking about their clients. But since his own role rules out supervising the actions of his consultees and restricts him to focusing only on issues that they raise, which are unlikely to include their own tendency to be insensitive, his contribution to identifying and remedying these difficulties will be limited.

This will specifically not be the case with a specialist using techniques of mental health collaboration. He has the explicit mission of supervising factors that influence the mental health outcome for clients of the caregiving institution. Clearly the issues that are the focus of our present discussion are of central importance in that mission. There is little benefit to be gained by promoting anticipatory guidance, crisis intervention, and support systems to be implemented by caregivers, if these services run the risk of reducing rather than augmenting the mental health of the client population. He should therefore not be satisfied just with personally modeling how to use these techniques and supervising how they are used in his presence. He should also monitor how they are being used in his absence; he should conduct a continual campaign of education about the ever-present dangers of inadvertent dehumanization and stereotyping; and he should vigilantly supervise the details of program implementation to identify and remedy such harmful side effects.

There is little that we can do to prevent distortion of our

messages by eventual dissemination to ever wider audiences. As long as we are in control of the communications, we should certainly ensure that our central themes are enunciated clearly. But inevitably what people do with them may come to bear little relationship to what we intended. Should we therefore choose to say nothing for wider use, for instance by publishing for a specialized audience or by restricting ourselves to communications within circumscribed settings where we may personally monitor how our views are interpreted?

Since this would clearly also prevent our doing good, we must accept our human limitations, which we share with all others who publish views about desirable practices to improve the quality of life. We must rely on the good sense of our readers to make constructive use of our ideas, which is likely to happen in most cases. And for the rest, who may distort our messages to fit their own previous ways of dealing with people in less desirable ways, we may realize that they would probably have behaved in much the same way if they had not heard of our concepts. We may also be reassured that in our democratic society, our sociolegal system and its guardians will safeguard the public from undue infringements on their privacy and from harmful dehumanizing or dependency-inducing practices. We must also remember that most members of the population have enough common sense and are robust and resilient enough to resist negative influences by caregivers and intervening outsiders.

— RECOMMENDED READINGS —

Alpert, J., and Associates. *Psychological Consultation in Educational Settings.* San Francisco: Jossey-Bass, 1982.

Alpert, J., and Silverstein, J. "Mental Health Consultation: Historical, Present, and Future Perspectives." In J. Bergan (ed.), *School Psychology in Contemporary Society.* Columbus, Ohio: Merrill, 1985.

Brook, A. "An Experiment in General Practitioner–Psychiatrist Cooperation." *Journal of the College of General Practitioners,* 1965, *13,* 127–131.

Brown, D., Pryzwansky, W. B., and Schultz, A. C. *Psychological Consultation: Introduction to Theory and Practice.* Needham Heights, Mass.: Allyn & Bacon, 1991.

Burton, R. *The Anatomy of Melancholy.* Everyman Library, vol. 1. London: J. M. Dent & Sons, 1968. (Originally published 1630.)

Bushard, B. L. "The U.S. Army's Mental Health Consultation Service." *Symposium on Preventive and Social Psychiatry.* Walter Reed Army Institute of Research, Apr. 1957. Washington, D.C.: U.S. Government Printing Office, 1958.

Caplan, G. "A Public Health Approach to Child Psychiatry." *Mental Hygiene,* 1951, *35,* 235–247.

Caplan, G. "Recent Trends in Preventive Psychiatry." In G. Caplan (ed.), *Emotional Problems of Early Childhood.* New York: Basic Books, 1955.

Caplan, G. "Mental Health Consultation in Schools." In E. M. Gruenberg and F. G. Boudreau (eds.), *The Elements of a Community Mental Health Program.* New York: Millbank Memorial Fund, 1956.

Caplan, G. *Concepts of Mental Health and Consultation.* Children's Bureau Publication no. 373. Washington, D.C.: Department of Health, Education, and Welfare, 1959a.

Caplan, G. "Practical Steps for the Family Physician in the Prevention of Emotional Disorder." *Journal of the American Medical Association,* 1959b, *170,* 1497–1506.

Caplan, G. *An Approach to Community Mental Health.* New York: Grune & Stratton, 1961.

Caplan, G. *Manual for Psychiatrists Participating in the Peace Corps Program.* Washington, D.C.: Medical Program Division, Peace Corps, 1962.

Caplan, G. "Opportunities for School Psychologists in the Primary Prevention of Mental Disorders in Children." *Mental Hygiene,* 1963a, *47,* 525–539.

Caplan, G. "Types of Mental Health Consultation." *American Journal of Orthopsychiatry,* 1963b, *33,* 470–481.

Caplan, G. *Principles of Preventive Psychiatry.* New York: Basic Books, 1964.

Caplan, G. "Opportunities for School Psychologists in the Primary Prevention of Mental Disorders in Children." In N. M. Lambert (ed.), *The Protection and Promotion of Mental Health in Schools.* Public Health Service Publication no. 1226. Washington, D.C.: Department of Health, Education, and Welfare, 1965.

Caplan, G. *Theory and Practice of Mental Health Consultation.* New York: Basic Books, 1970.

Caplan, G. *Support Systems and Community Mental Health: Lectures in Concept Development.* New York: Behavioral Publications, 1974.

Caplan, G. "An Approach to Preventive Intervention in Child Psychiatry." *Canadian Journal of Psychiatry,* 1980, *25,* 671–682.

Caplan, G. "Epilogue: Personal Reflections by Gerald Caplan." In H. C. Schulberg and M. Killilea (eds.), *The Modern Practice of Community Mental Health: A Volume in Honor of Gerald Caplan.* San Francisco: Jossey-Bass, 1982.

Caplan, G. "Preventing Psychological Disorders in Children of Divorce: Guidelines for the General Practitioner." *British Medical Journal,* 1986a, *292,* 1563–1566.

Caplan, G. "Recent Developments in Crisis Intervention and in the

Promotion of Support Services." In M. Kessler and S. E. Goldston (eds.), *A Decade of Progress in Primary Prevention*. Hanover: University Press of New England, 1986b.

Caplan, G. *Population-Oriented Psychiatry*. New York: Human Sciences Press, 1989.

Caplan, G., and Cadden, V. *Adjusting Overseas: A Message to Each Peace Corps Trainee*. Washington, D.C.: Peace Corps, 1962.

Caplan, G., and Caplan, R. B. "Development of Community Psychiatry Concepts." In A. M. Freedman and H. I. Kaplan (eds.), *Comprehensive Textbook of Psychiatry*. Baltimore: Williams & Wilkins, 1967.

Caplan, G., and Caplan, R. B. *Arab and Jew in Jerusalem*. Cambridge, Mass.: Harvard University Press, 1980.

Caplan, G., and Killilea, M. (eds.). *Support Systems and Mutual Help: Multidisciplinary Explorations*. New York: Grune & Stratton, 1976.

Caplan, G., Macht, L. B., and Wolf, A. *Manual for Mental Health Professionals Participating in the Job Corps Program*. Document no. JCH330-A. Washington, D.C.: Office of Economic Opportunity, 1969.

Caplan, R. B. *Psychiatry and the Community in Nineteenth-Century America: The Recurring Concern with Environment in the Prevention and Treatment of Mental Disorder*. New York: Basic Books, 1969.

Caplan, R. B. *Helping the Helpers to Help: The Development and Evaluation of Mental Health Consultation to Aid Clergymen in Pastoral Work*. New York: Seabury Press, 1972.

Caplan, R. B. "Deathbed Scenes and Graveyard Poetry: Death in Eighteenth-Century English Literature." In G. Caplan and M. Killilea (eds.), *Support Systems and Mutual Help: Multidisciplinary Explorations*. New York: Grune & Stratton, 1976.

Caplan, R. B. "Gerald Caplan: The Man and His Work." In H. C. Schulberg and M. Killilea (eds.), *The Modern Practice of Community Mental Health: A Volume in Honor of Gerald Caplan*. San Francisco: Jossey-Bass, 1982.

Conoley, J. C., and Conoley, C. W. *School Consultation: A Guide to Practice and Training*. Elmsford, N.Y.: Pergammon Press, 1982.

Conoley, J. C., and Conoley, C. W. "Useful Theories in School-Based Consultation." *Remedial and Special Education*, 1988, *6*, 14-20.

Erchul, W. P. "A Relational Communication Analysis of Control in School Consultation." *Professional School Psychology*, 1987, *2*, 113-124.

Erchul, W. P. "Gerald Caplan: A Major Attraction at the 1990 Convention." *The School Psychologist*, 1990, *44*(4), 4.

Erchul, W. P. (ed.). *Consultation in Community, School, and Organizational Practice: Gerald Caplan's Contributions to Professional Psychology.* Washington, D.C.: Hemisphere, 1993.

Erchul, W. P., and others. *Gerald Caplan's Contributions to American Psychology: Views from the Discipline.* Symposium presented at the meeting of the American Psychological Association, Boston, Aug. 1990. (Also available as cassette recording APA90-126 from Sound Images, Inc., Box 460519, Aurora, Colo. 80046.)

Gallessich, J. *The Profession and Practice of Consultation.* San Francisco: Jossey-Bass, 1982.

Gresham, F. M., and Kendell, G. K. "School Consultation Research: Methodological Critique and Future Research Directions." *School Psychology Review*, 1987, *16*, 306-316.

Gurin, G., Veroff, J., and Feld, S. *Americans View Their Mental Health.* New York: Basic Books, 1960.

Gutkin, T. B. "Relative Frequency of Consultee Lack of Knowledge, Skills, Confidence, and Objectivity in School Settings." *Journal of School Psychology*, 1981, *19*, 57-61.

Gutkin, T. B., and Curtis, M. J. "School-Based Consultation: Theory, Techniques, and Research." In T. B. Gutkin and C. R. Reynolds (eds.), *The Handbook of School Psychology.* (2nd ed.). New York: Wiley, 1990.

Hansen, J. C., Himes, B. S., and Meier, S. *Consultation: Concepts and Practices.* Englewood Cliffs, N.J.: Prentice-Hall, 1990.

Kaiser, R., and Propst, R. *Come Out, Come Out, Whoever You Are: The Community Service Unit of the H. Douglas Singer Zone Center.* Bloomington: NET Film Service, Audio-Visual Center, Indiana University, 1969.

Lambert, N. M. "Perspectives on Training School-Based Consultants." In J. Meyers and J. Alpert (eds.), *Training in Consultation:*

Perspectives from Behavioral, Mental Health and Organizational Consultation. Springfield, Ill.: Thomas, 1980.

Martin, R. "Expert and Referent Power: A Framework for Understanding and Maximising Consultation Effectiveness." *Journal of School Psychology,* 1978, *16,* 49-55.

Medway, F. J., and Updike, J. F. "Meta-Analysis of Consultation Outcome Studies." *American Journal of Community Psychology,* 1985, *13,* 489-505.

Menachem, S., Lipton, G. L., and Caplan, G. "The Psychologically Orientated Pediatrician and the Provision of Psychoanalytic Psychotherapy." *Child Psychiatry and Human Development,* 1981, *12,* 43-80.

Meyers, J. "Mental Health Consultation." In J. C. Conoley (ed.), *Consultation in Schools: Theory, Research, Procedures.* San Diego, Calif.: Academic Press, 1981.

Meyers, J., Parsons, R. D., and Martin, R. *Mental Health Consultation in the Schools.* San Francisco: Jossey-Bass, 1979.

Murray, H. A. *Thematic Apperception Test.* Cambridge, Mass.: Harvard University Press, 1943.

Oakland, T. "The Journal of School Psychology's First Twenty Years: Contributions and Contributors." *Journal of School Psychology,* 1984, *22,* 239-250.

Parsons, R. D., and Meyers, J. *Developing Consultation Skills.* San Francisco: Jossey-Bass, 1984.

Pryzwansky, W. B. "A Reconsideration of the Consultation Model for Delivery of School-Based Psychological Services." *American Journal of Orthopsychiatry,* 1974, *44,* 579-583.

Pryzwansky, W. B. "Collaboration or Consultation: Is There a Difference?" *Journal of Special Education,* 1977, *11,* 179-182.

Rosenfeld, J. M., and Caplan, G. "Techniques of Staff Consultation in an Immigrant Children's Organization in Israel." *American Journal of Orthopsychiatry,* 1953, *24,* 42-62.

Rosenfeld, S. *Instructional Consultation.* Elmsford, N.Y.: Pergamon Press, 1988.

Watkins, W.B.C. *Perilous Balance.* Princeton, N.J.: Princeton University Press, 1939.

West, J. F. "The Nature of Consultation vs. Collaboration: An Interview with Walter B. Pryzwansky." *The Consulting Edge,* 1990, *2*(1), 1-2.

West, J. F., and Idol, L. "School Consultation (Part I): An Interdisciplinary Perspective on Theory, Models, and Research." *Journal of Learning Disabilities,* 1987, *20,* 388-408.

Westbrook, D., and Hawton, K. "Liaison Meetings Between a Psychiatric Team and General Practitioners: Description and Evaluation of a Pilot Project." *Psychiatric Bulletin,* 1991, *15,* 388-329.

Zins, J. E., and Ponti, C. R. "Best Practices in School-Based Consultation." In A. Thomas and J. Grimes (eds.), *Best Practices in School Psychology—II.* Washington, D.C.: National Association of School Psychologists, 1990.

INDEX

ISBN 1-55542-478-3